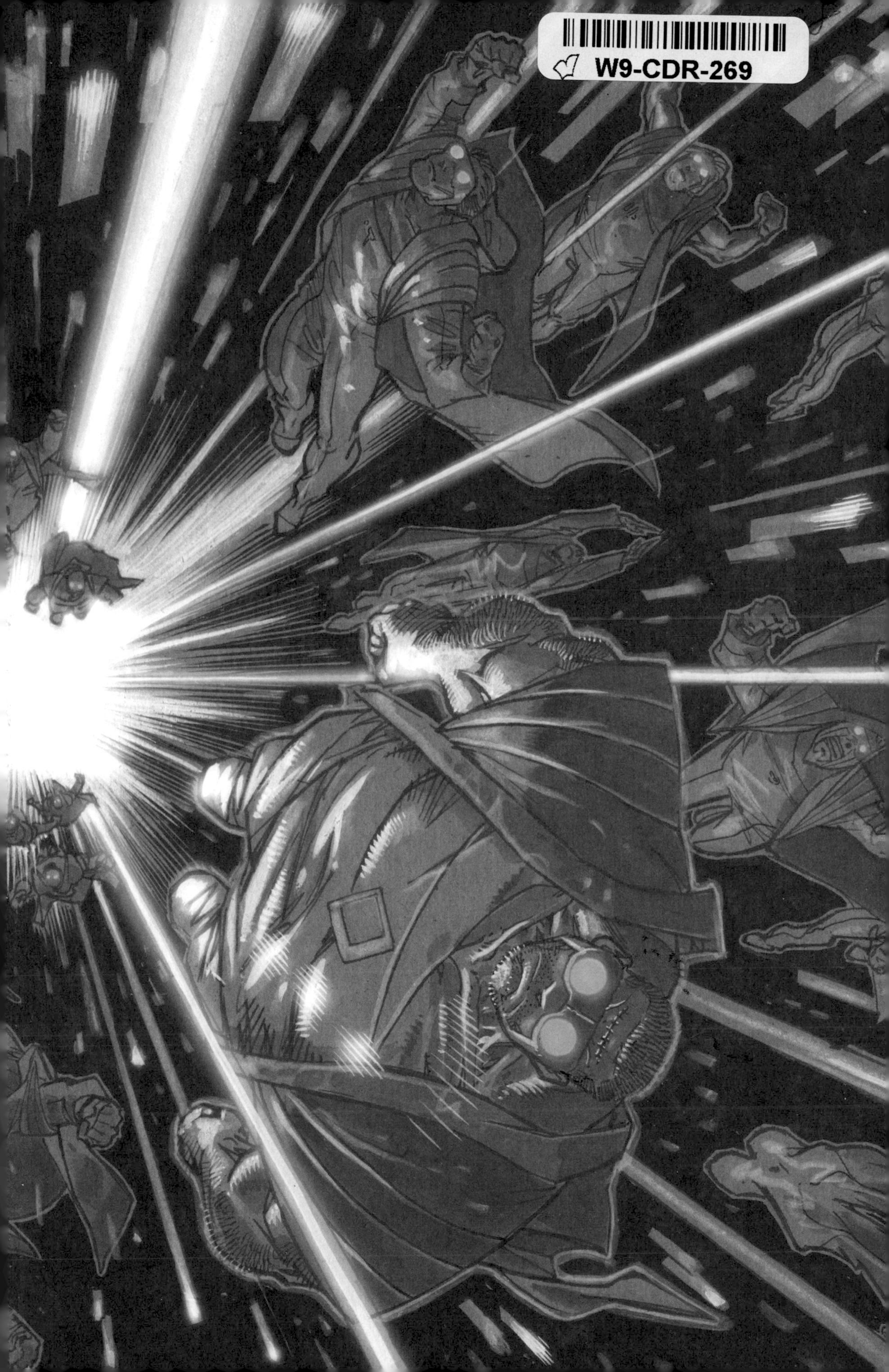

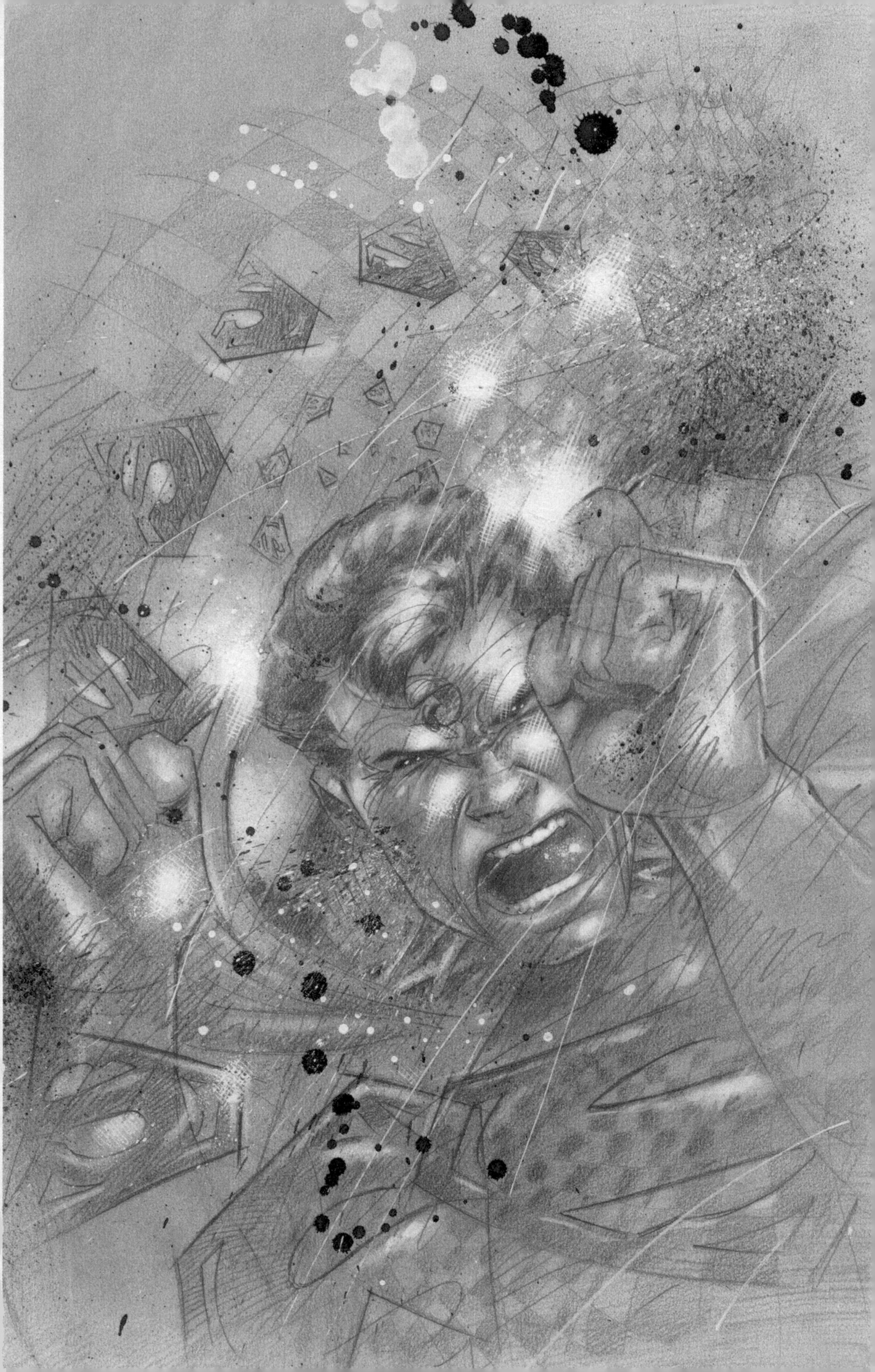

MATT IDELSON Senior Editor-original series
BOB HARRAS Editor-collected edition
SUPERMAN Senior Art Director | PAUL LEVITZ President & Publisher
VP-Design & DC Direct Creative | RICHARD BRUNING Senior VP-Creative Director
Executive VP-Finance & Operations | CHRIS CARAMALIS VP-Finance
CUNNINGHAM VP-Marketing | TERRI CUNNINGHAM VP-Managing Editor
GILL VP-Manufacturing | DAVID HYDE VP-Publicity | HANK KANALZ VP-General Manager, WildStorm
JIM LEE Editorial Director, WildStorm | PAULA LOWITT Senior VP-Business & Legal Affairs
MARYELLEN McLAUGHLIN VP-Advertising & Custom Publishing
JOHN NEE Senior VP-Business Development | GREGORY NOVECK Senior VP-Creative Affairs
SUE POHJA VP-Book Trade Sales | STEVE ROTTERDAM Senior VP-Sales & Marketing
CHERYL RUBIN Senior VP-Brand Management
JEFF TROJAN VP-Business Development, DC Direct | BOB WAYNE VP-Sales
Cover by Adam Kubert. Publication design by Amelia Grohman.

SUPERMAN: LAST SON
Published by DC Comics. Cover, text and compilation Copyright © 2008 DC Comics. All Rights Reserved.
Originally published in single magazine form in ACTION COMICS 844-846, 851 and ACTION COMICS ANNUAL 11.
Copyright © 2005, 2007, 2008 DC Comics. All Rights Reserved.
All characters, their distinctive likenesses and related elements featured in this publication are trademarks
of DC Comics. The stories, characters and incidents featured in this publication are entirely fictional.
DC Comics does not read or accept unsolicited submissions of ideas, stories or artwork.

DC Comics, 1700 Broadway, New York, NY 10019 | A Warner Bros. Entertainment Company
Printed in USA. First Printing. HC ISBN: 978-1-4012-1343-5 SC ISBN: 978-1-4012-1586-6

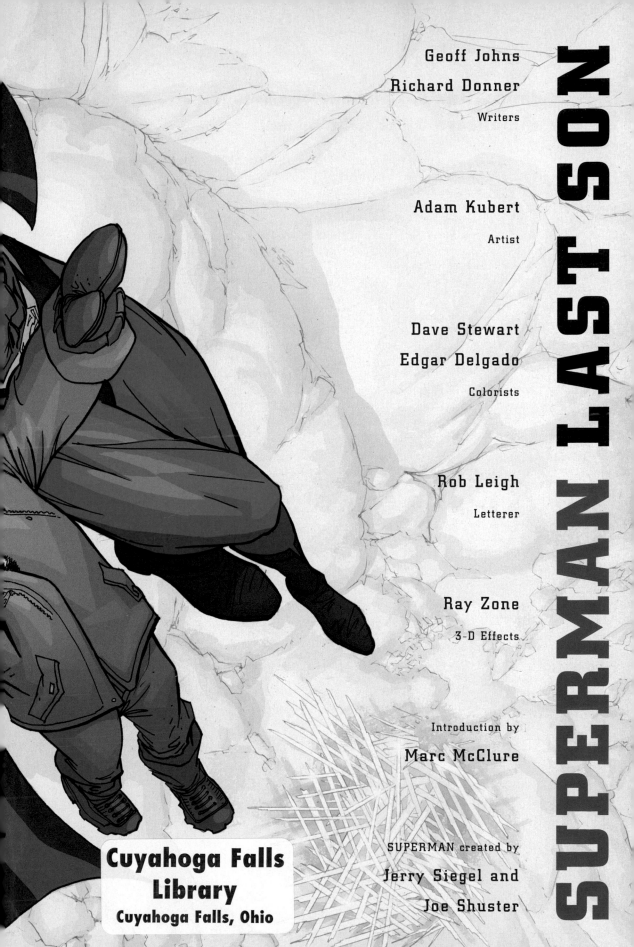

Geoff Johns
Richard Donner

Writers

Adam Kubert

Artist

Dave Stewart
Edgar Delgado

Colorists

Rob Leigh

Letterer

Ray Zone

3-D Effects

Introduction by

Marc McClure

SUPERMAN created by

Jerry Siegel and
Joe Shuster

SUPERMAN LAST SON

Before I go any further...Christopher Reeve is, and always will be, Superman.

1977... I'm twenty years old and living on a houseboat in Los Angeles. I get a call from my agent telling me I have an interview at Lynn Stalmaster's casting office. I show up and meet Lynn, Tom Mankiewicz and a kid named Richard Donner. Donner asked me what's been happening and I told him about the houseboat and how good life is. So Donner tells me he's always wanted to live on a boat so we ended up talking about boats.

After a while, he told me to get out and as I was heading for the door he asked if I knew who Jimmy Olsen was. I said, "Golly, Mr. Kent."

They laughed and I left.

Never even got to read for the part. About three months later, I get a call to see Donner again. I walked in and he said, "I just wanted to remember what you looked like."

A week later I was on a plane to London to play the role of Jimmy Olsen in *Superman: The Movie*.

You hear about being in the right place at the right time.... over thirty years ago, a great group of very talented individuals all found themselves together in the right place at the right time. They were there because of two men... Superman and Richard Donner.

I liked Donner from the start. Everyone likes Donner from the start. He's a larger-than-life kinda guy, and he reminded me of my father who I lost at a young age. They were both the loudest guys in the room, and both have big contagious laughs. I will always remember Donner telling me when I first arrived, if I needed anything or had any problems, to come and see him first. He protected everybody and that meant a lot to me.

Verisimilitude! It's a word that symbolizes truth. It was Donner's mantra throughout the filming of *Superman*. He has a gift as a filmmaker that lets you believe in what you're watching (and now, as he and Geoff Johns create a new series of stories about Superman in ACTION COMICS, that gift extends to his writing as well).

Geoff and I met in the nineties. He's been working with Donner a long time and they both share the same dream. Geoff has a real energy and passion for comics. Along with Donner's sensibility for story and truth, as well as Adam Kubert's amazing visual artistry, he takes us on adventures into worlds untold and shows us new possibilities we could only imagine. Clark, Lois and Jimmy and Christopher Kent! How great is that? Just close your eyes right now and see Chris Reeve standing there, smiling... and now with eyes wide open, you'll see Donner and Geoff smiling right back. I'm smiling too. Everybody is smiling. Trust me, this is all good.

It's amazing how life works. Donner, Geoff and Adam are meant to be doing these comics, and I know they feel fortunate and are aware of the responsibility involved with The Man of Steel. How they honored Chris is a testament to who they are.

Truth, Justice and the American Way. Superman is in good hands. He's with friends. He's with us. He will always be with us for lifetimes to come. I wish to thank all the creative forces involved in making these comics a reality and for putting all their talents together for such a wonderful cause. These comics will mean so much, to so many, on our planet.

Richard Donner always wondered what could have been if he had been allowed to direct all the Superman movies... the possibilities were endless. He loved the project and it was his baby... but if that had happened, we wouldn't have gotten to where we are now... this moment.

We have all learned so much from one man who became a teacher. How a person can rise above adversity and become a Superman in real life and also play him in the movies. How we learned about our own humanity and how precious life is. How we can all have reason for hope. How each day is a gift. I have learned there are no accidents in life. Everything happens for a reason. Understanding why they happen is our challenge. I remember Pa Kent telling a young Clark that he's here for a reason... I believe that to be true!

Respect each other and God Bless.

The Grateful One,

Marc McClure   **J.O**

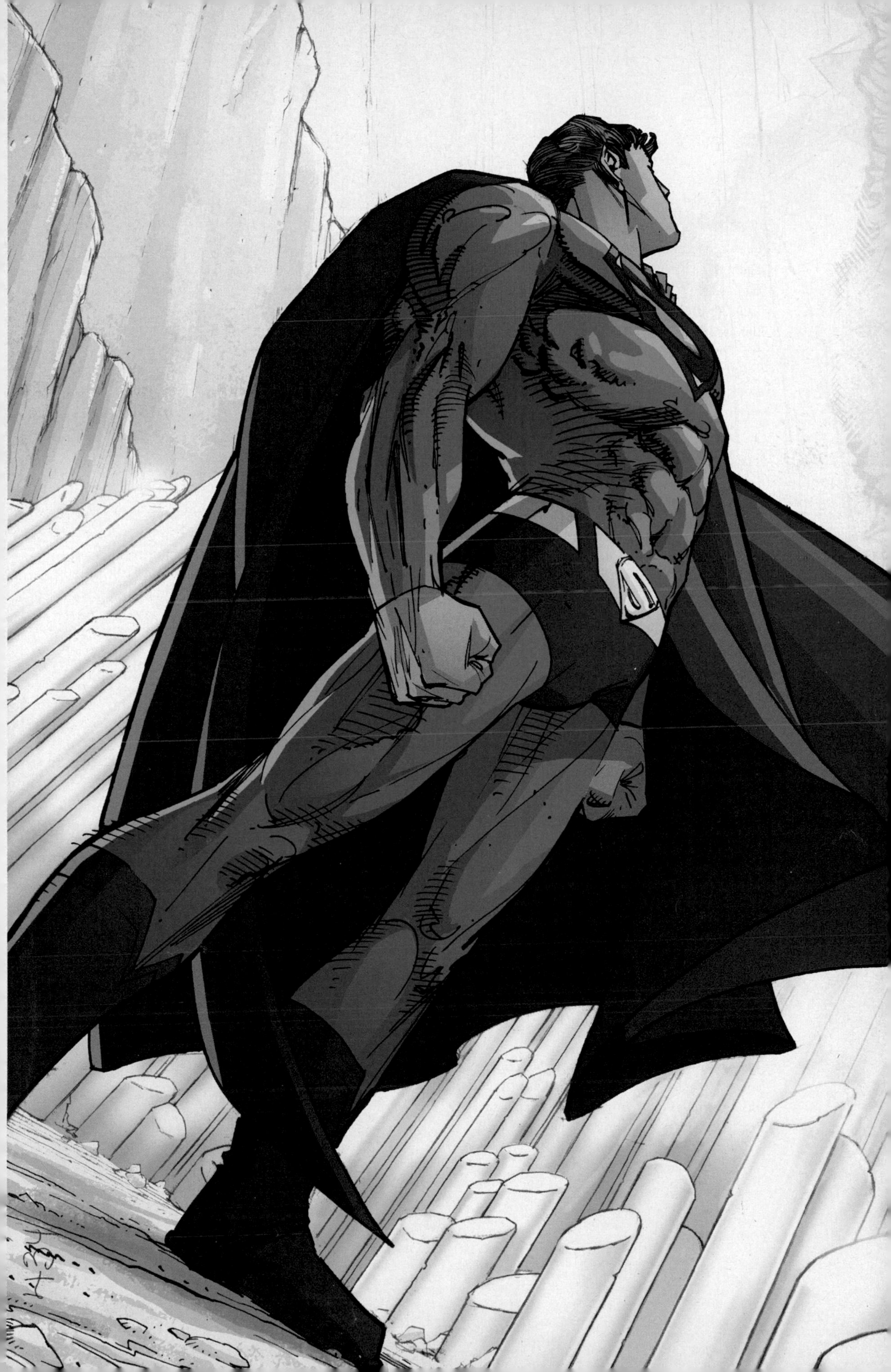

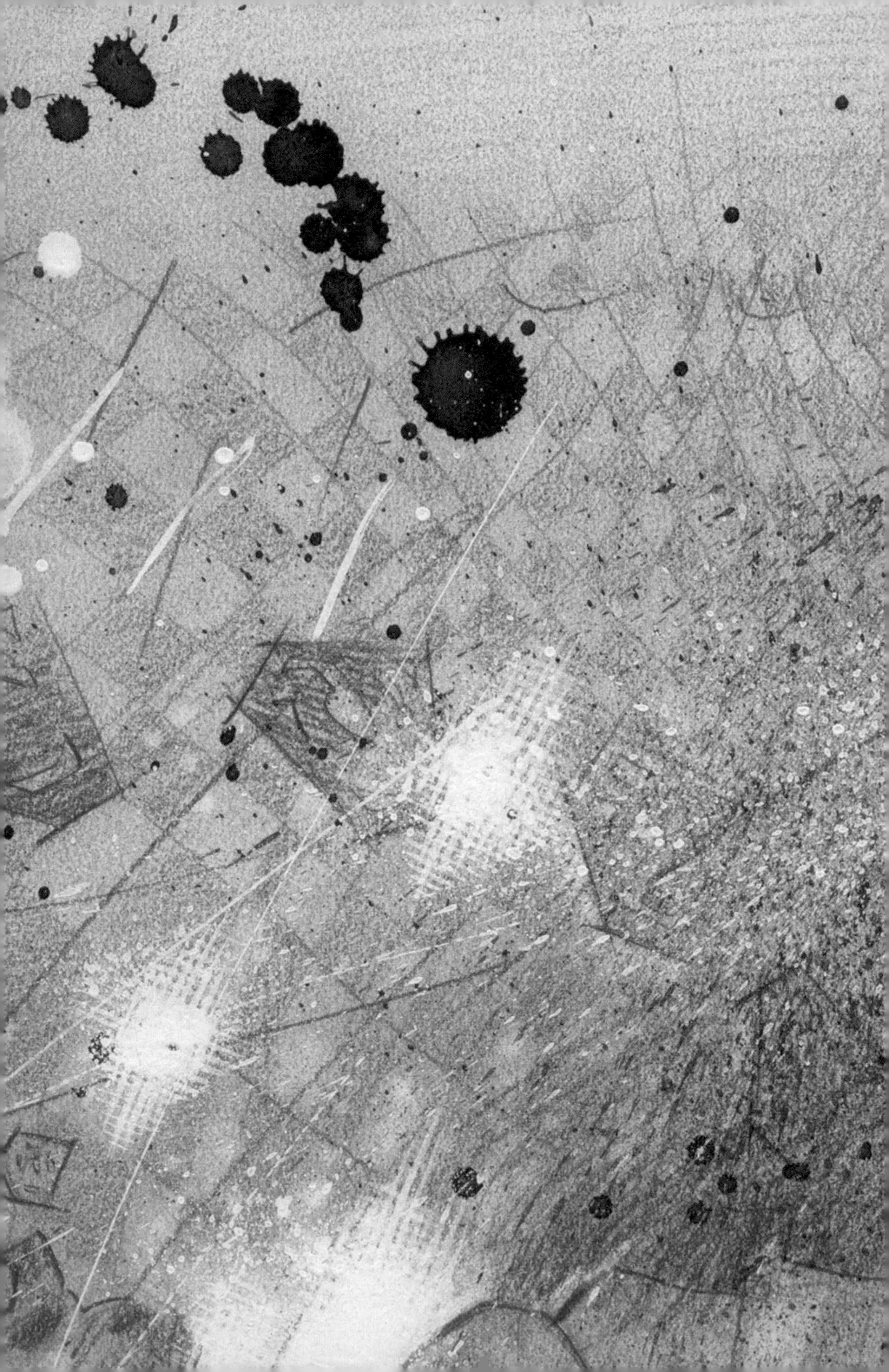

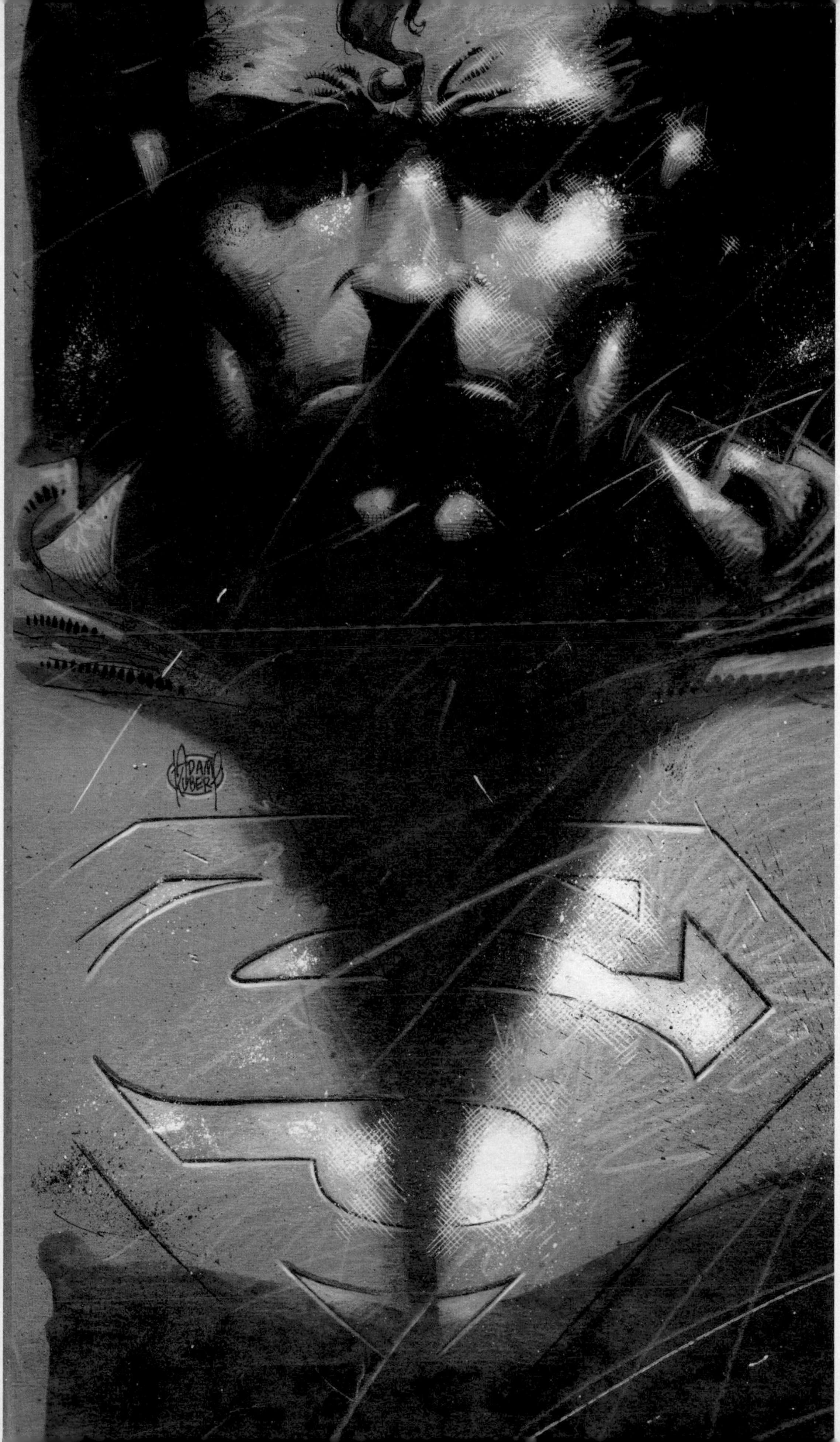

CHAPTER ONE

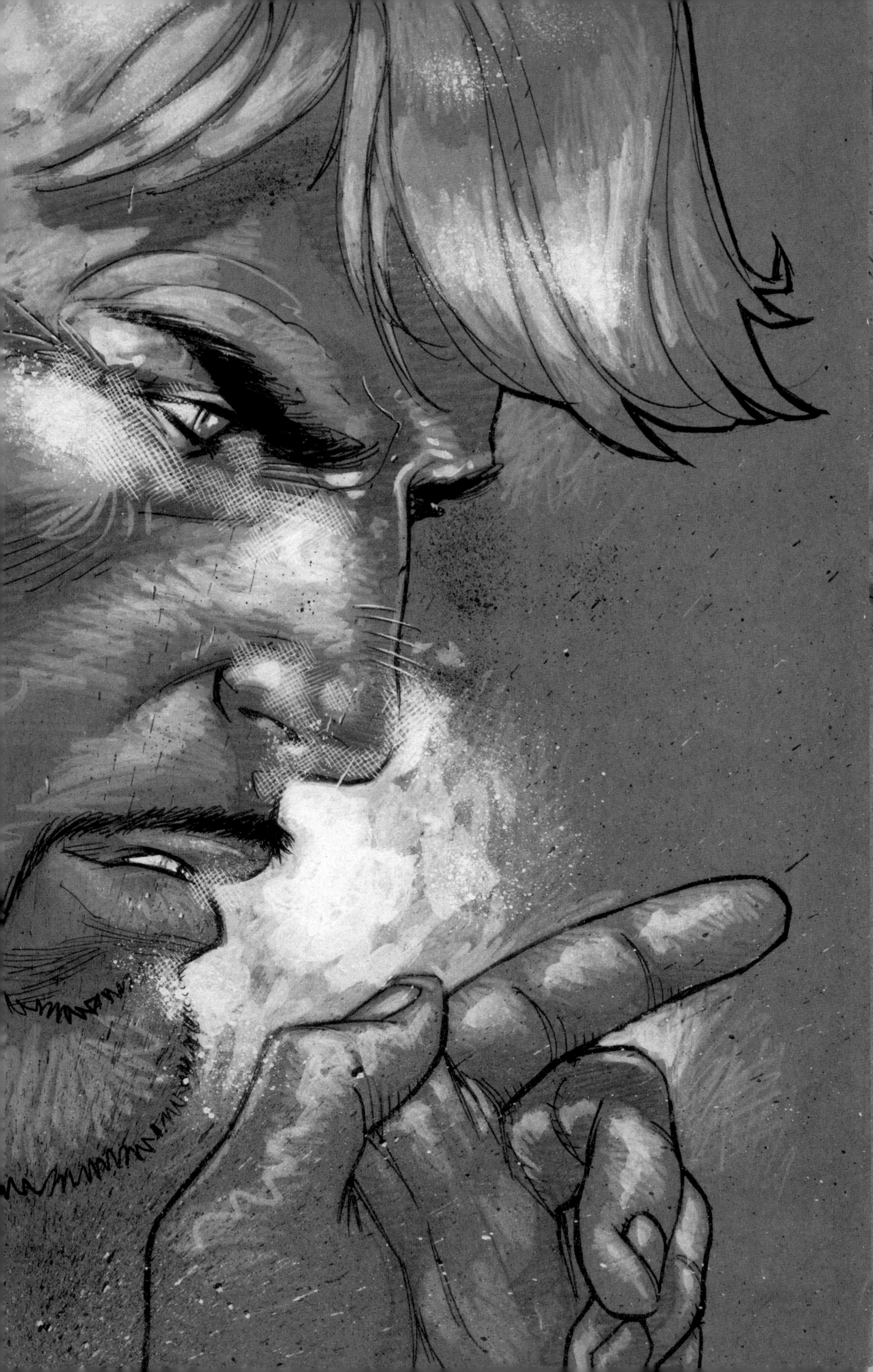

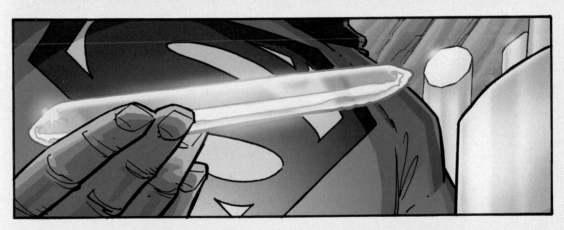

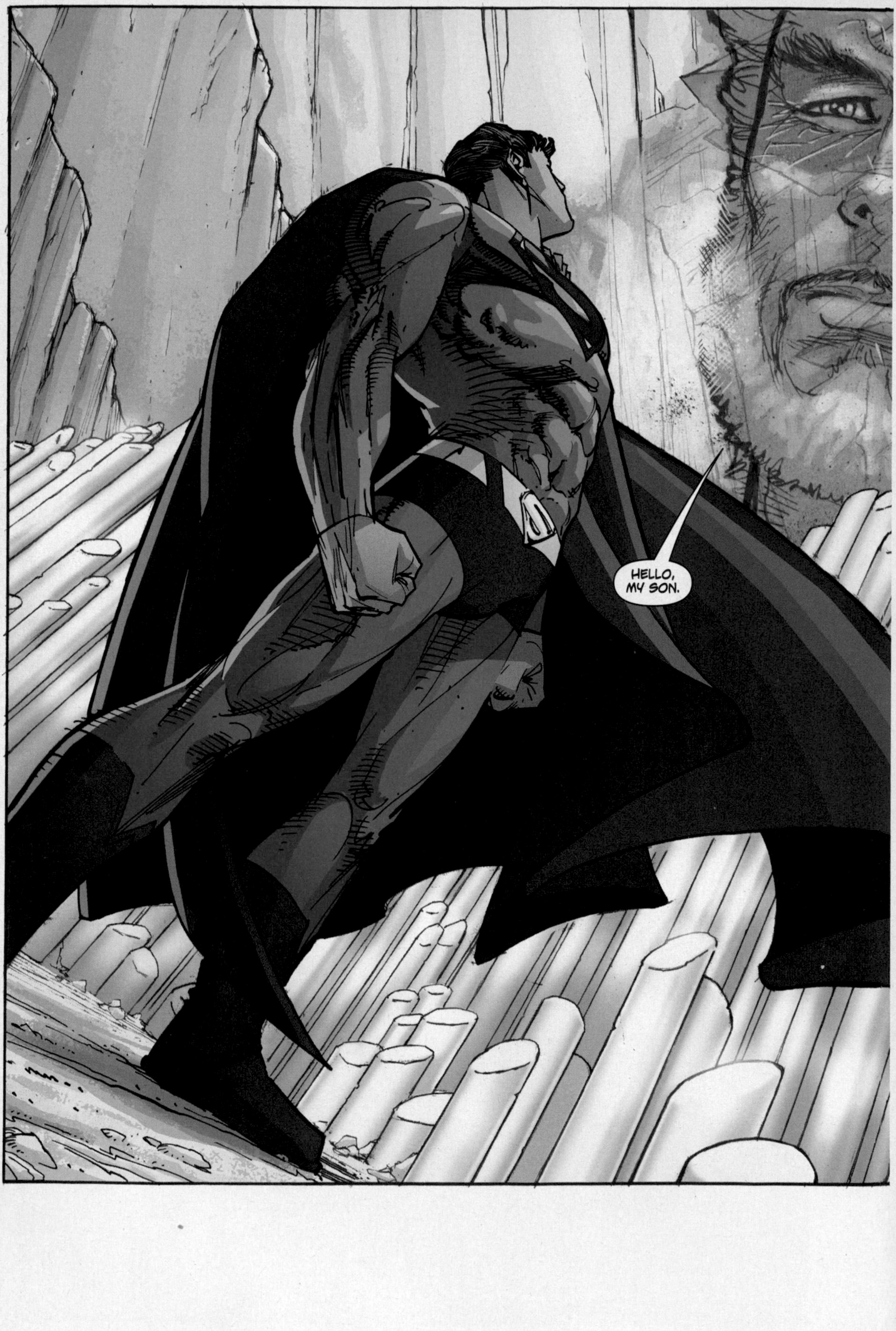
HELLO, MY SON.

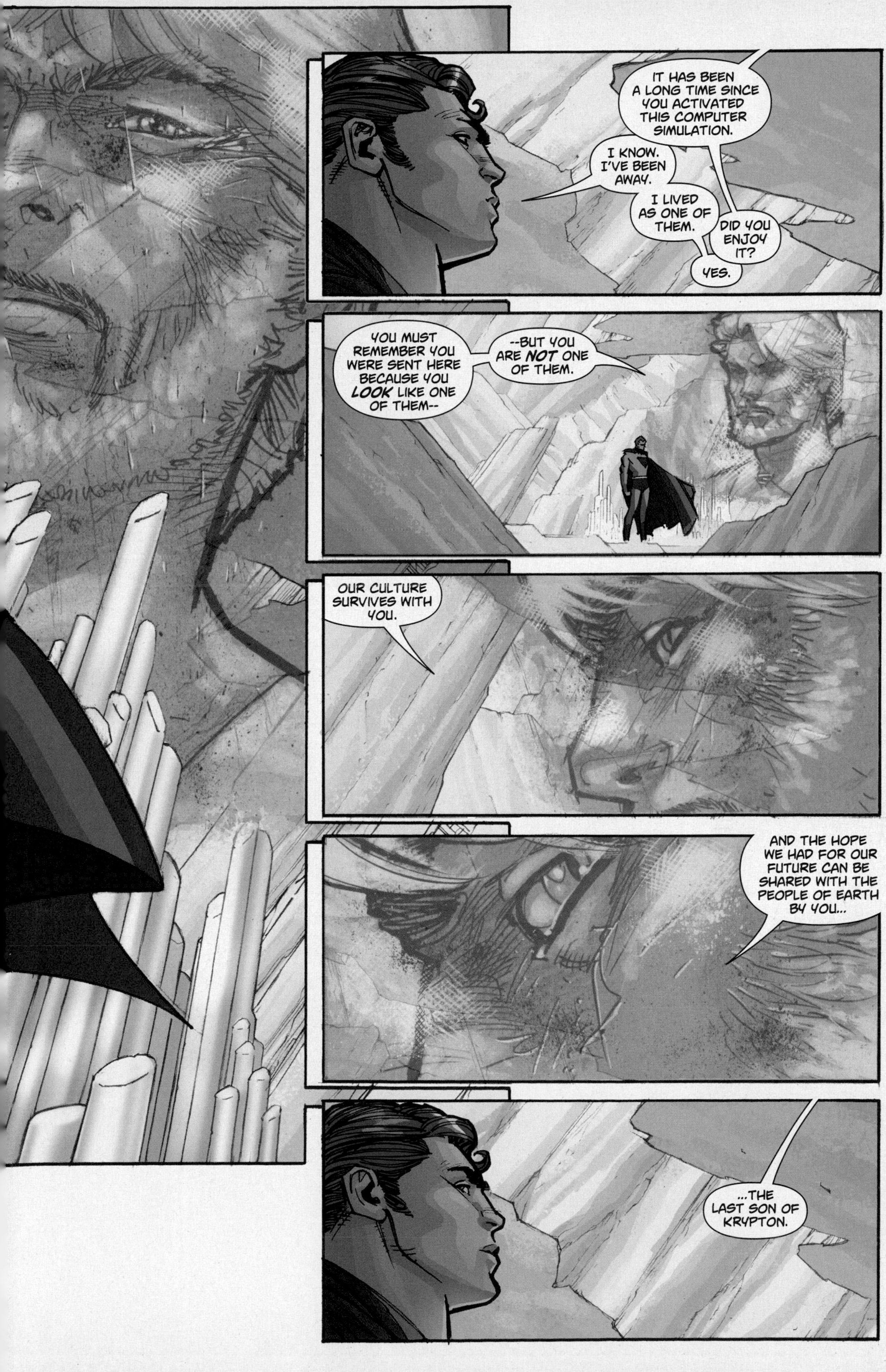
IT HAS BEEN A LONG TIME SINCE YOU ACTIVATED THIS COMPUTER SIMULATION.
I KNOW. I'VE BEEN AWAY.
I LIVED AS ONE OF THEM.
DID YOU ENJOY IT?
YES.
YOU MUST REMEMBER YOU WERE SENT HERE BECAUSE YOU LOOK LIKE ONE OF THEM--
--BUT YOU ARE NOT ONE OF THEM.
OUR CULTURE SURVIVES WITH YOU.
AND THE HOPE WE HAD FOR OUR FUTURE CAN BE SHARED WITH THE PEOPLE OF EARTH BY YOU...
...THE LAST SON OF KRYPTON.

WHAT AM I LOOKING AT, OLSEN?

SUPERMAN'S CAPE. THE CORNER OF IT. OR MAYBE IT'S HIS BOOT.

THAT'S *NOT* WHAT I'M LOOKING AT.

IT'S *NOT*?

I'M LOOKING AT A PHOTOGRAPHER WHO'S GOING TO BE OUT OF A *JOB* IF HE DOESN'T START SHOWING ME PICTURES INSTEAD OF WASTING MY TIME PLAYING *"GUESS WHAT I COULDN'T FOCUS ON!"*

Um, MR. WHITE, IF I COULD...

I *KNOW* WHAT HAPPENED, OLSEN!

THE *DAILY STAR* HAS A SHOT OF IT ON *THEIR* FRONT PAGE! YOU JUST HELPED THE COMPETITION SELL *TEN THOUSAND* MORE COPIES!

BUT--

COFFEE. TWO SUGARS. *NOW.*

SUPERMAN STOP UDD'S RAMPAG

YEAH, CHIEF.

A LITTLE HARD ON HIM, DON'T YOU THINK?

HARD ON HIM?

KENT, DO YOU KNOW WHAT *MY* EDITOR USED TO DO TO *ME* WHEN I BROUGHT HIM COFFEE THAT WAS TOO *COLD?*

LOOK!

KENT!?

UP IN THE SKY!

WHAT IS IT?!

OH, MY GOD! HELP!

KENT, ARE YOU LISTENING TO A WORD I'M SAYING?!

EXCUSE ME, MR. WHITE. I'VE GOT TO GO.

I'VE GOT A DENTIST APPOINTMENT I FORGOT ALL AB--

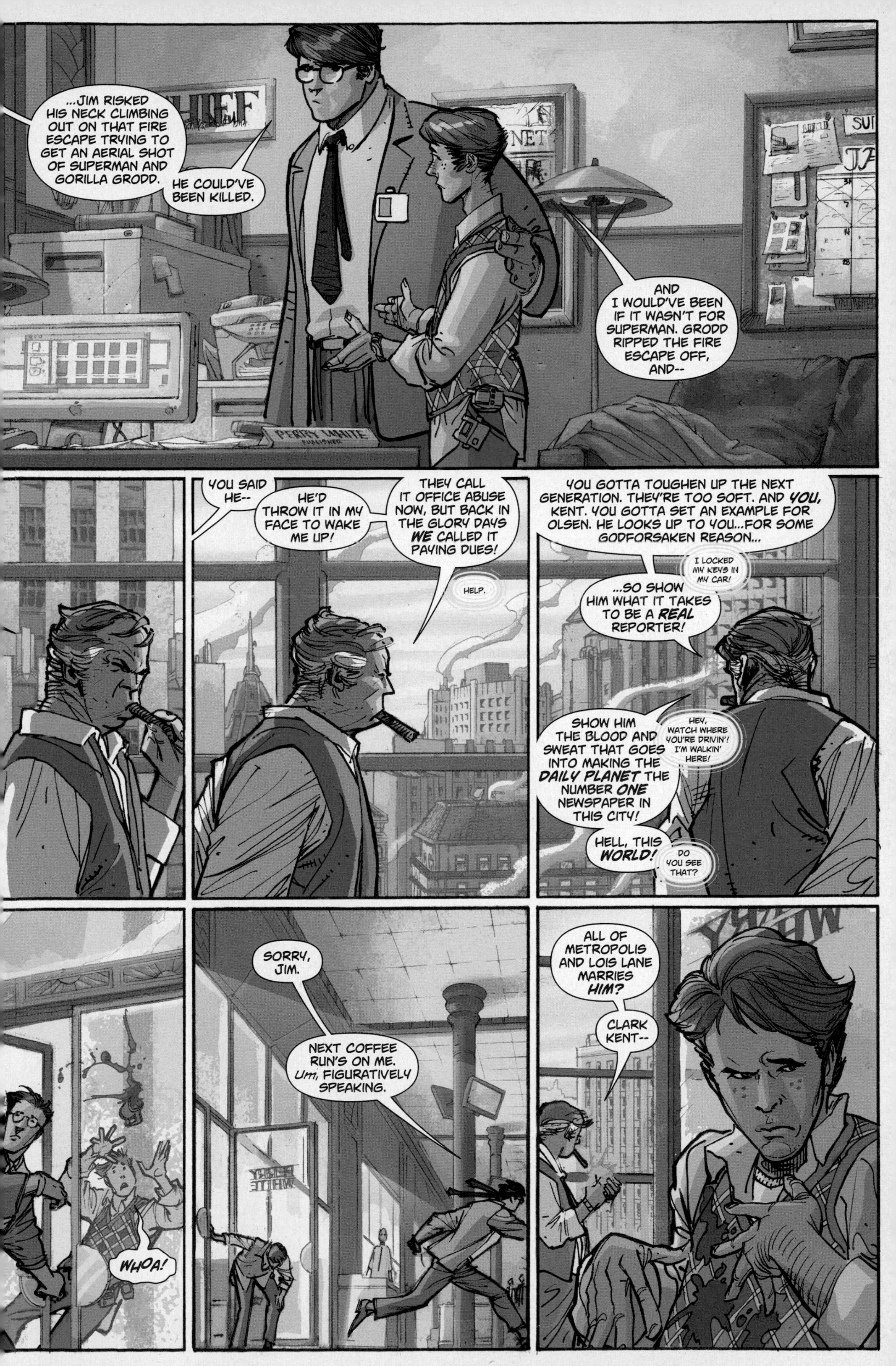
CHIEF
...JIM RISKED HIS NECK CLIMBING OUT ON THAT FIRE ESCAPE TRYING TO GET AN AERIAL SHOT OF SUPERMAN AND GORILLA GRODD.
HE COULD'VE BEEN KILLED.
AND I WOULD'VE BEEN IF IT WASN'T FOR SUPERMAN. GRODD RIPPED THE FIRE ESCAPE OFF, AND--
PERRY WHITE
PUBLISHER
YOU SAID HE--
HE'D THROW IT IN MY FACE TO WAKE ME UP!
THEY CALL IT OFFICE ABUSE NOW, BUT BACK IN THE GLORY DAYS WE CALLED IT PAYING DUES!
HELP.
YOU GOTTA TOUGHEN UP THE NEXT GENERATION. THEY'RE TOO SOFT. AND YOU, KENT. YOU GOTTA SET AN EXAMPLE FOR OLSEN. HE LOOKS UP TO YOU...FOR SOME GODFORSAKEN REASON...
I LOCKED MY KEYS IN MY CAR!
...SO SHOW HIM WHAT IT TAKES TO BE A REAL REPORTER!
SHOW HIM THE BLOOD AND SWEAT THAT GOES INTO MAKING THE DAILY PLANET THE NUMBER ONE NEWSPAPER IN THIS CITY!
HEY, WATCH WHERE YOU'RE DRIVIN'! I'M WALKIN' HERE!
HELL, THIS WORLD!
DO YOU SEE THAT?
WHOA!
SORRY, JIM.
NEXT COFFEE RUN'S ON ME. UM, FIGURATIVELY SPEAKING.
PERRY WHITE
ALL OF METROPOLIS AND LOIS LANE MARRIES HIM?
CLARK KENT--

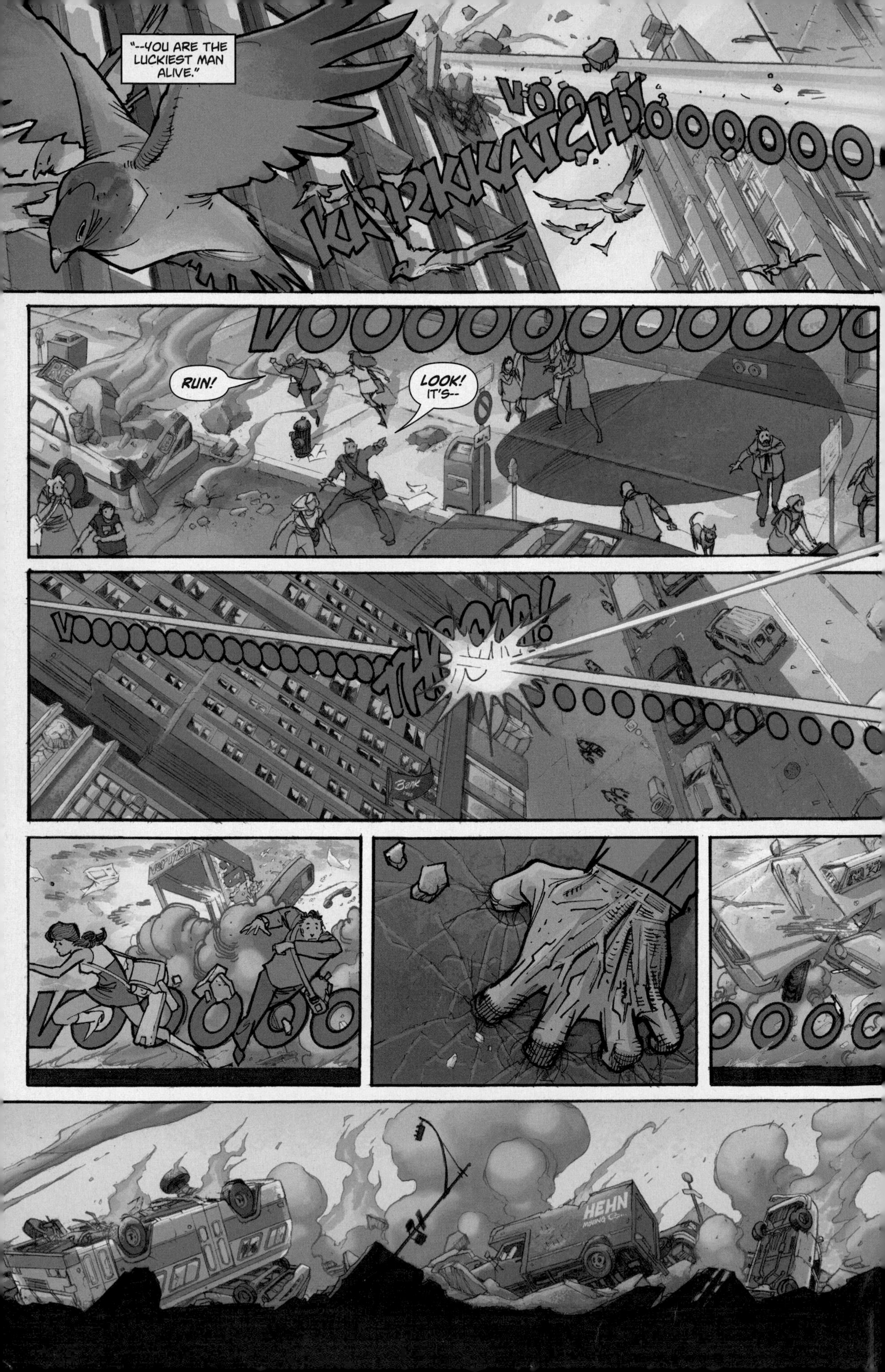
"--YOU ARE THE LUCKIEST MAN ALIVE."
KARKKATCH!
VOOOOOOOO
VOOOOOOOOOOOOC
RUN!
LOOK! IT'S--
VOOOOOOOOOOOOOOOOOO
THOOM!
OOOOOOOOOOOOOOOO
VOOOOO
OOOOOO
HEHN MOVING CO.
Bank

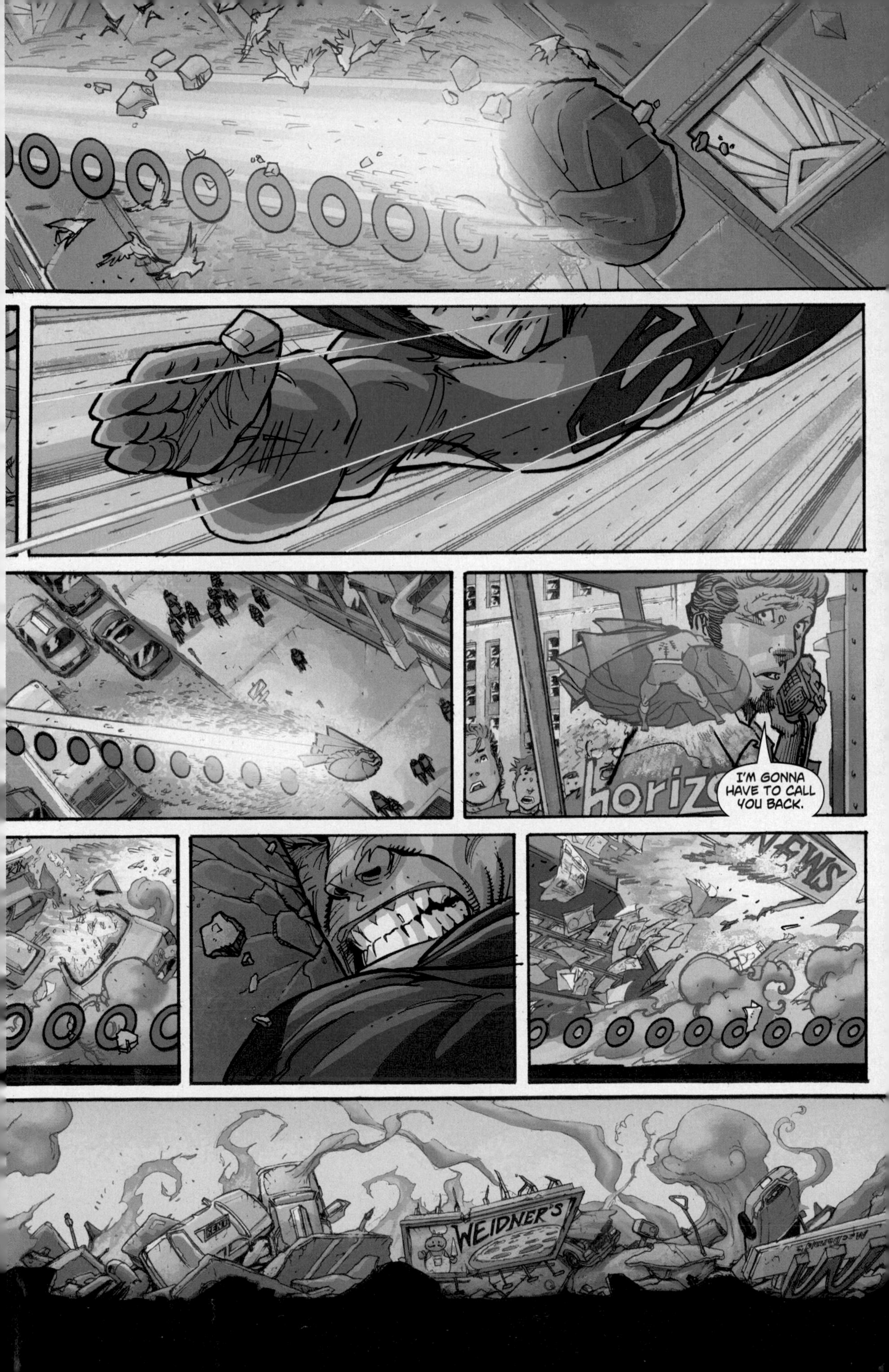
I'M GONNA HAVE TO CALL YOU BACK.
WEIDNER'S

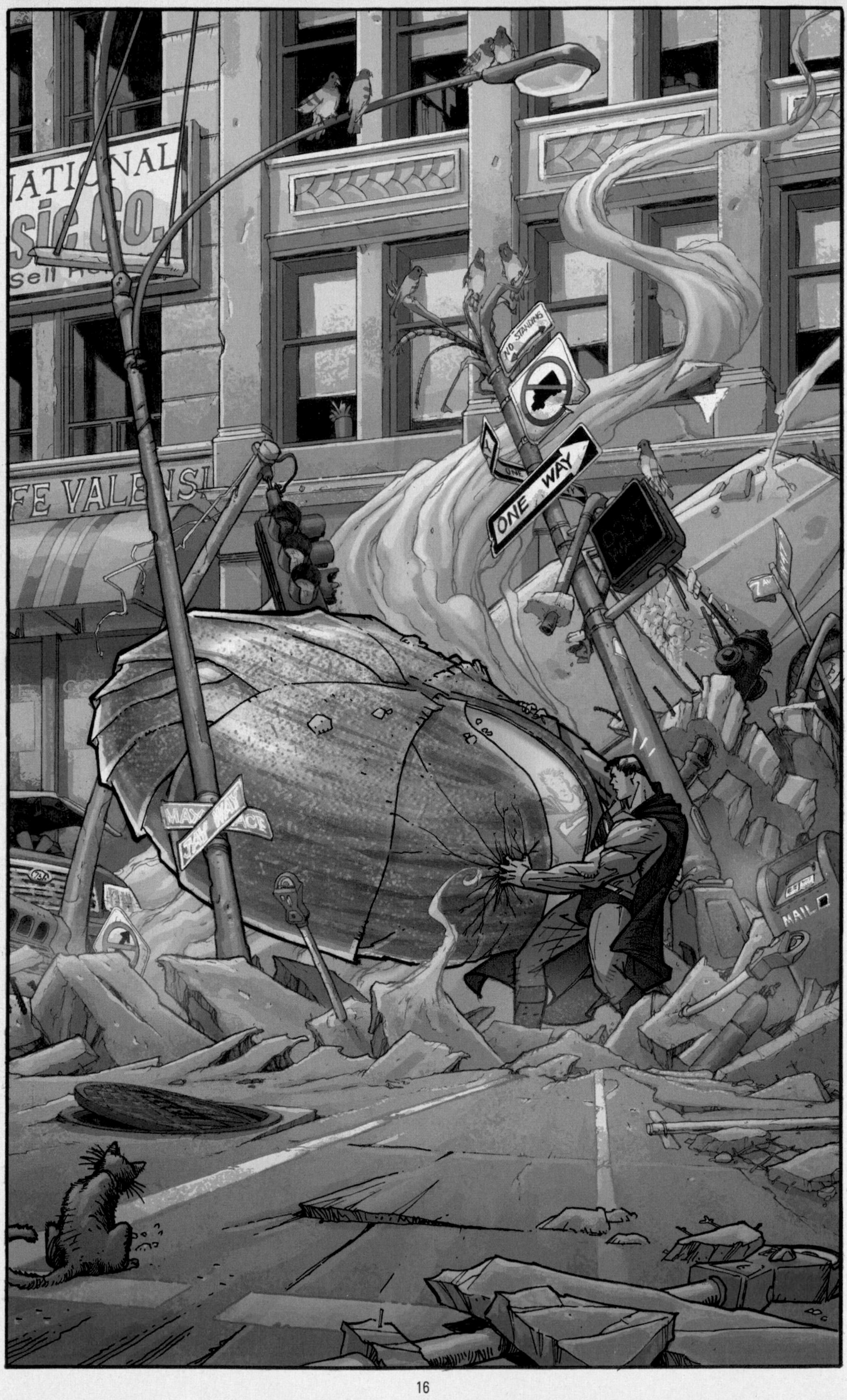
NATIONAL
sic CO.
FE VALENS
NO STANDING
ONE WAY
MAIL

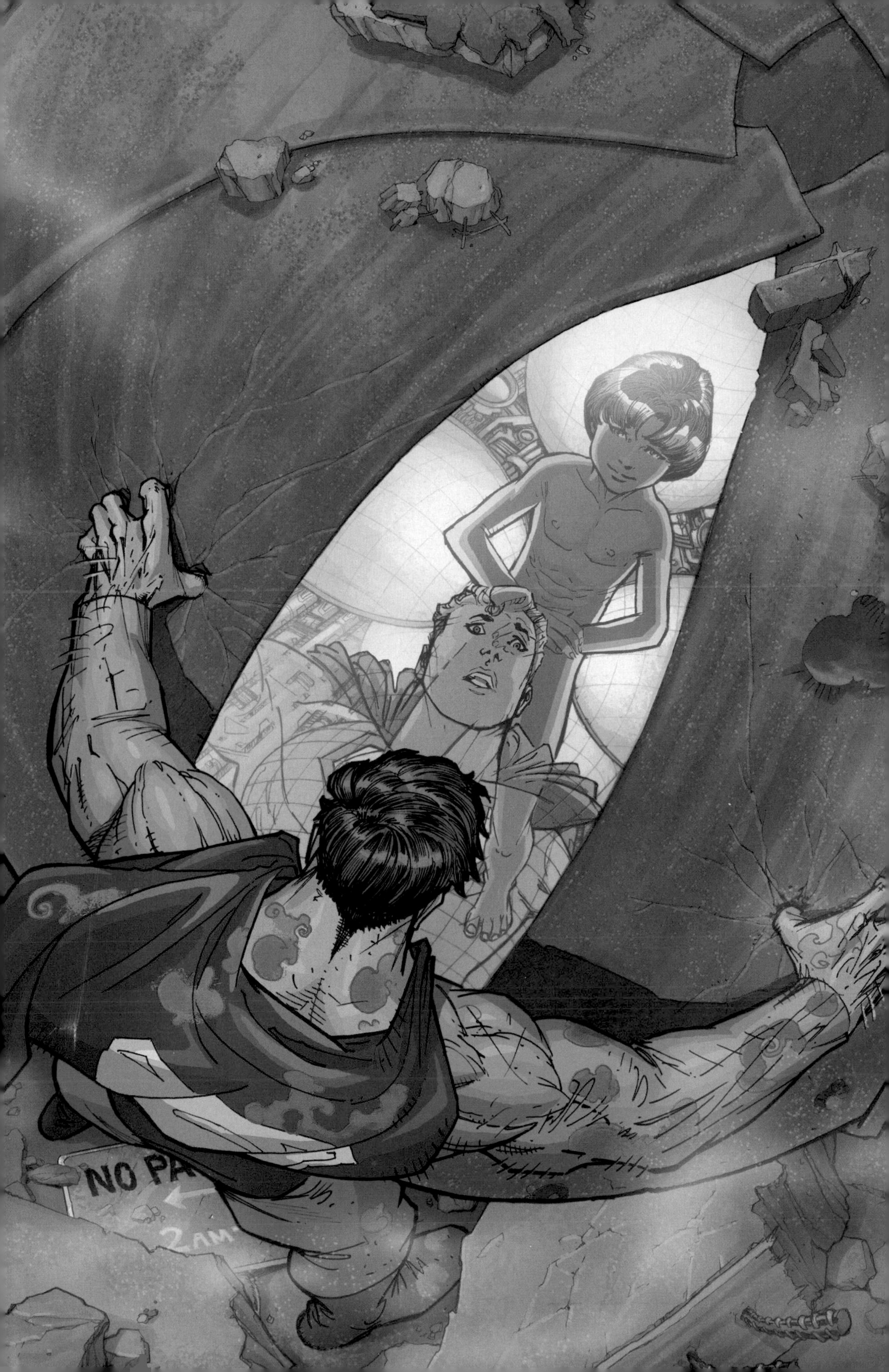
NO PA
2AM

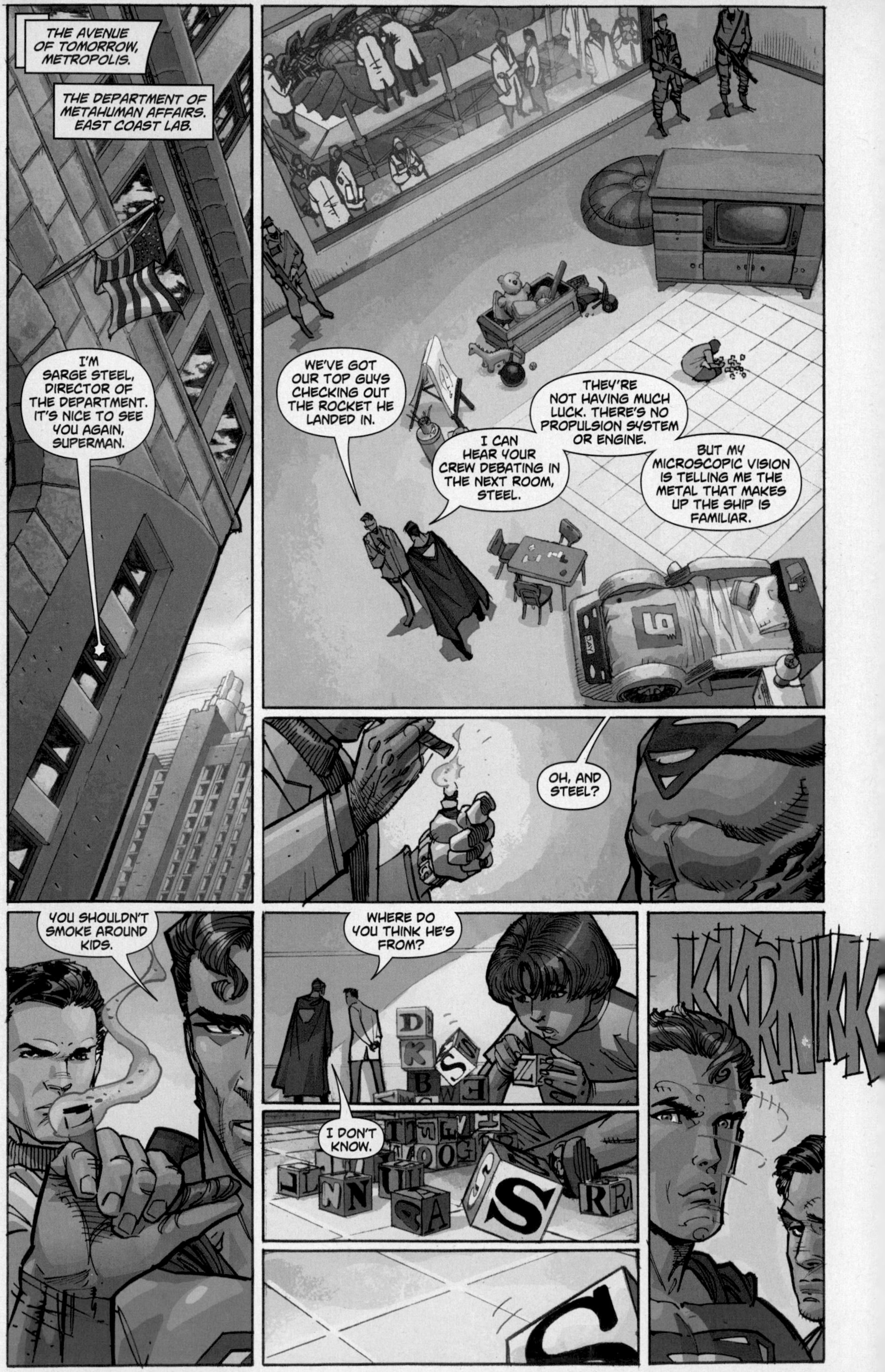
THE AVENUE OF TOMORROW, METROPOLIS.
THE DEPARTMENT OF METAHUMAN AFFAIRS. EAST COAST LAB.
I'M SARGE STEEL, DIRECTOR OF THE DEPARTMENT. IT'S NICE TO SEE YOU AGAIN, SUPERMAN.
WE'VE GOT OUR TOP GUYS CHECKING OUT THE ROCKET HE LANDED IN.
I CAN HEAR YOUR CREW DEBATING IN THE NEXT ROOM, STEEL.
THEY'RE NOT HAVING MUCH LUCK. THERE'S NO PROPULSION SYSTEM OR ENGINE.
BUT MY MICROSCOPIC VISION IS TELLING ME THE METAL THAT MAKES UP THE SHIP IS FAMILIAR.
OH, AND STEEL?
YOU SHOULDN'T SMOKE AROUND KIDS.
WHERE DO YOU THINK HE'S FROM?
I DON'T KNOW.
KKKRNKK

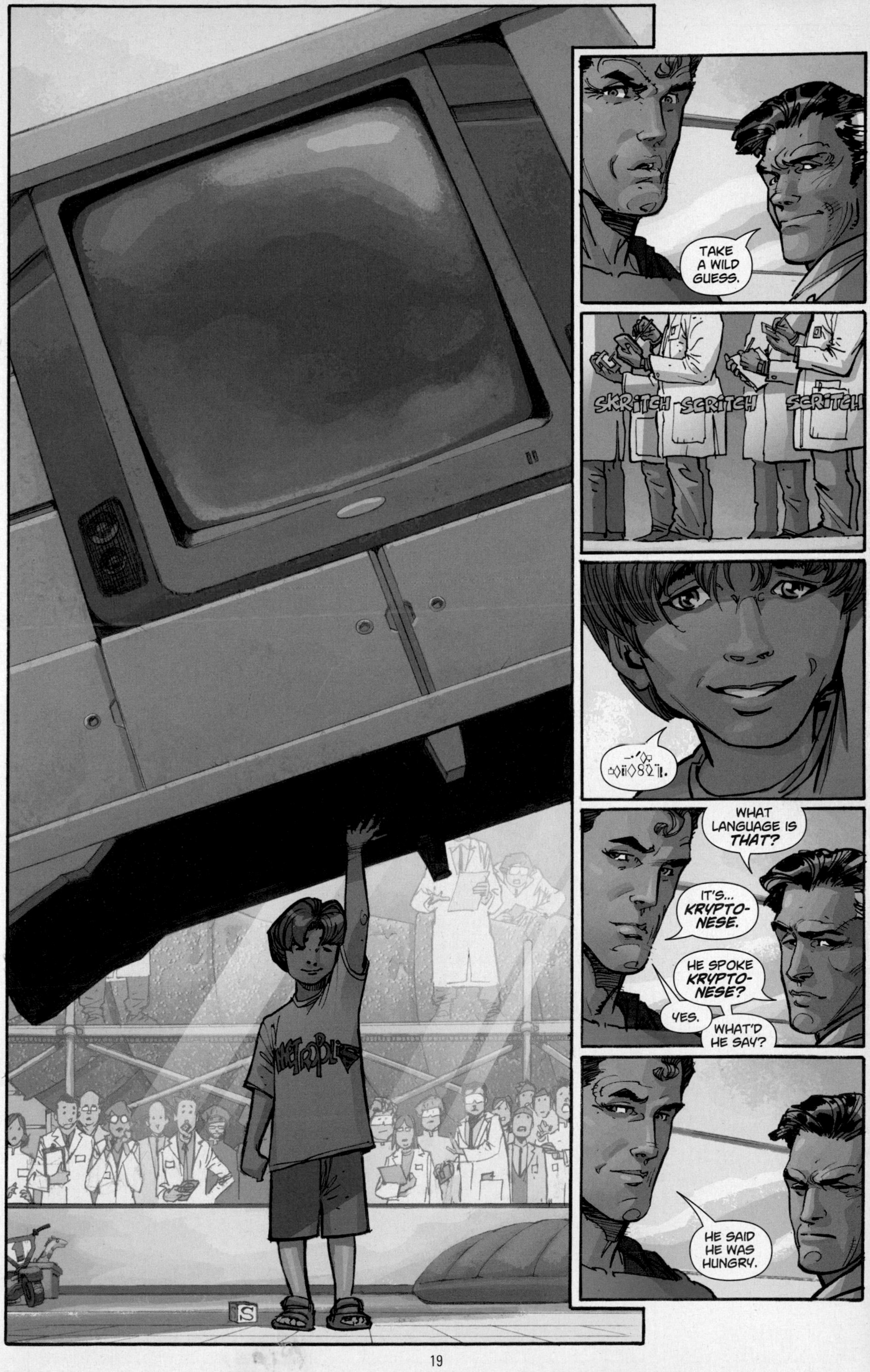

TAKE A WILD GUESS.
SKRITCH SCRITCH SCRITCH
WHAT LANGUAGE IS *THAT?*
IT'S... **KRYPTONESE.**
HE SPOKE **KRYPTONESE?**
YES.
WHAT'D HE SAY?
HE SAID HE WAS HUNGRY.

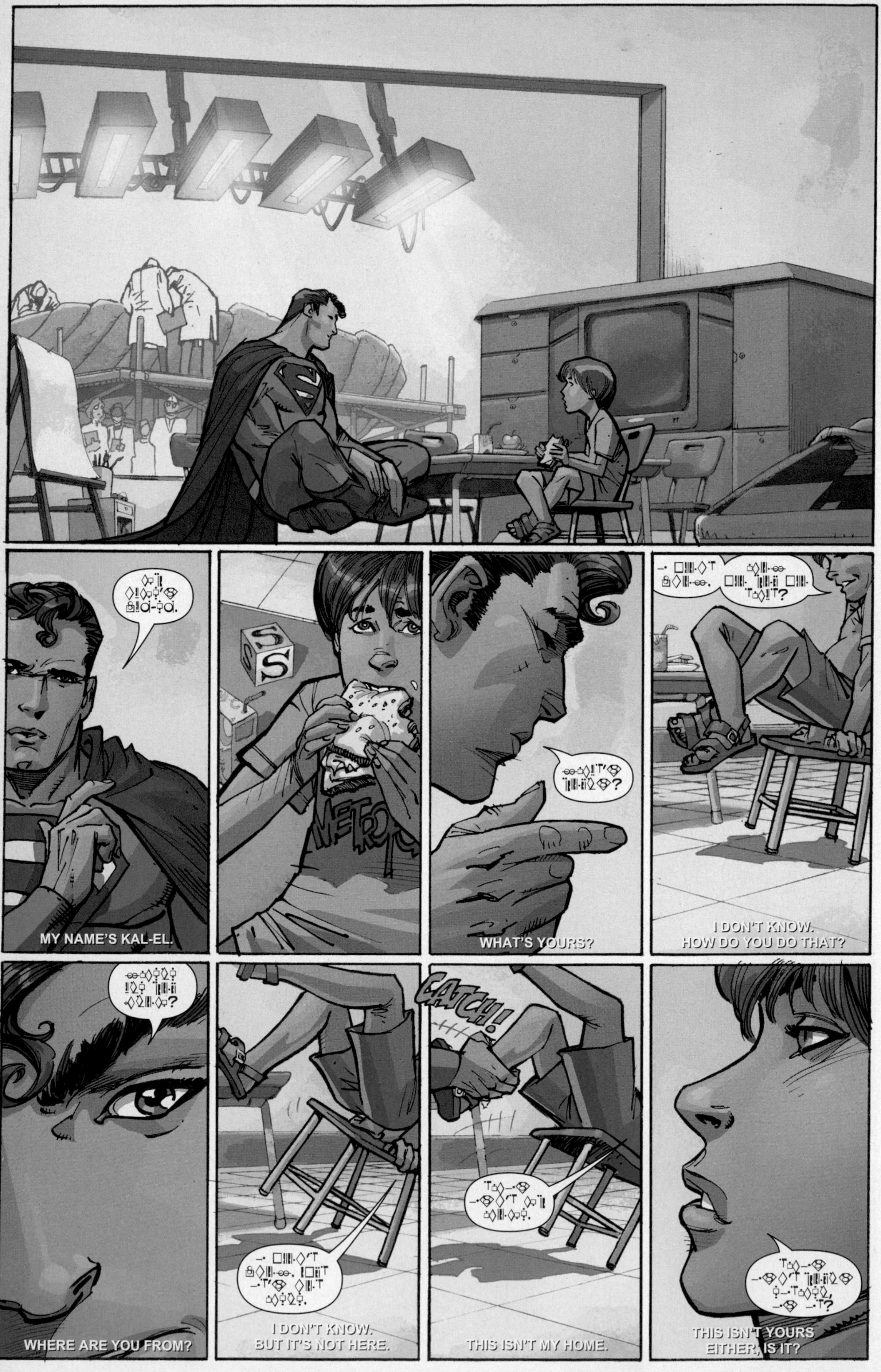
MY NAME'S KAL-EL.
WHAT'S YOURS?
I DON'T KNOW.
HOW DO YOU DO THAT?
WHERE ARE YOU FROM?
I DON'T KNOW.
BUT IT'S NOT HERE.
CATCH!
THIS ISN'T MY HOME.
THIS ISN'T YOURS
EITHER, IS IT?

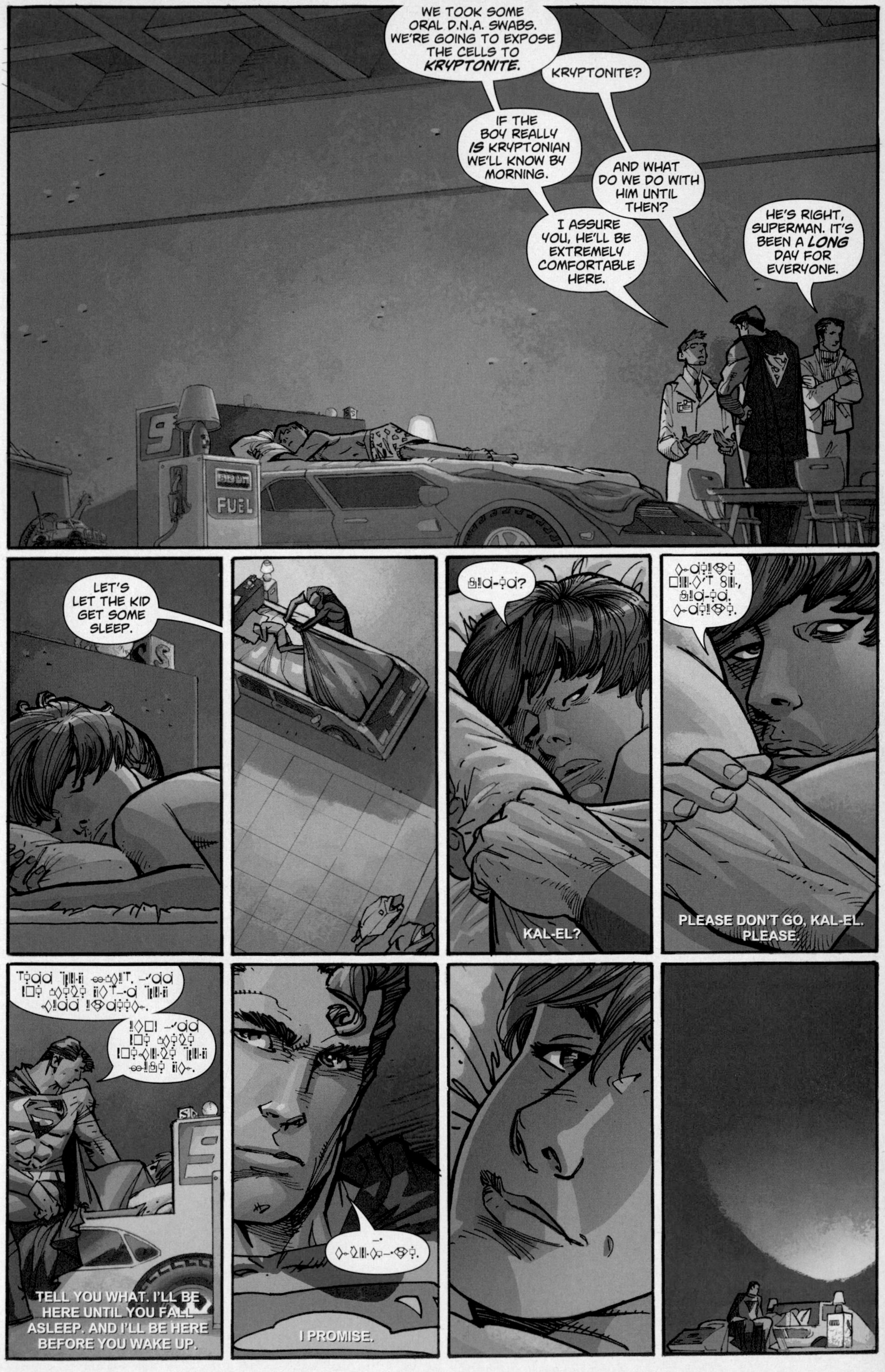
WE TOOK SOME ORAL D.N.A. SWABS. WE'RE GOING TO EXPOSE THE CELLS TO *KRYPTONITE.*
KRYPTONITE?
IF THE BOY REALLY *IS* KRYPTONIAN WE'LL KNOW BY MORNING.
AND WHAT DO WE DO WITH HIM UNTIL THEN?
I ASSURE YOU, HE'LL BE EXTREMELY COMFORTABLE HERE.
HE'S RIGHT, SUPERMAN. IT'S BEEN A *LONG* DAY FOR EVERYONE.
FUEL
LET'S LET THE KID GET SOME SLEEP.
KAL-EL?
PLEASE DON'T GO, KAL-EL. PLEASE.
TELL YOU WHAT. I'LL BE HERE UNTIL YOU FALL ASLEEP. AND I'LL BE HERE BEFORE YOU WAKE UP.
I PROMISE.

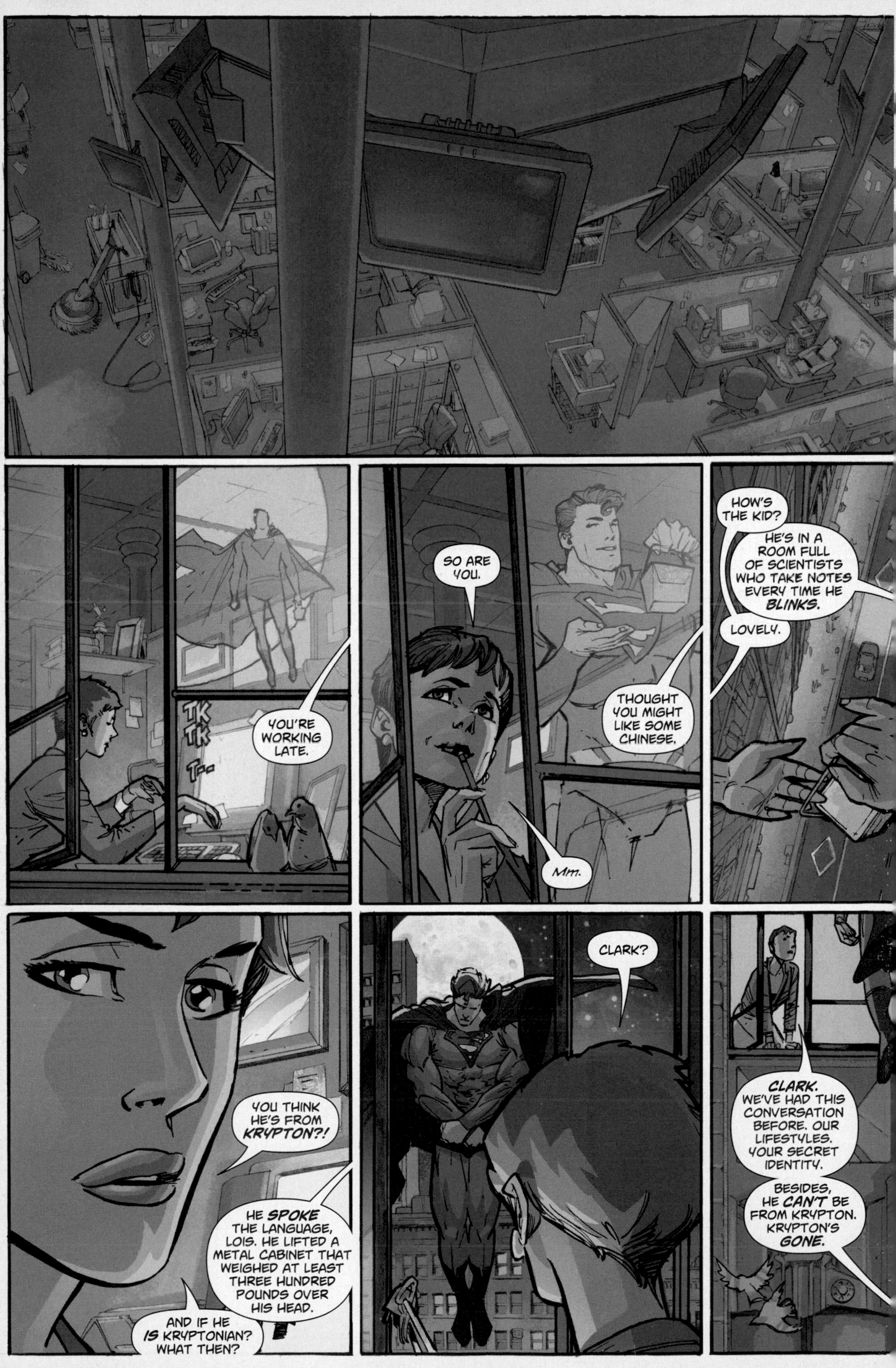
TK TK TK
YOU'RE WORKING LATE.
SO ARE YOU.
THOUGHT YOU MIGHT LIKE SOME CHINESE.
Mm.
HOW'S THE KID?
HE'S IN A ROOM FULL OF SCIENTISTS WHO TAKE NOTES EVERY TIME HE BLINKS.
LOVELY.
YOU THINK HE'S FROM KRYPTON?!
HE SPOKE THE LANGUAGE, LOIS. HE LIFTED A METAL CABINET THAT WEIGHED AT LEAST THREE HUNDRED POUNDS OVER HIS HEAD.
AND IF HE IS KRYPTONIAN? WHAT THEN?
CLARK?
CLARK. WE'VE HAD THIS CONVERSATION BEFORE. OUR LIFESTYLES. YOUR SECRET IDENTITY.
BESIDES, HE CAN'T BE FROM KRYPTON. KRYPTON'S GONE.

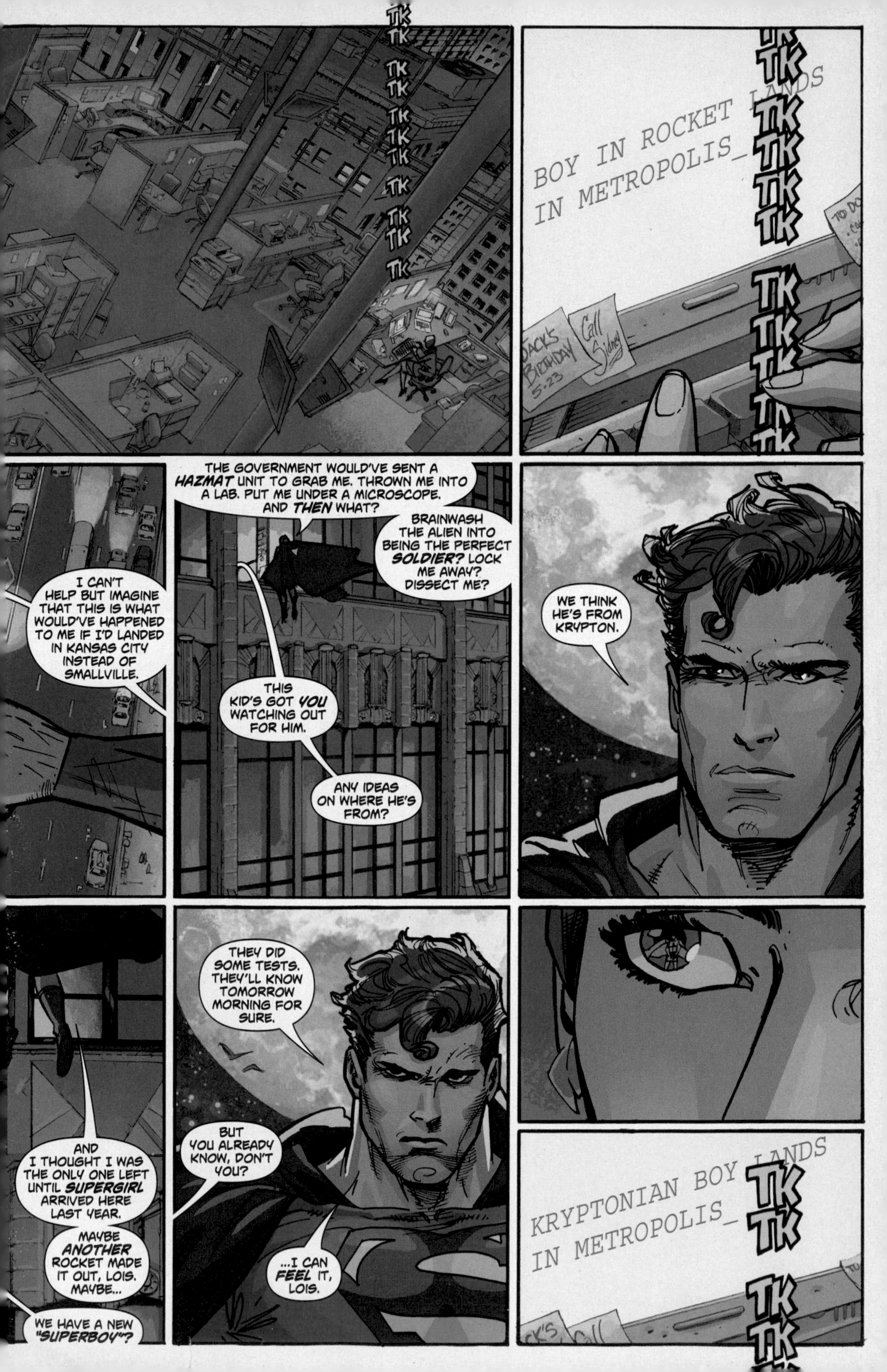
TK TK
TK TK
TK TK TK
TK
TK TK
TK
BOY IN ROCKET LANDS IN METROPOLIS_
TK TK TK TK
JACK'S BIRTHDAY 5.23
Call Sidney
TK TK TK
I CAN'T HELP BUT IMAGINE THAT THIS IS WHAT WOULD'VE HAPPENED TO ME IF I'D LANDED IN KANSAS CITY INSTEAD OF SMALLVILLE.
THE GOVERNMENT WOULD'VE SENT A HAZMAT UNIT TO GRAB ME. THROWN ME INTO A LAB. PUT ME UNDER A MICROSCOPE. AND THEN WHAT?
BRAINWASH THE ALIEN INTO BEING THE PERFECT SOLDIER? LOCK ME AWAY? DISSECT ME?
THIS KID'S GOT YOU WATCHING OUT FOR HIM.
ANY IDEAS ON WHERE HE'S FROM?
WE THINK HE'S FROM KRYPTON.
AND I THOUGHT I WAS THE ONLY ONE LEFT UNTIL SUPERGIRL ARRIVED HERE LAST YEAR.
MAYBE ANOTHER ROCKET MADE IT OUT, LOIS. MAYBE...
WE HAVE A NEW "SUPERBOY"?
THEY DID SOME TESTS. THEY'LL KNOW TOMORROW MORNING FOR SURE.
BUT YOU ALREADY KNOW, DON'T YOU?
...I CAN FEEL IT, LOIS.
KRYPTONIAN BOY LANDS IN METROPOLIS_
TK TK
TK TK

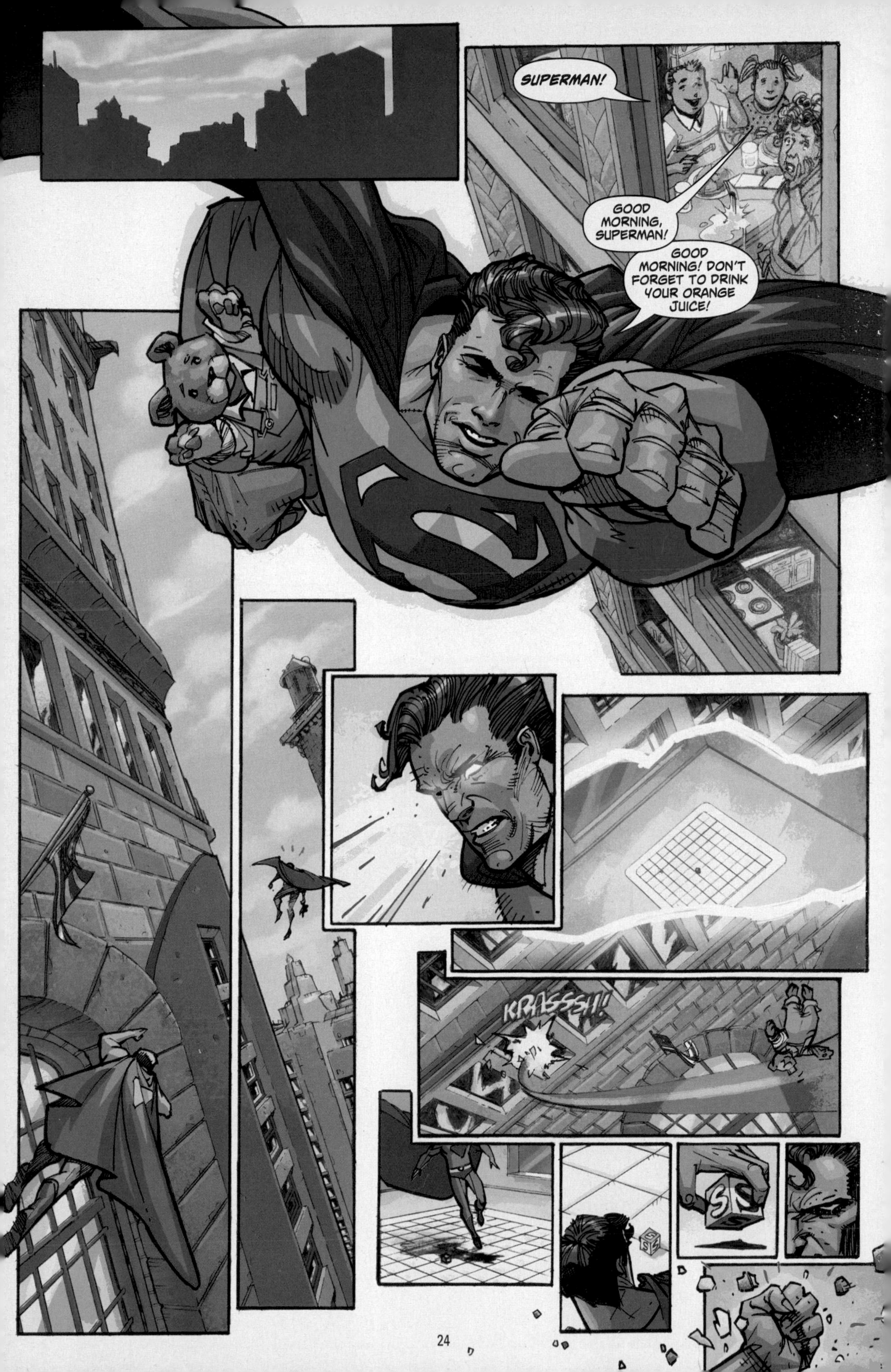
SUPERMAN!
GOOD MORNING, SUPERMAN!
GOOD MORNING! DON'T FORGET TO DRINK YOUR ORANGE JUICE!
KRASSSH!

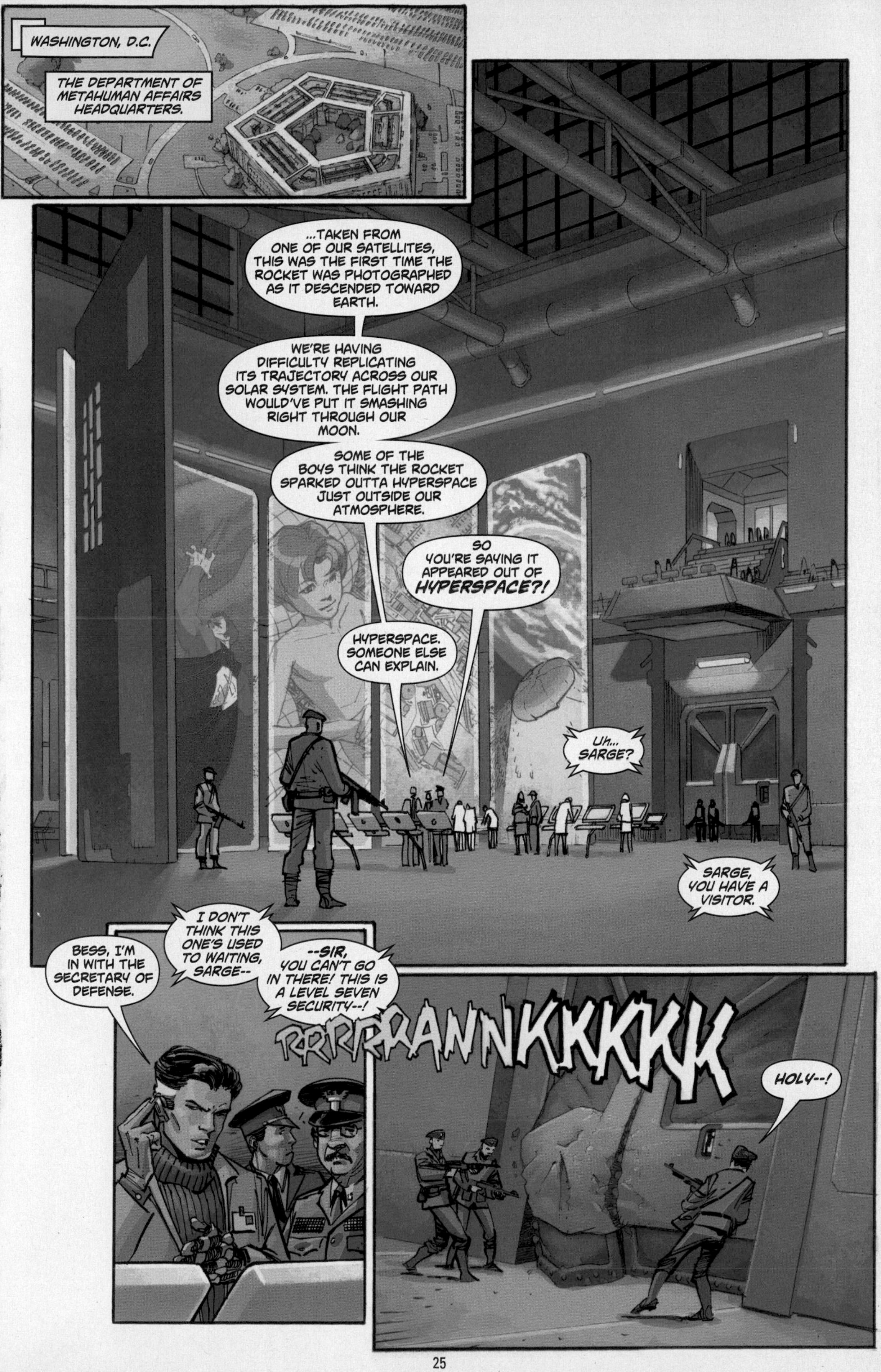
WASHINGTON, D.C.
THE DEPARTMENT OF METAHUMAN AFFAIRS HEADQUARTERS.
...TAKEN FROM ONE OF OUR SATELLITES, THIS WAS THE FIRST TIME THE ROCKET WAS PHOTOGRAPHED AS IT DESCENDED TOWARD EARTH.
WE'RE HAVING DIFFICULTY REPLICATING ITS TRAJECTORY ACROSS OUR SOLAR SYSTEM. THE FLIGHT PATH WOULD'VE PUT IT SMASHING RIGHT THROUGH OUR MOON.
SOME OF THE BOYS THINK THE ROCKET SPARKED OUTTA HYPERSPACE JUST OUTSIDE OUR ATMOSPHERE.
SO YOU'RE SAYING IT APPEARED OUT OF HYPERSPACE?!
HYPERSPACE. SOMEONE ELSE CAN EXPLAIN.
UH... SARGE?
SARGE, YOU HAVE A VISITOR.
BESS, I'M IN WITH THE SECRETARY OF DEFENSE.
I DON'T THINK THIS ONE'S USED TO WAITING, SARGE--
--SIR, YOU CAN'T GO IN THERE! THIS IS A LEVEL SEVEN SECURITY--!
RRRRRRANNKKKKKK
HOLY--!

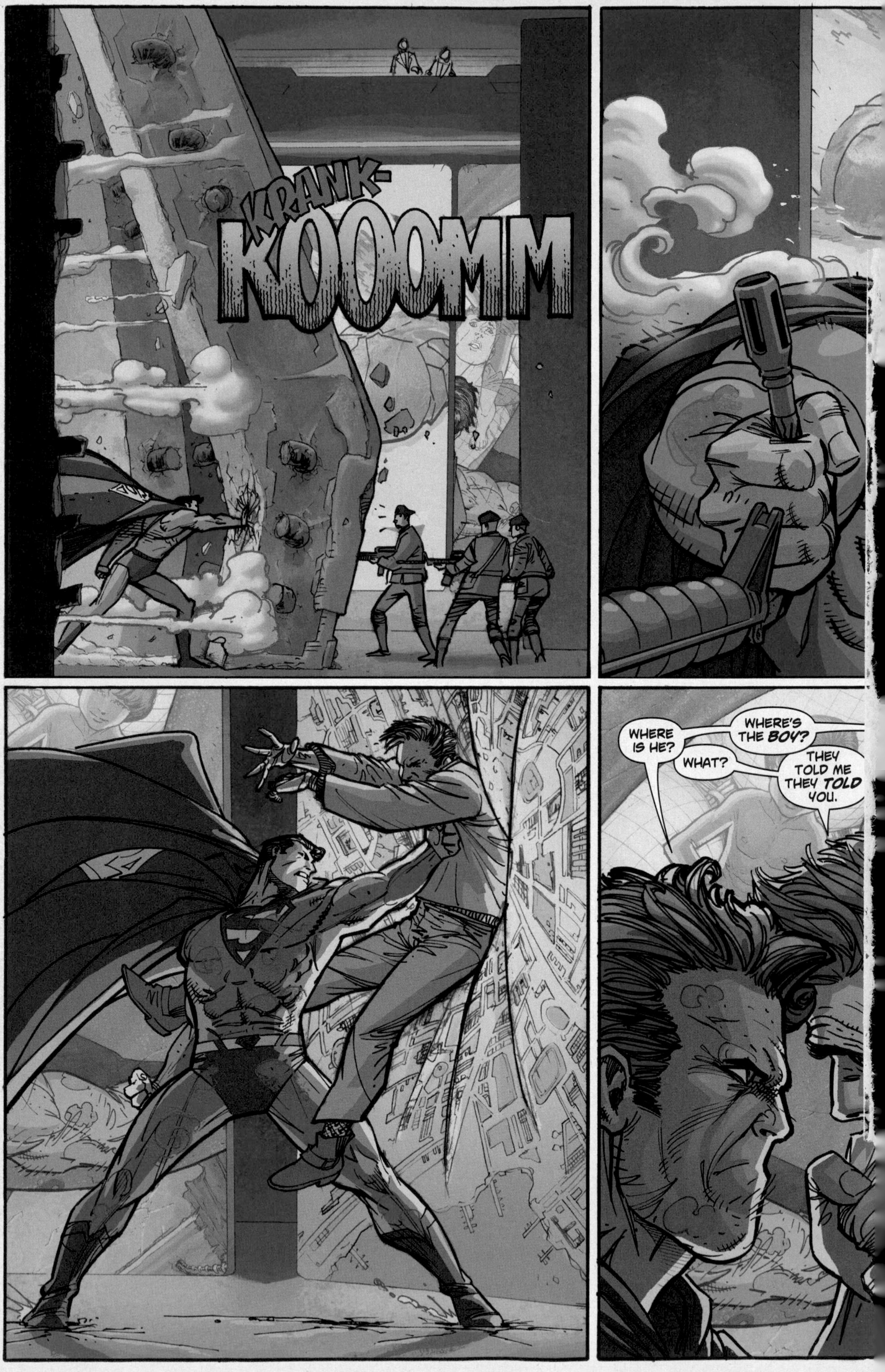
KRANK-
KOOOMM
WHERE IS HE?
WHERE'S THE BOY?
WHAT?
THEY TOLD ME THEY TOLD YOU.

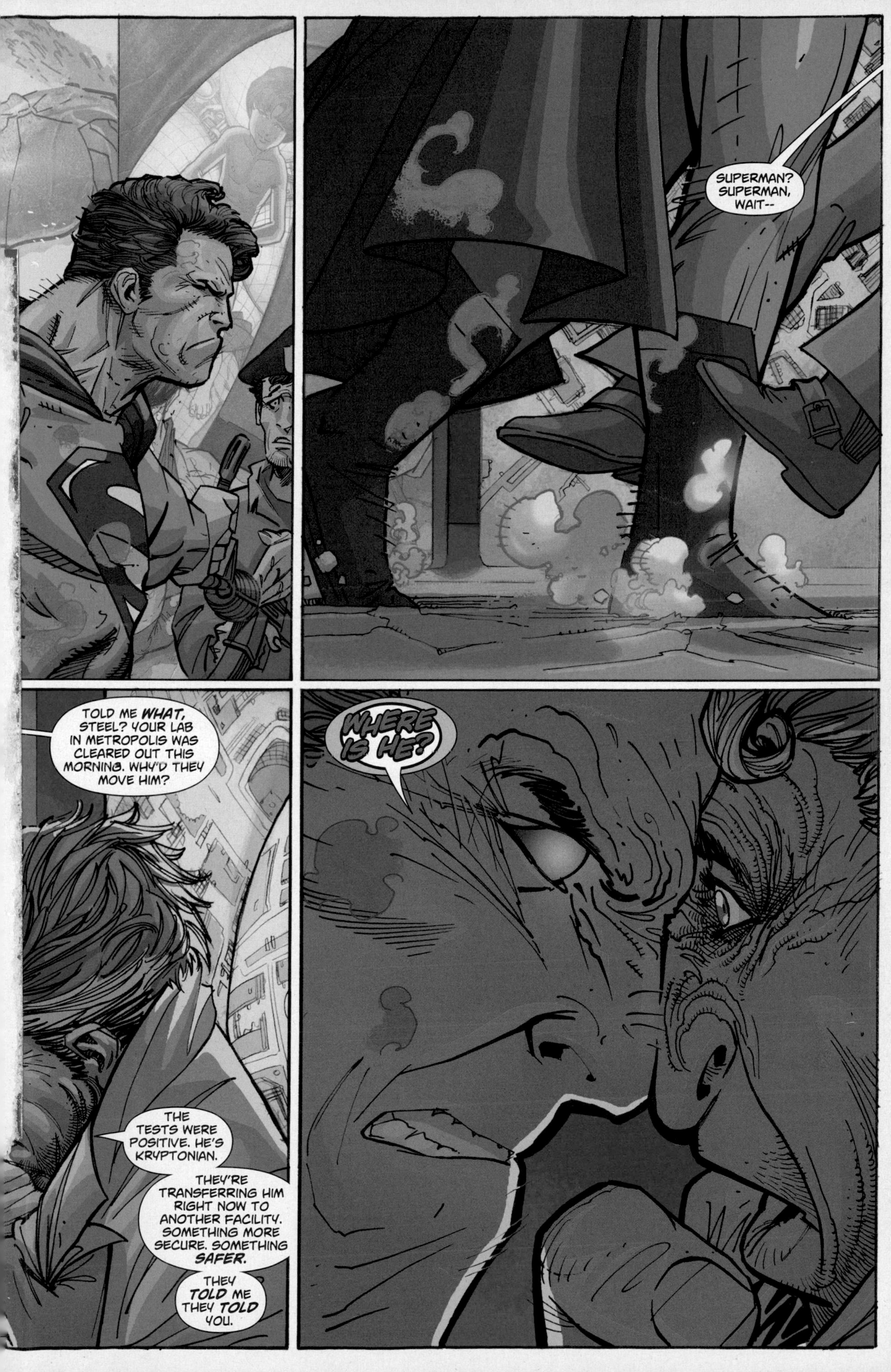
SUPERMAN? SUPERMAN, WAIT--
TOLD ME WHAT, STEEL? YOUR LAB IN METROPOLIS WAS CLEARED OUT THIS MORNING. WHY'D THEY MOVE HIM?
WHERE IS HE?
THE TESTS WERE POSITIVE. HE'S KRYPTONIAN.
THEY'RE TRANSFERRING HIM RIGHT NOW TO ANOTHER FACILITY. SOMETHING MORE SECURE. SOMETHING SAFER.
THEY TOLD ME THEY TOLD YOU.

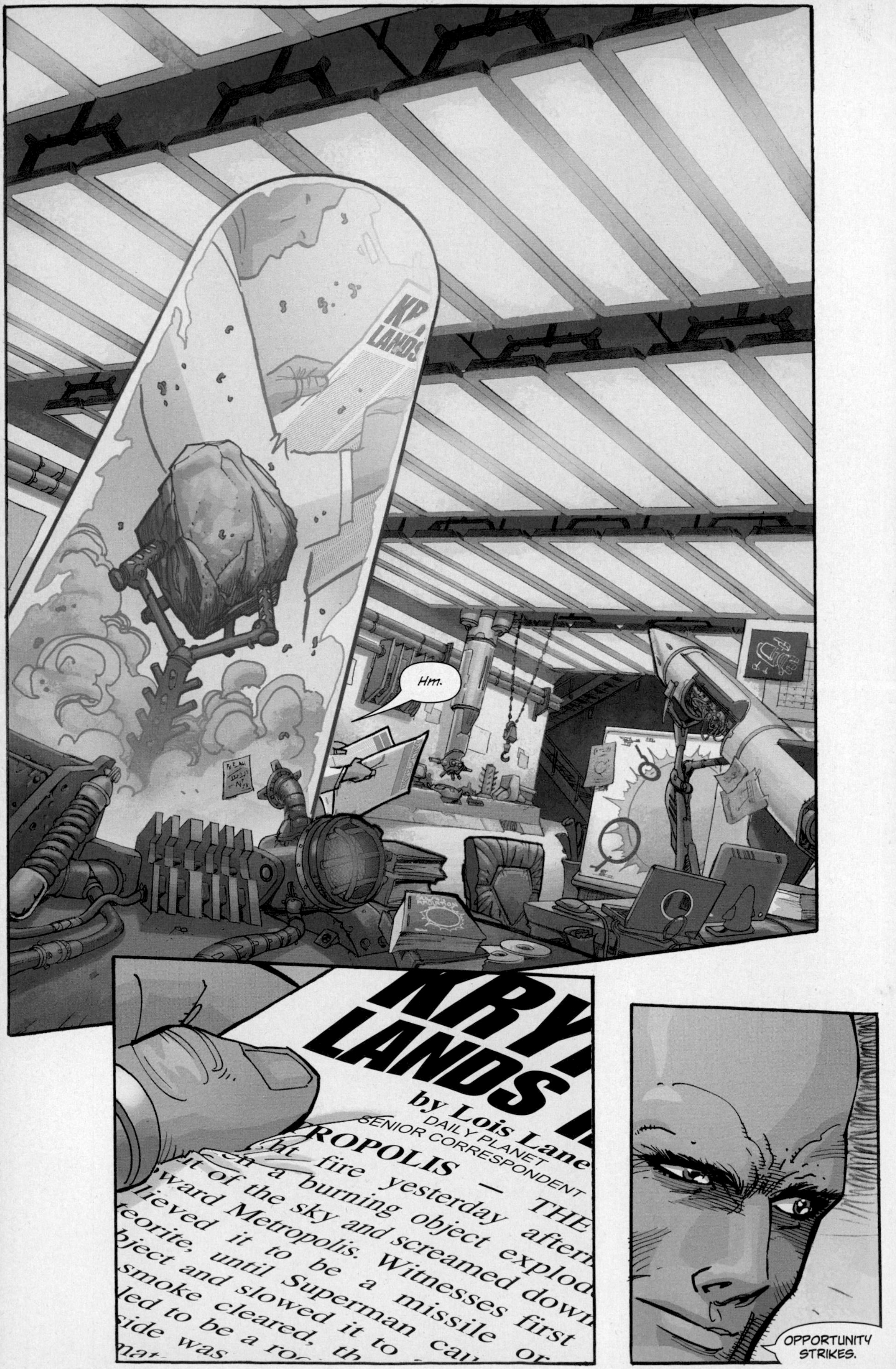
Hm.
KRY
LANDS
by Lois Lane
DAILY PLANET
SENIOR CORRESPONDENT
ROPOLIS — THE
fire yesterday after
n a burning object explod
t of the sky and screamed dow
ward Metropolis. Witnesses first
lieved it to be a missile or
eteorite, until Superman ca
object and slowed it to
smoke cleared, th
led to be a ro
side was
OPPORTUNITY STRIKES.

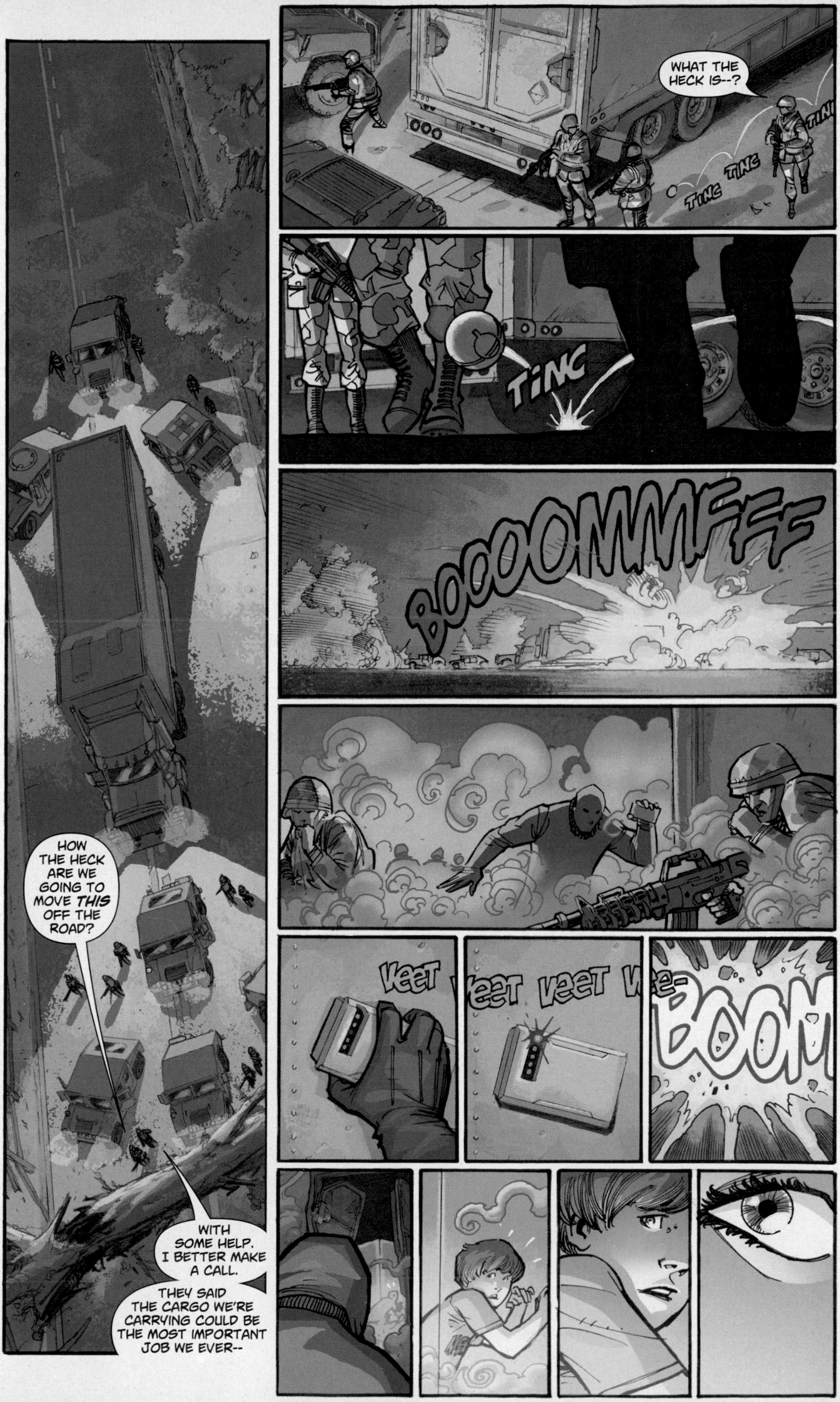
HOW THE HECK ARE WE GOING TO MOVE *THIS* OFF THE ROAD?
WITH SOME HELP. I BETTER MAKE A CALL.
THEY SAID THE CARGO WE'RE CARRYING COULD BE THE MOST IMPORTANT JOB WE EVER--
WHAT THE HECK IS--?
TINC
TINC
TINC
TINC
BOOOOMMFFF
VEET VEET VEET VEE-
BOOM

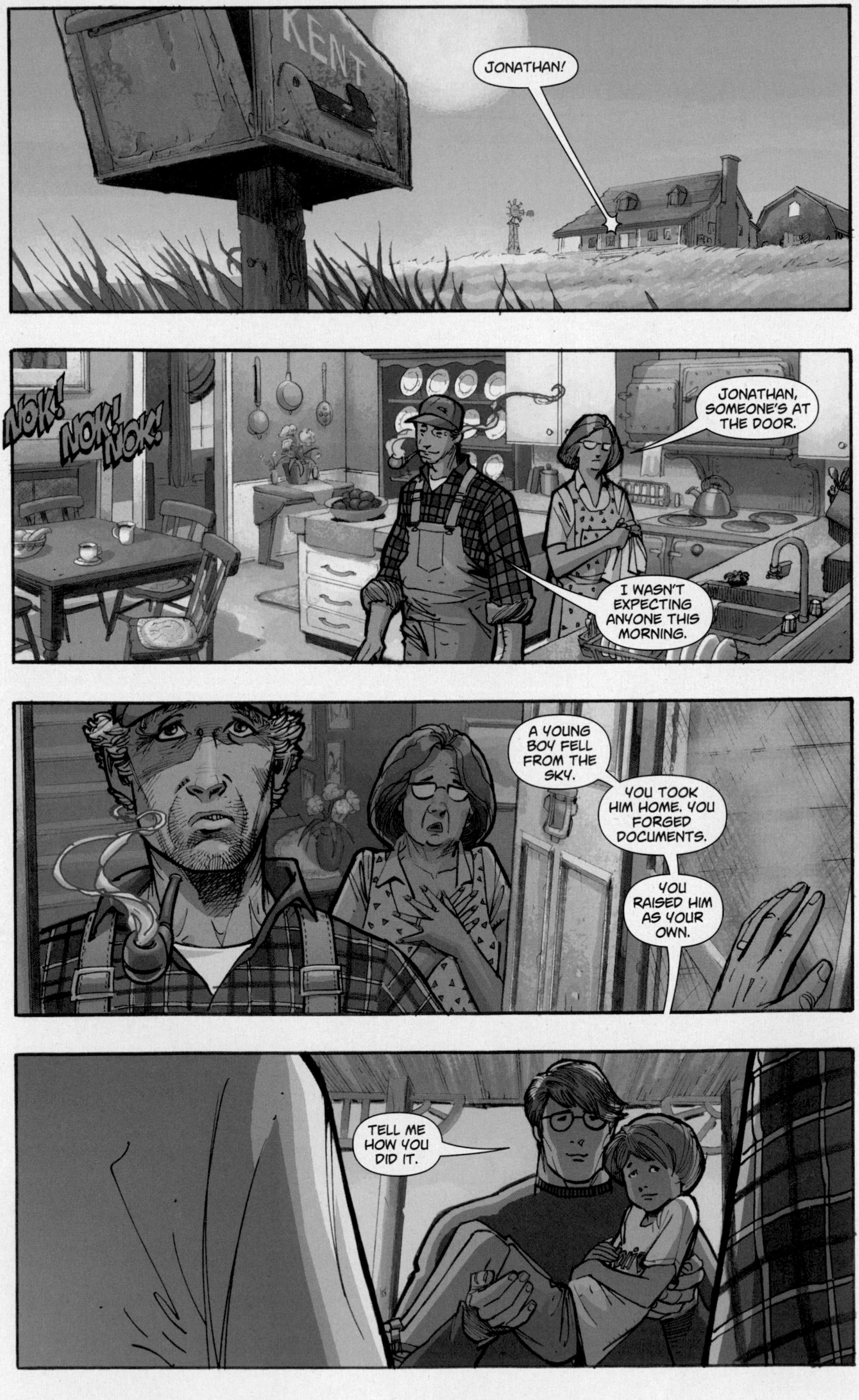
KENT
JONATHAN!
NOK! NOK! NOK!
JONATHAN, SOMEONE'S AT THE DOOR.
I WASN'T EXPECTING ANYONE THIS MORNING.
A YOUNG BOY FELL FROM THE SKY.
YOU TOOK HIM HOME. YOU FORGED DOCUMENTS.
YOU RAISED HIM AS YOUR OWN.
TELL ME HOW YOU DID IT.

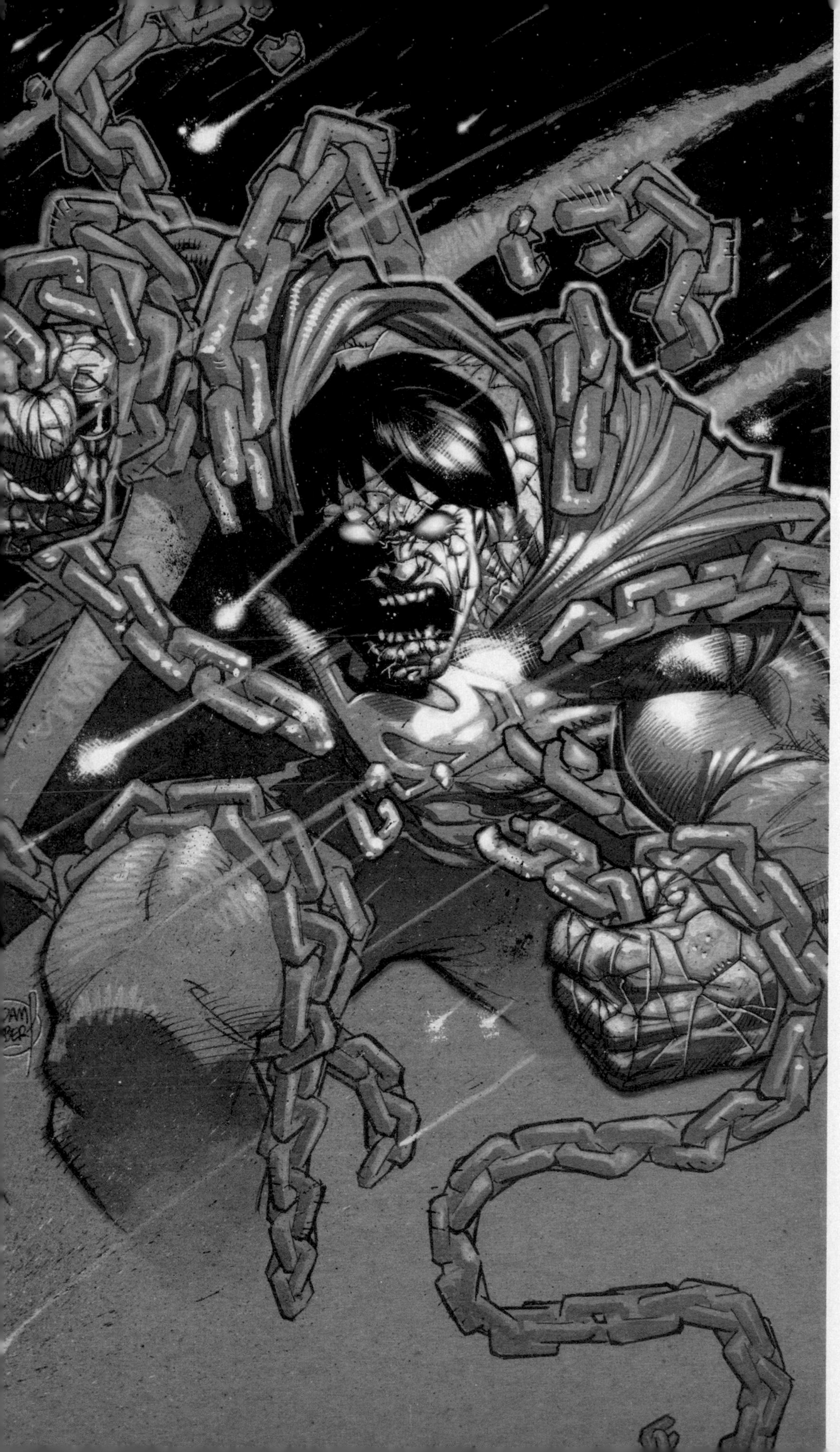

CHAPTER TWO

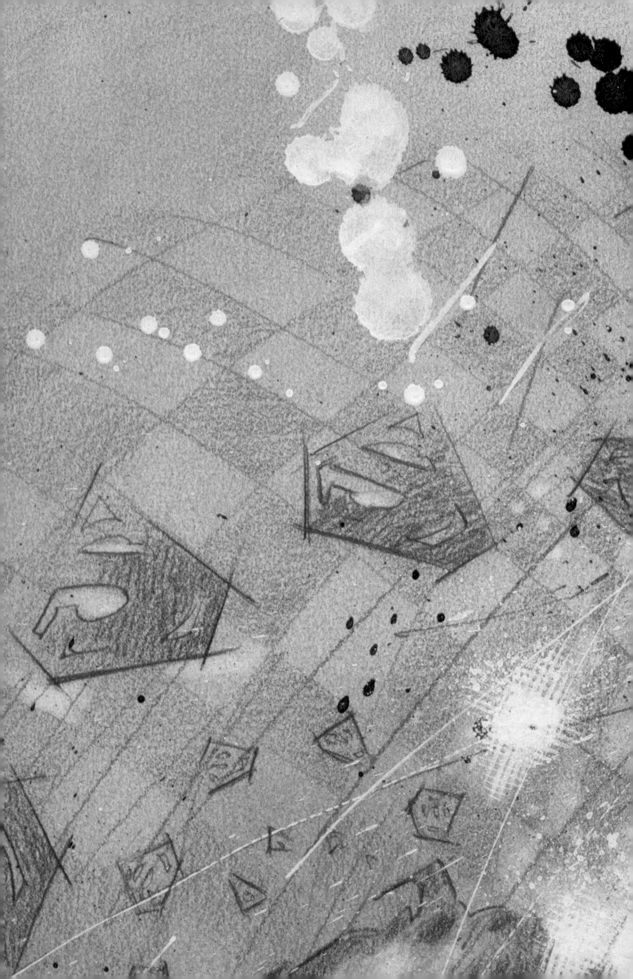

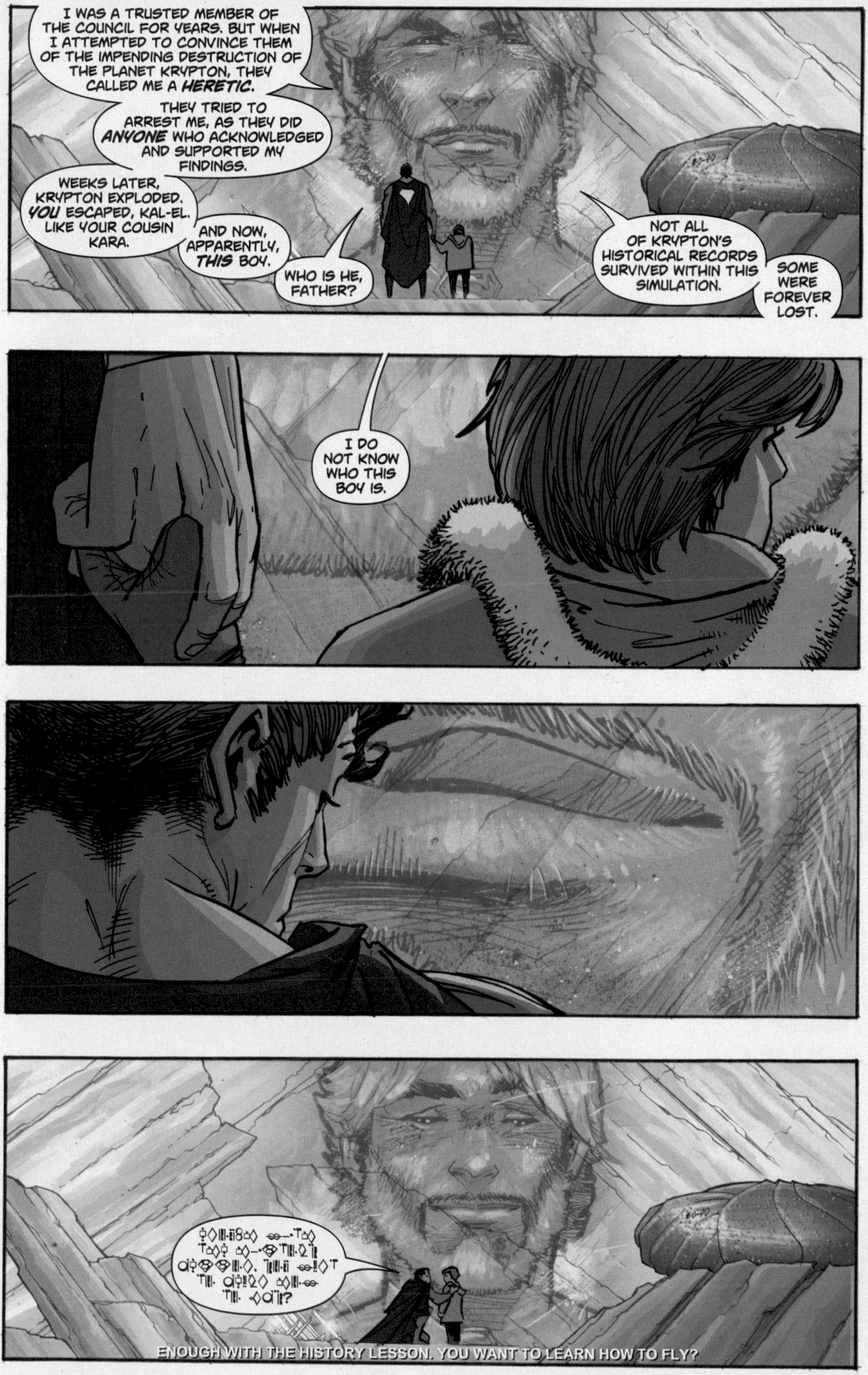

I WAS A TRUSTED MEMBER OF THE COUNCIL FOR YEARS. BUT WHEN I ATTEMPTED TO CONVINCE THEM OF THE IMPENDING DESTRUCTION OF THE PLANET KRYPTON, THEY CALLED ME A HERETIC.
THEY TRIED TO ARREST ME, AS THEY DID ANYONE WHO ACKNOWLEDGED AND SUPPORTED MY FINDINGS.
WEEKS LATER, KRYPTON EXPLODED. YOU ESCAPED, KAL-EL. LIKE YOUR COUSIN KARA.
AND NOW, APPARENTLY, THIS BOY.
WHO IS HE, FATHER?
NOT ALL OF KRYPTON'S HISTORICAL RECORDS SURVIVED WITHIN THIS SIMULATION.
SOME WERE FOREVER LOST.
I DO NOT KNOW WHO THIS BOY IS.
ENOUGH WITH THE HISTORY LESSON. YOU WANT TO LEARN HOW TO FLY?

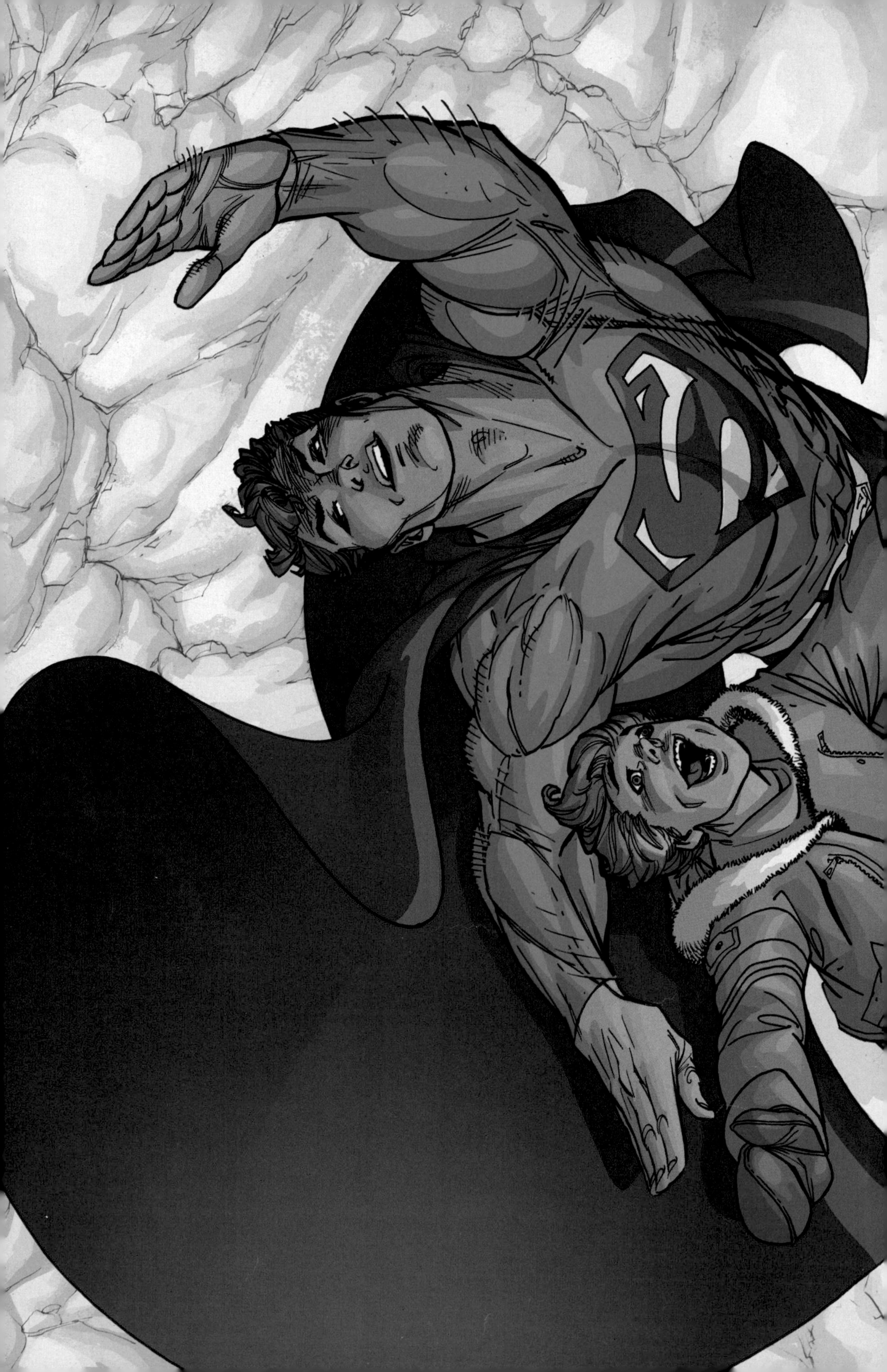

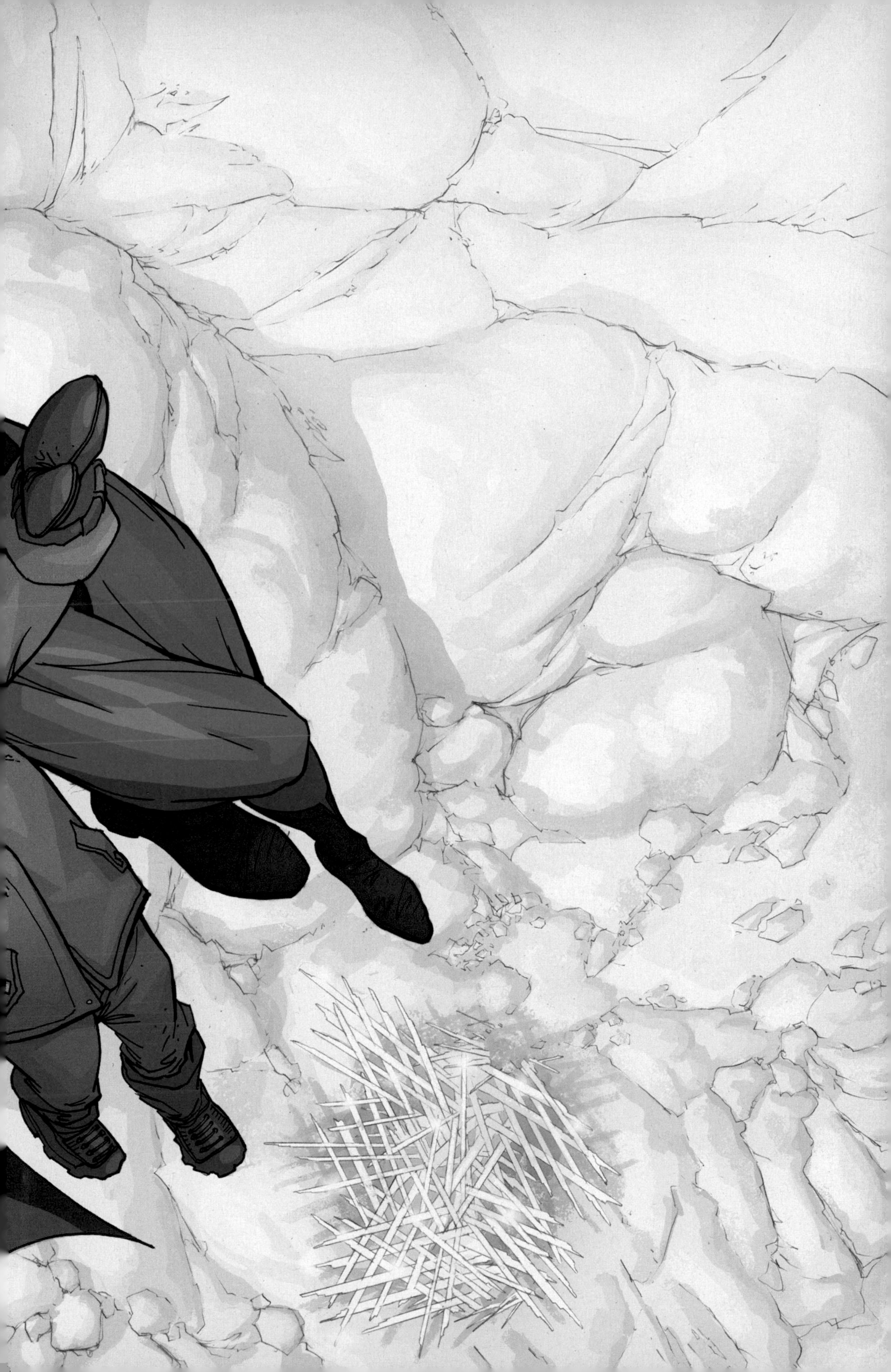

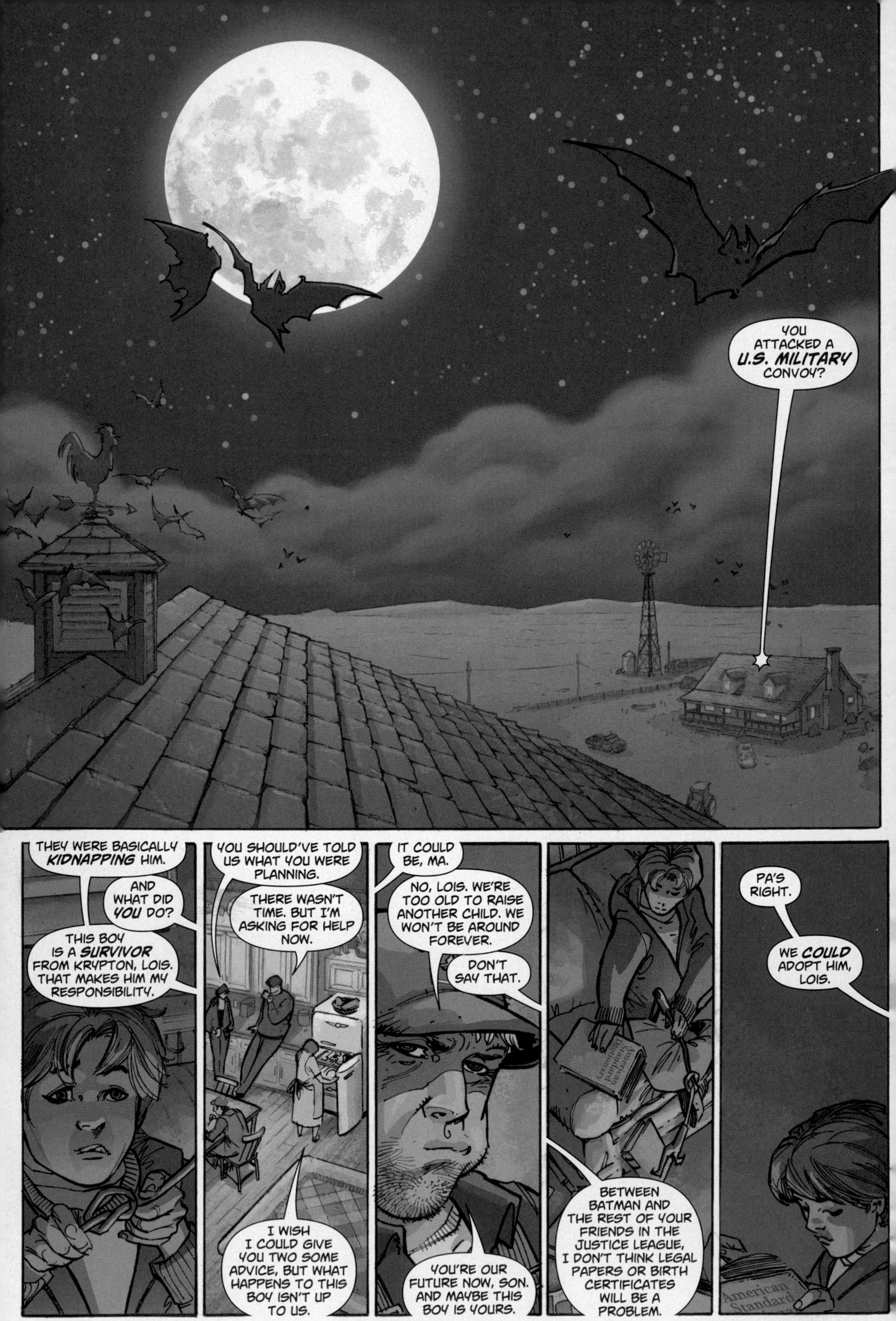

YOU ATTACKED A U.S. MILITARY CONVOY?
THEY WERE BASICALLY KIDNAPPING HIM.
AND WHAT DID YOU DO?
THIS BOY IS A SURVIVOR FROM KRYPTON, LOIS. THAT MAKES HIM MY RESPONSIBILITY.
YOU SHOULD'VE TOLD US WHAT YOU WERE PLANNING.
THERE WASN'T TIME. BUT I'M ASKING FOR HELP NOW.
I WISH I COULD GIVE YOU TWO SOME ADVICE, BUT WHAT HAPPENS TO THIS BOY ISN'T UP TO US.
IT COULD BE, MA.
NO, LOIS. WE'RE TOO OLD TO RAISE ANOTHER CHILD. WE WON'T BE AROUND FOREVER.
DON'T SAY THAT.
YOU'RE OUR FUTURE NOW, SON. AND MAYBE THIS BOY IS YOURS.
BETWEEN BATMAN AND THE REST OF YOUR FRIENDS IN THE JUSTICE LEAGUE, I DON'T THINK LEGAL PAPERS OR BIRTH CERTIFICATES WILL BE A PROBLEM.
PA'S RIGHT.
WE COULD ADOPT HIM, LOIS.

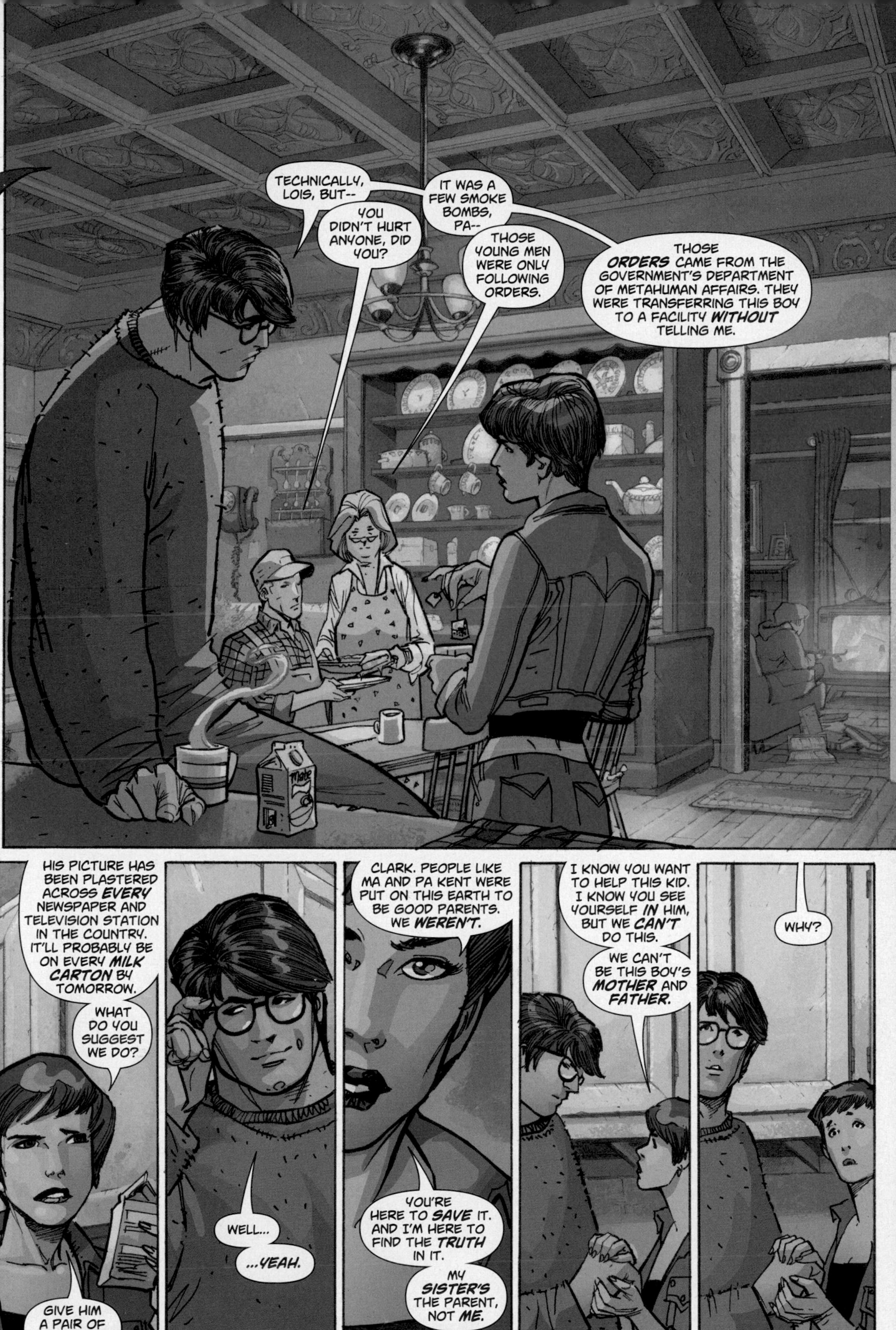
TECHNICALLY, LOIS, BUT--
IT WAS A FEW SMOKE BOMBS, PA--
YOU DIDN'T HURT ANYONE, DID YOU?
THOSE YOUNG MEN WERE ONLY FOLLOWING ORDERS.
THOSE ORDERS CAME FROM THE GOVERNMENT'S DEPARTMENT OF METAHUMAN AFFAIRS. THEY WERE TRANSFERRING THIS BOY TO A FACILITY WITHOUT TELLING ME.
HIS PICTURE HAS BEEN PLASTERED ACROSS EVERY NEWSPAPER AND TELEVISION STATION IN THE COUNTRY. IT'LL PROBABLY BE ON EVERY MILK CARTON BY TOMORROW.
WHAT DO YOU SUGGEST WE DO?
GIVE HIM A PAIR OF GLASSES?
WELL...
...YEAH.
CLARK. PEOPLE LIKE MA AND PA KENT WERE PUT ON THIS EARTH TO BE GOOD PARENTS. WE WEREN'T.
YOU'RE HERE TO SAVE IT. AND I'M HERE TO FIND THE TRUTH IN IT.
MY SISTER'S THE PARENT, NOT ME.
I KNOW YOU WANT TO HELP THIS KID. I KNOW YOU SEE YOURSELF IN HIM, BUT WE CAN'T DO THIS.
WE CAN'T BE THIS BOY'S MOTHER AND FATHER.
WHY?

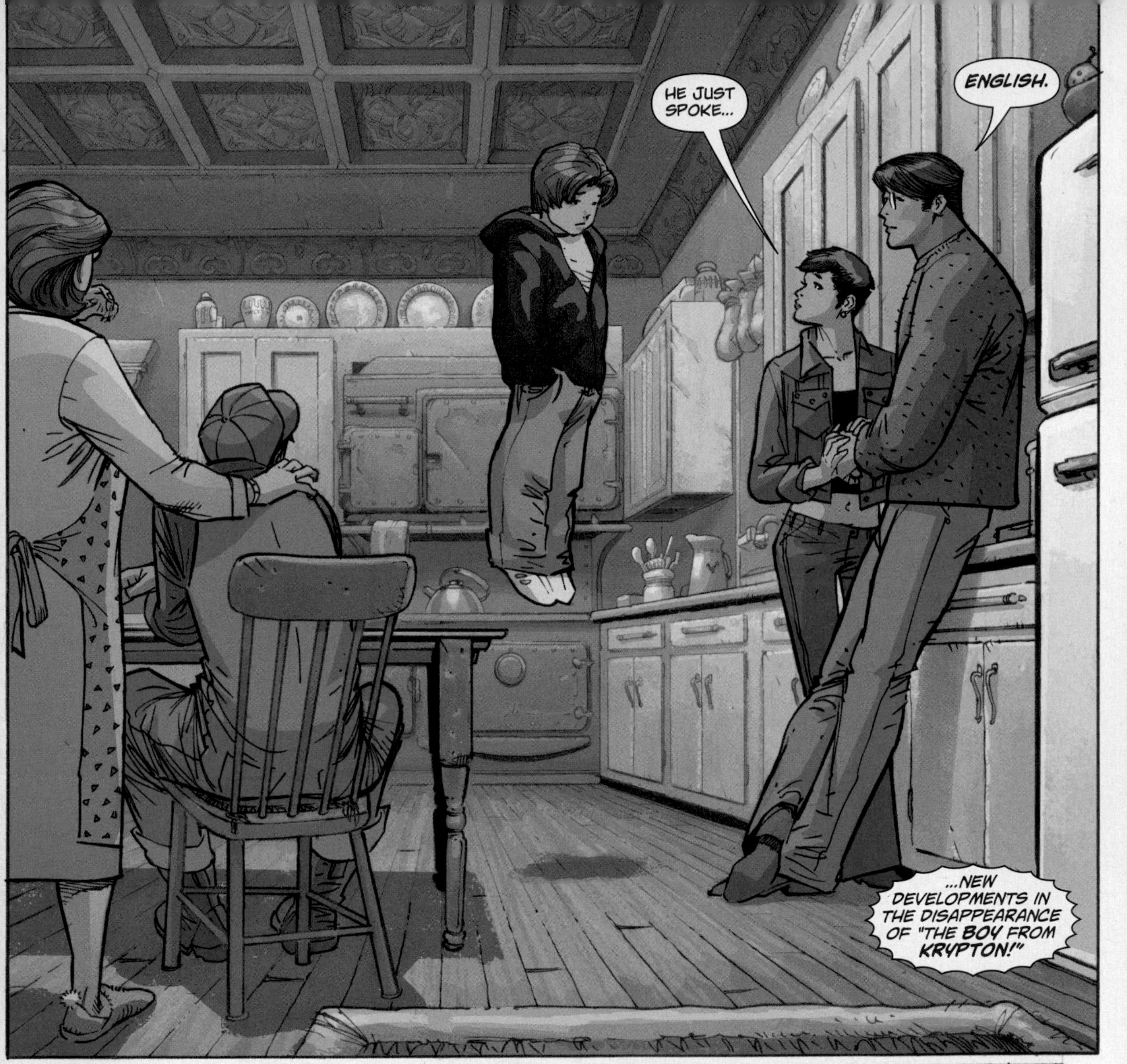
HE JUST SPOKE...
ENGLISH.
...NEW DEVELOPMENTS IN THE DISAPPEARANCE OF "THE BOY FROM KRYPTON!"

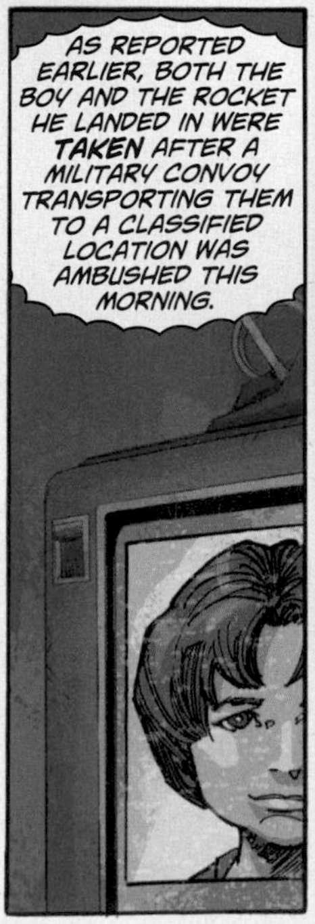
AS REPORTED EARLIER, BOTH THE BOY AND THE ROCKET HE LANDED IN WERE TAKEN AFTER A MILITARY CONVOY TRANSPORTING THEM TO A CLASSIFIED LOCATION WAS AMBUSHED THIS MORNING.

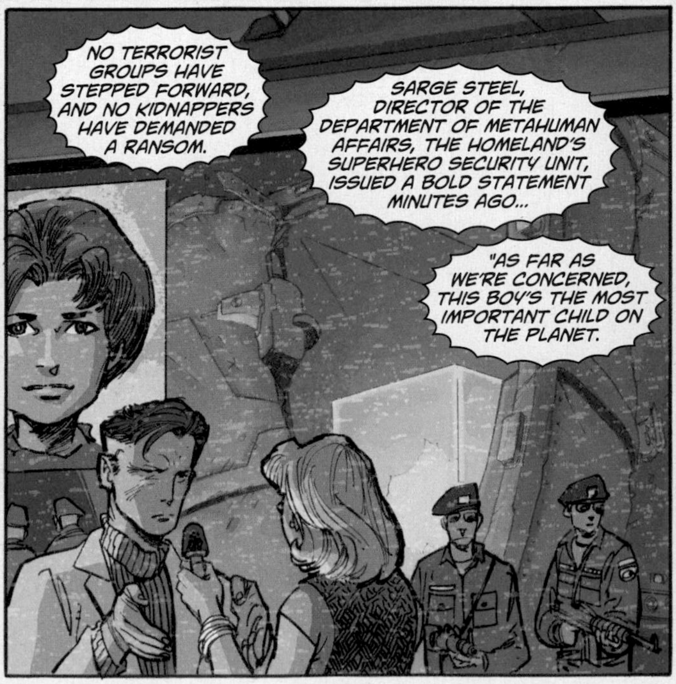
NO TERRORIST GROUPS HAVE STEPPED FORWARD, AND NO KIDNAPPERS HAVE DEMANDED A RANSOM.
SARGE STEEL, DIRECTOR OF THE DEPARTMENT OF METAHUMAN AFFAIRS, THE HOMELAND'S SUPERHERO SECURITY UNIT, ISSUED A BOLD STATEMENT MINUTES AGO...
"AS FAR AS WE'RE CONCERNED, THIS BOY'S THE MOST IMPORTANT CHILD ON THE PLANET.

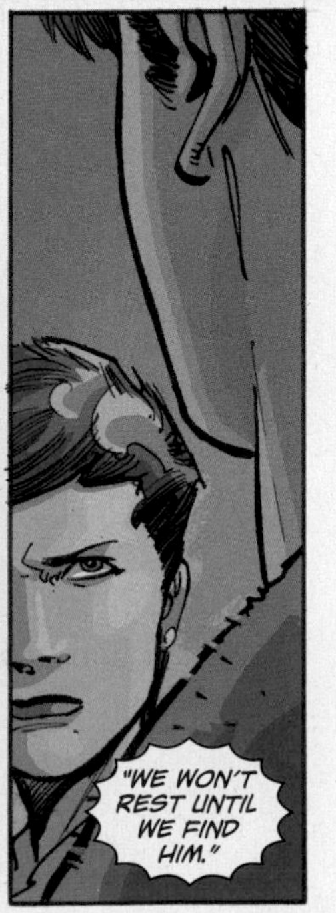
"WE WON'T REST UNTIL WE FIND HIM."

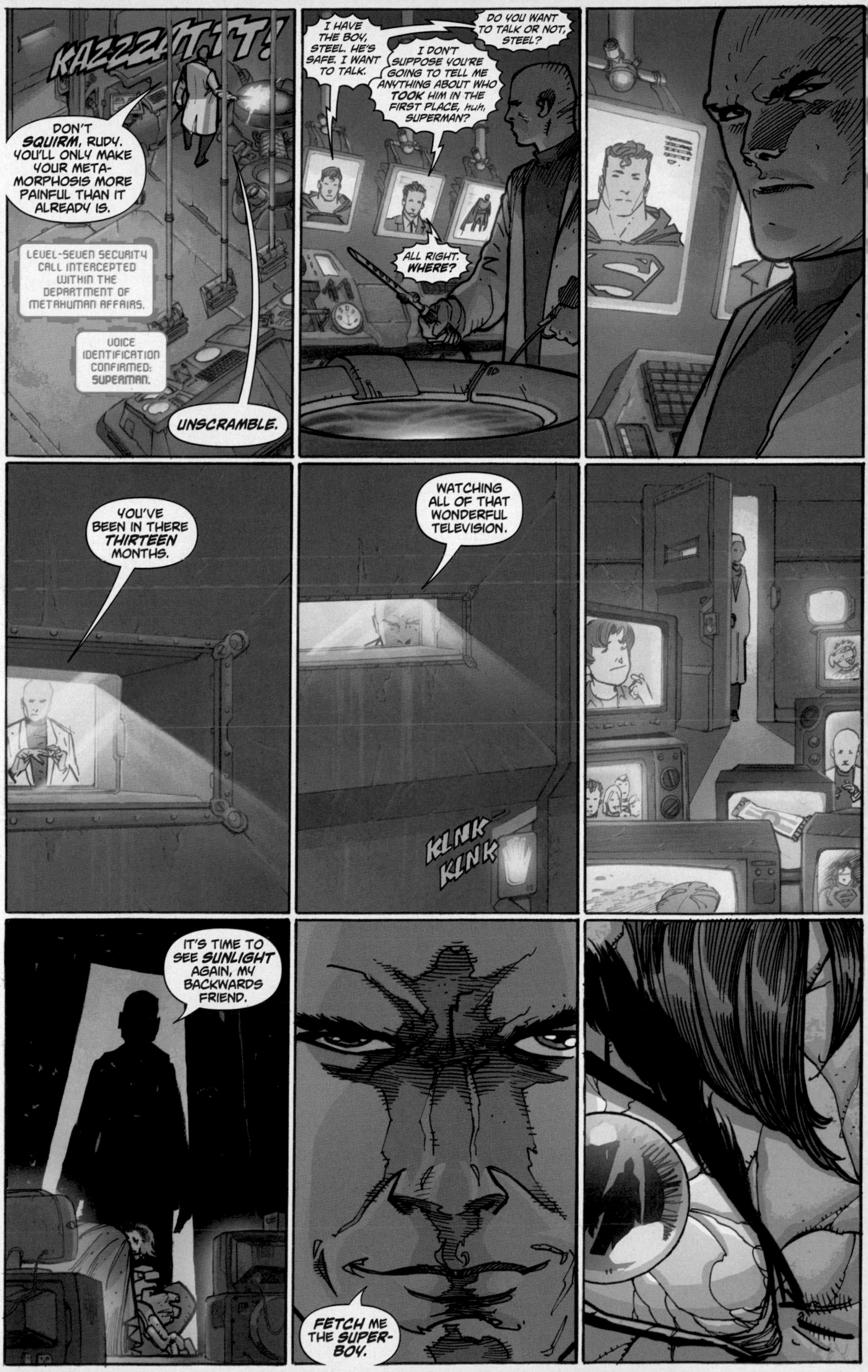
KAZZZATTTT!
DON'T SQUIRM, RUDY. YOU'LL ONLY MAKE YOUR METAMORPHOSIS MORE PAINFUL THAN IT ALREADY IS.
LEVEL-SEVEN SECURITY CALL INTERCEPTED WITHIN THE DEPARTMENT OF METAHUMAN AFFAIRS.
VOICE IDENTIFICATION CONFIRMED: SUPERMAN.
UNSCRAMBLE.
I HAVE THE BOY, STEEL. HE'S SAFE. I WANT TO TALK.
I DON'T SUPPOSE YOU'RE GOING TO TELL ME ANYTHING ABOUT WHO TOOK HIM IN THE FIRST PLACE, huh, SUPERMAN?
DO YOU WANT TO TALK OR NOT, STEEL?
ALL RIGHT. WHERE?
YOU'VE BEEN IN THERE THIRTEEN MONTHS.
WATCHING ALL OF THAT WONDERFUL TELEVISION.
KLNK KLNK
IT'S TIME TO SEE SUNLIGHT AGAIN, MY BACKWARDS FRIEND.
FETCH ME THE SUPER-BOY.

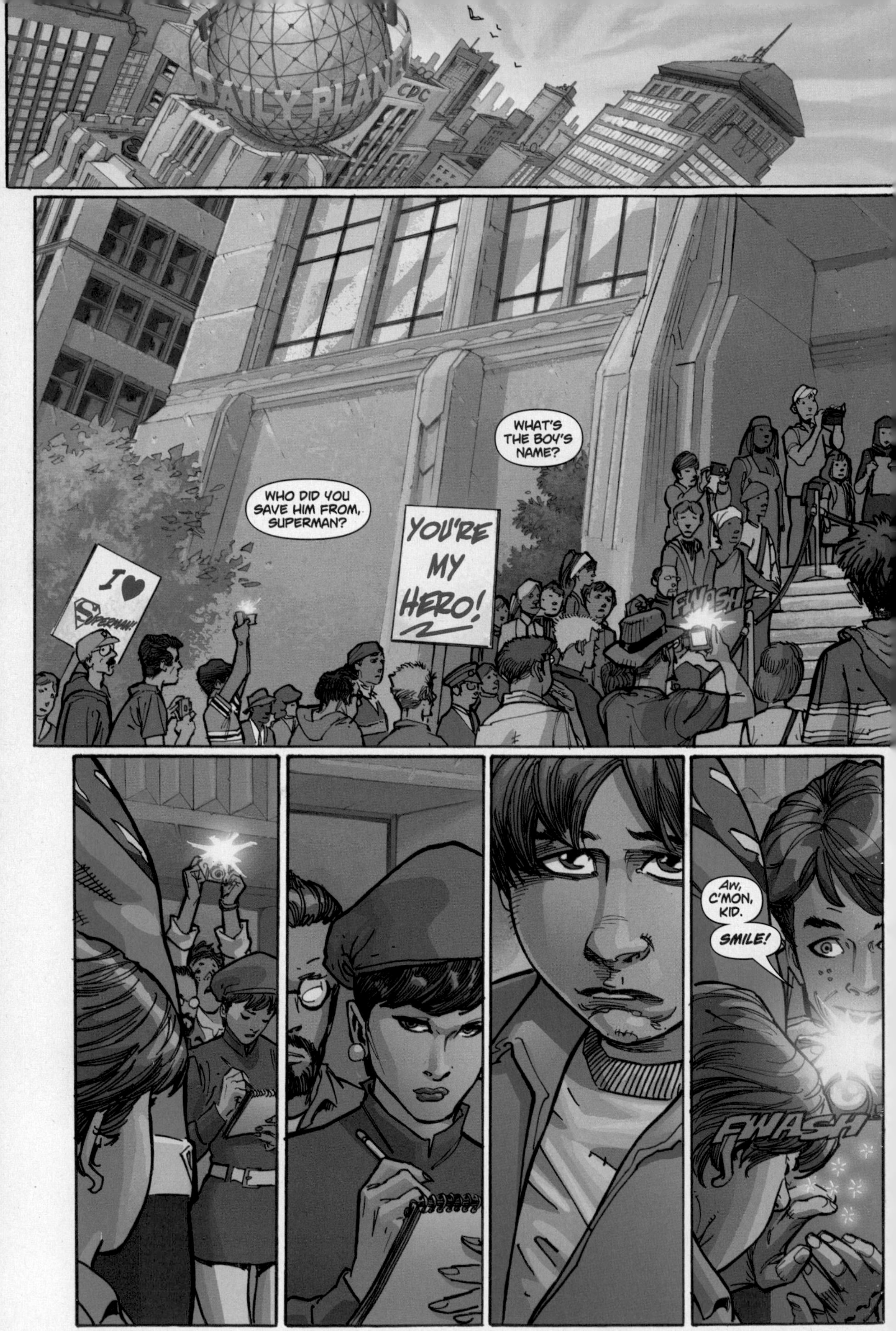
CDC
WHO DID YOU SAVE HIM FROM, SUPERMAN?
WHAT'S THE BOY'S NAME?
I ♥ SUPERMAN!
YOU'RE MY HERO!
FWASH
AW, C'MON, KID.
SMILE!
FWASH

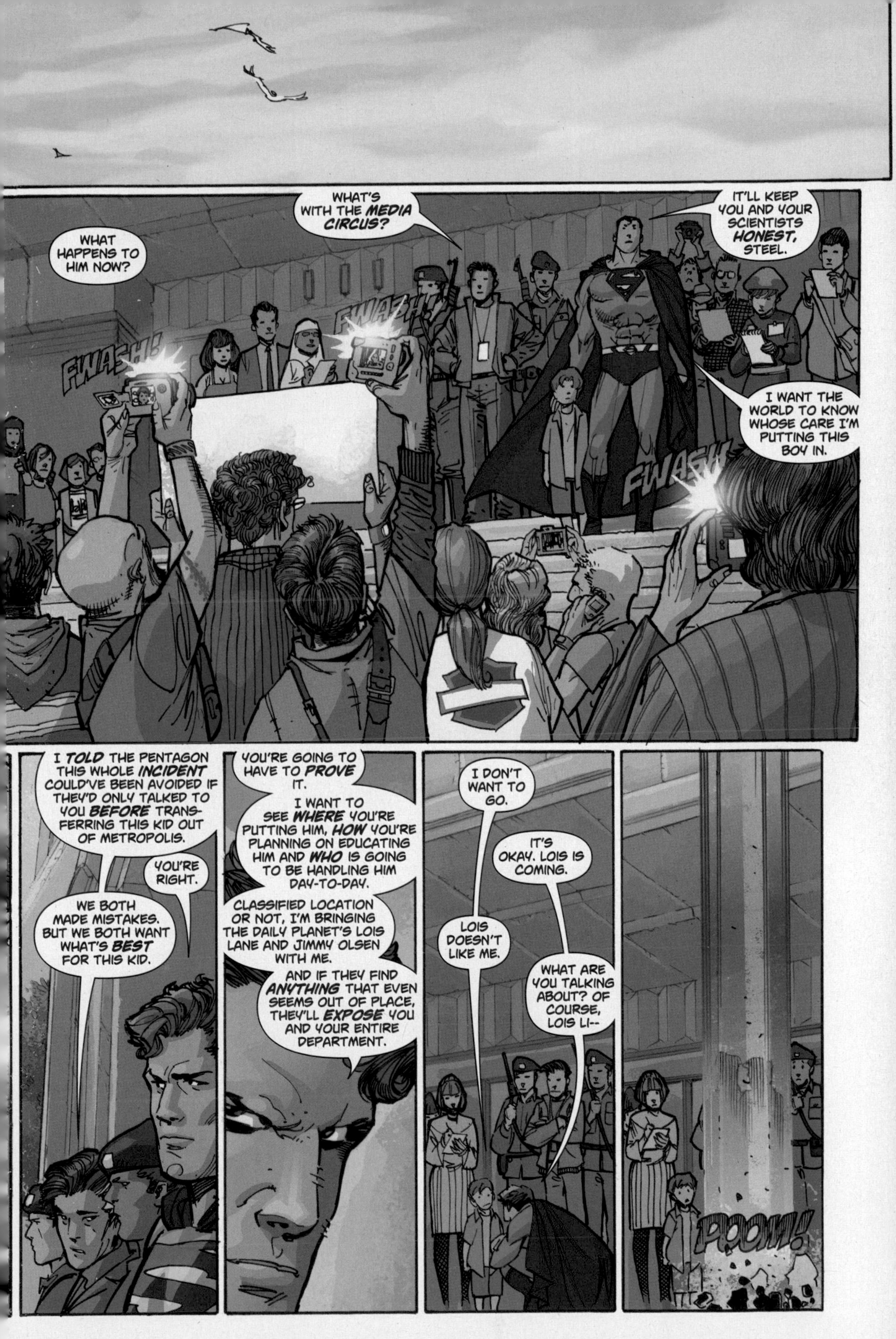
WHAT HAPPENS TO HIM NOW?
WHAT'S WITH THE MEDIA CIRCUS?
FWASH!
FWASH!
IT'LL KEEP YOU AND YOUR SCIENTISTS HONEST, STEEL.
I WANT THE WORLD TO KNOW WHOSE CARE I'M PUTTING THIS BOY IN.
FWASH
I TOLD THE PENTAGON THIS WHOLE INCIDENT COULD'VE BEEN AVOIDED IF THEY'D ONLY TALKED TO YOU BEFORE TRANSFERRING THIS KID OUT OF METROPOLIS.
YOU'RE RIGHT.
WE BOTH MADE MISTAKES. BUT WE BOTH WANT WHAT'S BEST FOR THIS KID.
YOU'RE GOING TO HAVE TO PROVE IT.
I WANT TO SEE WHERE YOU'RE PUTTING HIM, HOW YOU'RE PLANNING ON EDUCATING HIM AND WHO IS GOING TO BE HANDLING HIM DAY-TO-DAY.
CLASSIFIED LOCATION OR NOT, I'M BRINGING THE DAILY PLANET'S LOIS LANE AND JIMMY OLSEN WITH ME.
AND IF THEY FIND ANYTHING THAT EVEN SEEMS OUT OF PLACE, THEY'LL EXPOSE YOU AND YOUR ENTIRE DEPARTMENT.
I DON'T WANT TO GO.
IT'S OKAY. LOIS IS COMING.
LOIS DOESN'T LIKE ME.
WHAT ARE YOU TALKING ABOUT? OF COURSE, LOIS LI--
POOM!

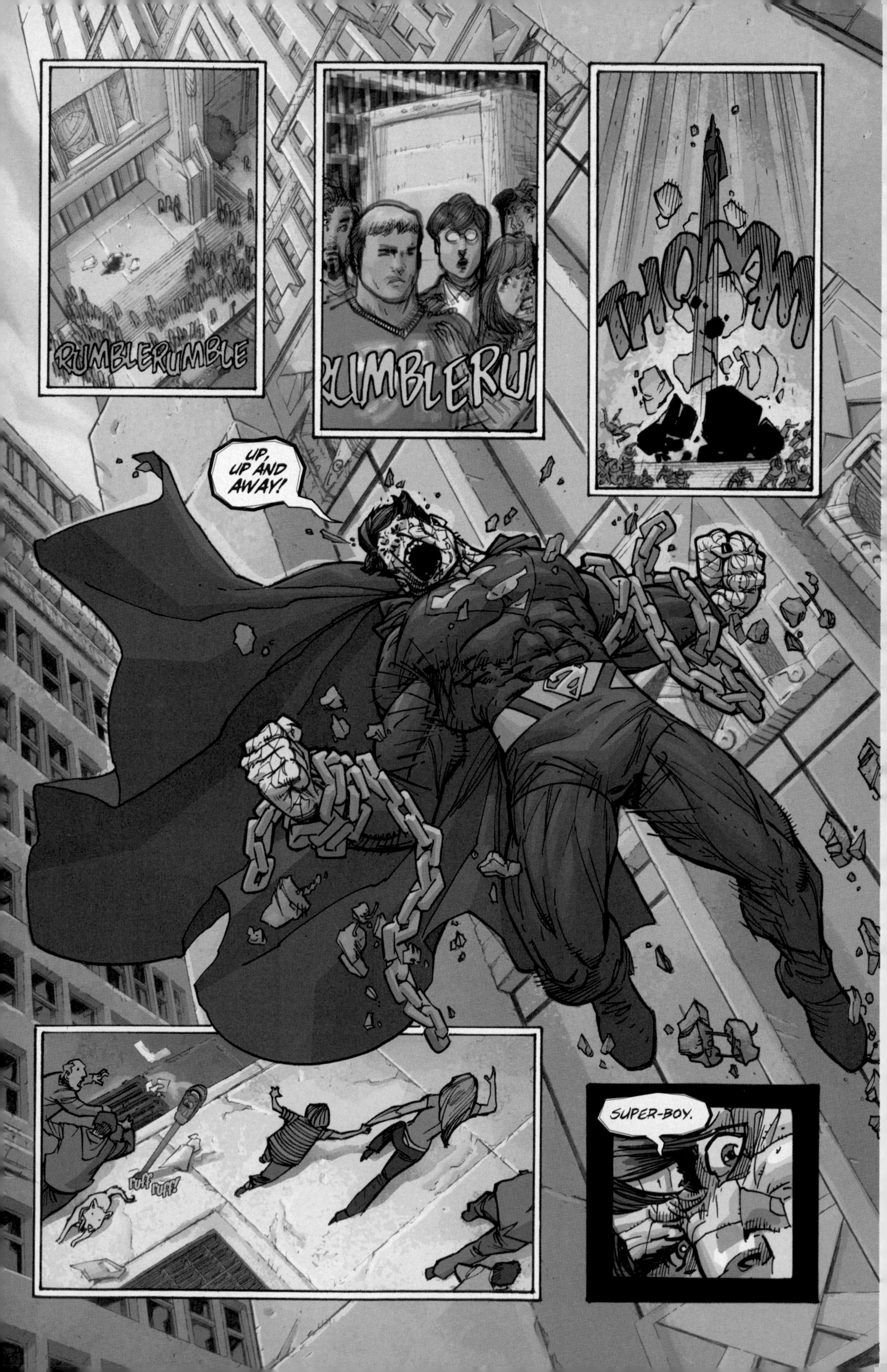
RUMBLERUMBLE
RUMBLERU
THOOM
UP, UP AND AWAY!
RUFF RUFF!
SUPER-BOY.

SNATCH!

AAHH!!

SNAP

YOU AM NOT SUPER-BOY.

YOU BREAK.

WHO WILL NOT BREAK?

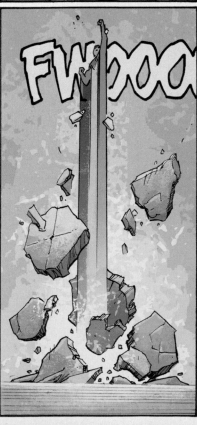

FWOOO

OOOSH!

FETCH.

SUPER-BOY.

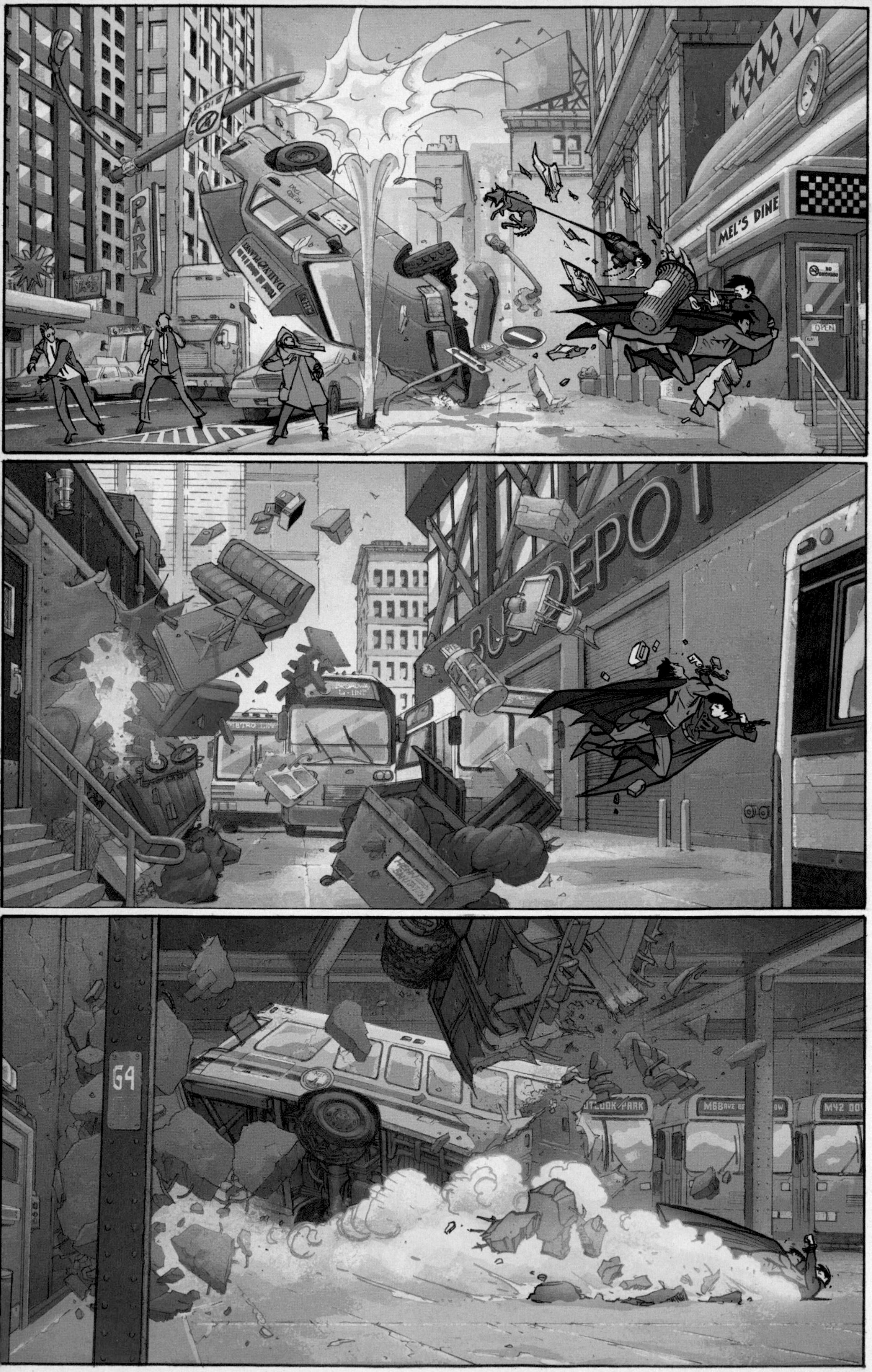
PARK
MEL'S DINE
OPEN
DEPOT
G4

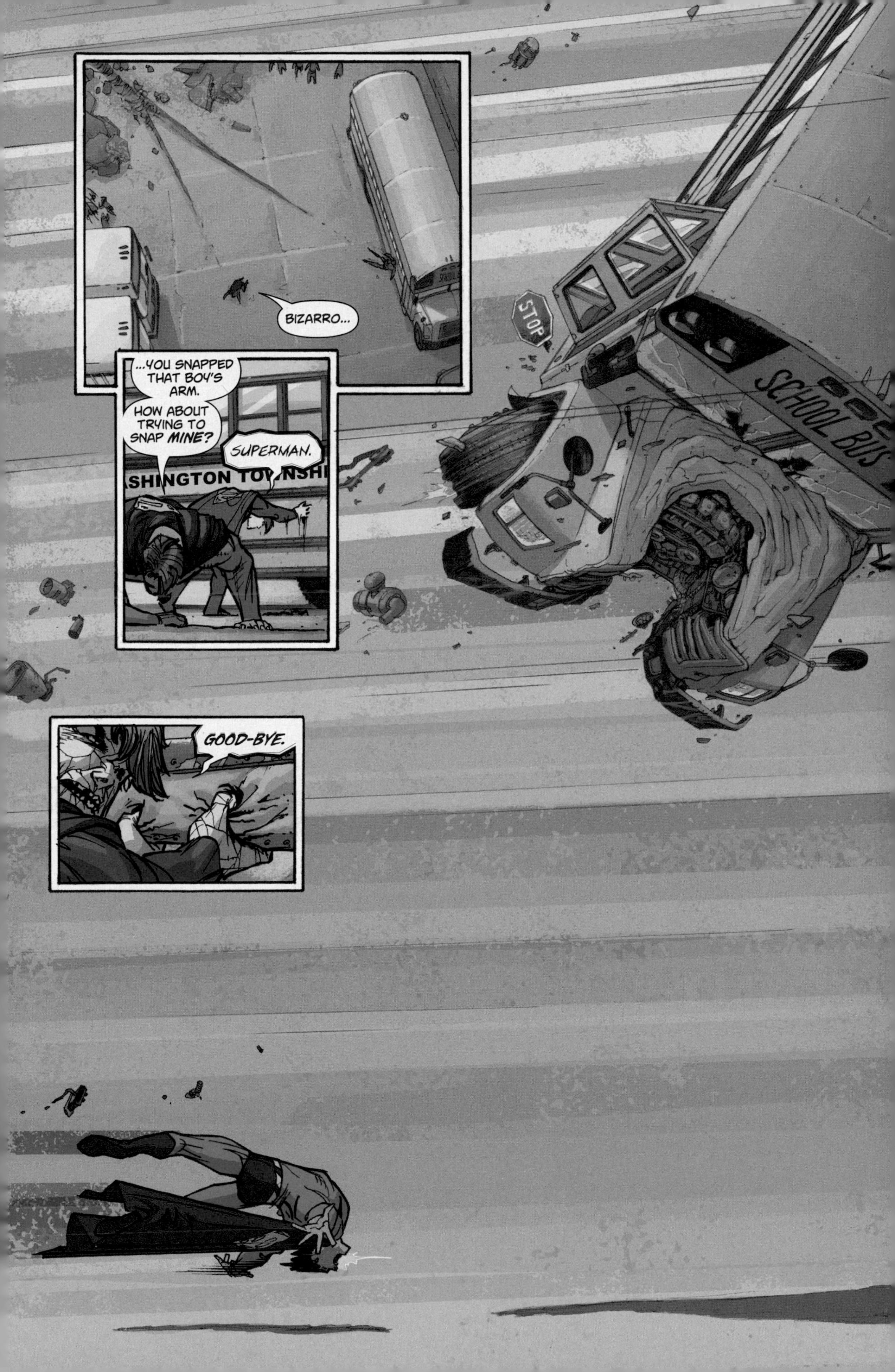

BIZARRO...
...YOU SNAPPED THAT BOY'S ARM.
HOW ABOUT TRYING TO SNAP MINE?
SUPERMAN.
ASHINGTON TOWNSHI
GOOD-BYE.
STOP
SCHOOL BUS

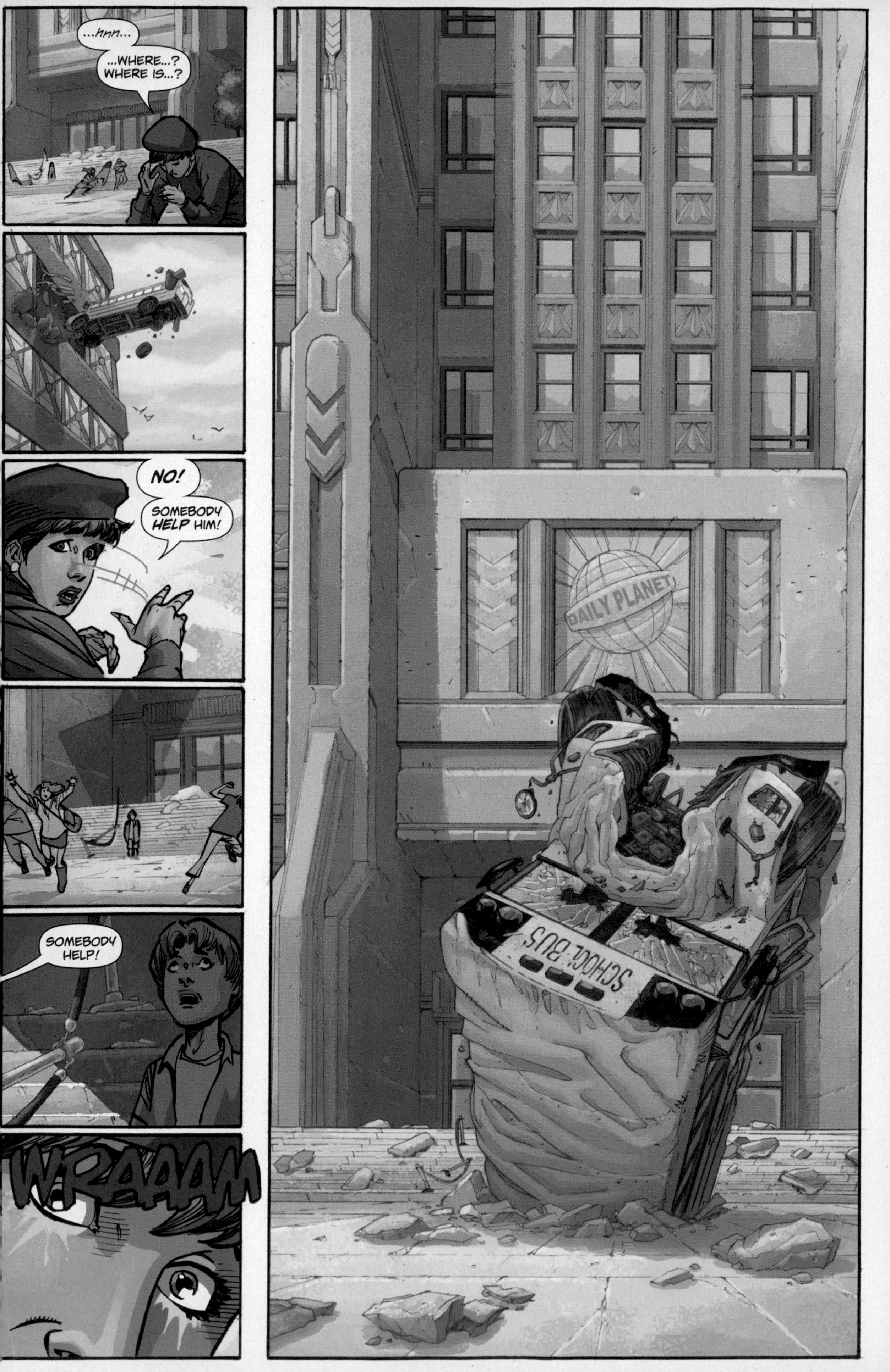
...hnn...
...WHERE...? WHERE IS...?
NO!
SOMEBODY HELP HIM!
SOMEBODY HELP!
WRAAAM
DAILY PLANET
SCHOOL BUS

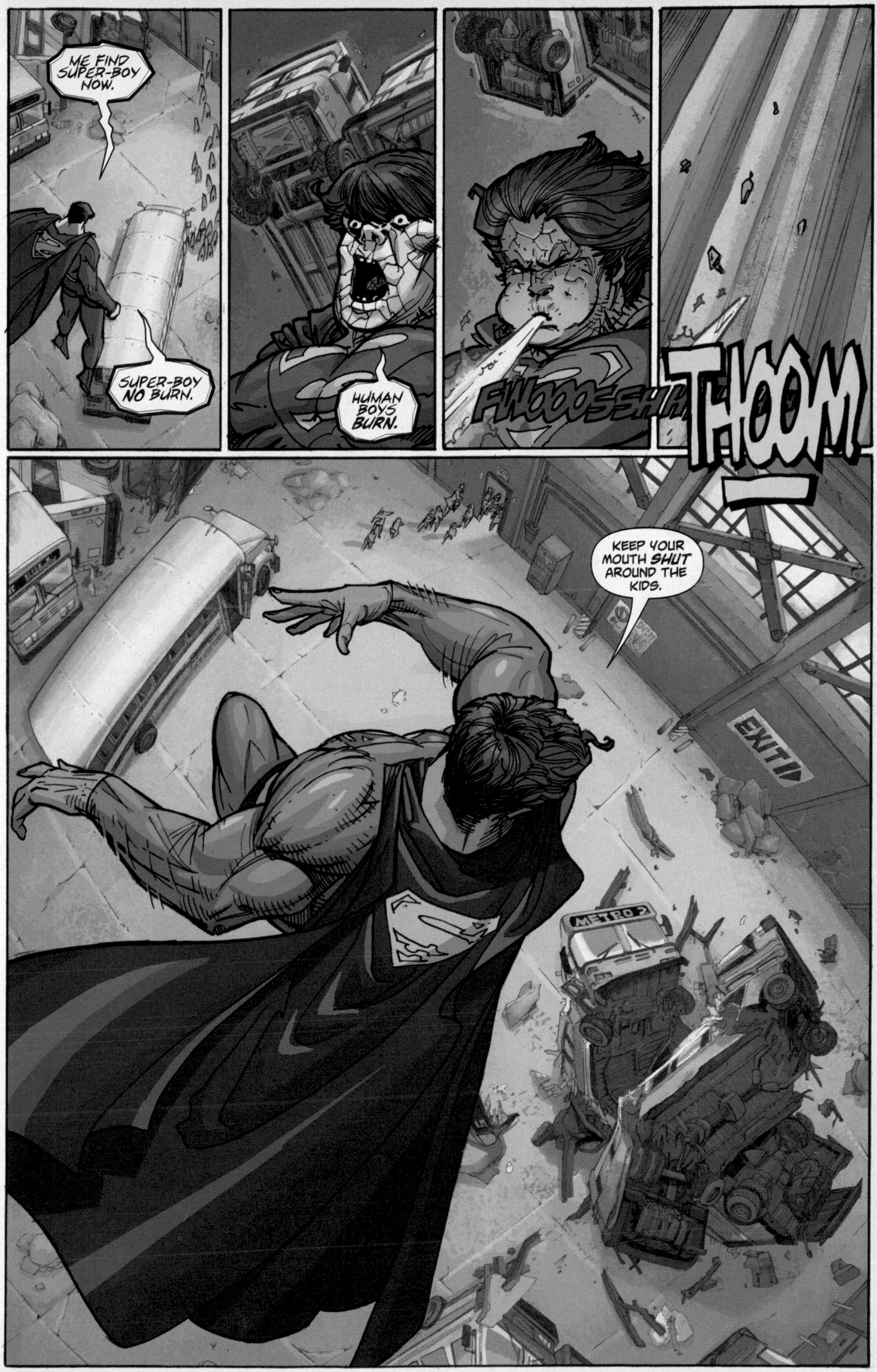
ME FIND SUPER-BOY NOW.
SUPER-BOY NO BURN.
HUMAN BOYS BURN.
FWOOOOSSHHH
THOOM
KEEP YOUR MOUTH SHUT AROUND THE KIDS.
EXIT
METRO 2

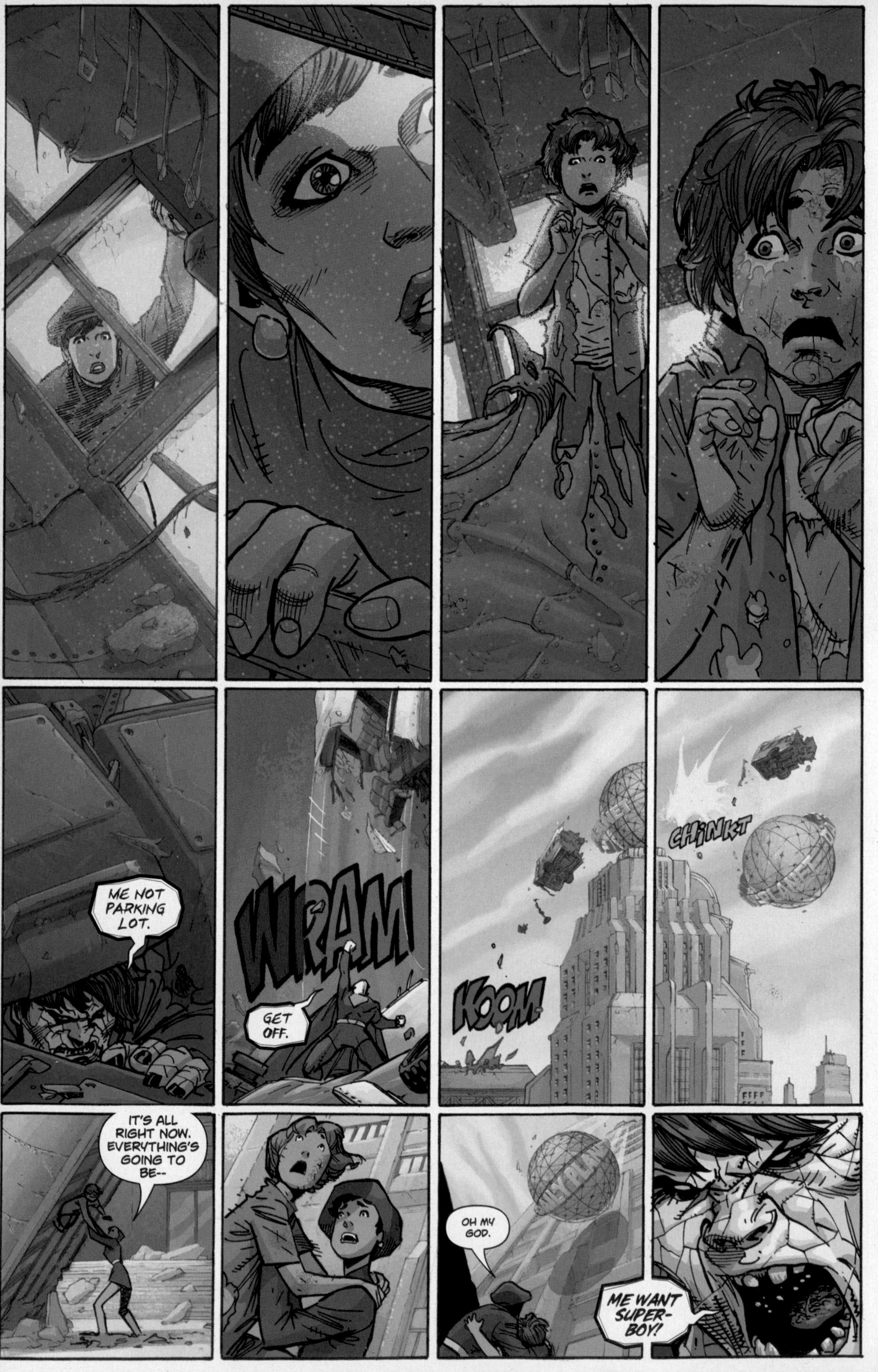
ME NOT PARKING LOT.
WRAM
GET OFF.
KOOM
CHINKT
IT'S ALL RIGHT NOW. EVERYTHING'S GOING TO BE--
OH MY GOD.
ME WANT SUPER-BOY!

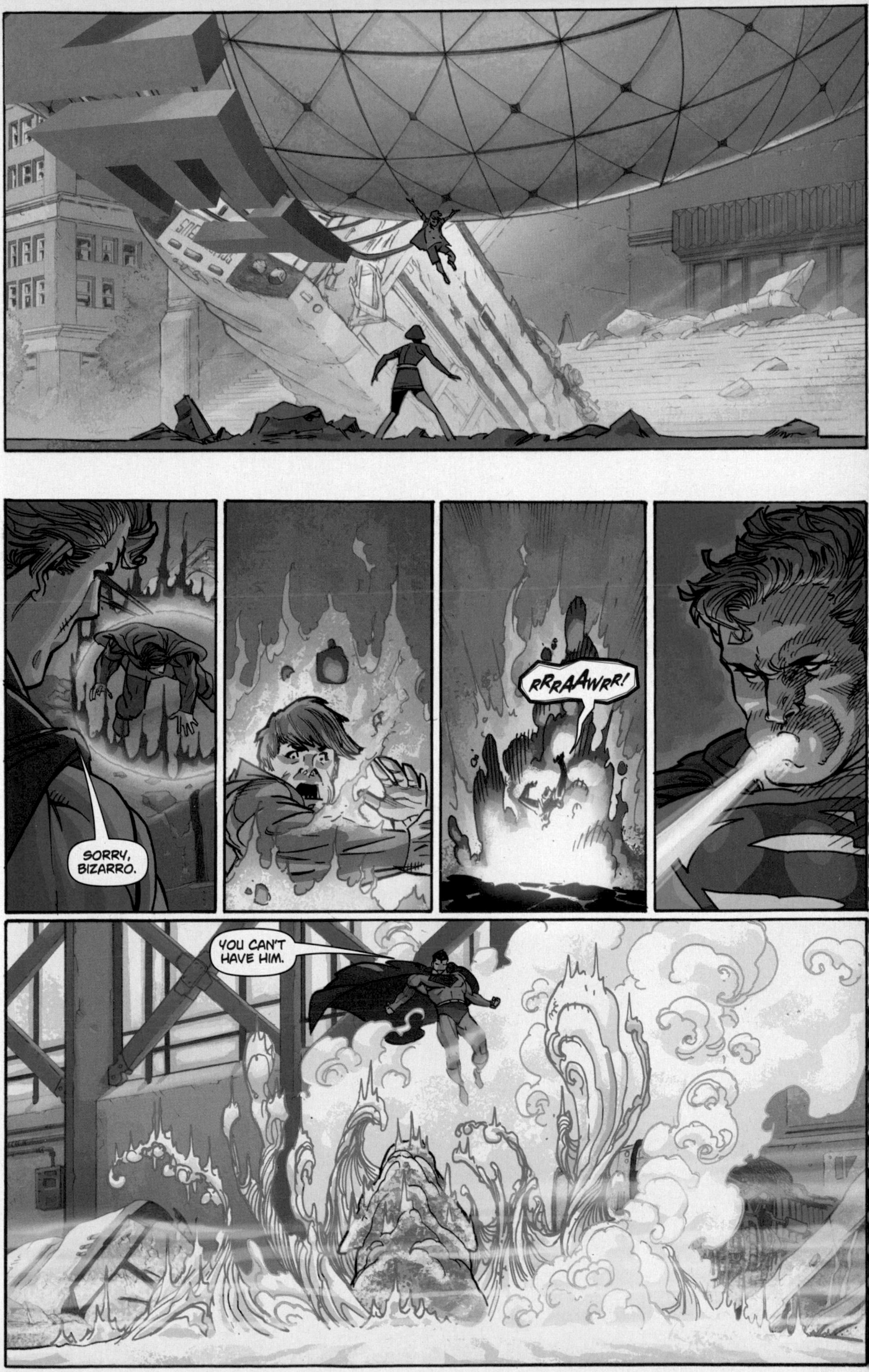
SORRY, BIZARRO.
RRRAAWRR!
YOU CAN'T HAVE HIM.

HEY, OLSEN! *SMILE!*

CHIEF'S GONNA KILL ME.

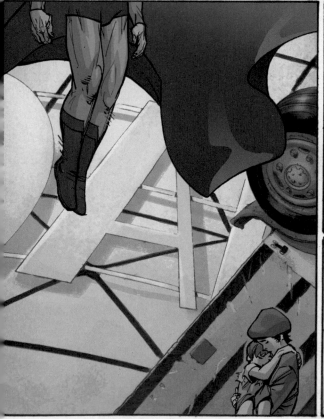

I SAID WE COULDN'T DO IT.

BUT I WANT TO *TRY.*

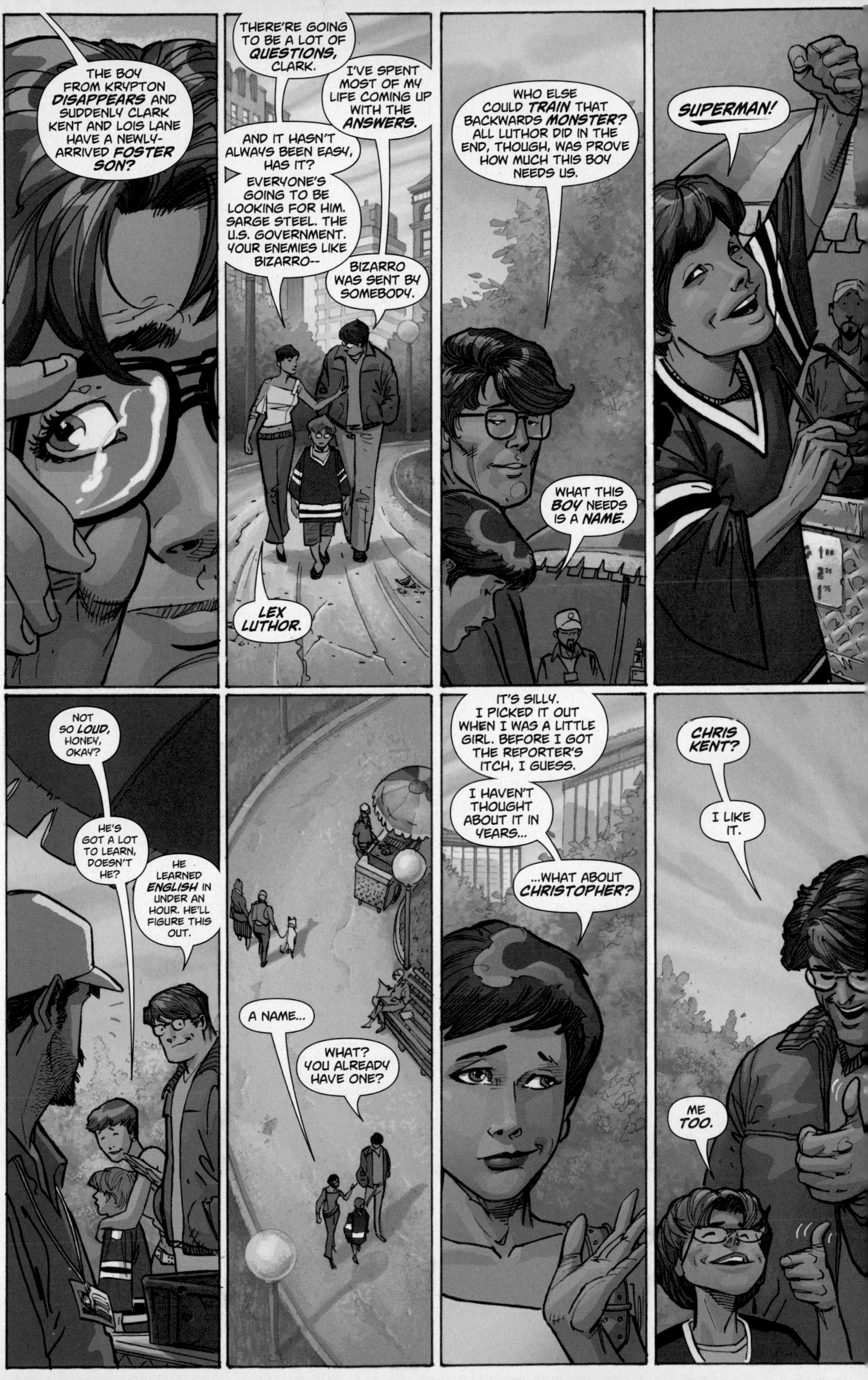
THE BOY FROM KRYPTON DISAPPEARS AND SUDDENLY CLARK KENT AND LOIS LANE HAVE A NEWLY-ARRIVED FOSTER SON?
THERE'RE GOING TO BE A LOT OF QUESTIONS, CLARK.
I'VE SPENT MOST OF MY LIFE COMING UP WITH THE ANSWERS.
AND IT HASN'T ALWAYS BEEN EASY, HAS IT?
EVERYONE'S GOING TO BE LOOKING FOR HIM. SARGE STEEL. THE U.S. GOVERNMENT. YOUR ENEMIES LIKE BIZARRO--
BIZARRO WAS SENT BY SOMEBODY.
LEX LUTHOR.
WHO ELSE COULD TRAIN THAT BACKWARDS MONSTER? ALL LUTHOR DID IN THE END, THOUGH, WAS PROVE HOW MUCH THIS BOY NEEDS US.
WHAT THIS BOY NEEDS IS A NAME.
SUPERMAN!
NOT SO LOUD, HONEY, OKAY?
HE'S GOT A LOT TO LEARN, DOESN'T HE?
HE LEARNED ENGLISH IN UNDER AN HOUR. HE'LL FIGURE THIS OUT.
A NAME...
WHAT? YOU ALREADY HAVE ONE?
IT'S SILLY. I PICKED IT OUT WHEN I WAS A LITTLE GIRL. BEFORE I GOT THE REPORTER'S ITCH, I GUESS.
I HAVEN'T THOUGHT ABOUT IT IN YEARS...
...WHAT ABOUT CHRISTOPHER?
CHRIS KENT?
I LIKE IT.
ME TOO.

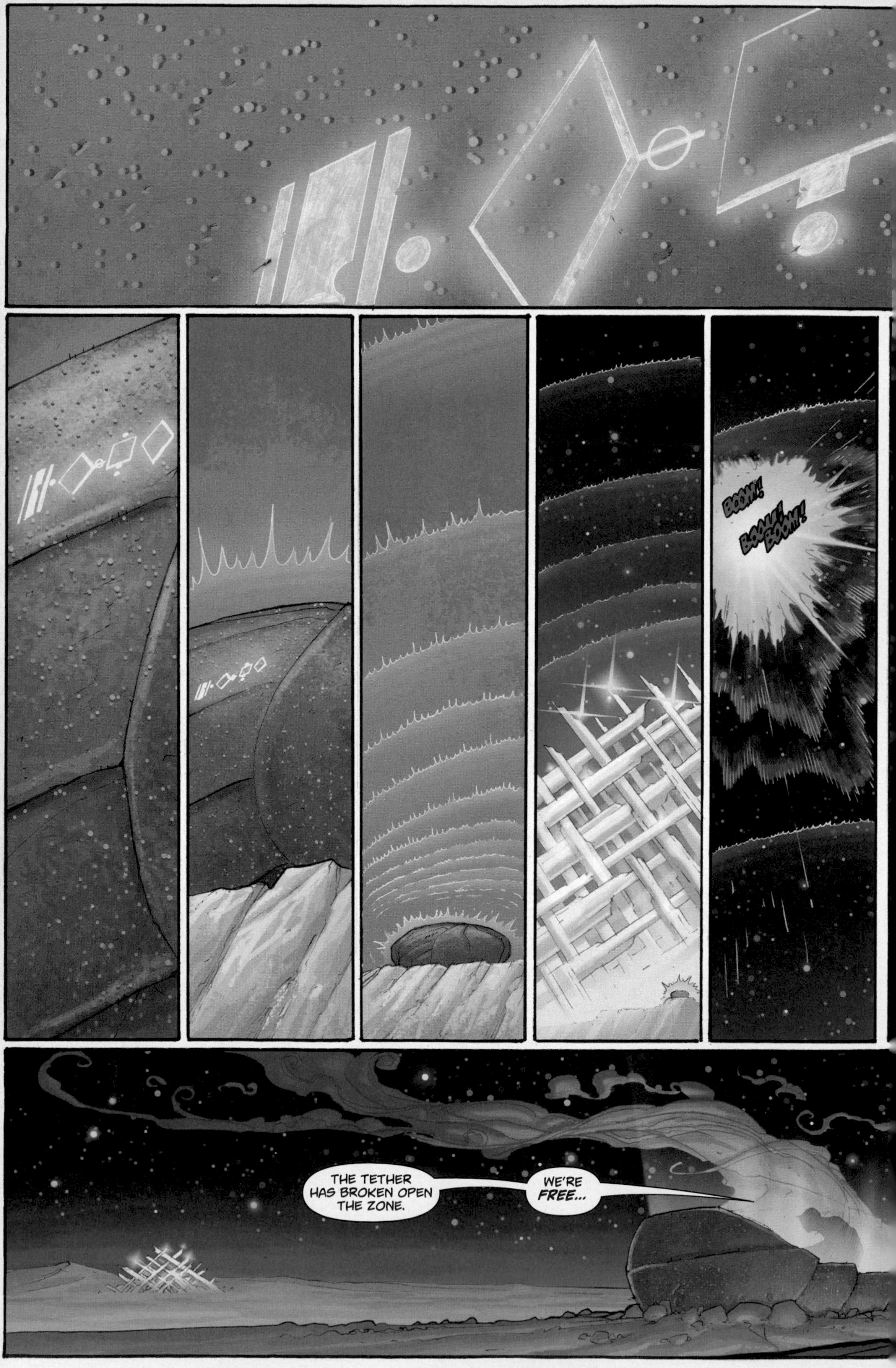
BOOM!
BOOM!
BOOM!
THE TETHER HAS BROKEN OPEN THE ZONE.
WE'RE *FREE*...

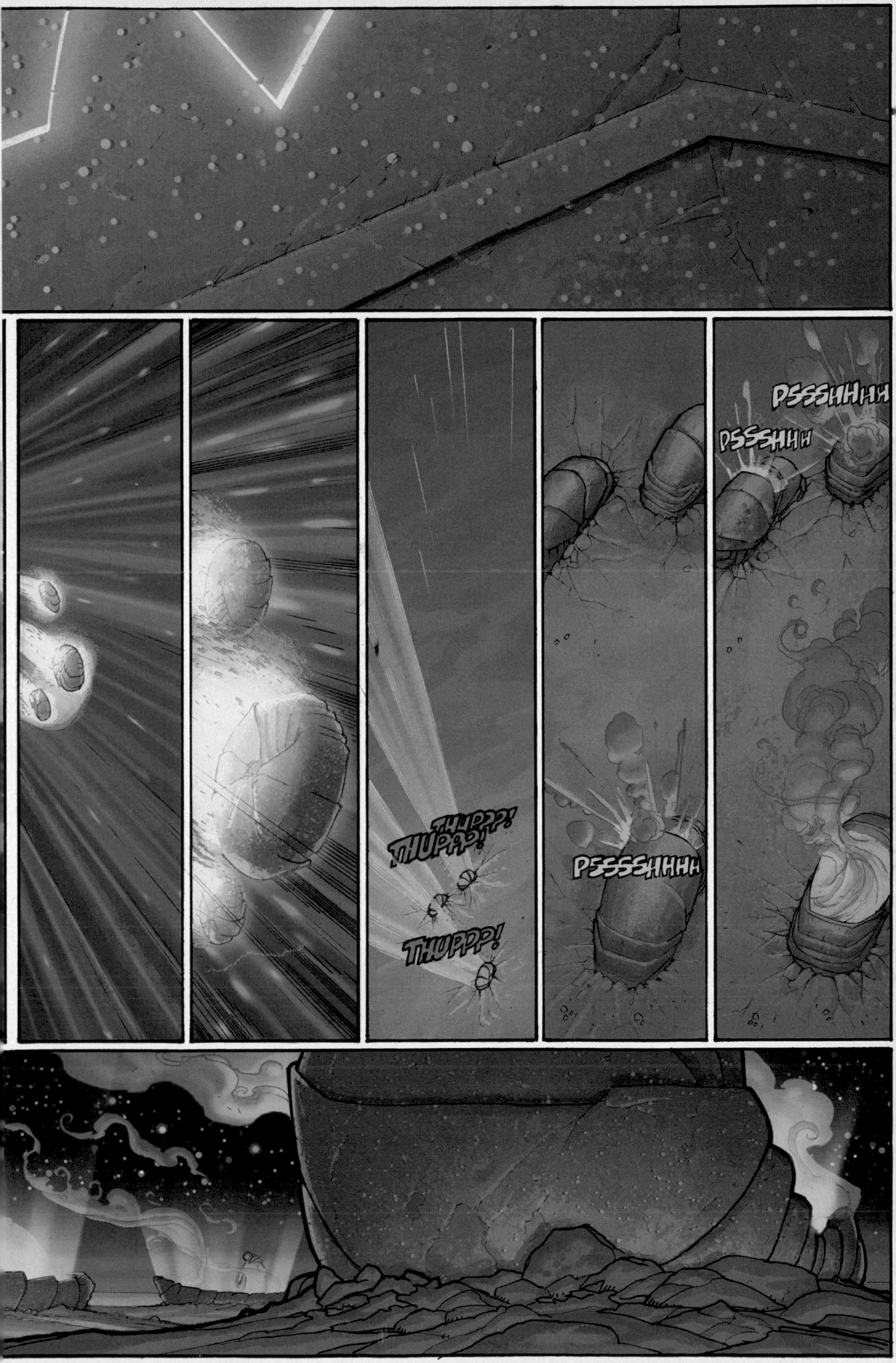
THUPPP!
THUPPP!
THUPPP!
PSSSSHHHH
PSSSHHH
PSSSHHHHH

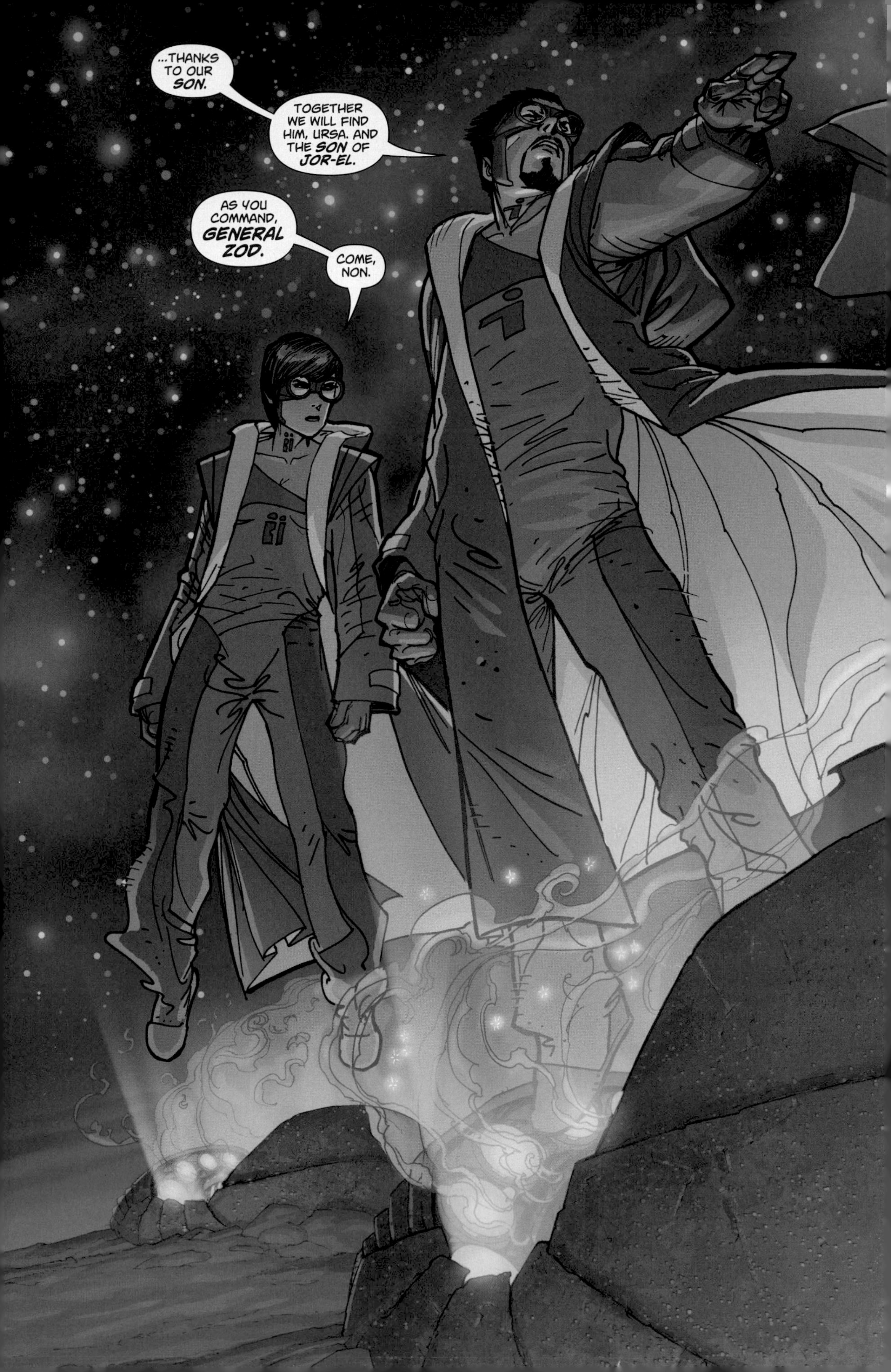
...THANKS TO OUR SON.
TOGETHER WE WILL FIND HIM, URSA. AND THE SON OF JOR-EL.
AS YOU COMMAND, GENERAL ZOD.
COME, NON.

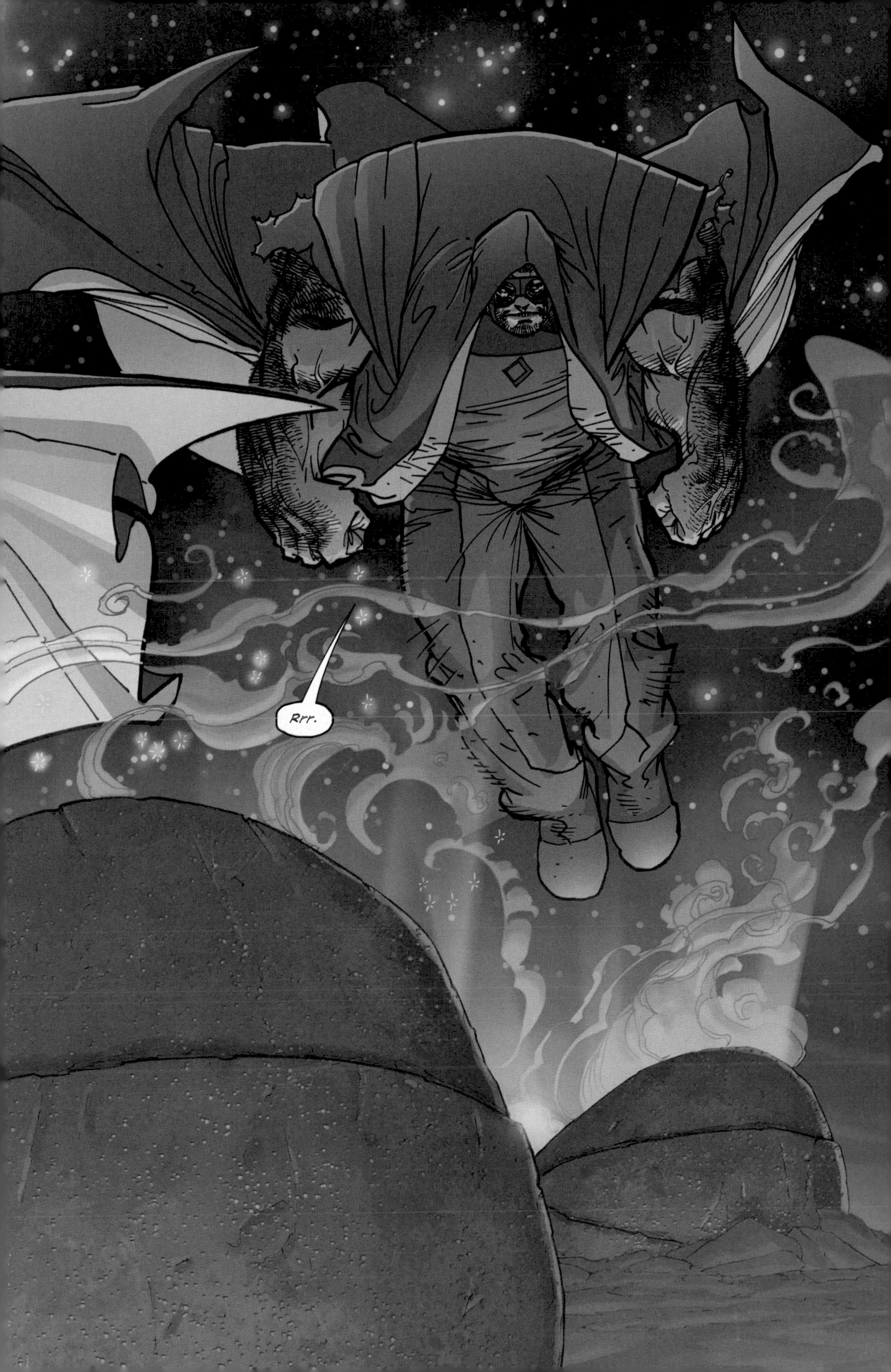
Rrr.

CHAPTER THREE

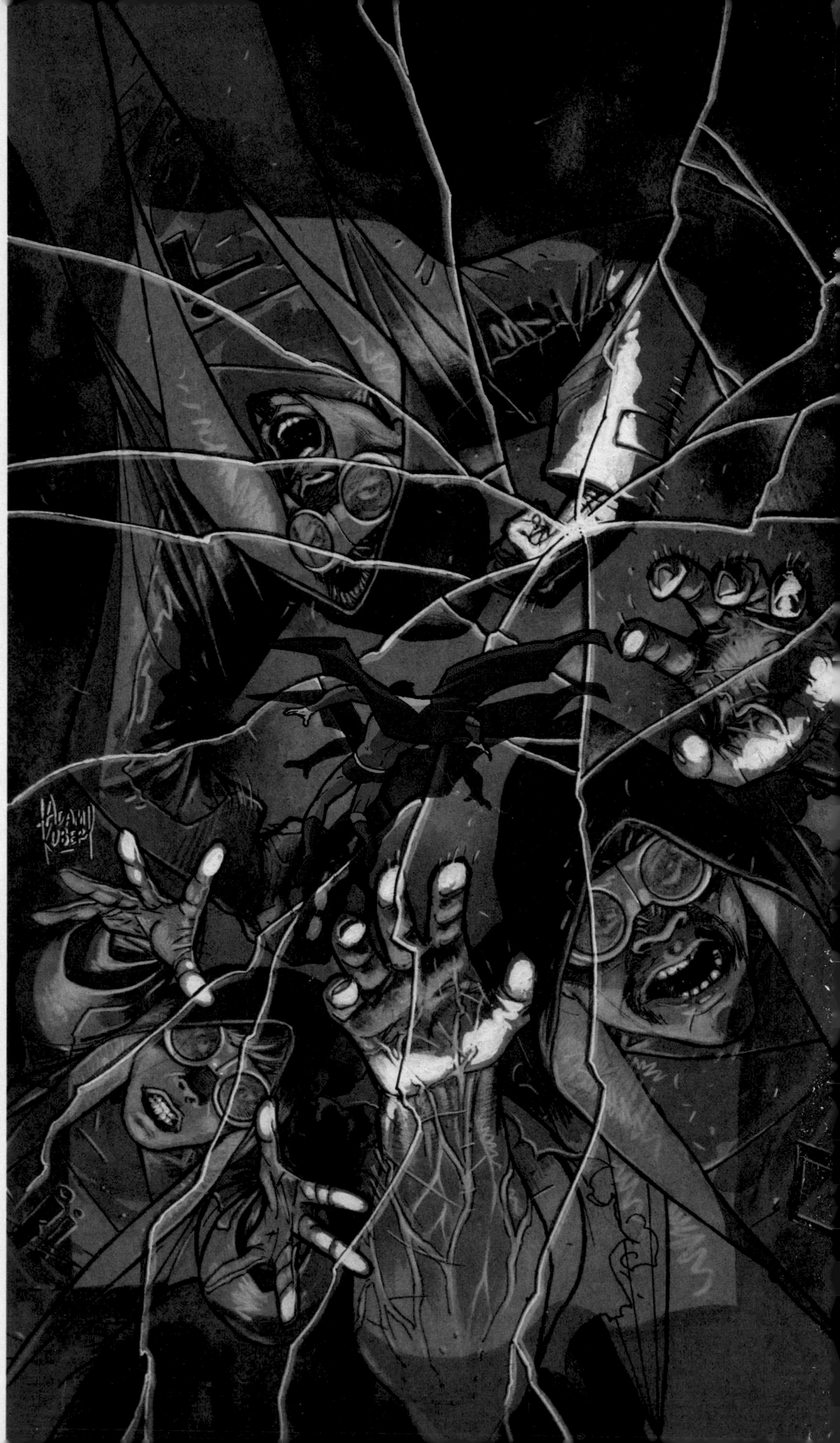

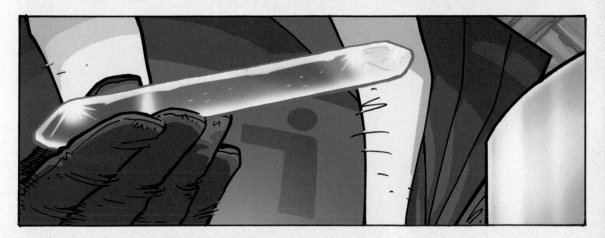

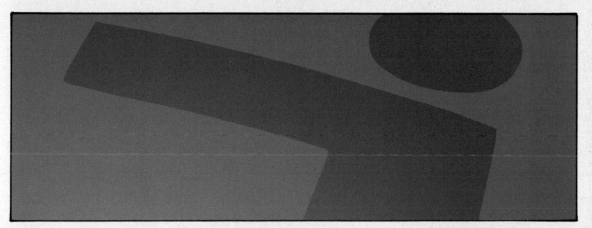

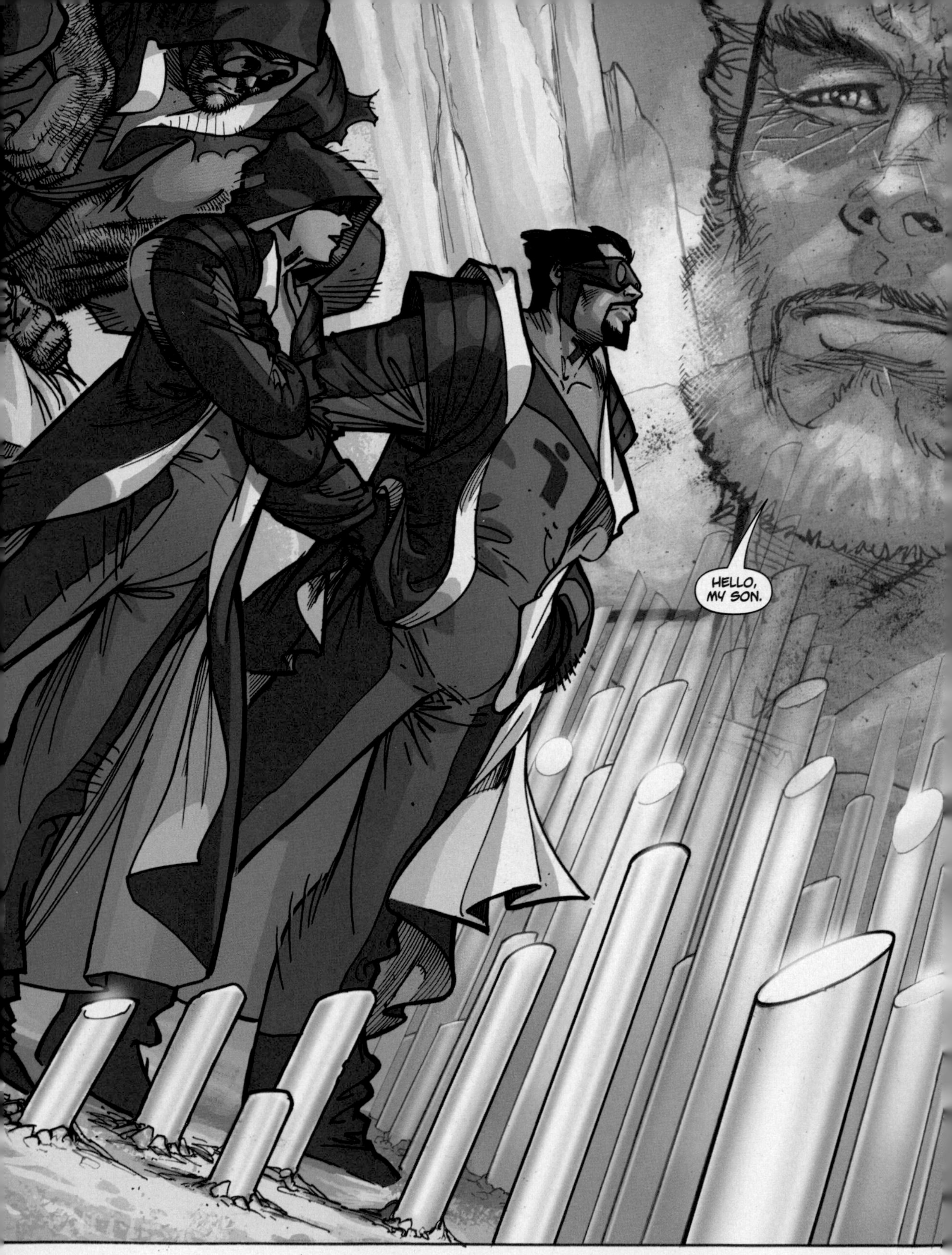
HELLO,
MY SON.

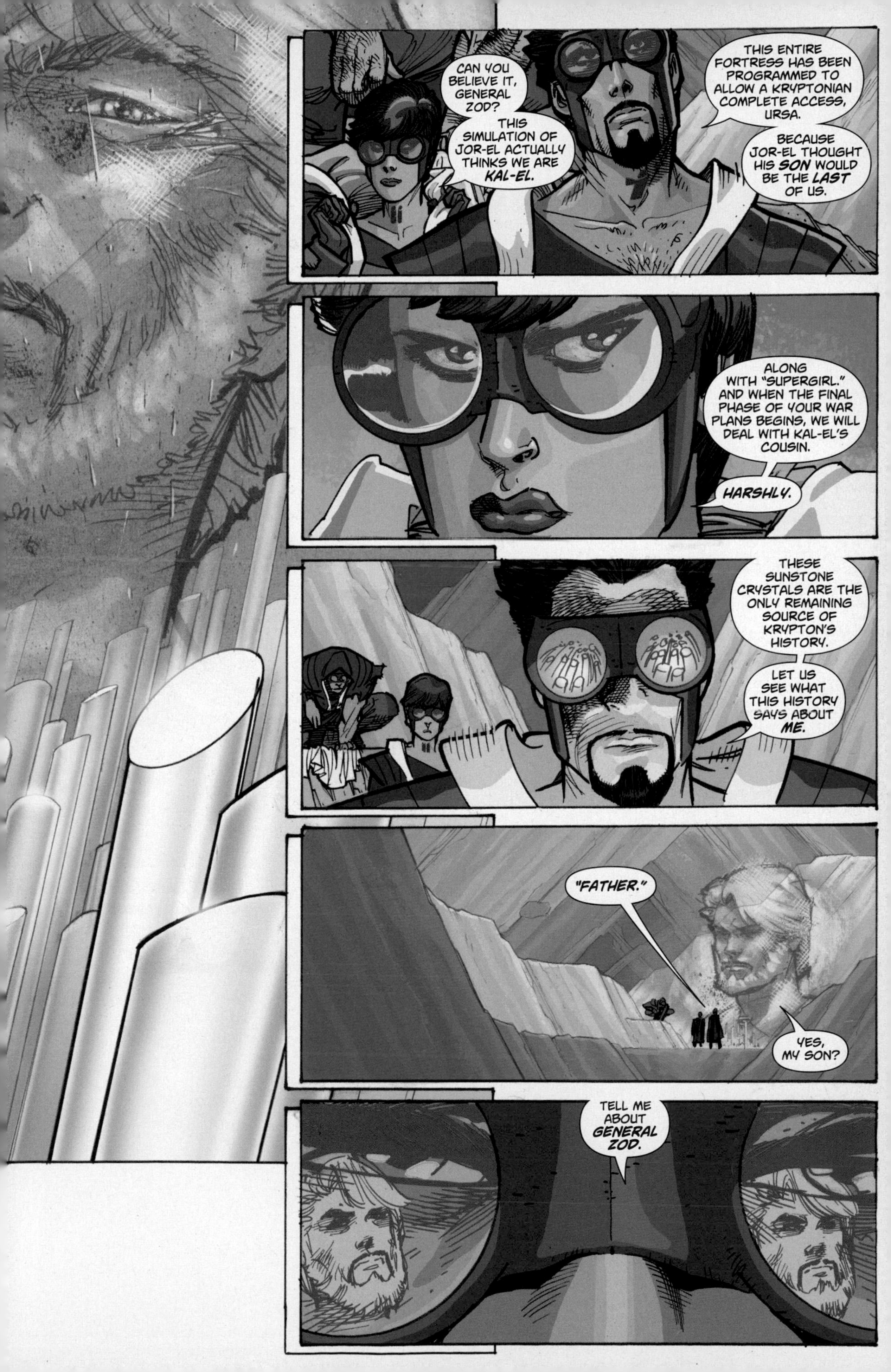
CAN YOU BELIEVE IT, GENERAL ZOD?
THIS SIMULATION OF JOR-EL ACTUALLY THINKS WE ARE KAL-EL.
THIS ENTIRE FORTRESS HAS BEEN PROGRAMMED TO ALLOW A KRYPTONIAN COMPLETE ACCESS, URSA.
BECAUSE JOR-EL THOUGHT HIS SON WOULD BE THE LAST OF US.
ALONG WITH "SUPERGIRL." AND WHEN THE FINAL PHASE OF YOUR WAR PLANS BEGINS, WE WILL DEAL WITH KAL-EL'S COUSIN.
HARSHLY.
THESE SUNSTONE CRYSTALS ARE THE ONLY REMAINING SOURCE OF KRYPTON'S HISTORY.
LET US SEE WHAT THIS HISTORY SAYS ABOUT ME.
"FATHER."
YES, MY SON?
TELL ME ABOUT GENERAL ZOD.

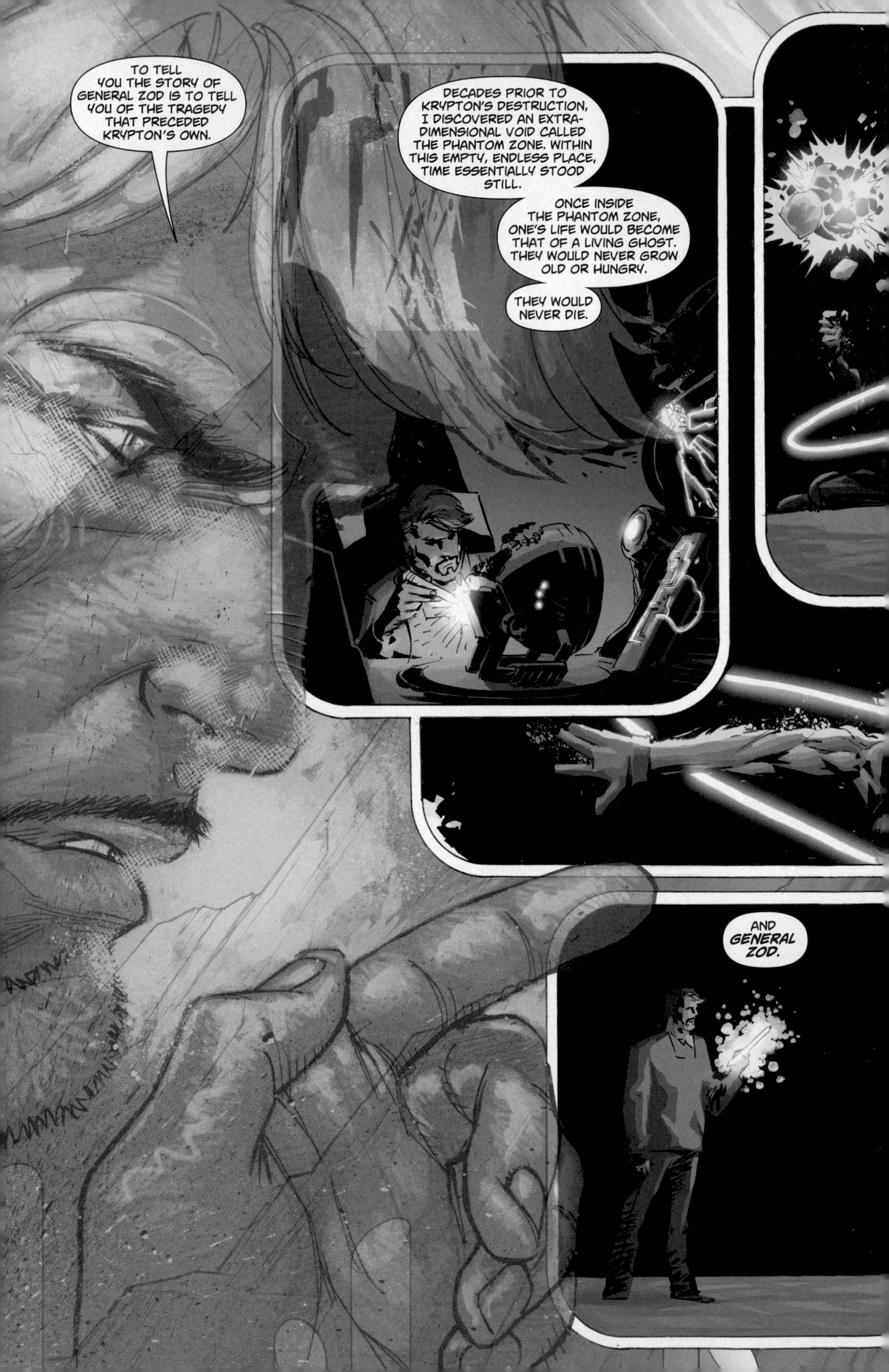
TO TELL YOU THE STORY OF GENERAL ZOD IS TO TELL YOU OF THE TRAGEDY THAT PRECEDED KRYPTON'S OWN.
DECADES PRIOR TO KRYPTON'S DESTRUCTION, I DISCOVERED AN EXTRA-DIMENSIONAL VOID CALLED THE PHANTOM ZONE. WITHIN THIS EMPTY, ENDLESS PLACE, TIME ESSENTIALLY STOOD STILL.
ONCE INSIDE THE PHANTOM ZONE, ONE'S LIFE WOULD BECOME THAT OF A LIVING GHOST. THEY WOULD NEVER GROW OLD OR HUNGRY.
THEY WOULD NEVER DIE.
AND GENERAL ZOD.

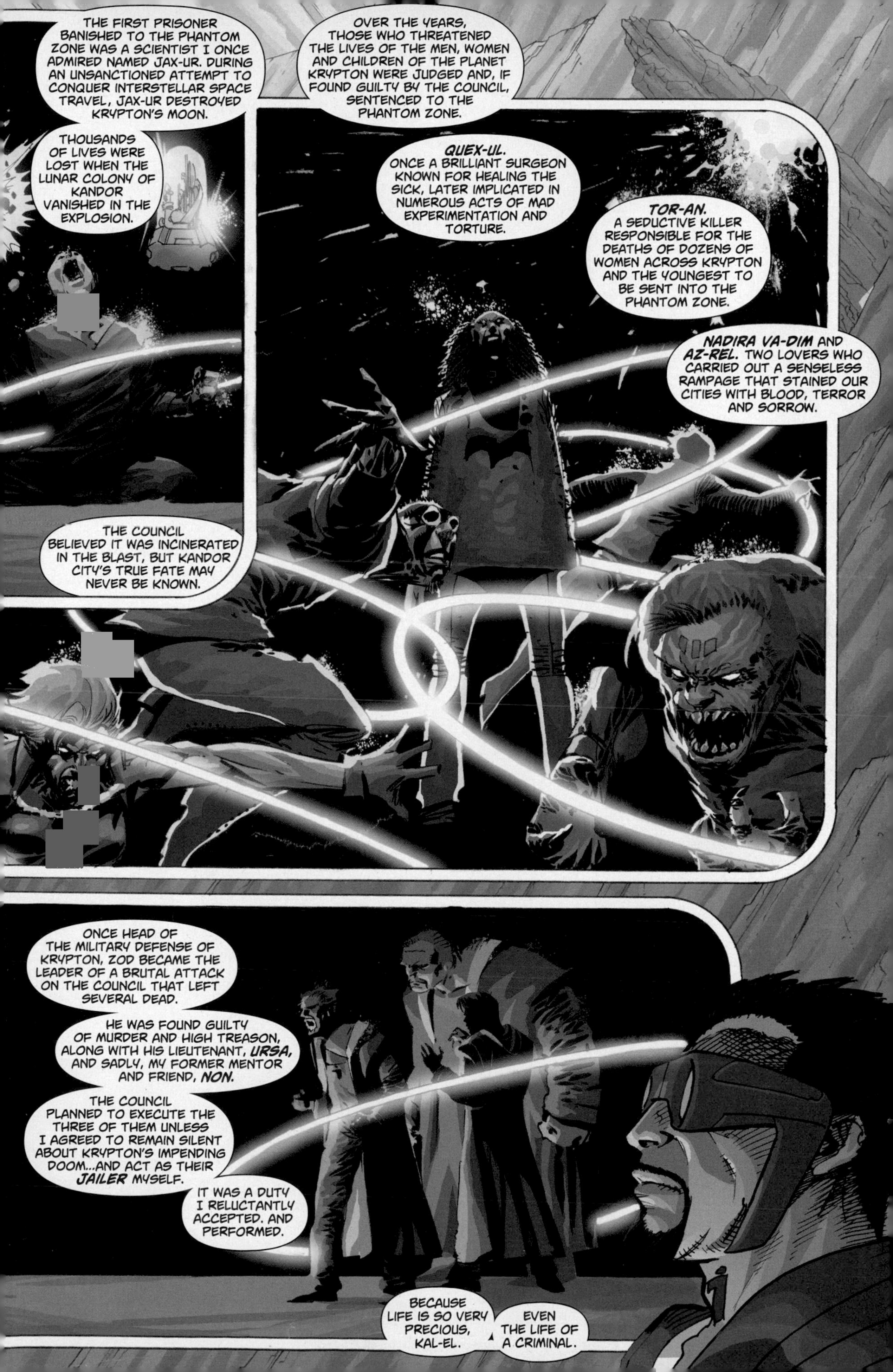
THE FIRST PRISONER BANISHED TO THE PHANTOM ZONE WAS A SCIENTIST I ONCE ADMIRED NAMED JAX-UR. DURING AN UNSANCTIONED ATTEMPT TO CONQUER INTERSTELLAR SPACE TRAVEL, JAX-UR DESTROYED KRYPTON'S MOON.
THOUSANDS OF LIVES WERE LOST WHEN THE LUNAR COLONY OF KANDOR VANISHED IN THE EXPLOSION.
THE COUNCIL BELIEVED IT WAS INCINERATED IN THE BLAST, BUT KANDOR CITY'S TRUE FATE MAY NEVER BE KNOWN.
OVER THE YEARS, THOSE WHO THREATENED THE LIVES OF THE MEN, WOMEN AND CHILDREN OF THE PLANET KRYPTON WERE JUDGED AND, IF FOUND GUILTY BY THE COUNCIL, SENTENCED TO THE PHANTOM ZONE.
QUEX-UL. ONCE A BRILLIANT SURGEON KNOWN FOR HEALING THE SICK, LATER IMPLICATED IN NUMEROUS ACTS OF MAD EXPERIMENTATION AND TORTURE.
TOR-AN. A SEDUCTIVE KILLER RESPONSIBLE FOR THE DEATHS OF DOZENS OF WOMEN ACROSS KRYPTON AND THE YOUNGEST TO BE SENT INTO THE PHANTOM ZONE.
NADIRA VA-DIM AND AZ-REL. TWO LOVERS WHO CARRIED OUT A SENSELESS RAMPAGE THAT STAINED OUR CITIES WITH BLOOD, TERROR AND SORROW.
ONCE HEAD OF THE MILITARY DEFENSE OF KRYPTON, ZOD BECAME THE LEADER OF A BRUTAL ATTACK ON THE COUNCIL THAT LEFT SEVERAL DEAD.
HE WAS FOUND GUILTY OF MURDER AND HIGH TREASON, ALONG WITH HIS LIEUTENANT, URSA, AND SADLY, MY FORMER MENTOR AND FRIEND, NON.
THE COUNCIL PLANNED TO EXECUTE THE THREE OF THEM UNLESS I AGREED TO REMAIN SILENT ABOUT KRYPTON'S IMPENDING DOOM...AND ACT AS THEIR JAILER MYSELF.
IT WAS A DUTY I RELUCTANTLY ACCEPTED. AND PERFORMED.
BECAUSE LIFE IS SO VERY PRECIOUS, KAL-EL.
EVEN THE LIFE OF A CRIMINAL.

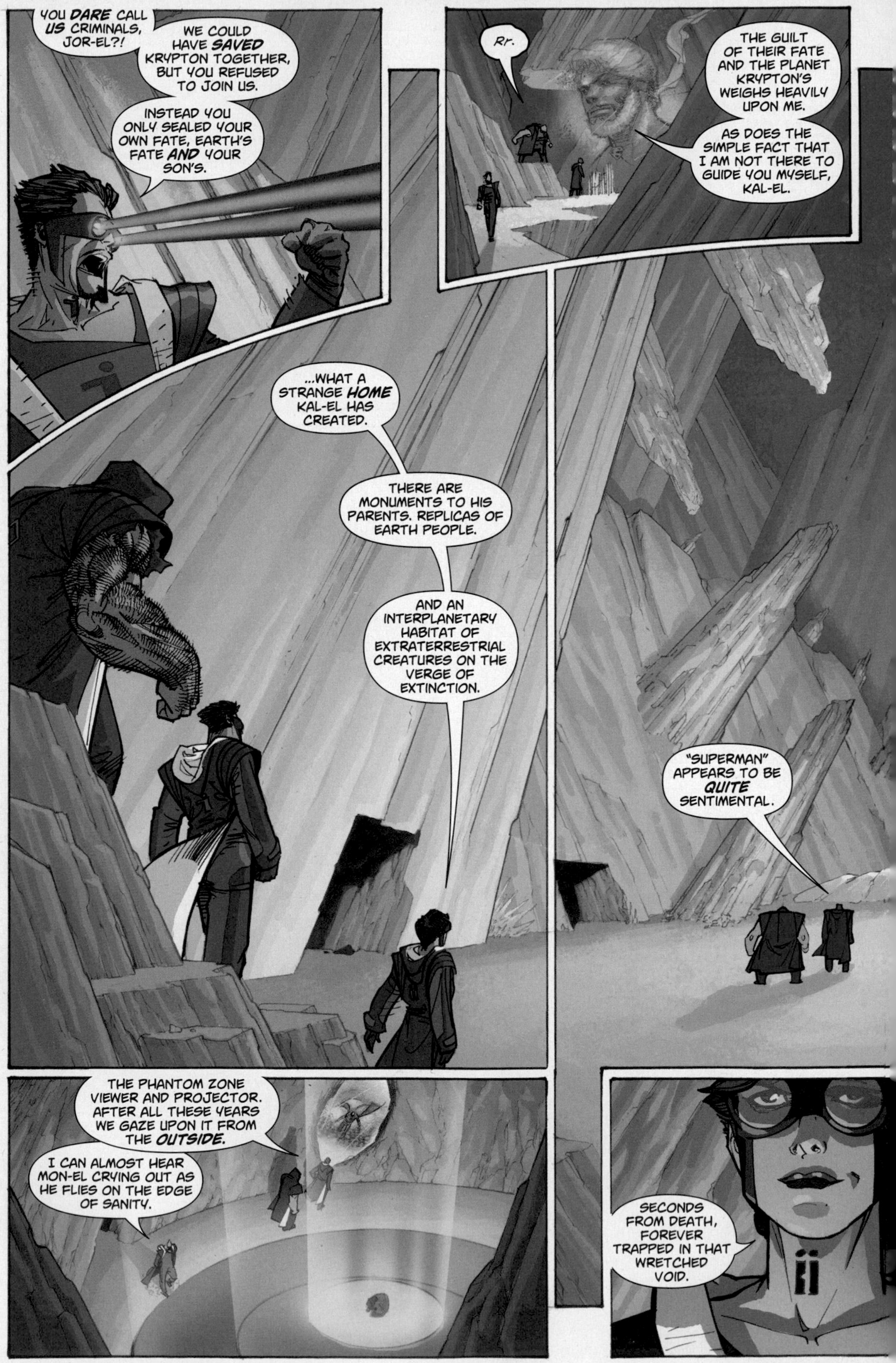
YOU DARE CALL US CRIMINALS, JOR-EL?!
WE COULD HAVE SAVED KRYPTON TOGETHER, BUT YOU REFUSED TO JOIN US.
INSTEAD YOU ONLY SEALED YOUR OWN FATE, EARTH'S FATE AND YOUR SON'S.
Rr.
THE GUILT OF THEIR FATE AND THE PLANET KRYPTON'S WEIGHS HEAVILY UPON ME.
AS DOES THE SIMPLE FACT THAT I AM NOT THERE TO GUIDE YOU MYSELF, KAL-EL.
...WHAT A STRANGE HOME KAL-EL HAS CREATED.
THERE ARE MONUMENTS TO HIS PARENTS. REPLICAS OF EARTH PEOPLE.
AND AN INTERPLANETARY HABITAT OF EXTRATERRESTRIAL CREATURES ON THE VERGE OF EXTINCTION.
"SUPERMAN" APPEARS TO BE QUITE SENTIMENTAL.
THE PHANTOM ZONE VIEWER AND PROJECTOR. AFTER ALL THESE YEARS WE GAZE UPON IT FROM THE OUTSIDE.
I CAN ALMOST HEAR MON-EL CRYING OUT AS HE FLIES ON THE EDGE OF SANITY.
SECONDS FROM DEATH, FOREVER TRAPPED IN THAT WRETCHED VOID.

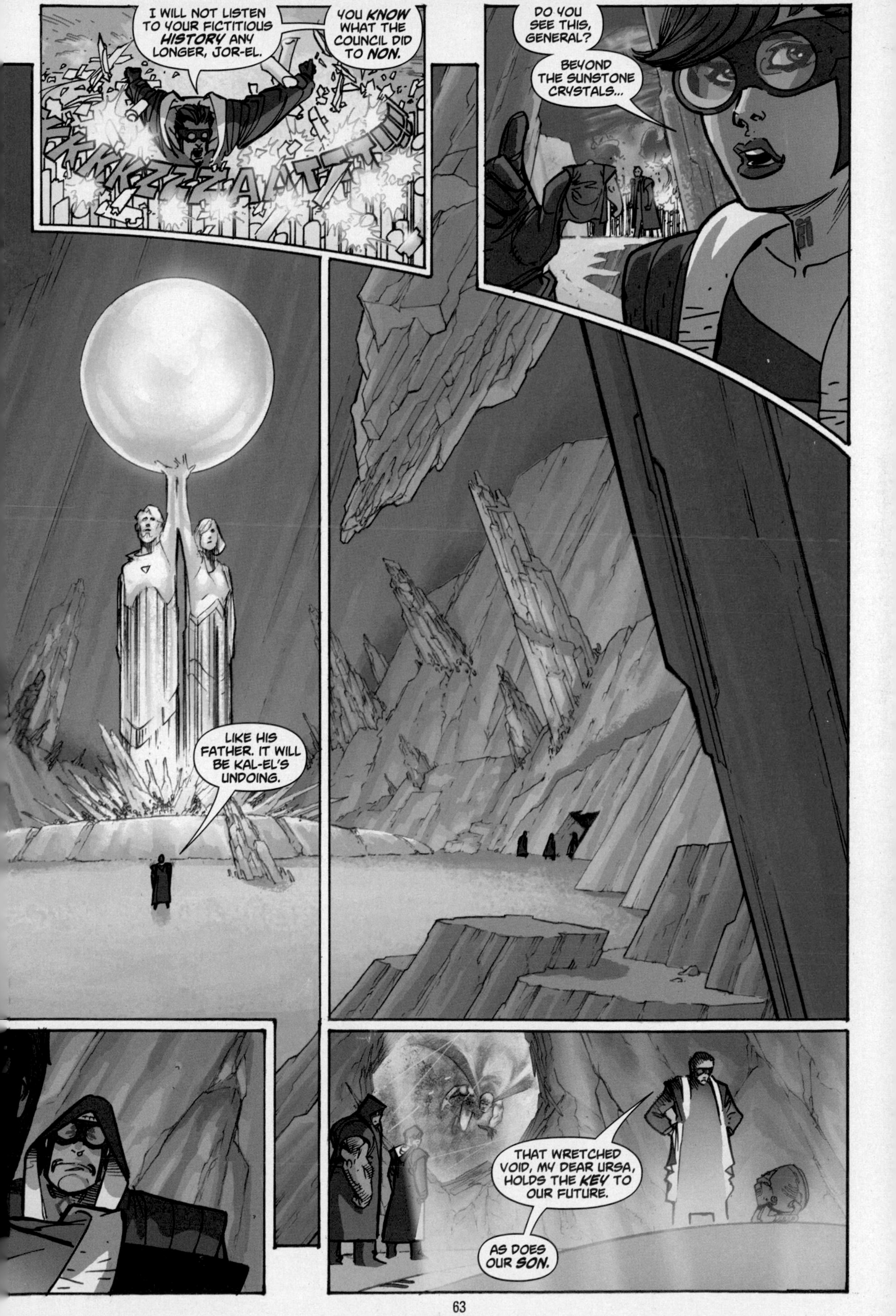
I WILL NOT LISTEN TO YOUR FICTITIOUS HISTORY ANY LONGER, JOR-EL.
YOU KNOW WHAT THE COUNCIL DID TO NON.
KKKZZZAAATT
DO YOU SEE THIS, GENERAL?
BEYOND THE SUNSTONE CRYSTALS...
LIKE HIS FATHER. IT WILL BE KAL-EL'S UNDOING.
THAT WRETCHED VOID, MY DEAR URSA, HOLDS THE KEY TO OUR FUTURE.
AS DOES OUR SON.

SO WE HAVE OUR STORIES STRAIGHT?

I THINK SO...

...HIS NAME IS CHRISTOPHER.

HE'S TWELVE YEARS OLD.

HE'S FROM NEW YORK CITY.

AND HE'S MY COUSIN'S SON.

I THOUGHT HE WAS *MY* COUSIN'S SON.

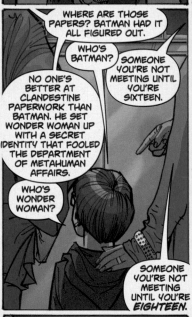

WHERE ARE THOSE PAPERS? BATMAN HAD IT ALL FIGURED OUT.

WHO'S BATMAN?

SOMEONE YOU'RE NOT MEETING UNTIL YOU'RE SIXTEEN.

NO ONE'S BETTER AT CLANDESTINE PAPERWORK THAN BATMAN. HE SET WONDER WOMAN UP WITH A SECRET IDENTITY THAT FOOLED THE DEPARTMENT OF METAHUMAN AFFAIRS.

WHO'S WONDER WOMAN?

SOMEONE YOU'RE NOT MEETING UNTIL YOU'RE *EIGHTEEN.*

DO YOU REMEMBER WHAT YOU'RE GOING TO SAY?

"HI! IT'S NICE TO MEET YOU!"

AND WHAT *ELSE?*

NOTHING!

GREAT.

DING!

TWENTY-FIFTH FLOOR. REPORTERS AND KRYPTONIANS.

LOIS, RELAX.

THIS IS GOING TO BE AS *EASY* AS PUTTING ON A PAIR OF *GLASSES.*

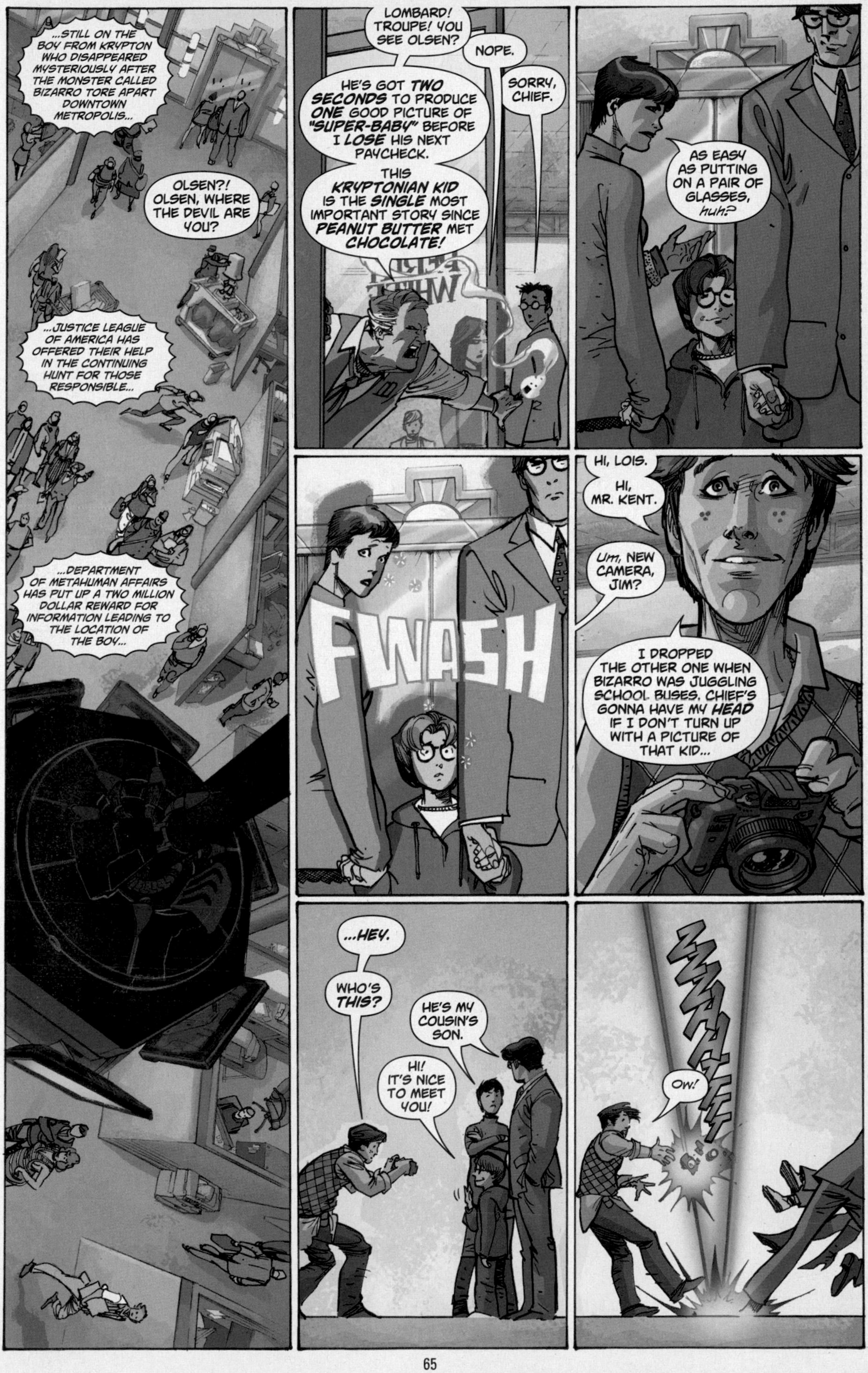
...STILL ON THE BOY FROM KRYPTON WHO DISAPPEARED MYSTERIOUSLY AFTER THE MONSTER CALLED BIZARRO TORE APART DOWNTOWN METROPOLIS...
OLSEN?! OLSEN, WHERE THE DEVIL ARE YOU?
...JUSTICE LEAGUE OF AMERICA HAS OFFERED THEIR HELP IN THE CONTINUING HUNT FOR THOSE RESPONSIBLE...
...DEPARTMENT OF METAHUMAN AFFAIRS HAS PUT UP A TWO MILLION DOLLAR REWARD FOR INFORMATION LEADING TO THE LOCATION OF THE BOY...
LOMBARD! TROUPE! YOU SEE OLSEN?
NOPE.
SORRY, CHIEF.
HE'S GOT TWO SECONDS TO PRODUCE ONE GOOD PICTURE OF "SUPER-BABY" BEFORE I LOSE HIS NEXT PAYCHECK.
THIS KRYPTONIAN KID IS THE SINGLE MOST IMPORTANT STORY SINCE PEANUT BUTTER MET CHOCOLATE!
AS EASY AS PUTTING ON A PAIR OF GLASSES, huh?
FWASH
HI, LOIS.
HI, MR. KENT.
Um, NEW CAMERA, JIM?
I DROPPED THE OTHER ONE WHEN BIZARRO WAS JUGGLING SCHOOL BUSES. CHIEF'S GONNA HAVE MY HEAD IF I DON'T TURN UP WITH A PICTURE OF THAT KID...
...HEY.
WHO'S THIS?
HE'S MY COUSIN'S SON.
HI! IT'S NICE TO MEET YOU!
OW!

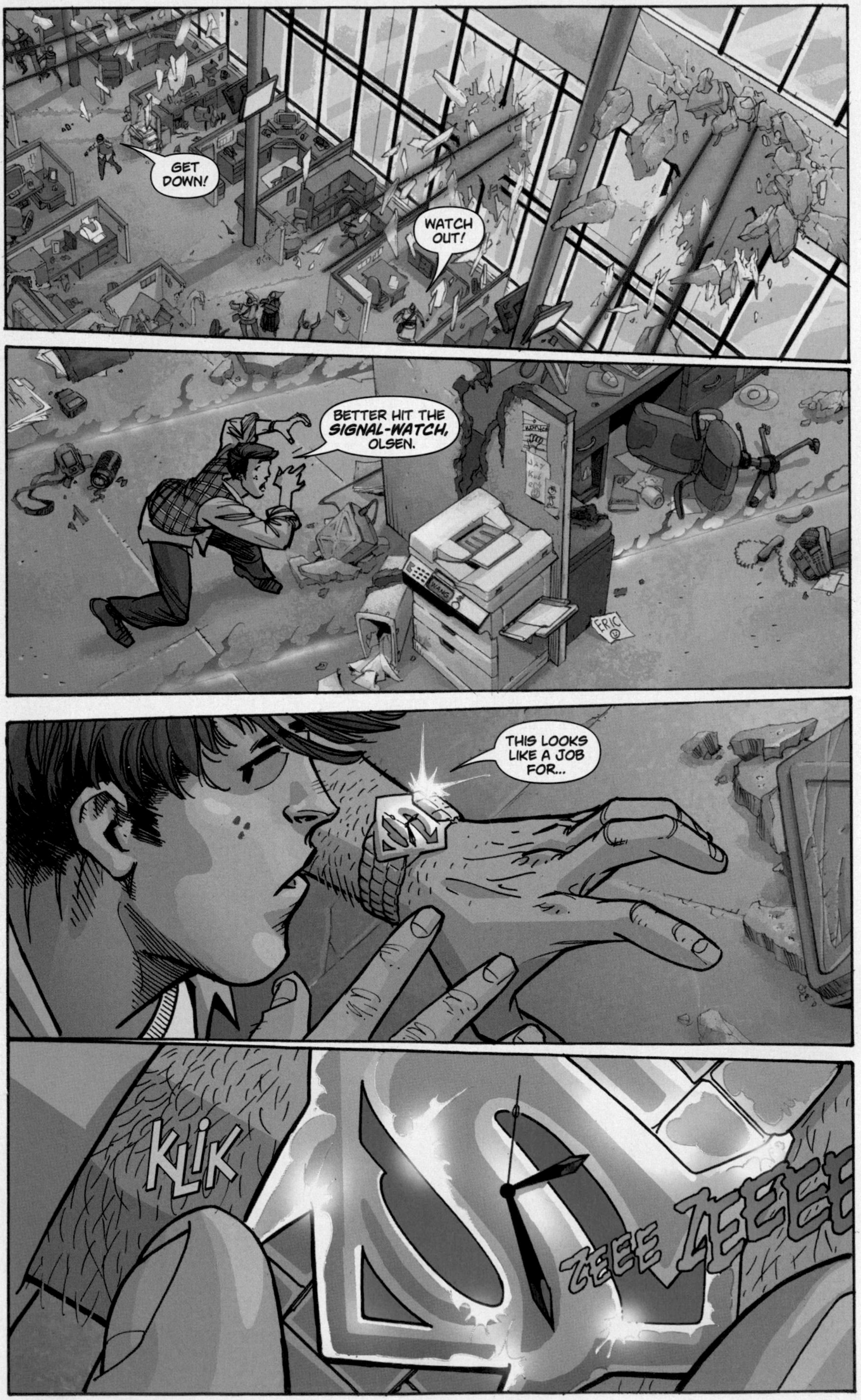
GET DOWN!
WATCH OUT!
BETTER HIT THE SIGNAL-WATCH, OLSEN.
WANG
ERIC
THIS LOOKS LIKE A JOB FOR...
KLIK
ZEEE ZEEEE

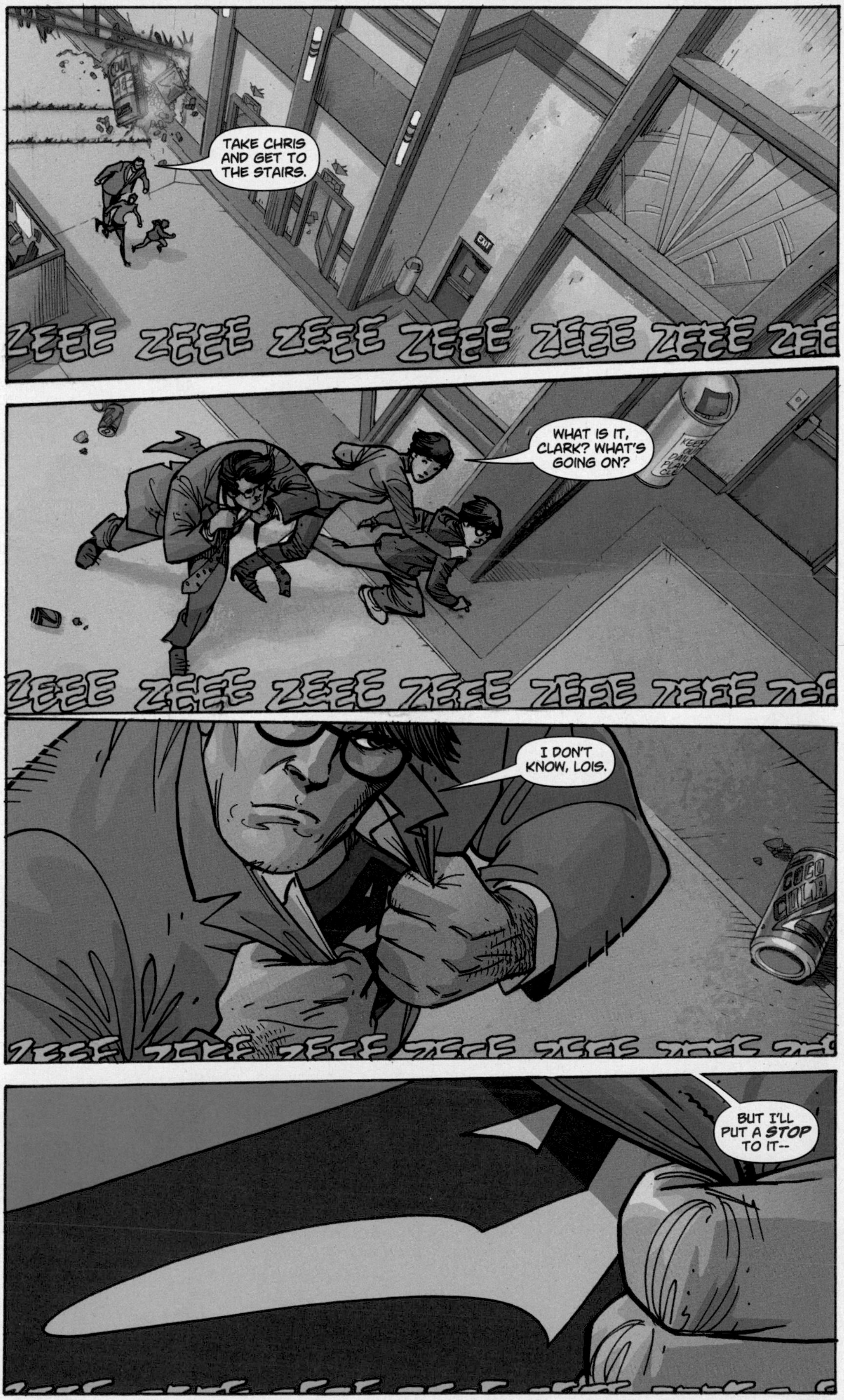
TAKE CHRIS AND GET TO THE STAIRS.
ZEEE ZEEE ZEEE ZEEE ZEEE ZEEE
WHAT IS IT, CLARK? WHAT'S GOING ON?
ZEEE ZEEE ZEEE ZEEE ZEEE ZEEE
I DON'T KNOW, LOIS.
BUT I'LL PUT A STOP TO IT--

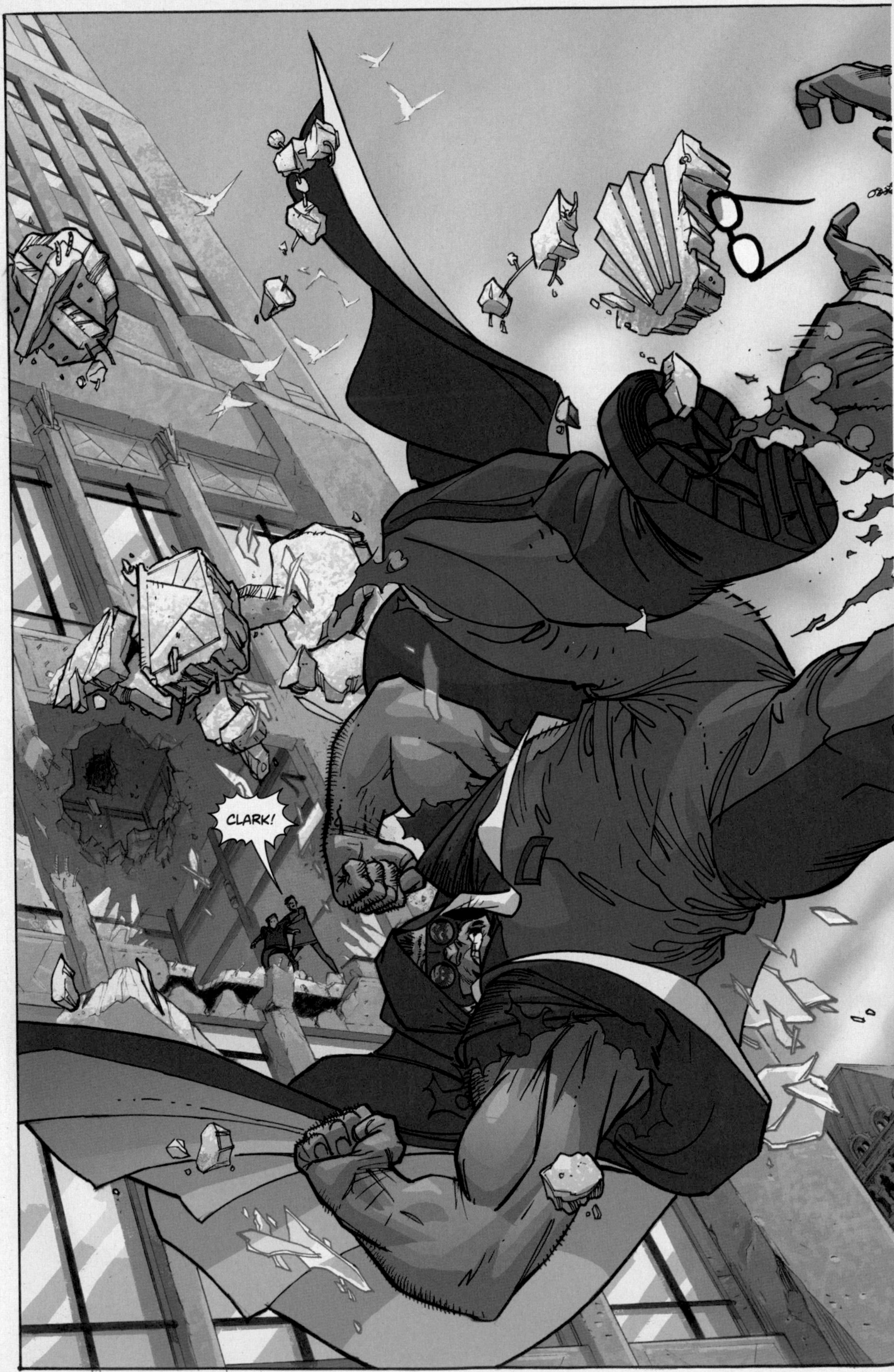
CLARK!

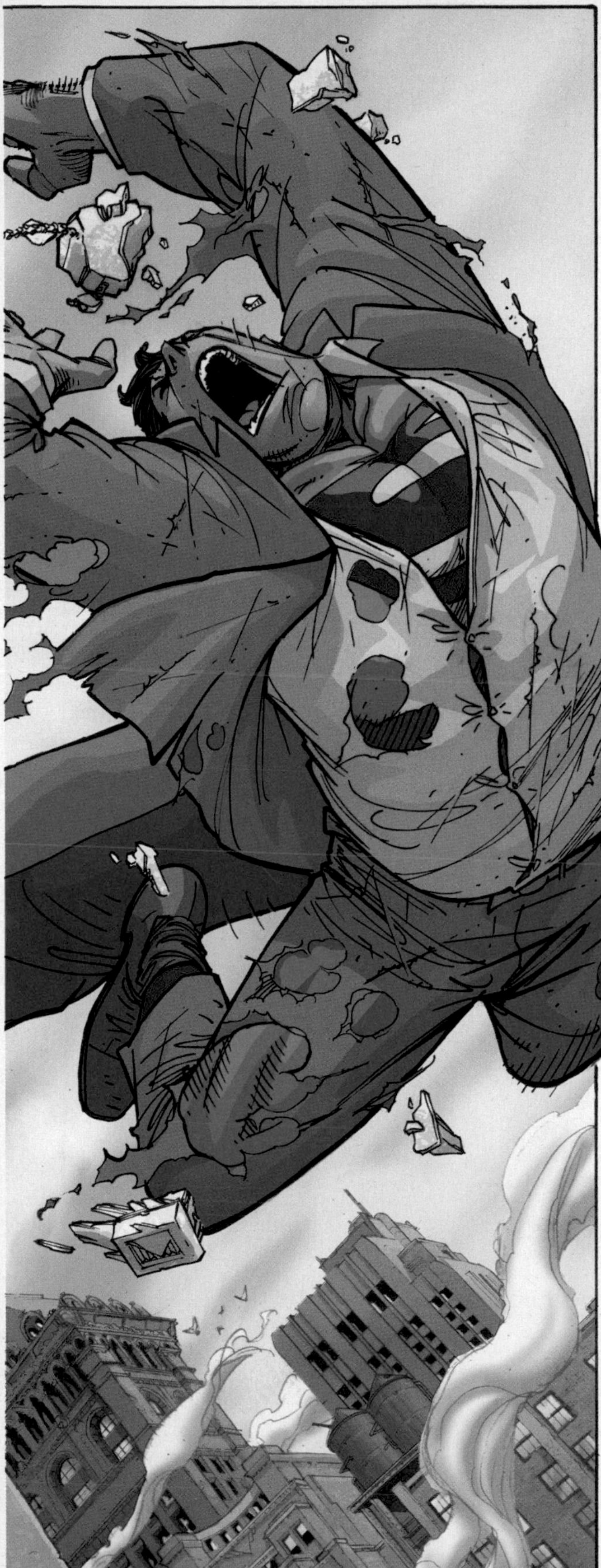

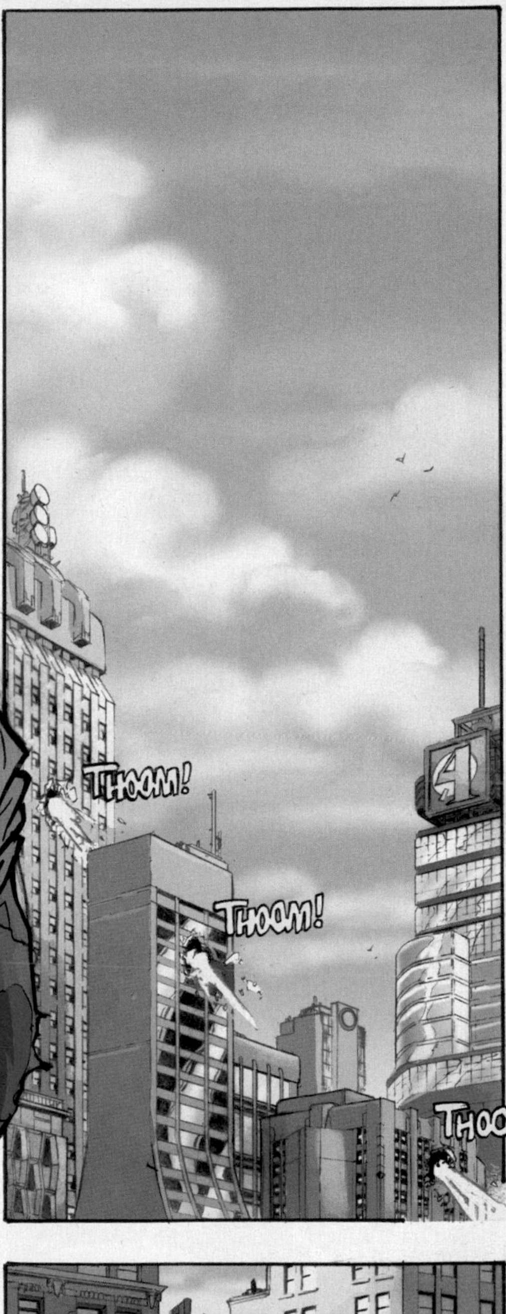
THOOM!
THOOM!
THOOM!

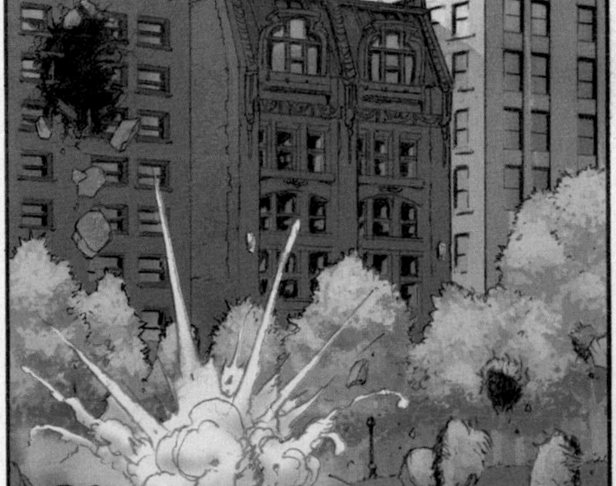

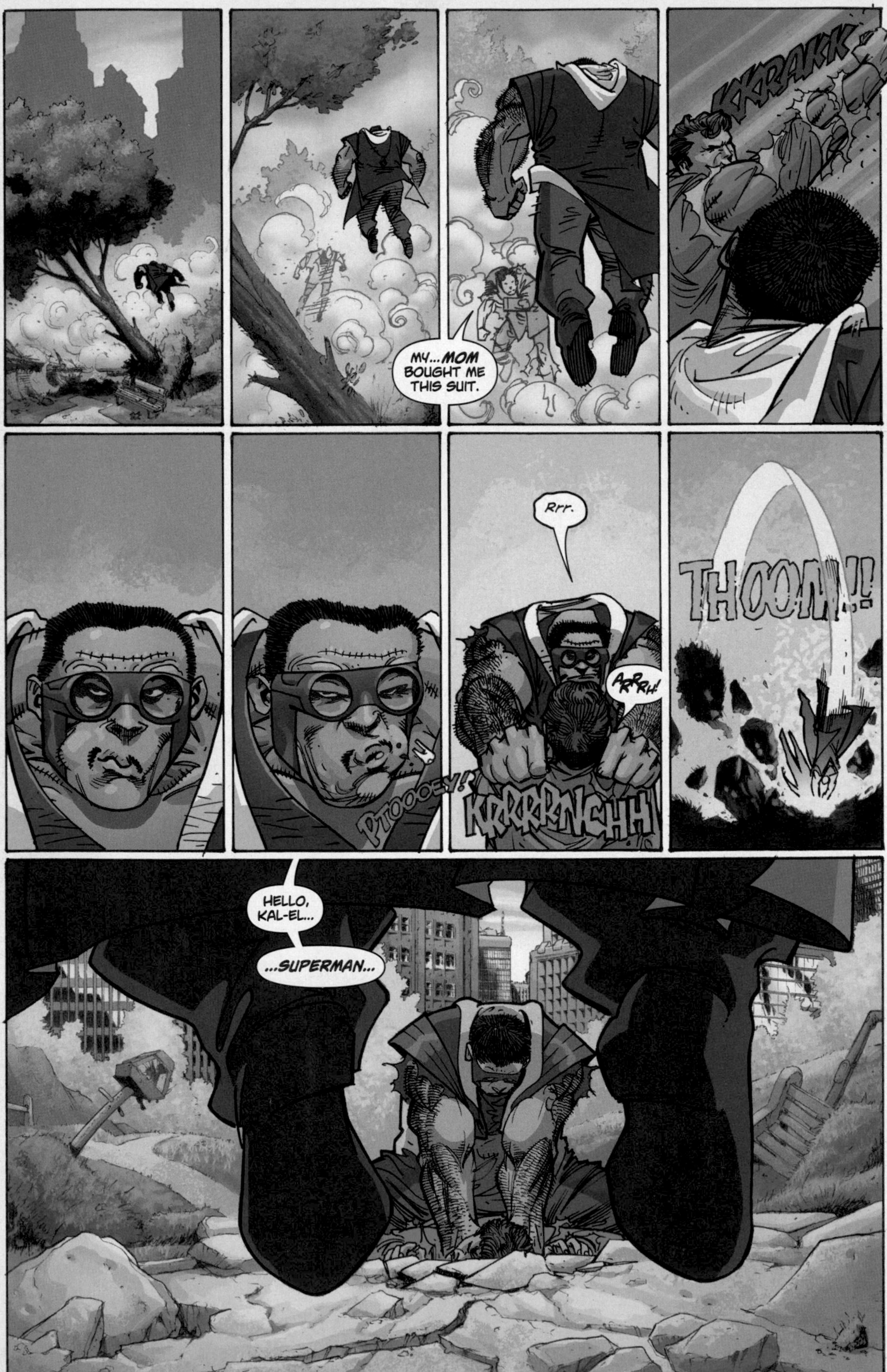
MY...MOM BOUGHT ME THIS SUIT.
KKRAKK
Rrr.
THOOM!!
PTOOOEY!
ARRRH!
KRRRRNCHH
HELLO, KAL-EL...
...SUPERMAN...

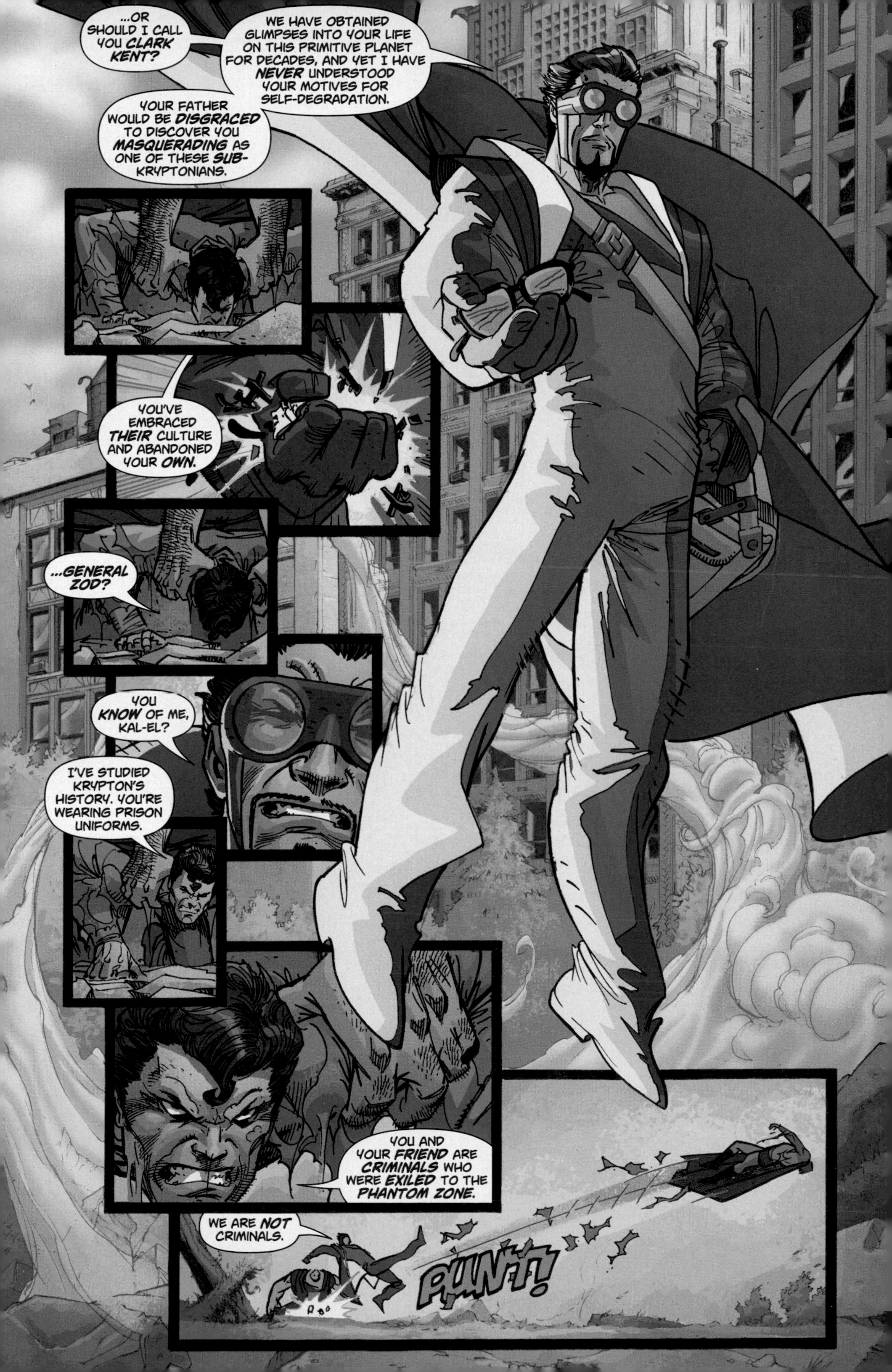
...OR SHOULD I CALL YOU CLARK KENT?
WE HAVE OBTAINED GLIMPSES INTO YOUR LIFE ON THIS PRIMITIVE PLANET FOR DECADES, AND YET I HAVE NEVER UNDERSTOOD YOUR MOTIVES FOR SELF-DEGRADATION.
YOUR FATHER WOULD BE DISGRACED TO DISCOVER YOU MASQUERADING AS ONE OF THESE SUB-KRYPTONIANS.
YOU'VE EMBRACED THEIR CULTURE AND ABANDONED YOUR OWN.
...GENERAL ZOD?
YOU KNOW OF ME, KAL-EL?
I'VE STUDIED KRYPTON'S HISTORY. YOU'RE WEARING PRISON UNIFORMS.
YOU AND YOUR FRIEND ARE CRIMINALS WHO WERE EXILED TO THE PHANTOM ZONE.
WE ARE NOT CRIMINALS.
PUNT!

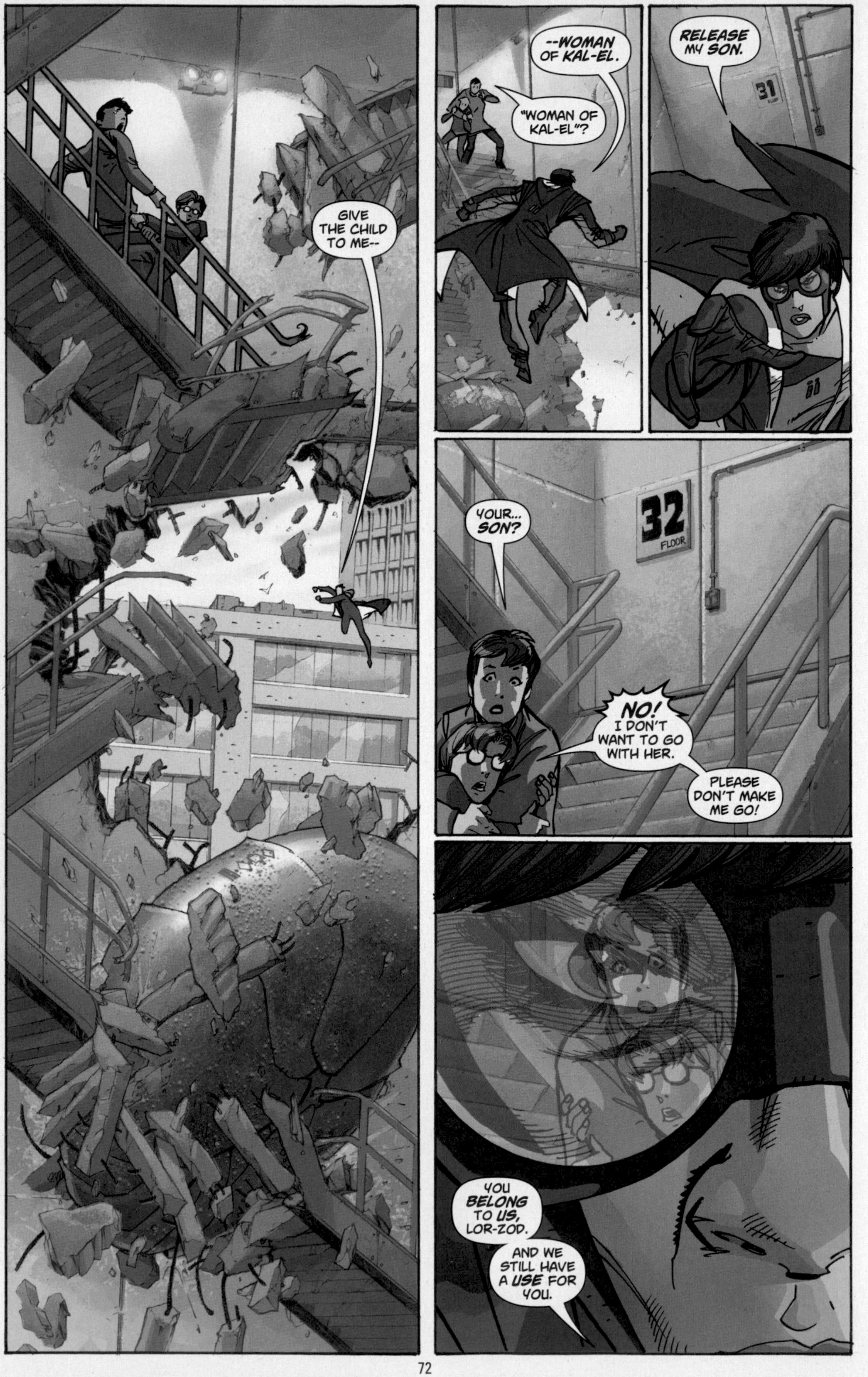
GIVE THE CHILD TO ME--
--WOMAN OF KAL-EL.
"WOMAN OF KAL-EL"?
RELEASE MY SON.
31
YOUR... SON?
32 FLOOR
NO! I DON'T WANT TO GO WITH HER.
PLEASE DON'T MAKE ME GO!
YOU BELONG TO US, LOR-ZOD.
AND WE STILL HAVE A USE FOR YOU.

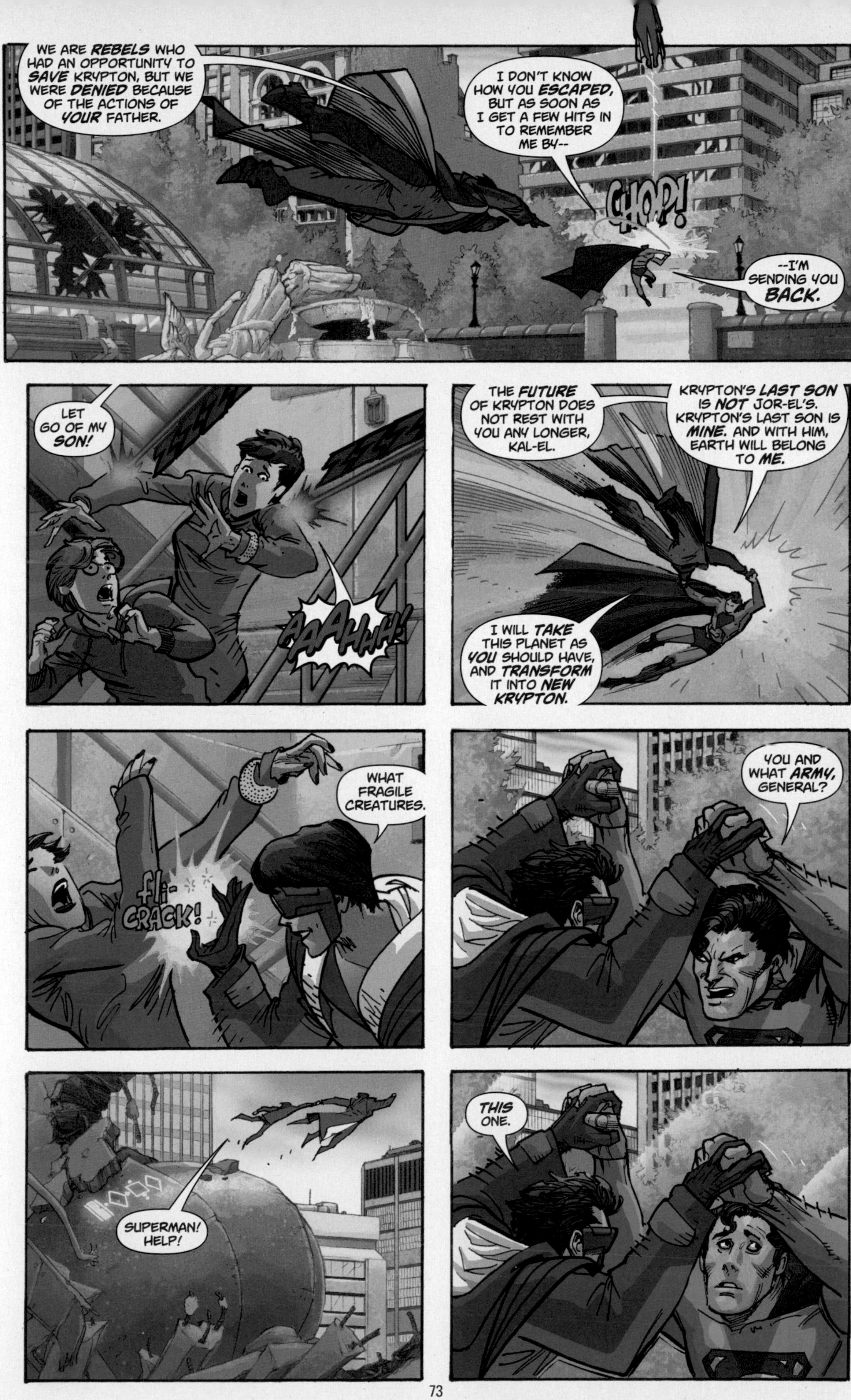
WE ARE REBELS WHO HAD AN OPPORTUNITY TO SAVE KRYPTON, BUT WE WERE DENIED BECAUSE OF THE ACTIONS OF YOUR FATHER.
I DON'T KNOW HOW YOU ESCAPED, BUT AS SOON AS I GET A FEW HITS IN TO REMEMBER ME BY--
CHOP!
--I'M SENDING YOU BACK.
LET GO OF MY SON!
AAAHHH!
THE FUTURE OF KRYPTON DOES NOT REST WITH YOU ANY LONGER, KAL-EL.
KRYPTON'S LAST SON IS NOT JOR-EL'S. KRYPTON'S LAST SON IS MINE. AND WITH HIM, EARTH WILL BELONG TO ME.
I WILL TAKE THIS PLANET AS YOU SHOULD HAVE, AND TRANSFORM IT INTO NEW KRYPTON.
WHAT FRAGILE CREATURES.
fli-CRACK!
YOU AND WHAT ARMY, GENERAL?
SUPERMAN! HELP!
THIS ONE.

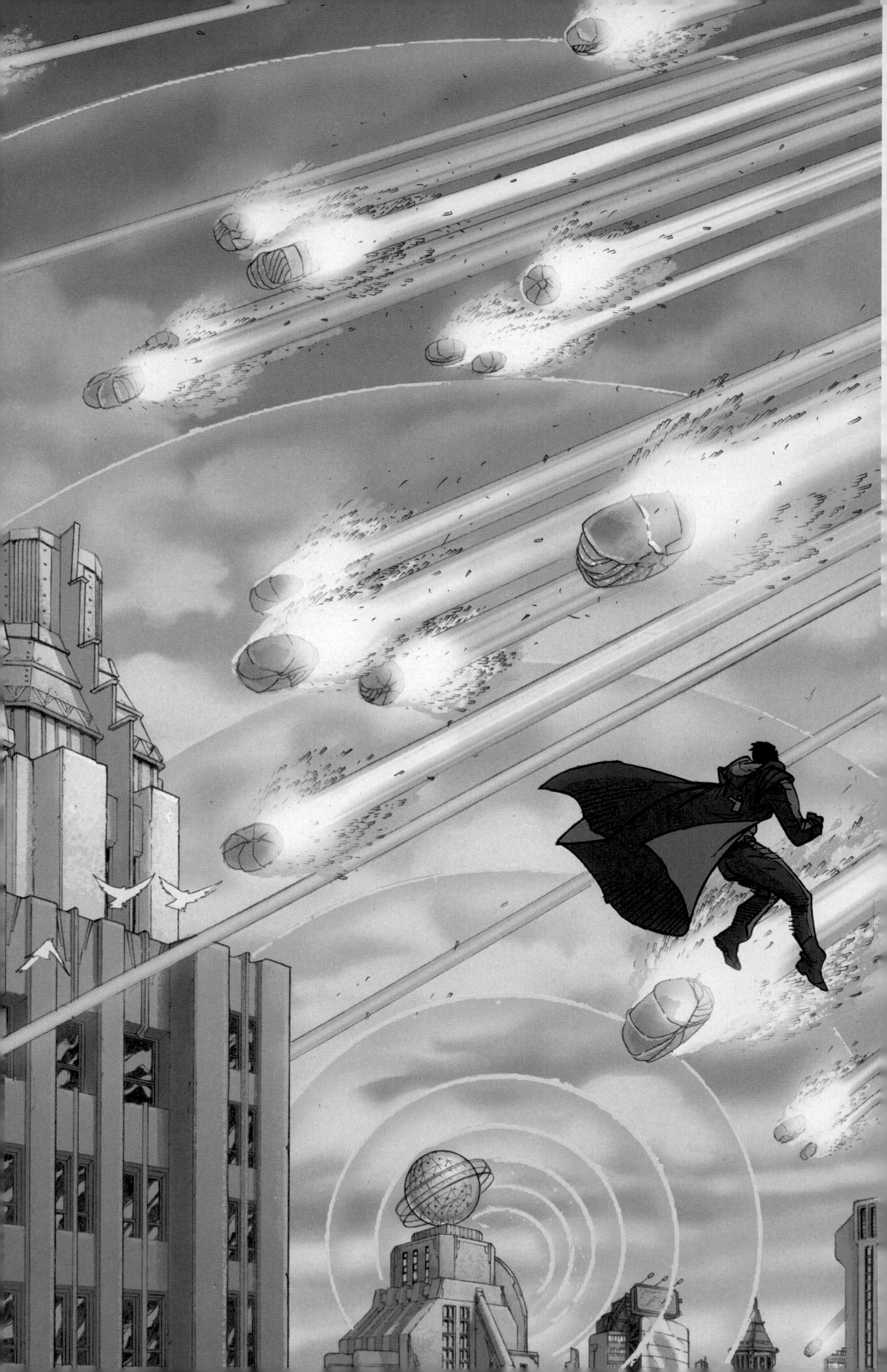

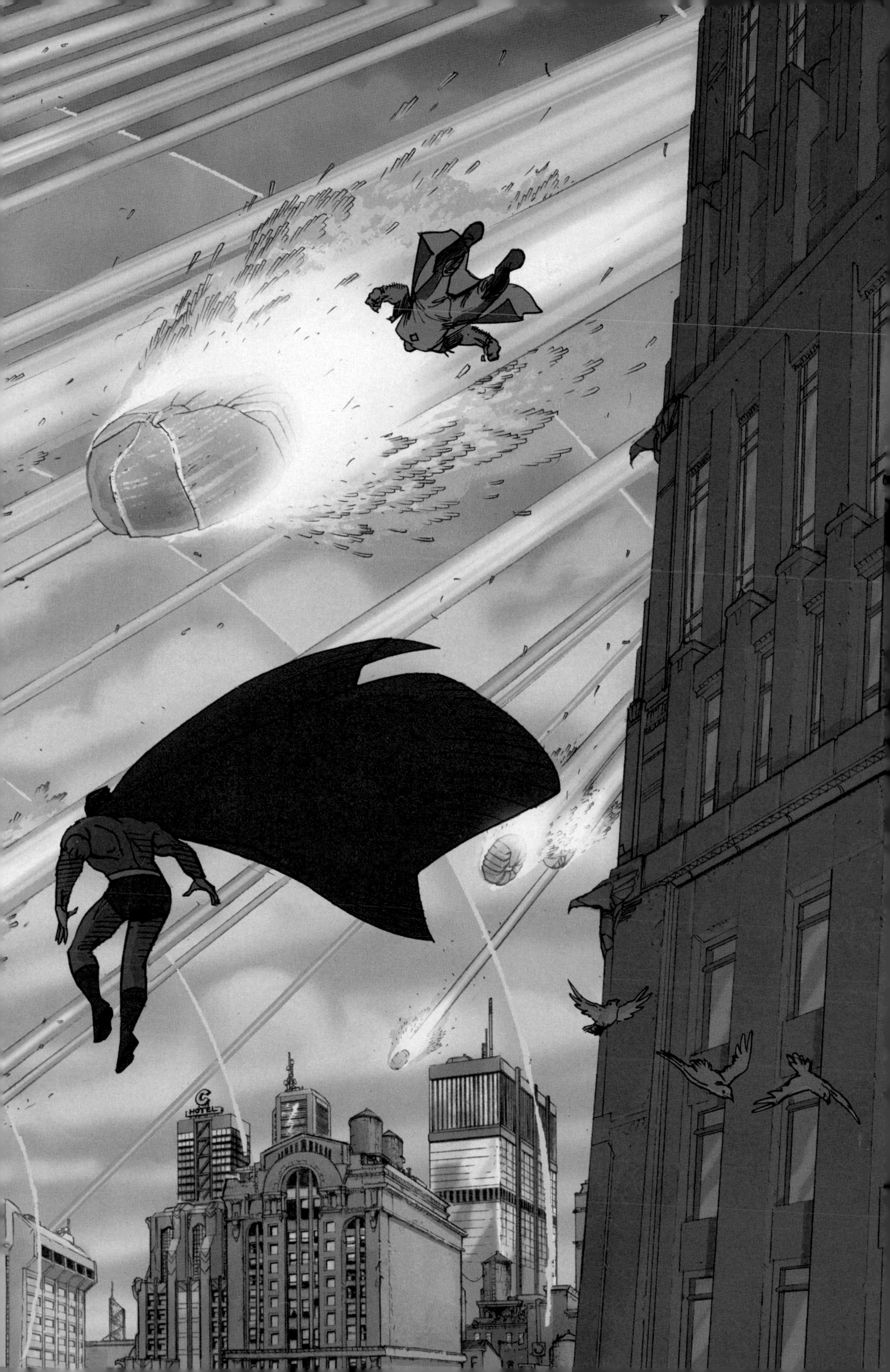
HOTEL

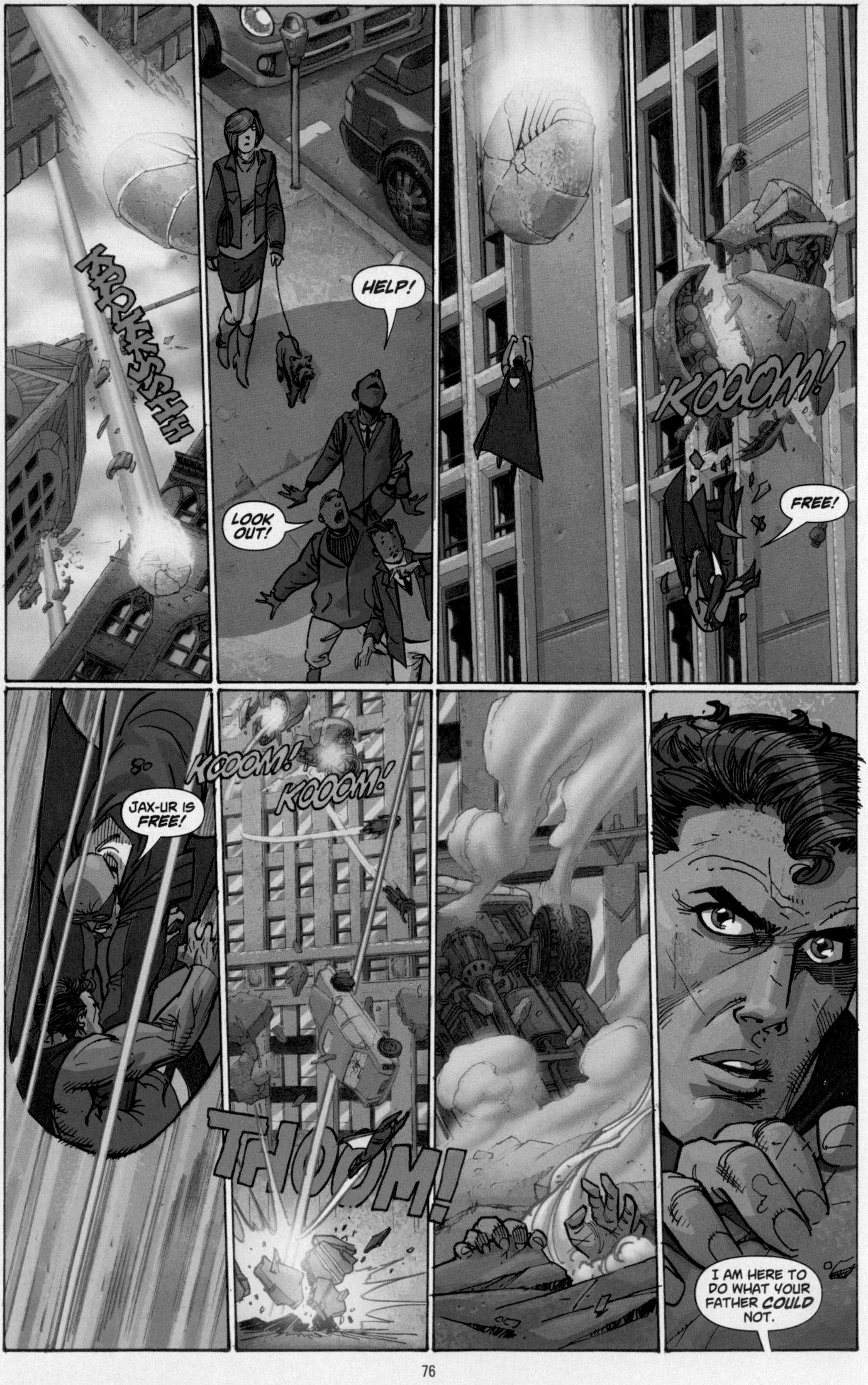
KRKKSHH
HELP!
LOOK OUT!
KOOOM!
FREE!
JAX-UR IS FREE!
KOOOM!
KOOOM!
THOOM!
I AM HERE TO DO WHAT YOUR FATHER COULD NOT.

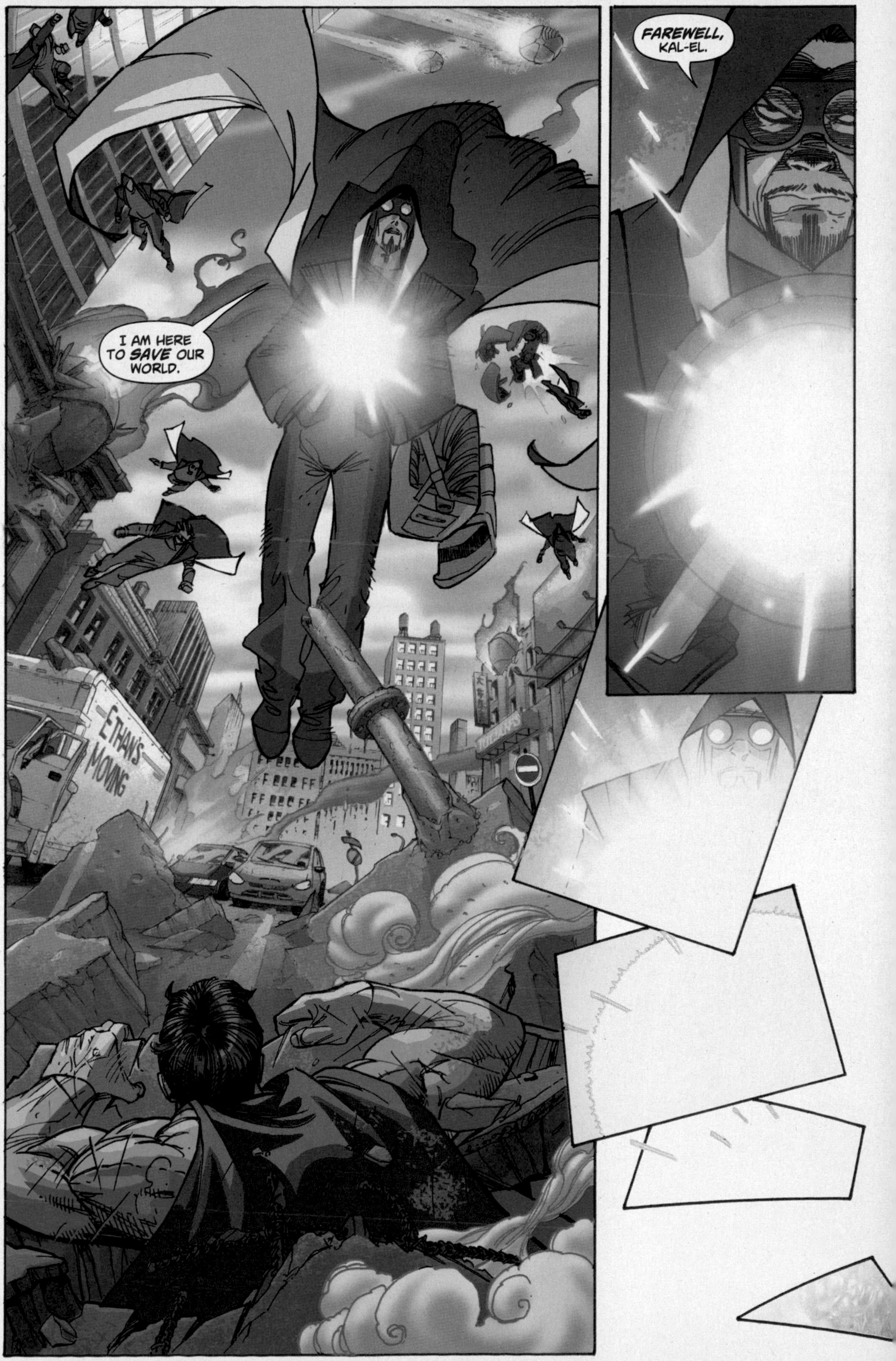
I AM HERE TO SAVE OUR WORLD.
ETHAN'S MOVING
FAREWELL, KAL-EL.

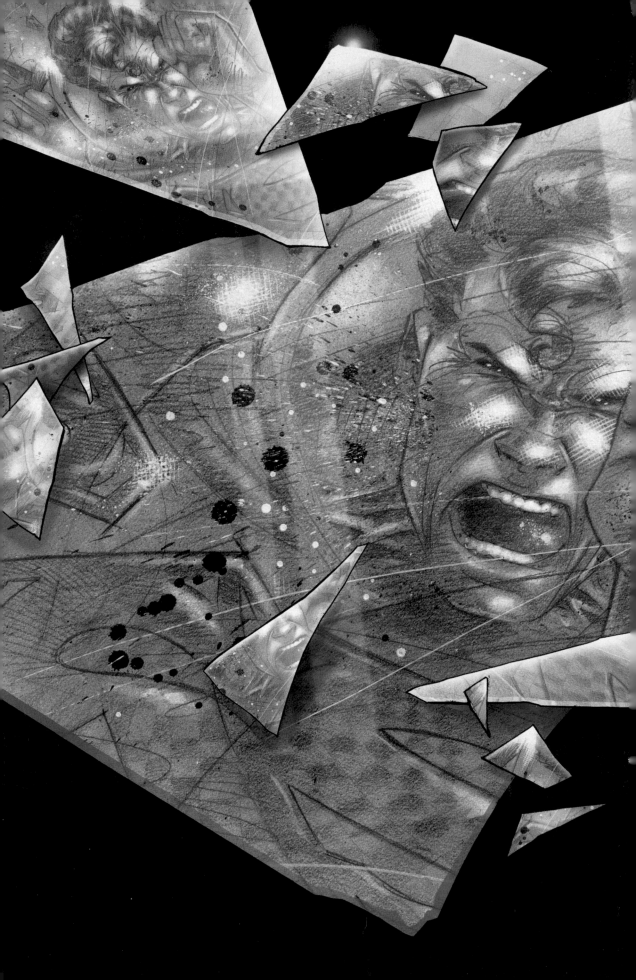

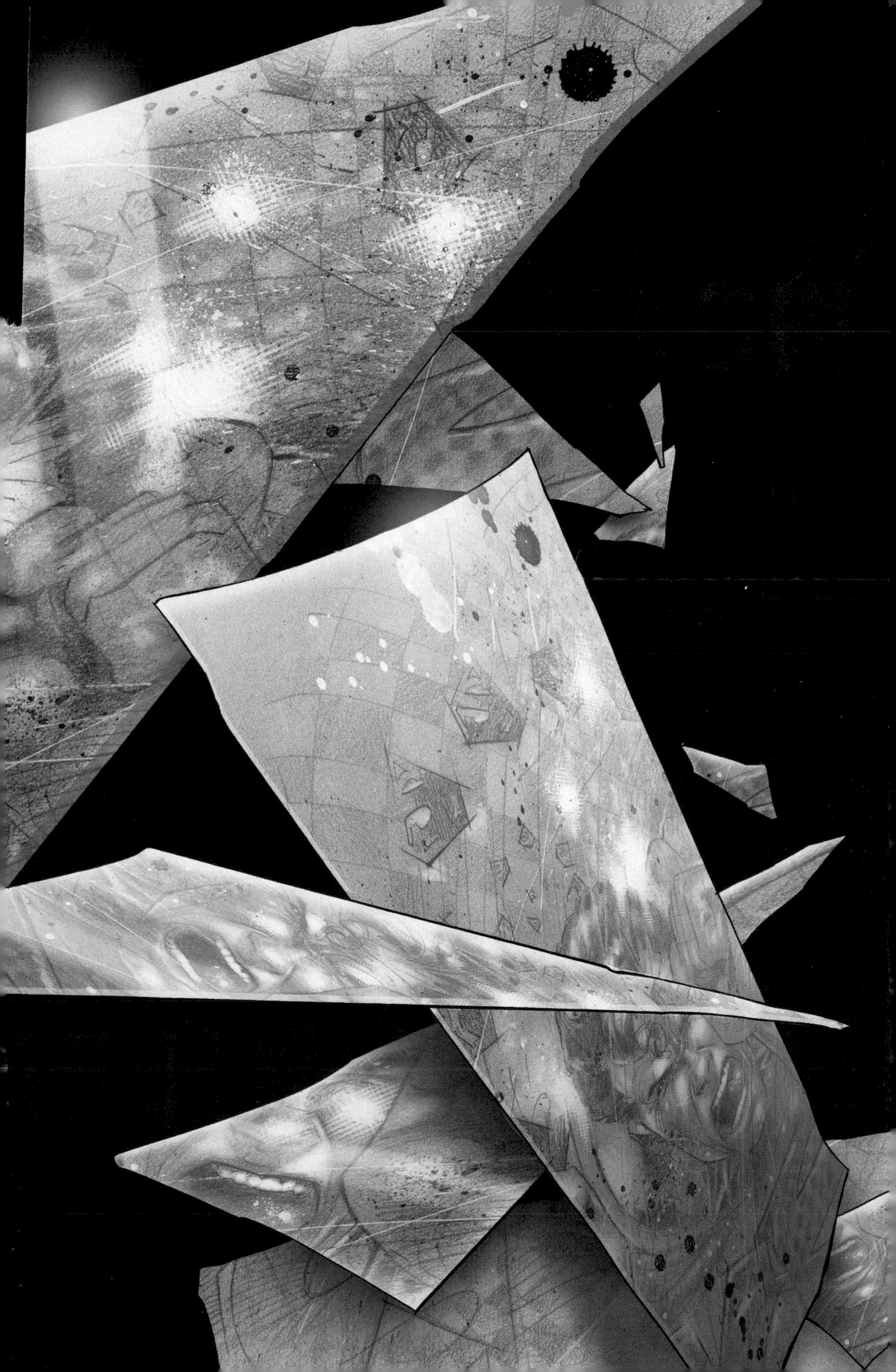

CHAPTER FOUR

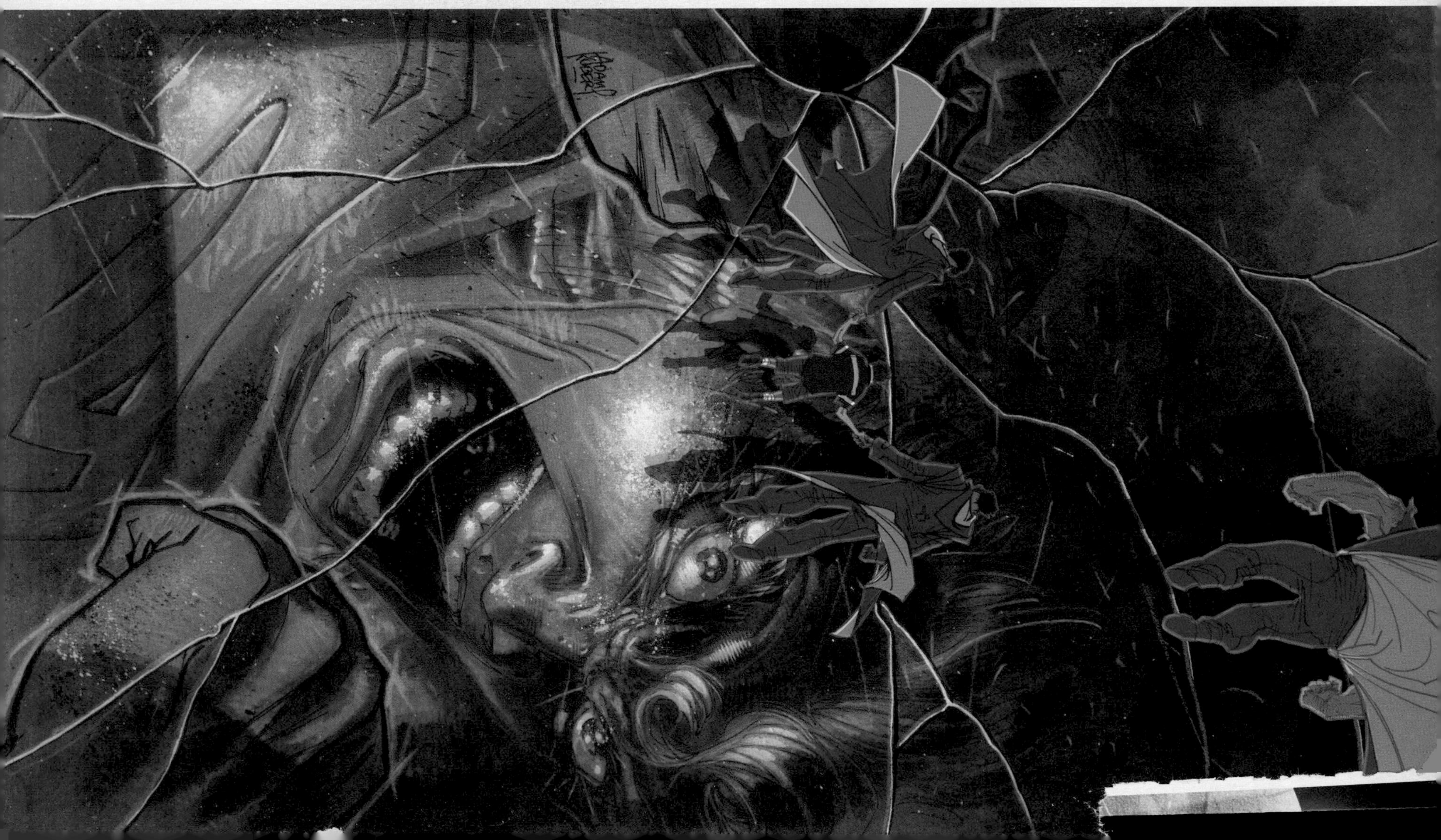

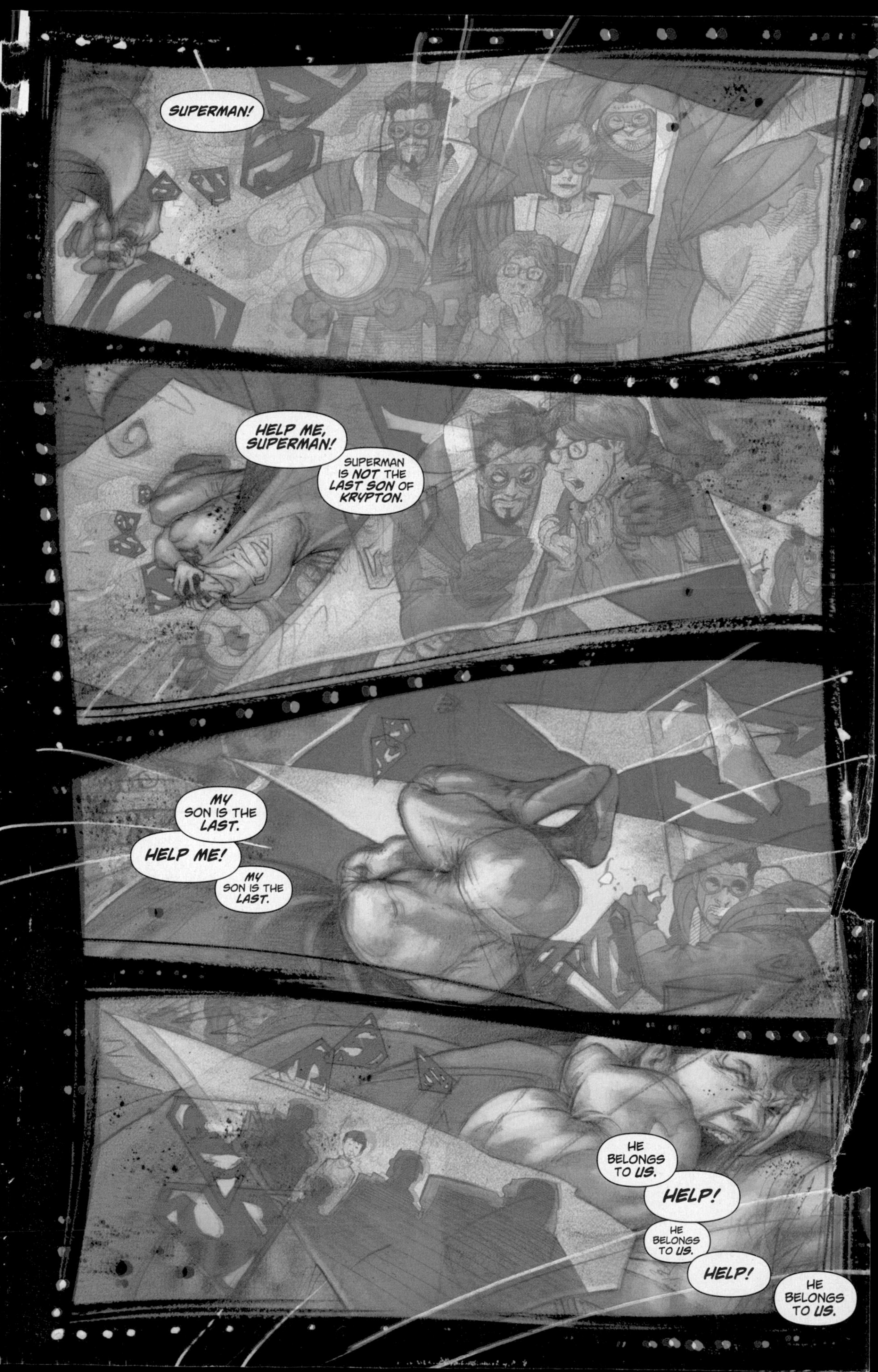
SUPERMAN!
HELP ME, SUPERMAN!
SUPERMAN IS NOT THE LAST SON OF KRYPTON.
MY SON IS THE LAST.
HELP ME!
MY SON IS THE LAST.
HE BELONGS TO US.
HELP!
HE BELONGS TO US.
HELP!
HE BELONGS TO US.

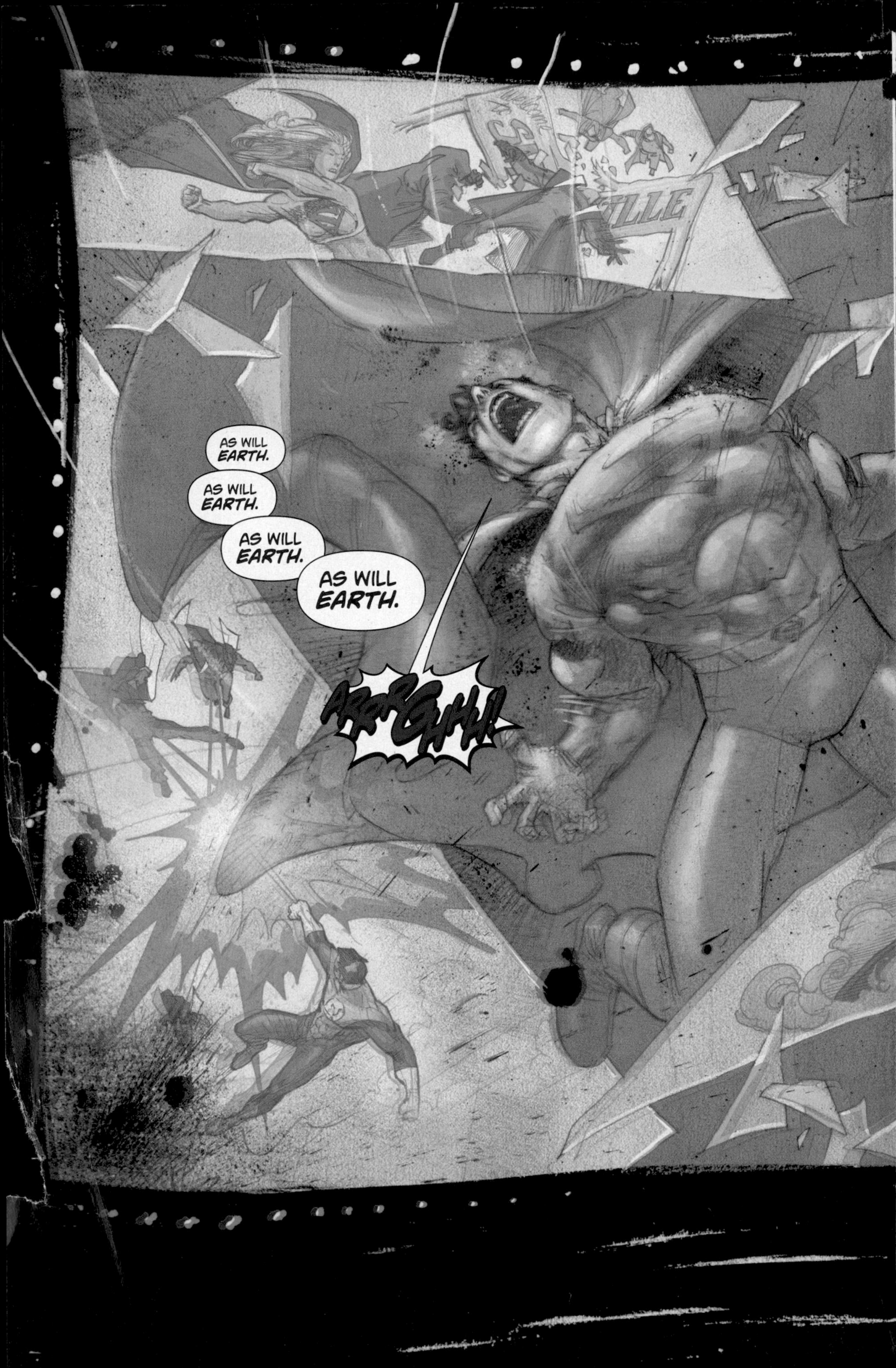
AS WILL EARTH.
AS WILL EARTH.
AS WILL EARTH.
AS WILL EARTH.
ARRRGHHH!

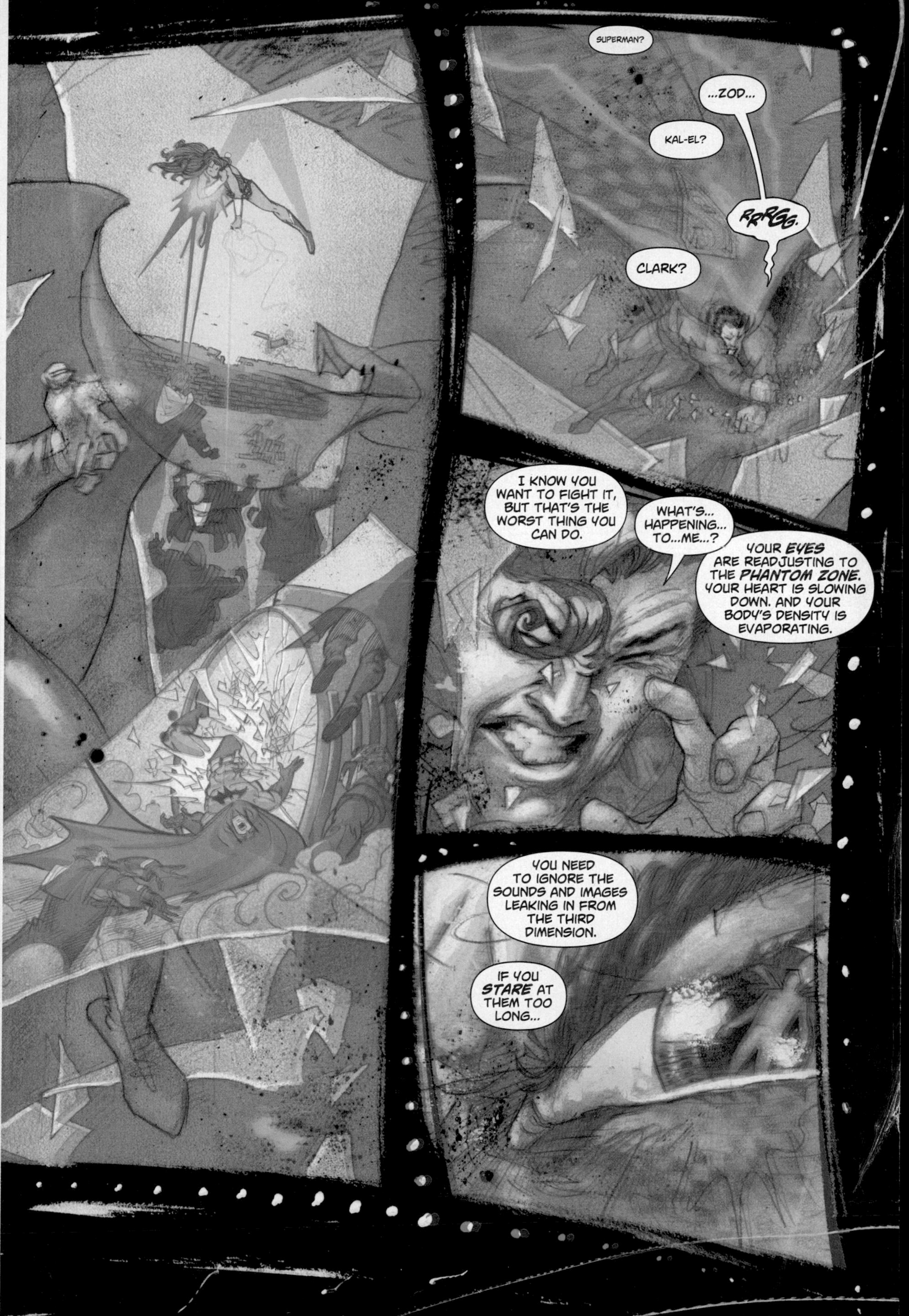
SUPERMAN?
...ZOD...
KAL-EL?
RRRGG.
CLARK?
I KNOW YOU WANT TO FIGHT IT, BUT THAT'S THE WORST THING YOU CAN DO.
WHAT'S... HAPPENING... TO...ME...?
YOUR EYES ARE READJUSTING TO THE PHANTOM ZONE. YOUR HEART IS SLOWING DOWN. AND YOUR BODY'S DENSITY IS EVAPORATING.
YOU NEED TO IGNORE THE SOUNDS AND IMAGES LEAKING IN FROM THE THIRD DIMENSION.
IF YOU STARE AT THEM TOO LONG...

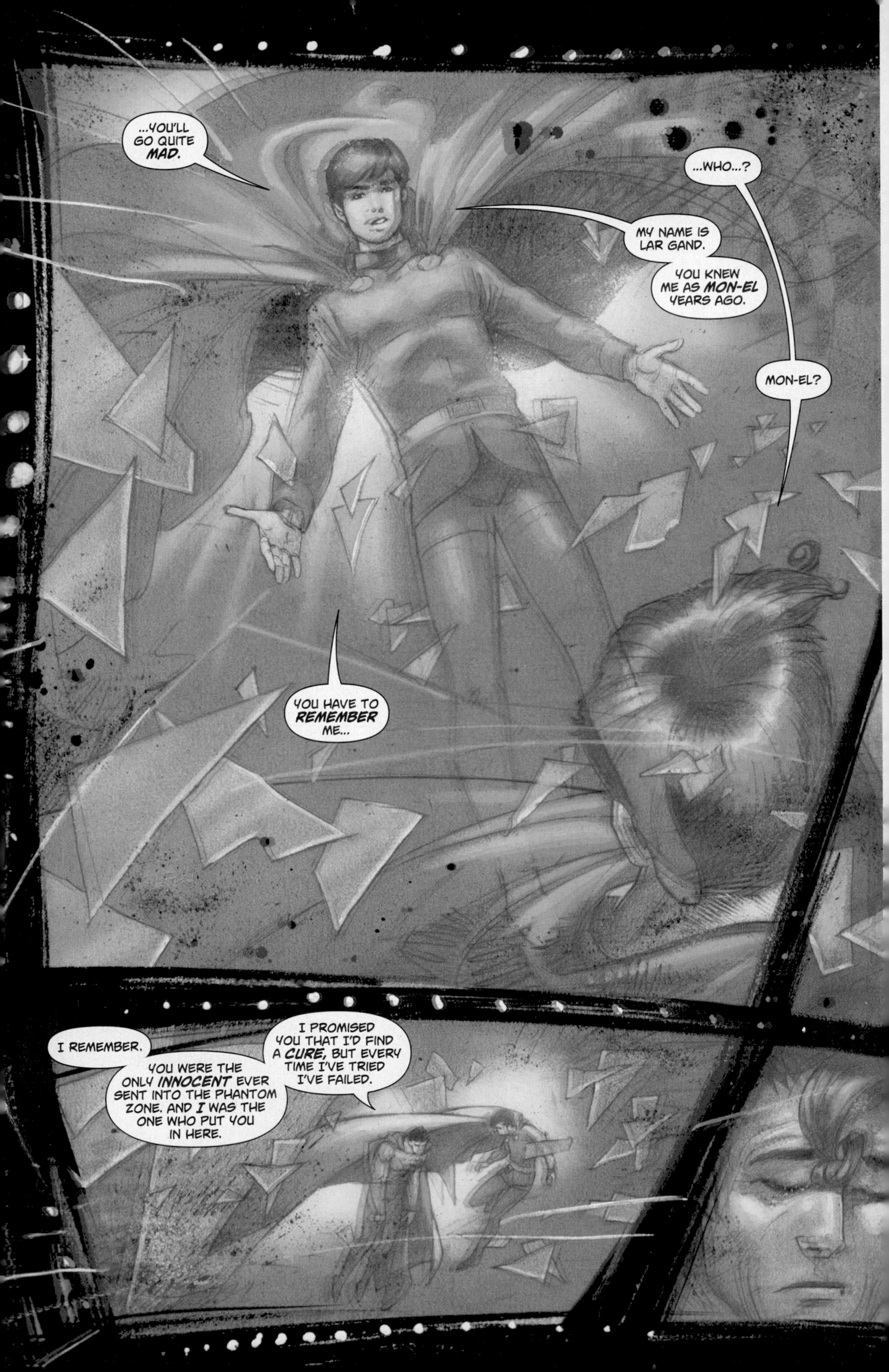
...YOU'LL GO QUITE MAD.
...WHO...?
MY NAME IS LAR GAND.
YOU KNEW ME AS MON-EL YEARS AGO.
MON-EL?
YOU HAVE TO REMEMBER ME...
I REMEMBER.
YOU WERE THE ONLY INNOCENT EVER SENT INTO THE PHANTOM ZONE. AND I WAS THE ONE WHO PUT YOU IN HERE.
I PROMISED YOU THAT I'D FIND A CURE, BUT EVERY TIME I'VE TRIED I'VE FAILED.

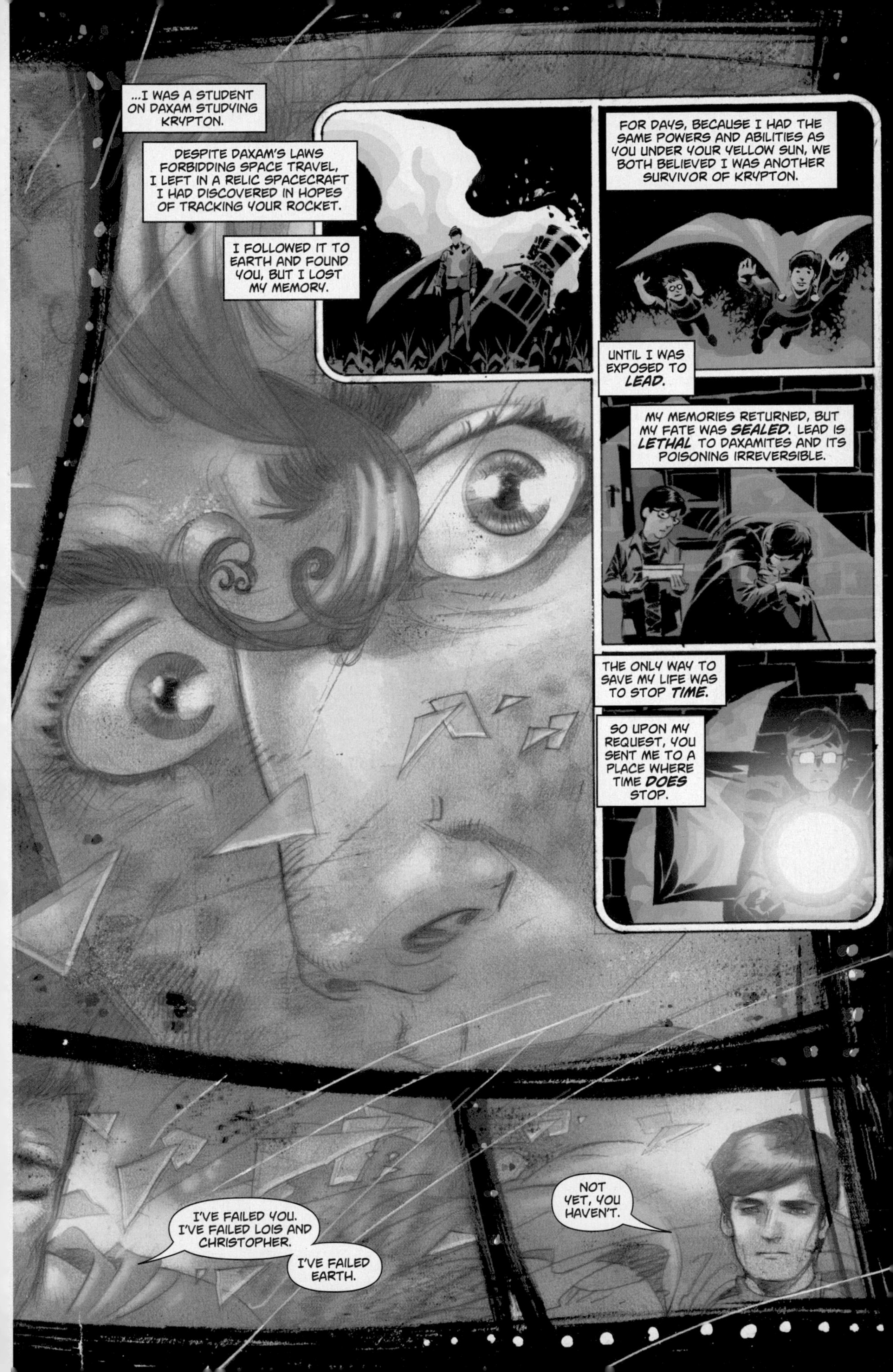
...I WAS A STUDENT ON DAXAM STUDYING KRYPTON.
DESPITE DAXAM'S LAWS FORBIDDING SPACE TRAVEL, I LEFT IN A RELIC SPACECRAFT I HAD DISCOVERED IN HOPES OF TRACKING YOUR ROCKET.
I FOLLOWED IT TO EARTH AND FOUND YOU, BUT I LOST MY MEMORY.
FOR DAYS, BECAUSE I HAD THE SAME POWERS AND ABILITIES AS YOU UNDER YOUR YELLOW SUN, WE BOTH BELIEVED I WAS ANOTHER SURVIVOR OF KRYPTON.
UNTIL I WAS EXPOSED TO LEAD.
MY MEMORIES RETURNED, BUT MY FATE WAS SEALED. LEAD IS LETHAL TO DAXAMITES AND ITS POISONING IRREVERSIBLE.
THE ONLY WAY TO SAVE MY LIFE WAS TO STOP TIME.
SO UPON MY REQUEST, YOU SENT ME TO A PLACE WHERE TIME DOES STOP.
I'VE FAILED YOU. I'VE FAILED LOIS AND CHRISTOPHER.
I'VE FAILED EARTH.
NOT YET, YOU HAVEN'T.

IT ALL STARTED WHEN GENERAL ZOD FOUND *THIS.*
IT WAS A KRYPTONIAN PRISON CALLED FORT ROZZ.
HOW DID IT GET INTO THE PHANTOM ZONE?
DEV-EM WAS TO BE SENT HERE FOR CRIMES OF *MURDER* AND *PERVERSION,* BUT BEFORE HIS JAILERS COULD ACTIVATE THE PHANTOM ZONE PROJECTOR A *RIOT* BROKE OUT.
DURING THE REVOLT, THE PROJECTOR EXPLODED AND THE ENTIRE PRISON WAS TRANSPORTED HERE.
THE METAL'S... *SOLID?*
AND IF ANYONE ENTERS, THEY BECOME SOLID TOO. UNLIKE THE REST OF THE PHANTOM ZONE, TIME PASSES INSIDE FORT ROZZ.
SO THAT'S HOW GENERAL ZOD HAD CHRISTOPHER.
CHRISTOPHER'S REAL NAME IS LOR-ZOD.
HE SHOULD BE, KAL.
IT'S HARD TO BELIEVE HE'S ONE OF THEM.
HE SEEMED SO TERRIFIED WHEN HE SAW HIS FATHER.
ZOD AND URSA HAVE BEEN ABUSING THEIR SON FOR YEARS.

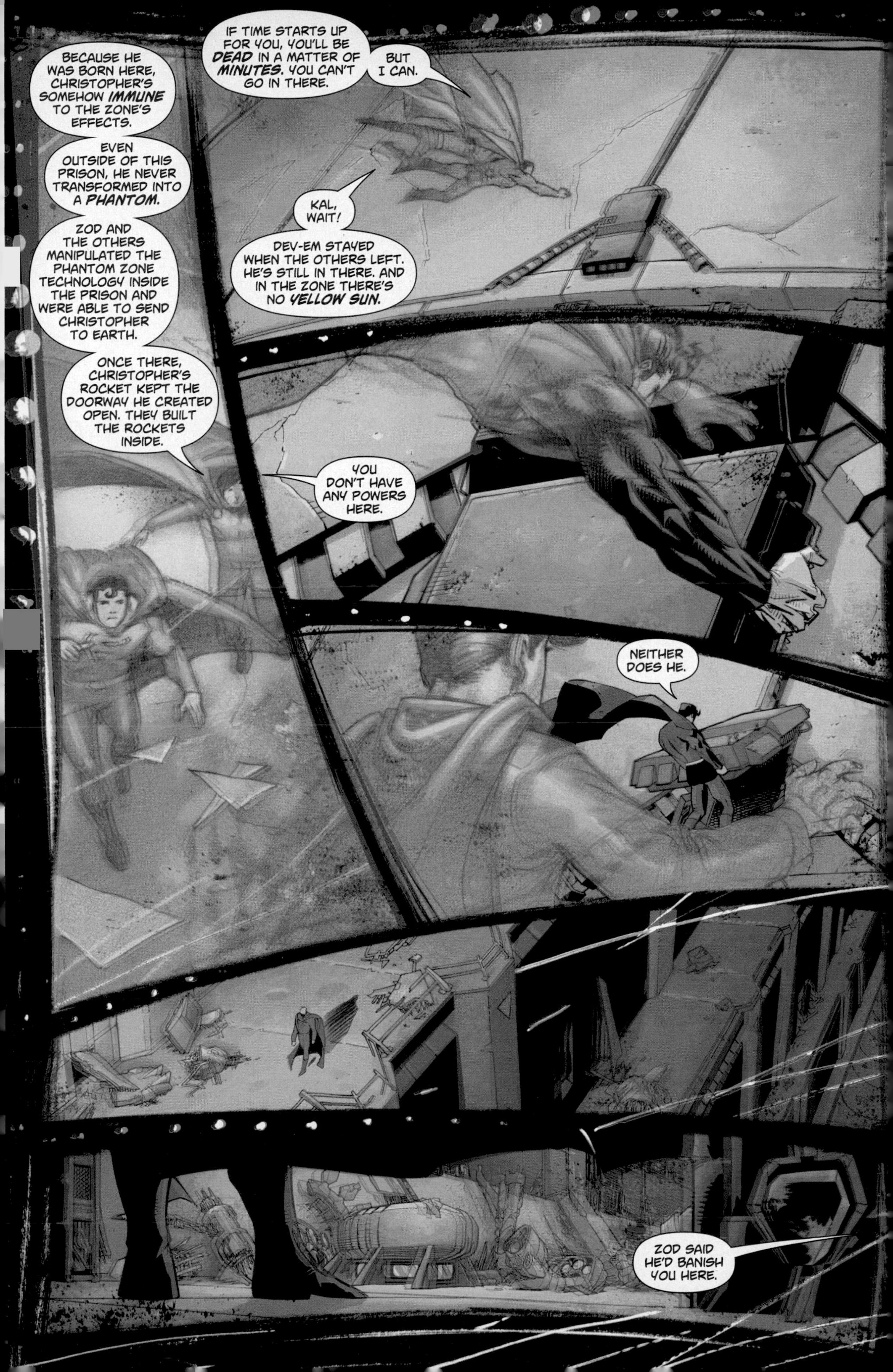
IF TIME STARTS UP FOR YOU, YOU'LL BE DEAD IN A MATTER OF MINUTES. YOU CAN'T GO IN THERE.
BUT I CAN.
BECAUSE HE WAS BORN HERE, CHRISTOPHER'S SOMEHOW IMMUNE TO THE ZONE'S EFFECTS.
EVEN OUTSIDE OF THIS PRISON, HE NEVER TRANSFORMED INTO A PHANTOM.
ZOD AND THE OTHERS MANIPULATED THE PHANTOM ZONE TECHNOLOGY INSIDE THE PRISON AND WERE ABLE TO SEND CHRISTOPHER TO EARTH.
ONCE THERE, CHRISTOPHER'S ROCKET KEPT THE DOORWAY HE CREATED OPEN. THEY BUILT THE ROCKETS INSIDE.
KAL, WAIT!
DEV-EM STAYED WHEN THE OTHERS LEFT. HE'S STILL IN THERE. AND IN THE ZONE THERE'S NO YELLOW SUN.
YOU DON'T HAVE ANY POWERS HERE.
NEITHER DOES HE.
ZOD SAID HE'D BANISH YOU HERE.

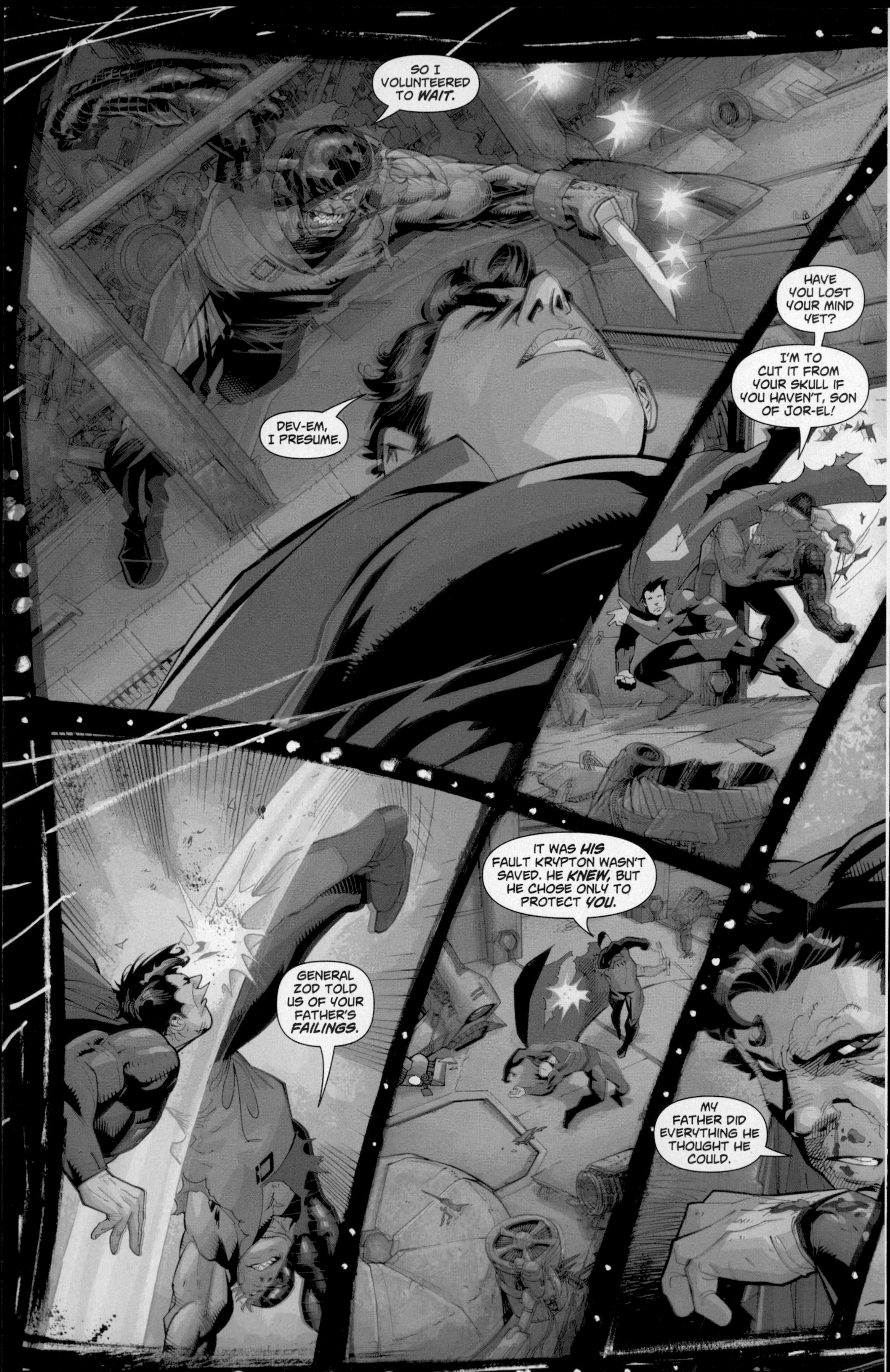
SO I VOLUNTEERED TO WAIT.
DEV-EM, I PRESUME.
HAVE YOU LOST YOUR MIND YET?
I'M TO CUT IT FROM YOUR SKULL IF YOU HAVEN'T, SON OF JOR-EL!
GENERAL ZOD TOLD US OF YOUR FATHER'S FAILINGS.
IT WAS HIS FAULT KRYPTON WASN'T SAVED. HE KNEW, BUT HE CHOSE ONLY TO PROTECT YOU.
MY FATHER DID EVERYTHING HE THOUGHT HE COULD.

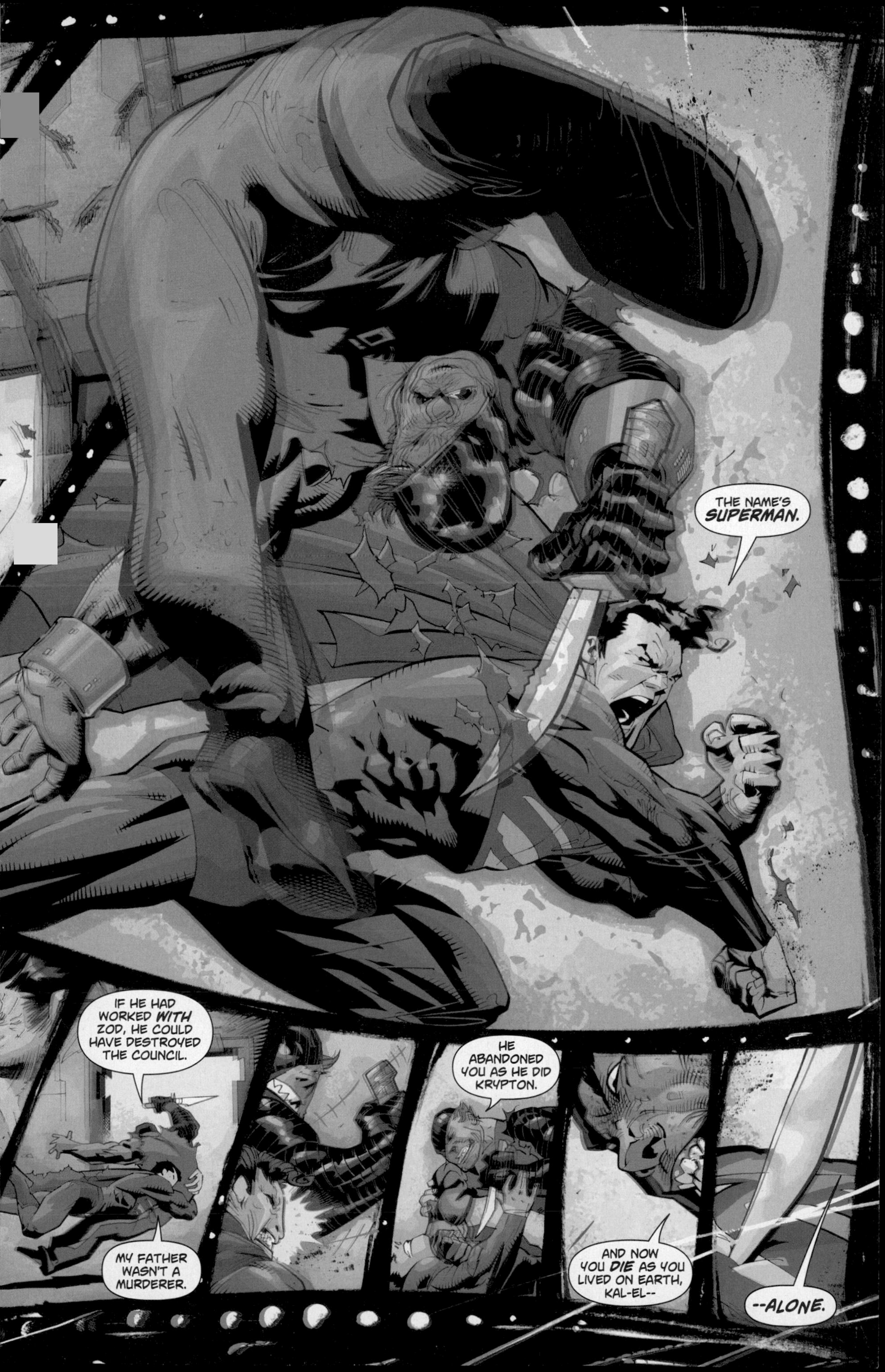
THE NAME'S SUPERMAN.
IF HE HAD WORKED WITH ZOD, HE COULD HAVE DESTROYED THE COUNCIL.
MY FATHER WASN'T A MURDERER.
HE ABANDONED YOU AS HE DID KRYPTON.
AND NOW YOU DIE AS YOU LIVED ON EARTH, KAL-EL--
--ALONE.

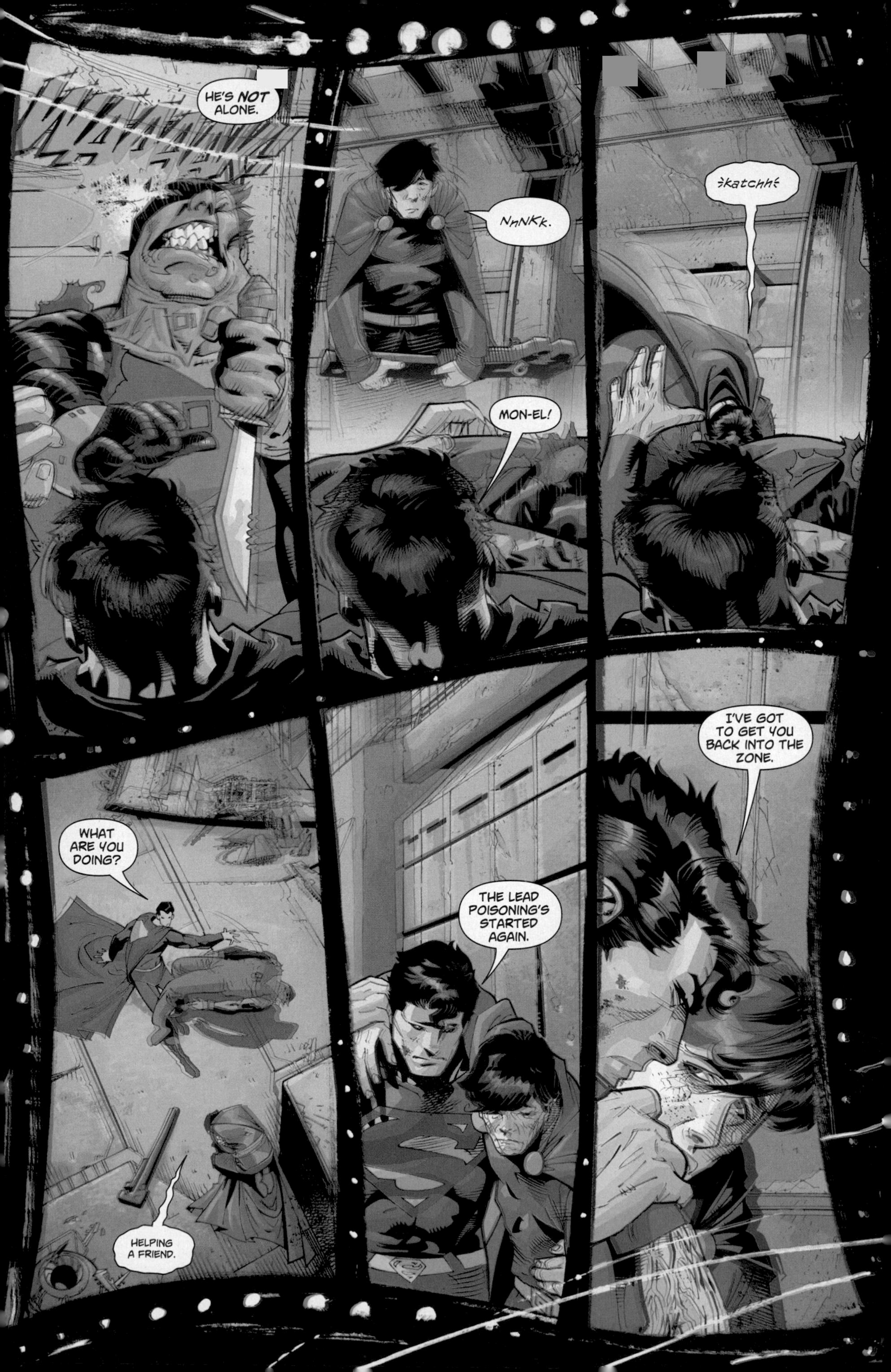
HE'S **NOT** ALONE.
NnNKk.
MON-EL!
katchh
WHAT ARE YOU DOING?
HELPING A FRIEND.
THE LEAD POISONING'S STARTED AGAIN.
I'VE GOT TO GET YOU BACK INTO THE ZONE.

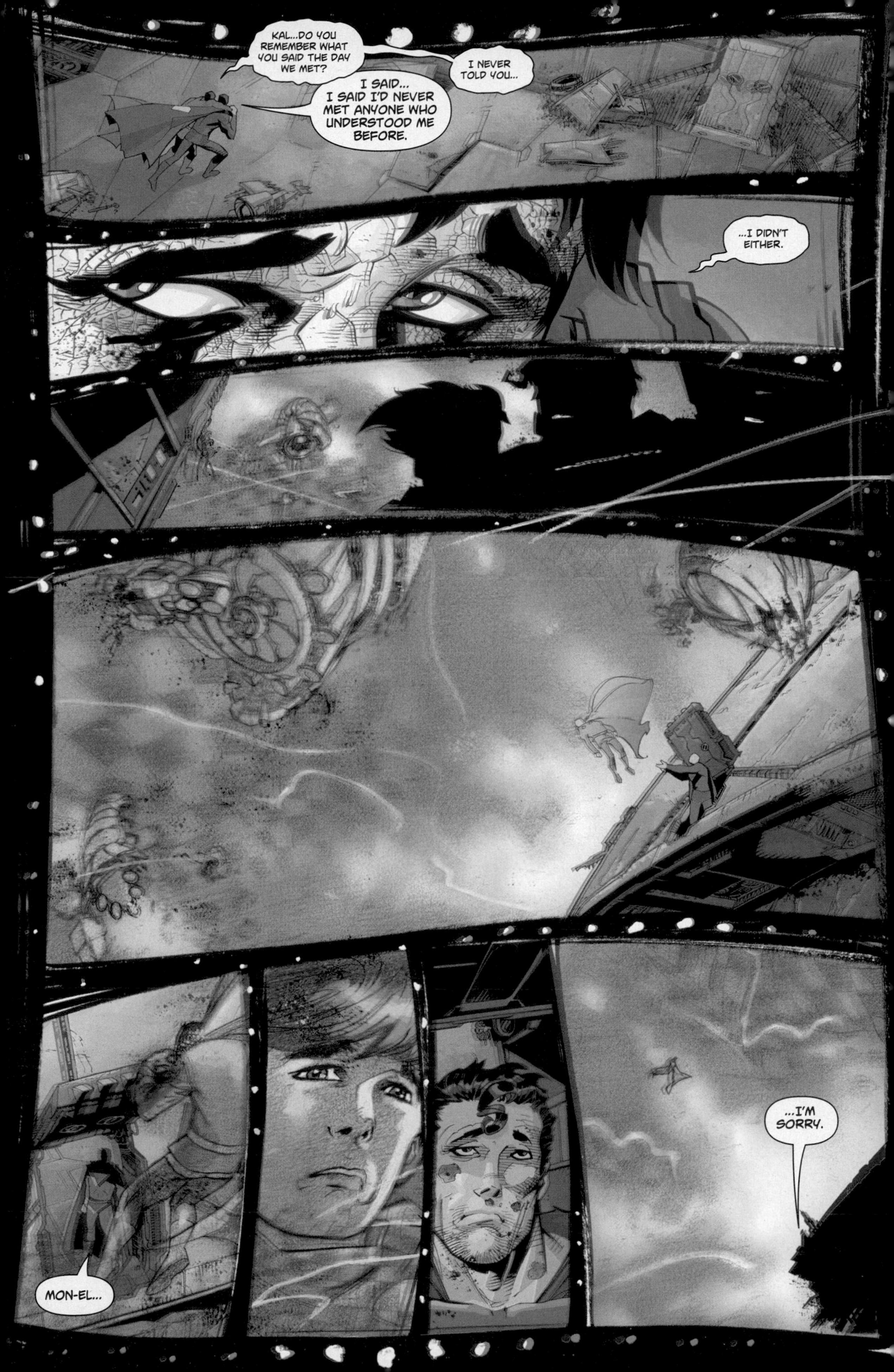
KAL...DO YOU REMEMBER WHAT YOU SAID THE DAY WE MET?
I NEVER TOLD YOU...
I SAID... I SAID I'D NEVER MET ANYONE WHO UNDERSTOOD ME BEFORE.
...I DIDN'T EITHER.
MON-EL...
...I'M SORRY.

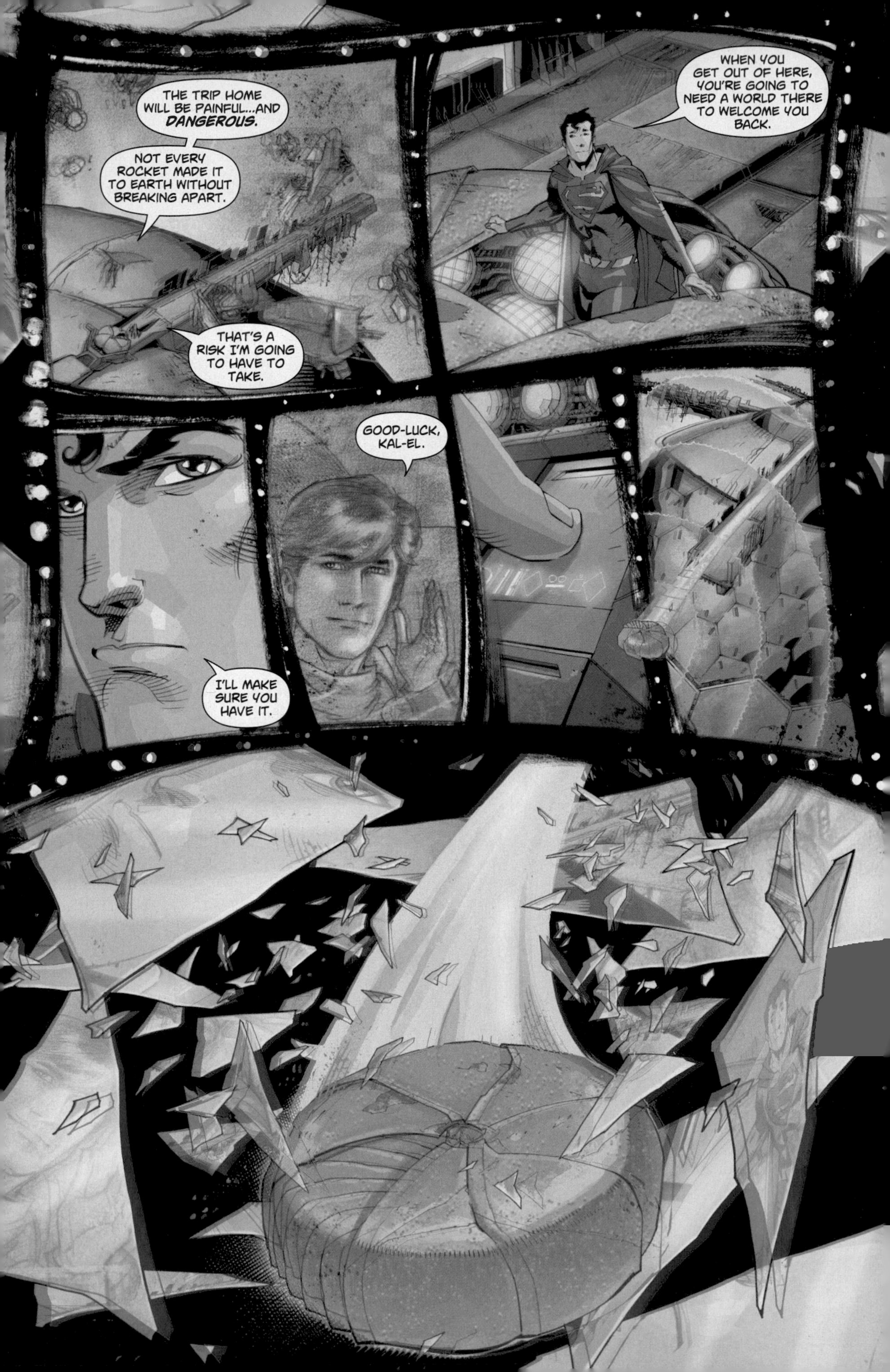
THE TRIP HOME WILL BE PAINFUL...AND **DANGEROUS.**
NOT EVERY ROCKET MADE IT TO EARTH WITHOUT BREAKING APART.
THAT'S A RISK I'M GOING TO HAVE TO TAKE.
WHEN YOU GET OUT OF HERE, YOU'RE GOING TO NEED A WORLD THERE TO WELCOME YOU BACK.
I'LL MAKE SURE YOU HAVE IT.
GOOD-LUCK, KAL-EL.

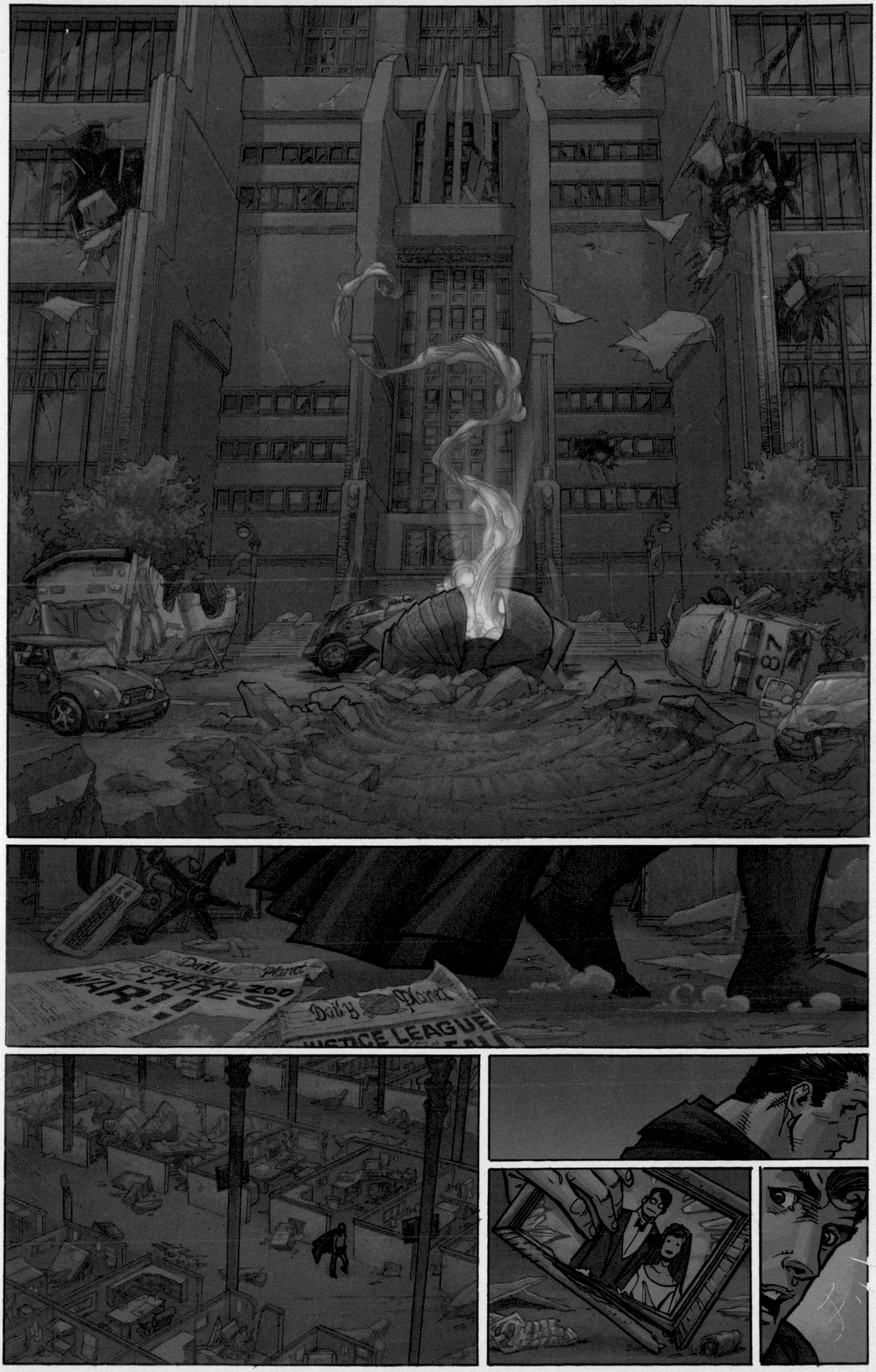

Daily Planet
GENERAL ZOD
WAR!!
Daily Planet
JUSTICE LEAGUE

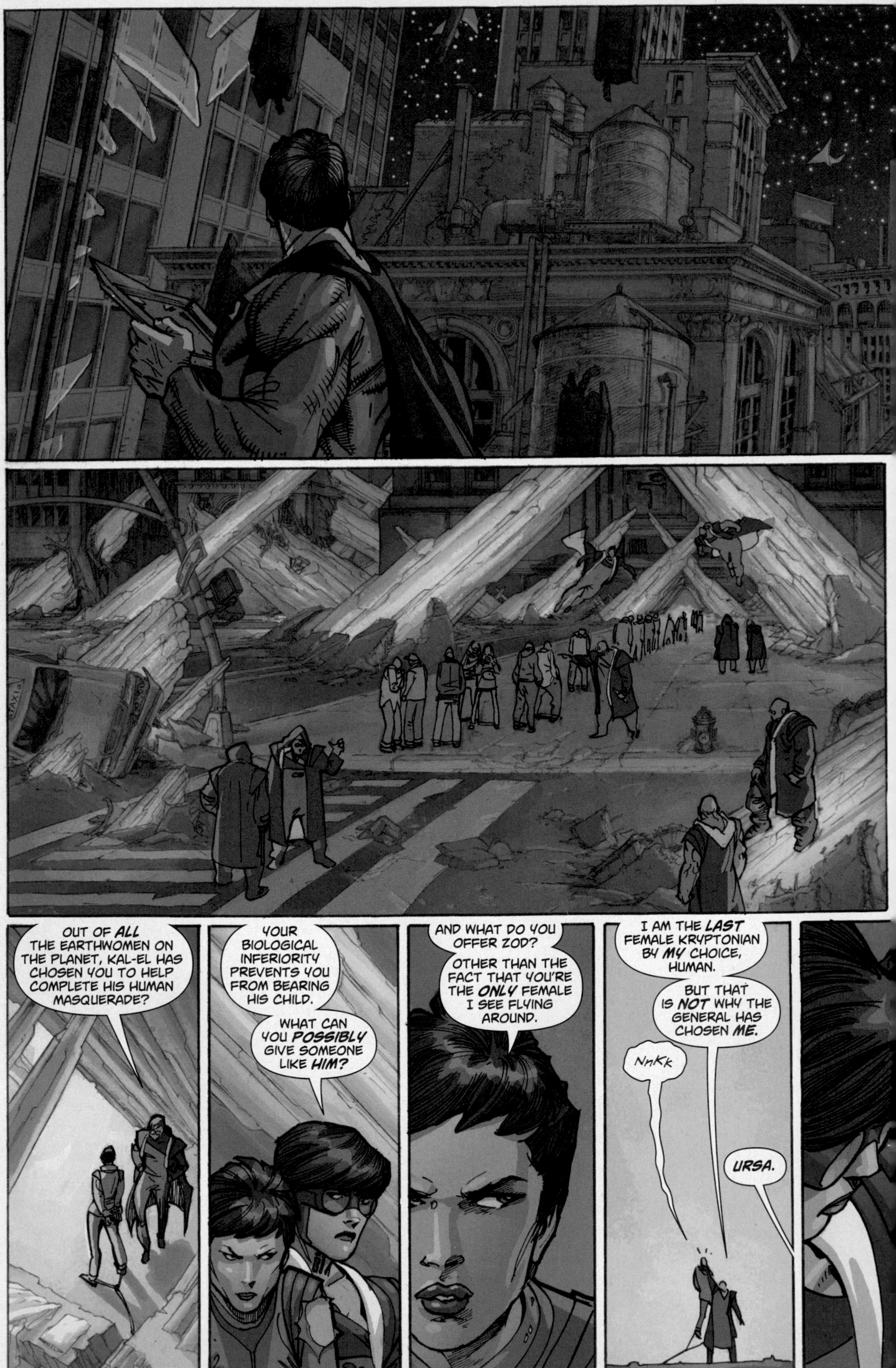
OUT OF ALL THE EARTHWOMEN ON THE PLANET, KAL-EL HAS CHOSEN YOU TO HELP COMPLETE HIS HUMAN MASQUERADE?
YOUR BIOLOGICAL INFERIORITY PREVENTS YOU FROM BEARING HIS CHILD.
WHAT CAN YOU POSSIBLY GIVE SOMEONE LIKE HIM?
AND WHAT DO YOU OFFER ZOD?
OTHER THAN THE FACT THAT YOU'RE THE ONLY FEMALE I SEE FLYING AROUND.
I AM THE LAST FEMALE KRYPTONIAN BY MY CHOICE, HUMAN.
BUT THAT IS NOT WHY THE GENERAL HAS CHOSEN ME.
NnKk
URSA.

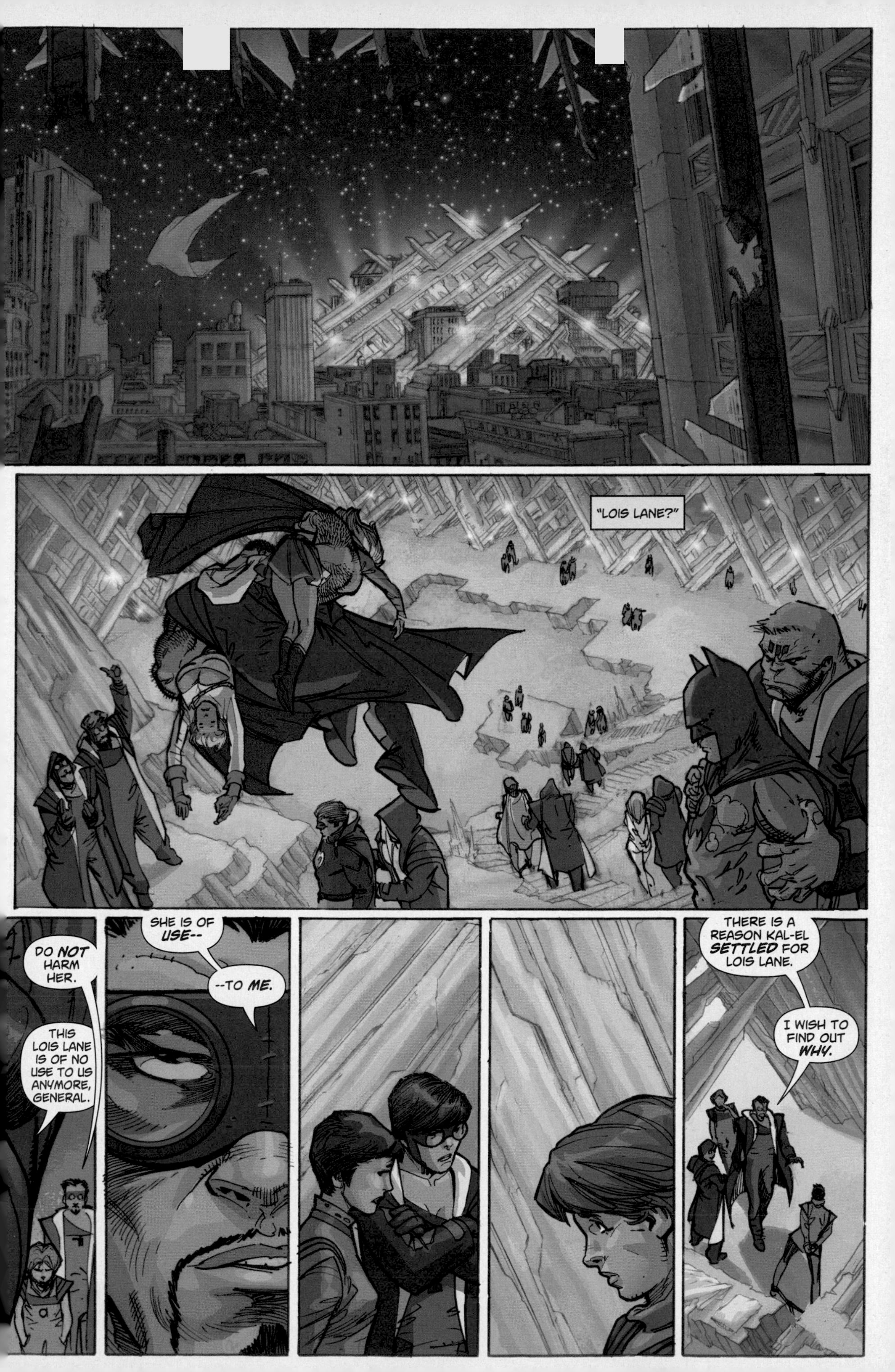
"LOIS LANE?"
DO NOT HARM HER.
THIS LOIS LANE IS OF NO USE TO US ANYMORE, GENERAL.
SHE IS OF USE--
--TO ME.
THERE IS A REASON KAL-EL SETTLED FOR LOIS LANE.
I WISH TO FIND OUT WHY.

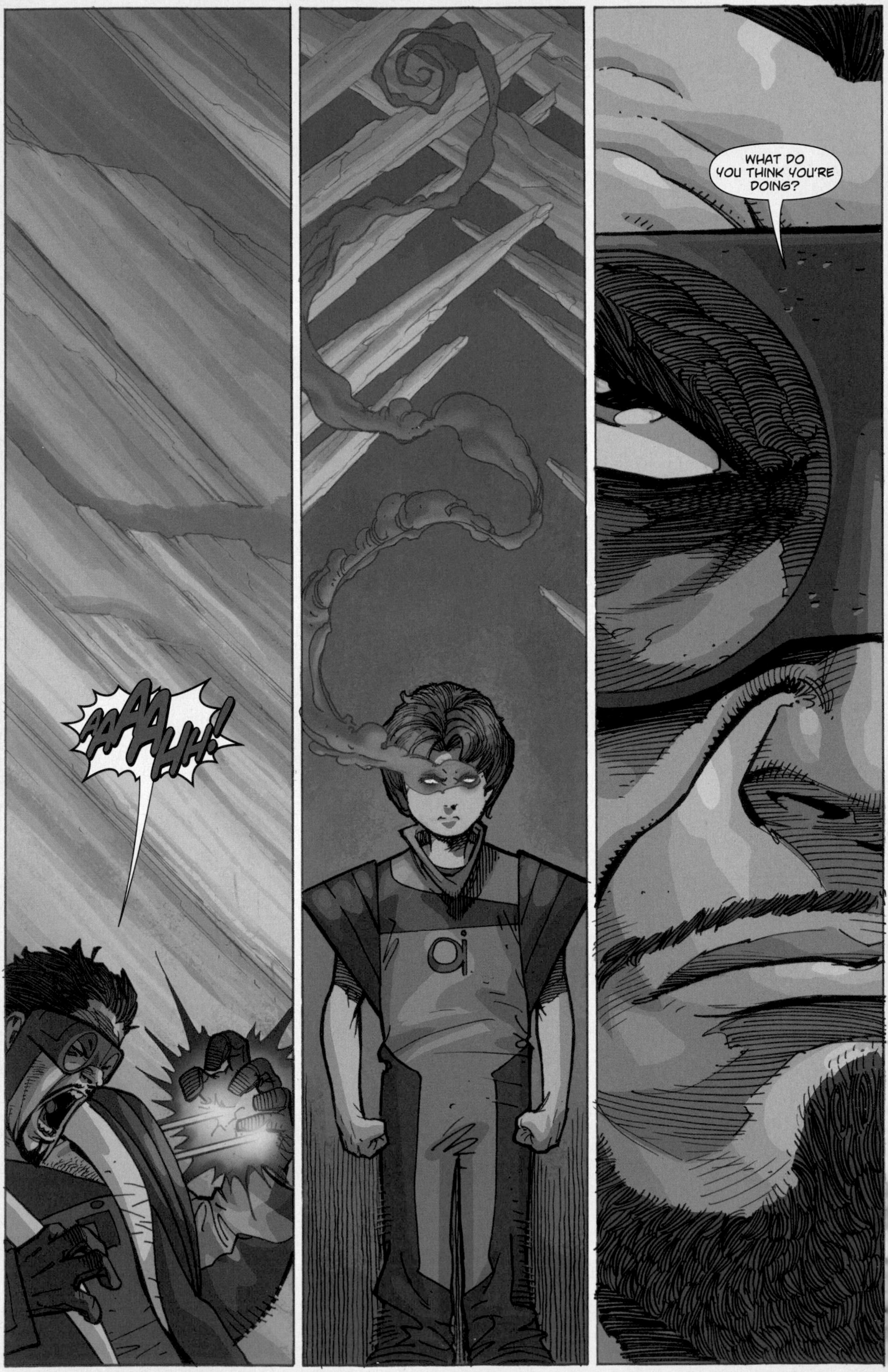
AAAAHH!
WHAT DO YOU THINK YOU'RE DOING?

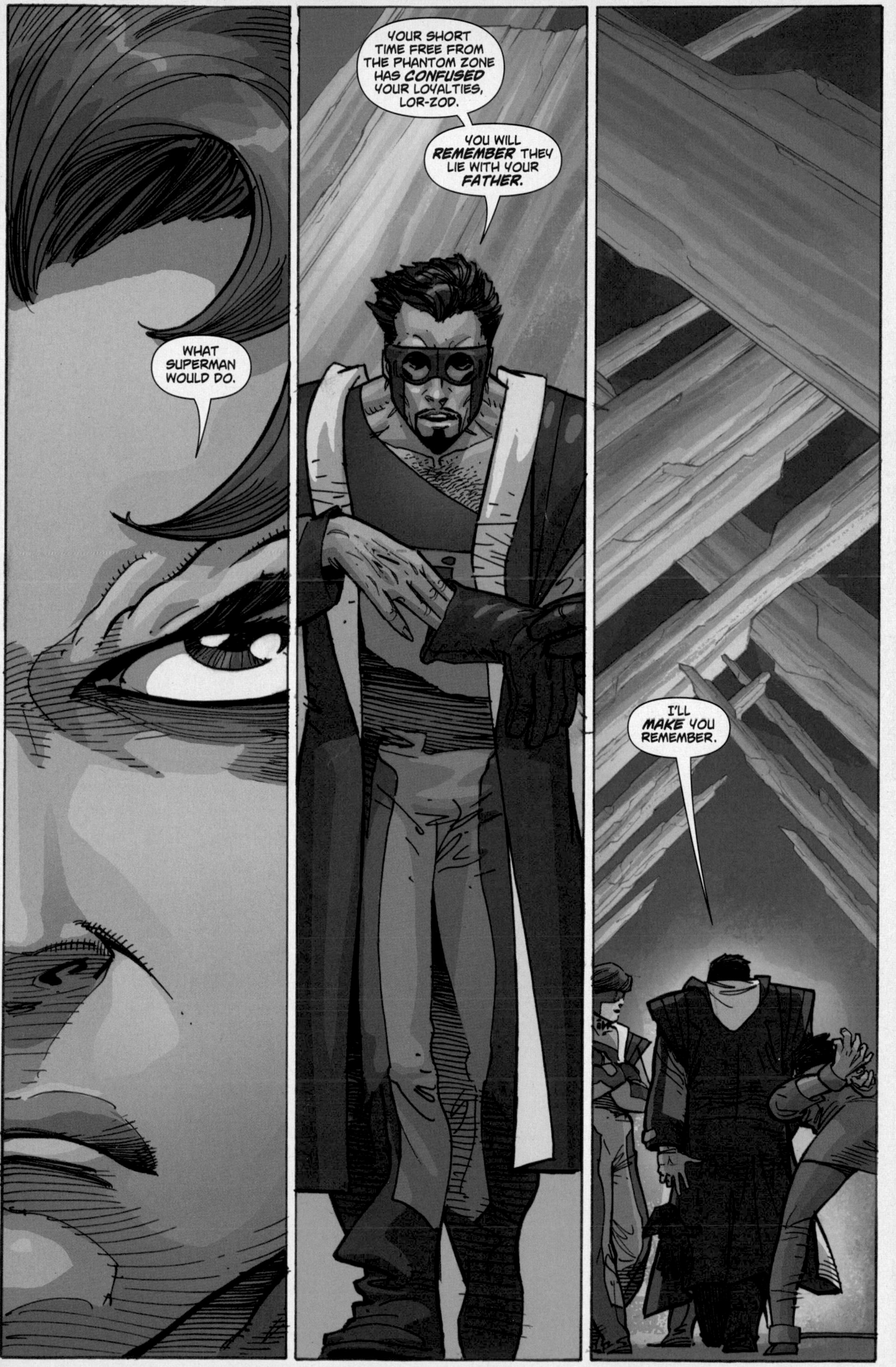
WHAT SUPERMAN WOULD DO.
YOUR SHORT TIME FREE FROM THE PHANTOM ZONE HAS CONFUSED YOUR LOYALTIES, LOR-ZOD.
YOU WILL REMEMBER THEY LIE WITH YOUR FATHER.
I'LL MAKE YOU REMEMBER.

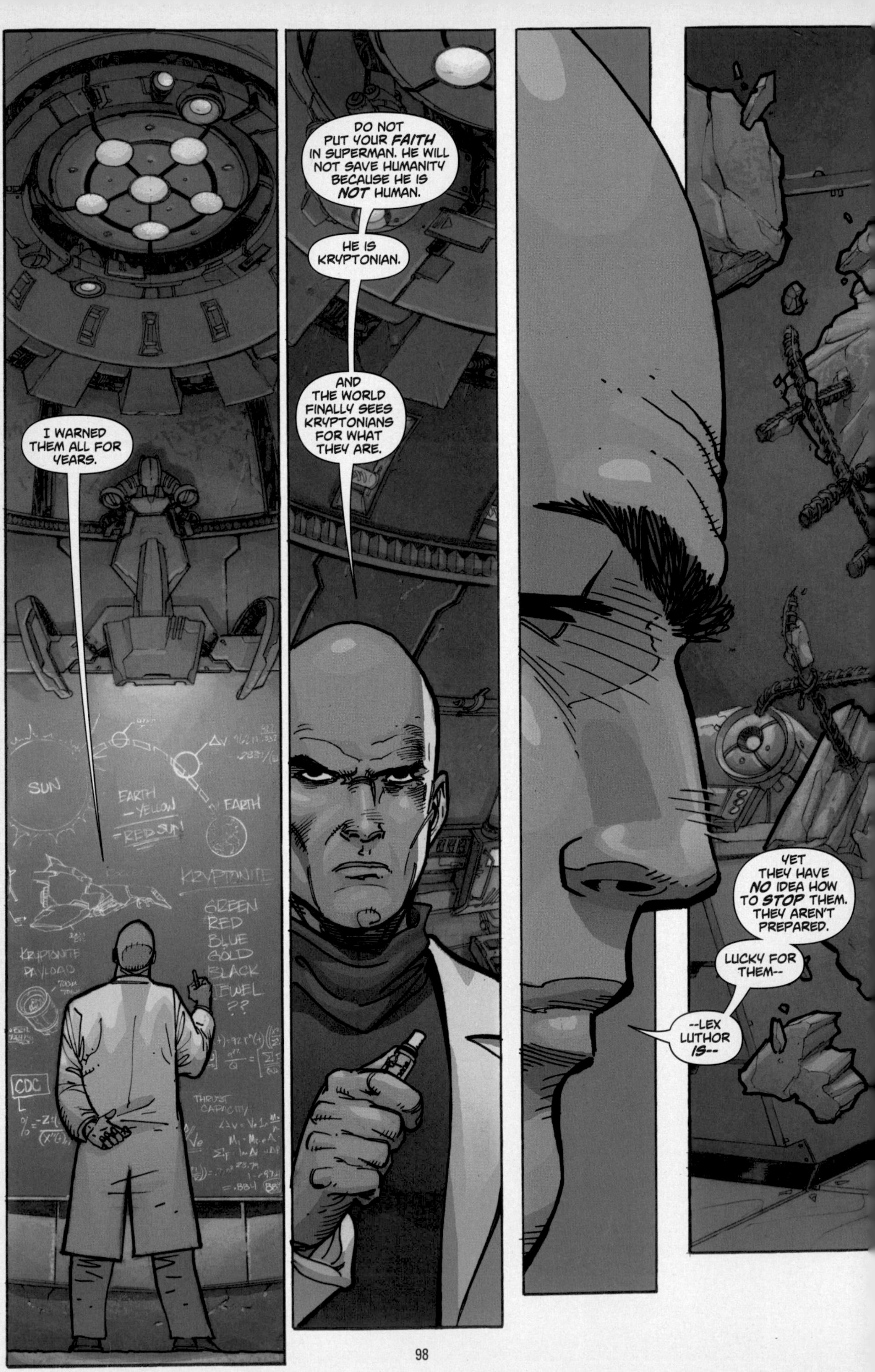

I WARNED THEM ALL FOR YEARS.
SUN
EARTH
EARTH -YELLOW
=RED SUN
KRYPTONITE
GREEN
RED
BLUE
GOLD
BLACK
JEWEL
??
KRYPTONITE PAYLOAD
CDC
THRUST CAPACITY
DO NOT PUT YOUR FAITH IN SUPERMAN. HE WILL NOT SAVE HUMANITY BECAUSE HE IS NOT HUMAN.
HE IS KRYPTONIAN.
AND THE WORLD FINALLY SEES KRYPTONIANS FOR WHAT THEY ARE.
YET THEY HAVE NO IDEA HOW TO STOP THEM. THEY AREN'T PREPARED.
LUCKY FOR THEM--
--LEX LUTHOR IS--

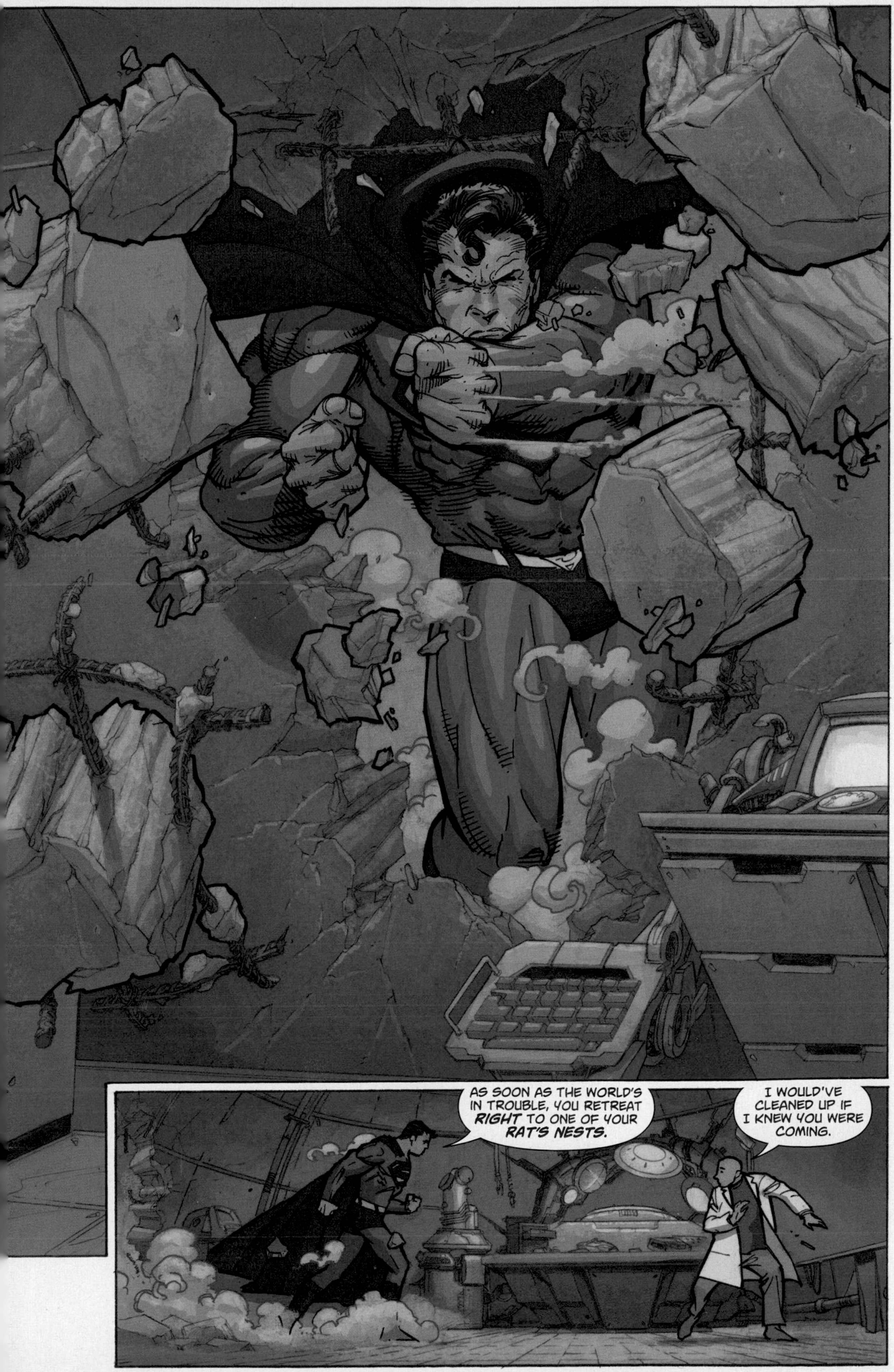
AS SOON AS THE WORLD'S IN TROUBLE, YOU RETREAT RIGHT TO ONE OF YOUR RAT'S NESTS.
I WOULD'VE CLEANED UP IF I KNEW YOU WERE COMING.

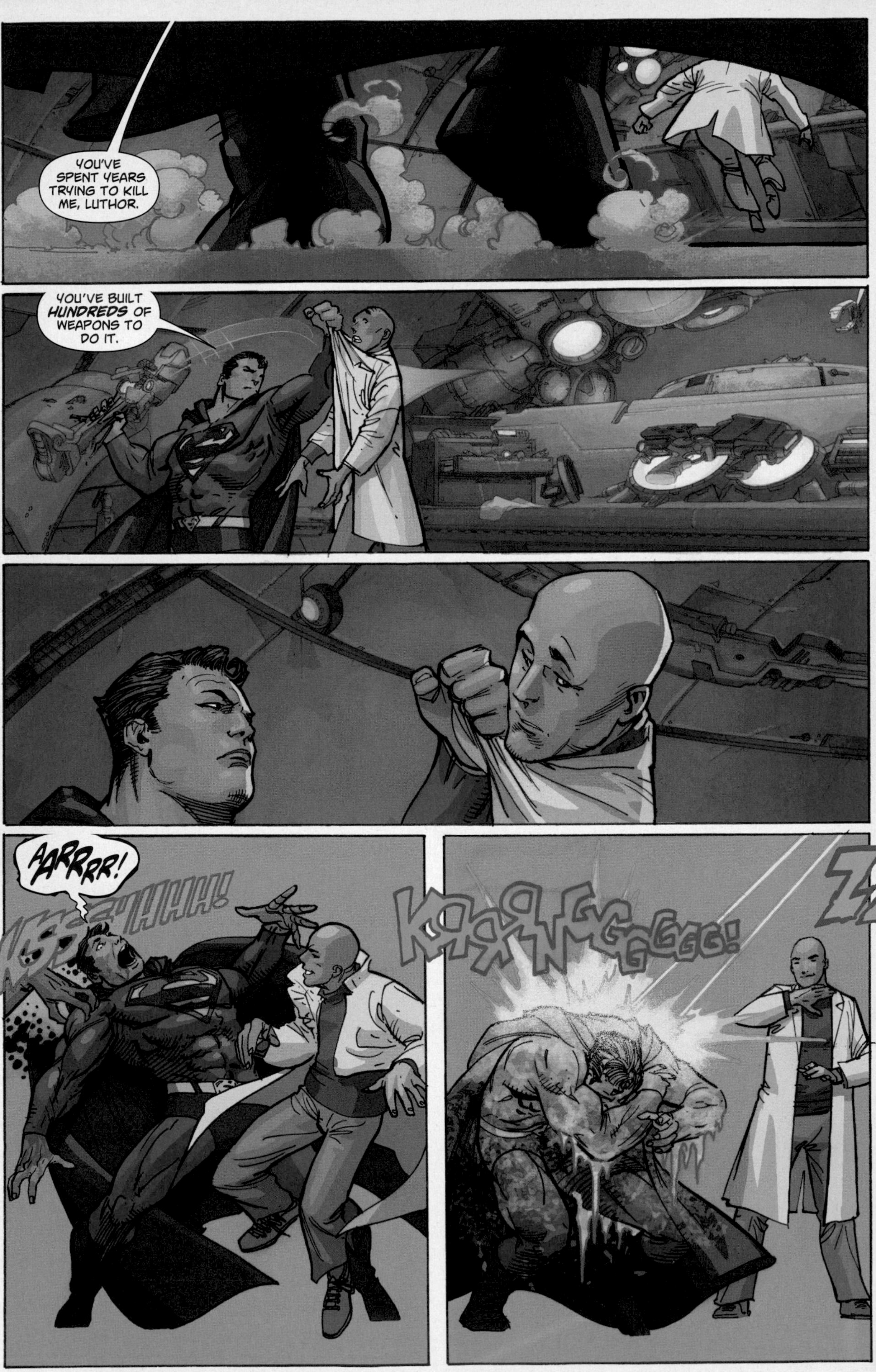

YOU'VE SPENT YEARS TRYING TO KILL ME, LUTHOR.
YOU'VE BUILT *HUNDREDS* OF WEAPONS TO DO IT.
AARRRR!
KRRRANGGGGGG!

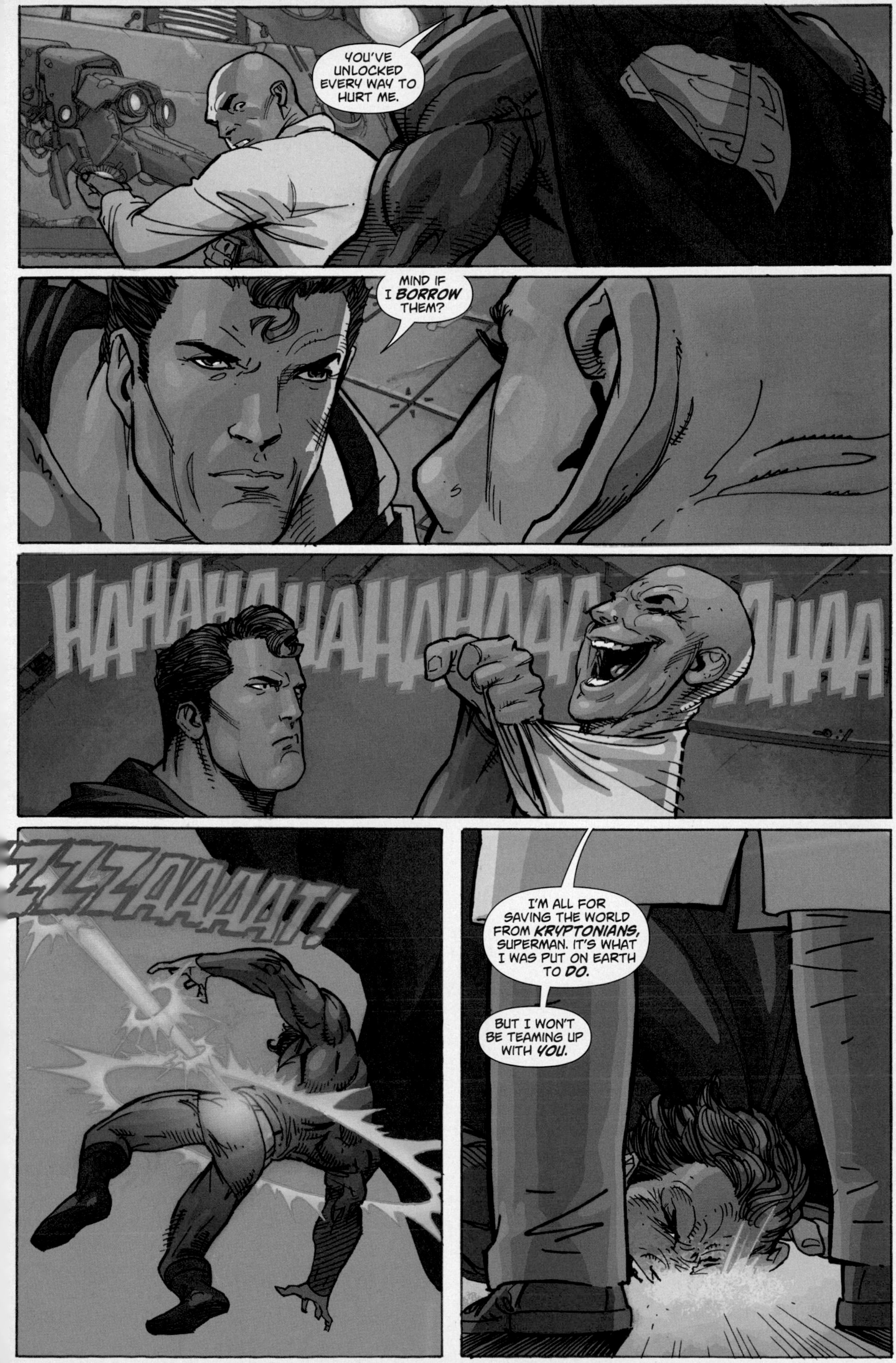
YOU'VE UNLOCKED EVERY WAY TO HURT ME.
MIND IF I BORROW THEM?
HAHAHAHAHAHAHAAAHAHAA
ZZZAAAAAT!
I'M ALL FOR SAVING THE WORLD FROM KRYPTONIANS, SUPERMAN. IT'S WHAT I WAS PUT ON EARTH TO DO.
BUT I WON'T BE TEAMING UP WITH YOU.

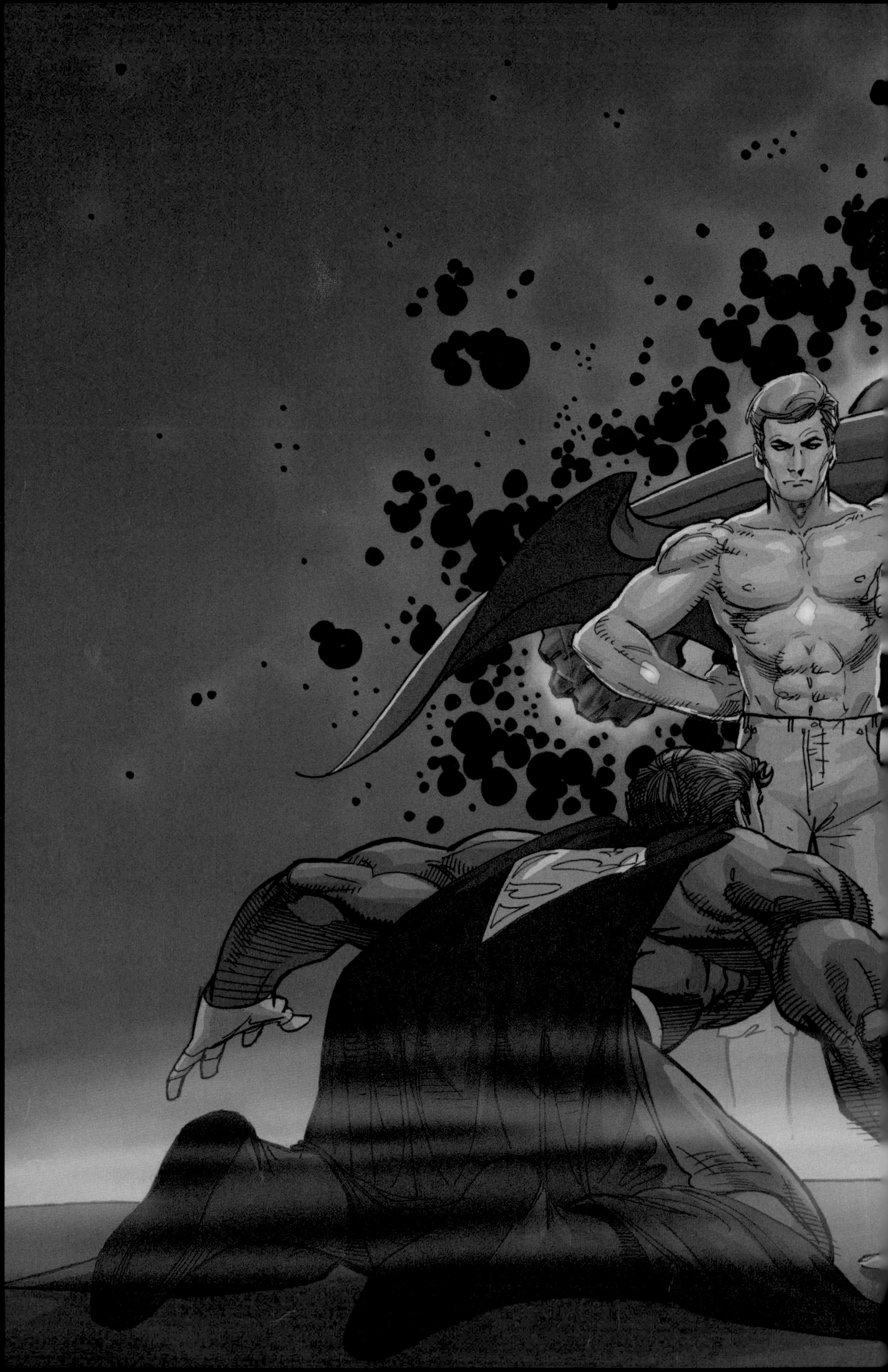

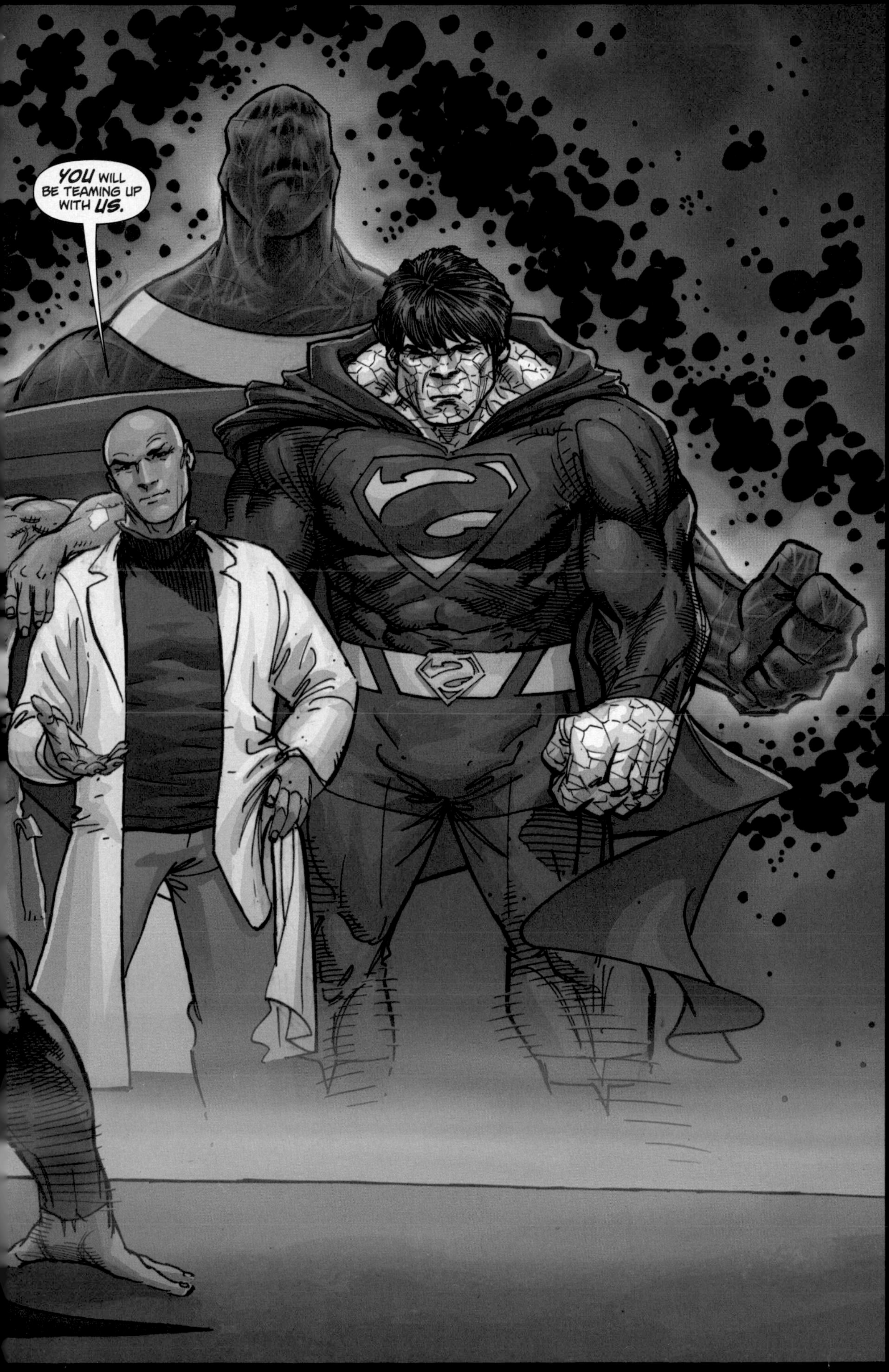
YOU WILL BE TEAMING UP WITH US.

CHAPTER FIVE

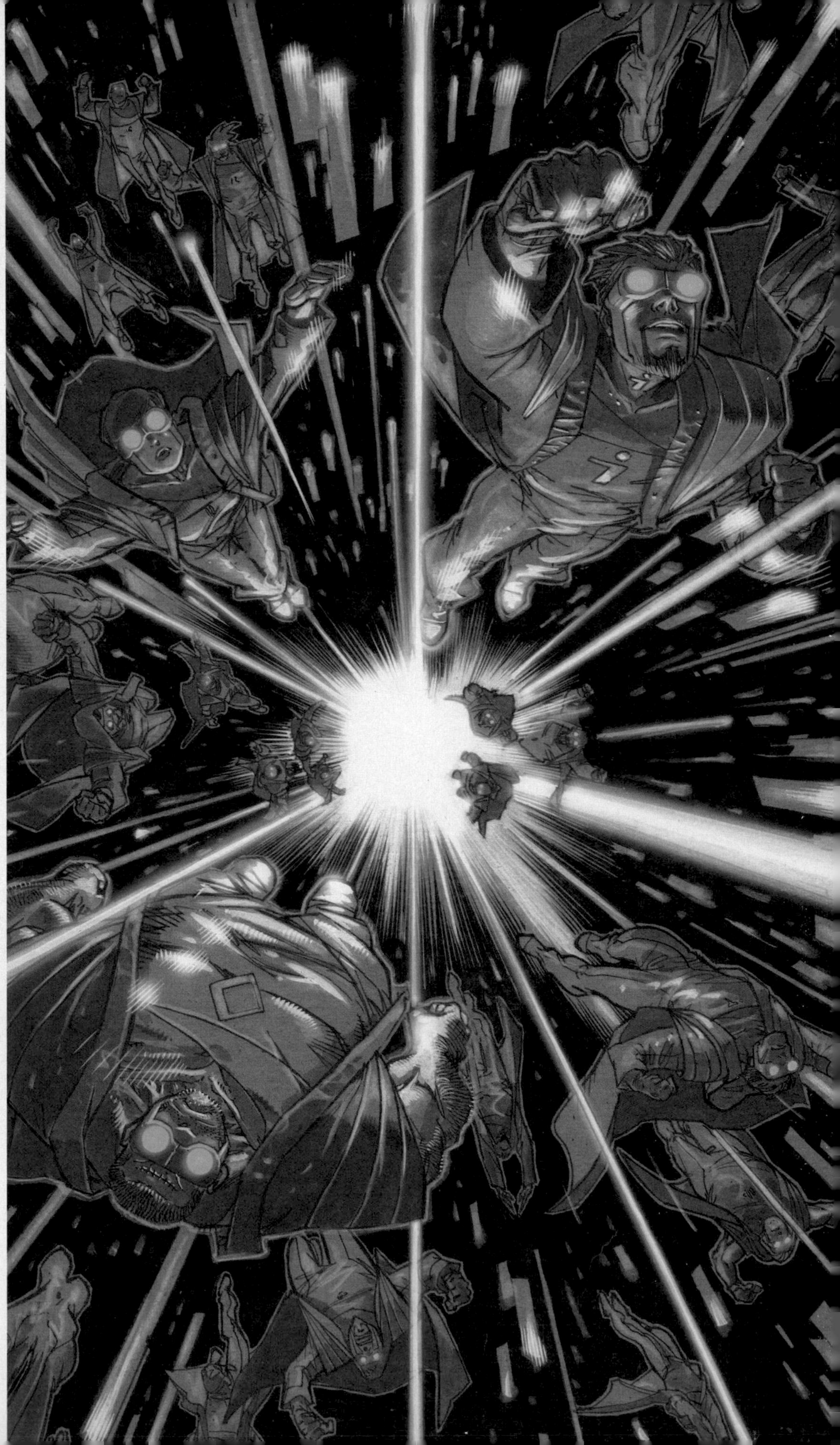

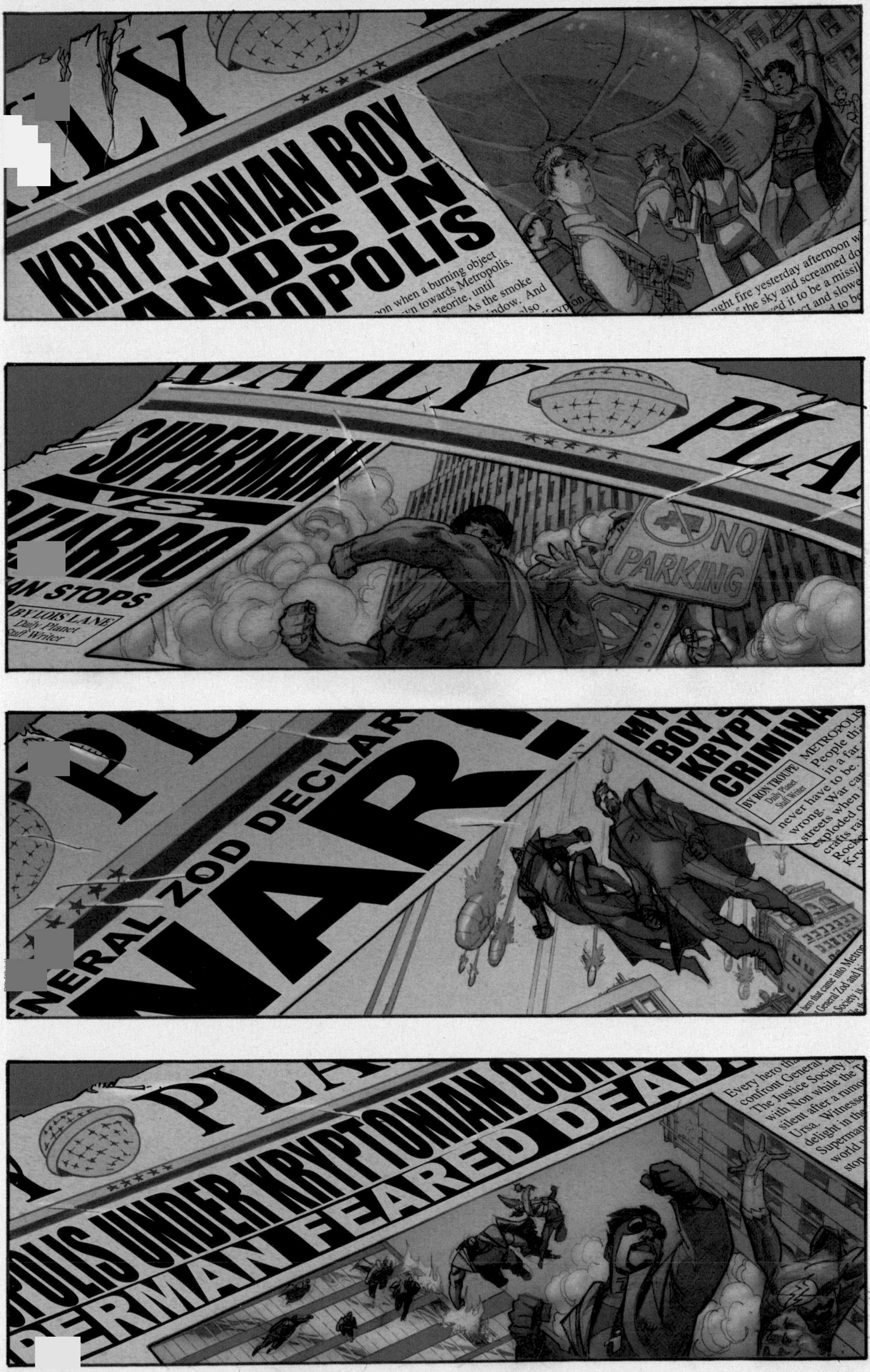

LY
KRYPTONIAN BOY
ANDS IN
ROPOLIS
DAILY
PLA
SUPERMAN
VS.
IZARRO
AN STOPS
BY LOIS LANE
Daily Planet
Staff Writer
NO PARKING
PL
ENERAL ZOD DECLAR
WAR
BOY
KRYPT
CRIMINA
BY RON TROUPE
Daily Planet
Staff Writer
PLA
POLIS UNDER KRYPTONIAN CON
ERMAN FEARED DEAD!

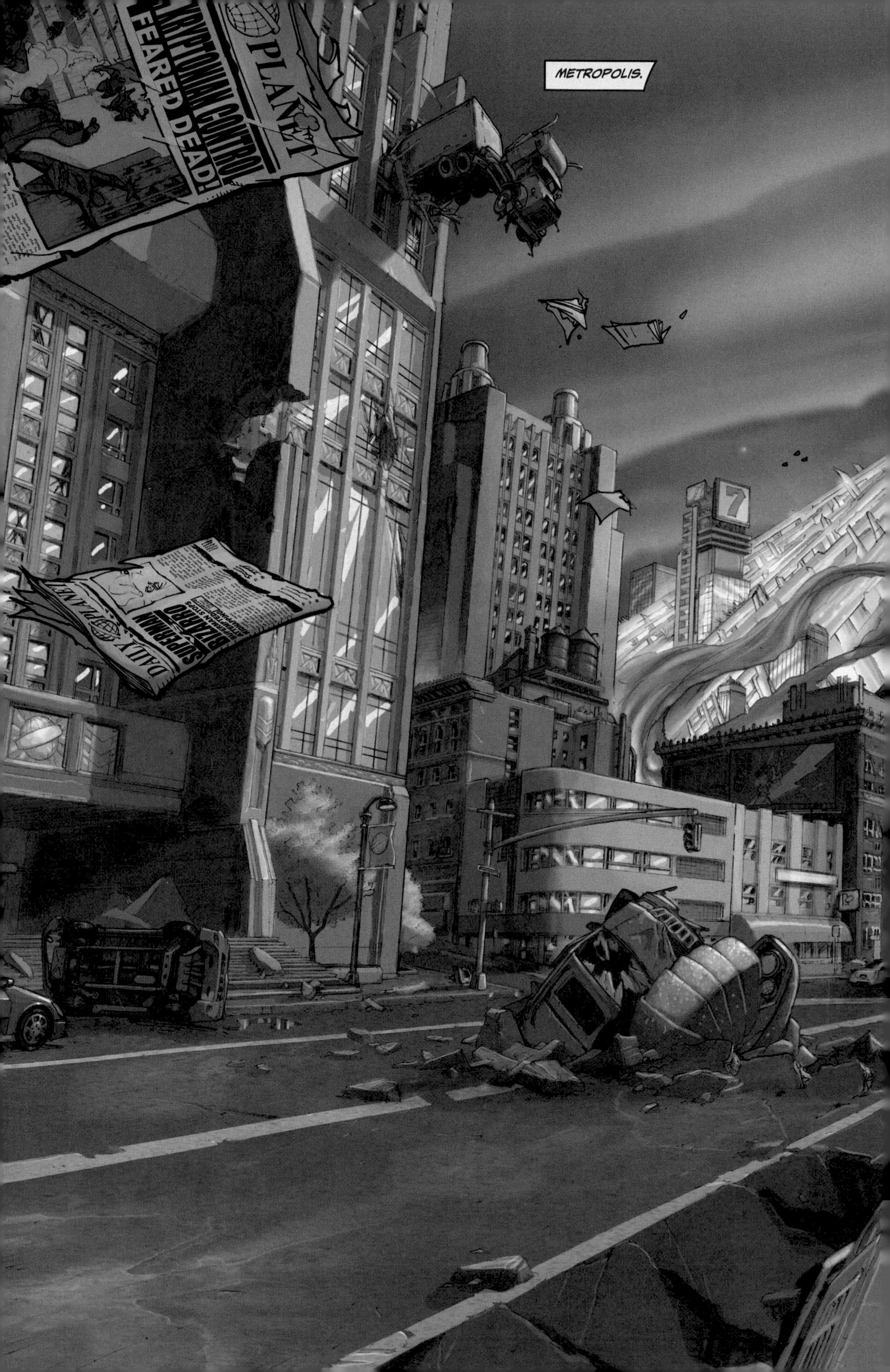
METROPOLIS.
PLANET
KRYPTONIAN CONTROL
FEARED DEAD!
DAILY PLANET
SUPERMAN
BIZARRO
7

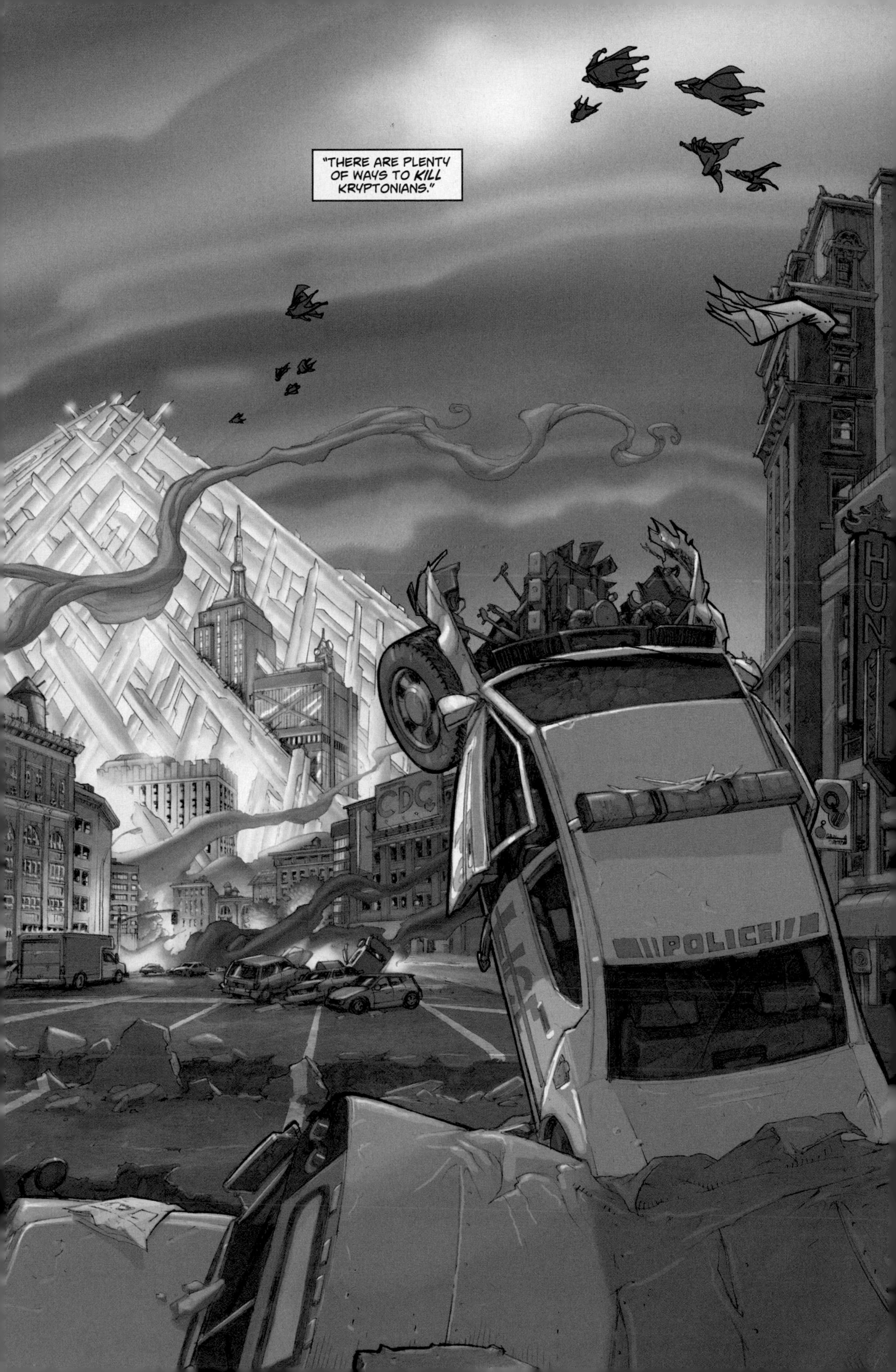
"THERE ARE PLENTY OF WAYS TO KILL KRYPTONIANS."
CDC
POLICE

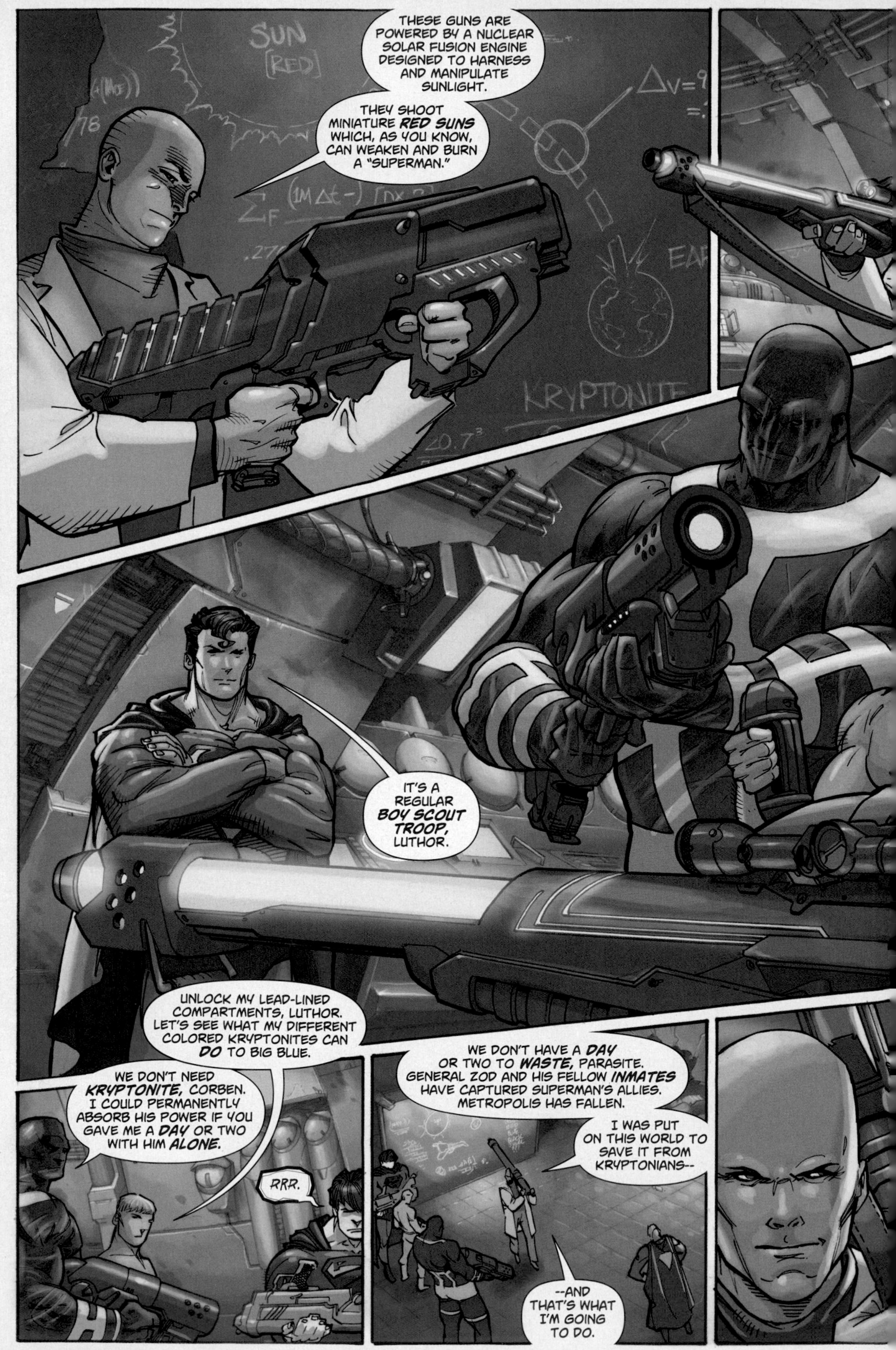
SUN
[RED]
THESE GUNS ARE POWERED BY A NUCLEAR SOLAR FUSION ENGINE DESIGNED TO HARNESS AND MANIPULATE SUNLIGHT.
THEY SHOOT MINIATURE RED SUNS WHICH, AS YOU KNOW, CAN WEAKEN AND BURN A "SUPERMAN."
KRYPTONITE
IT'S A REGULAR BOY SCOUT TROOP, LUTHOR.
UNLOCK MY LEAD-LINED COMPARTMENTS, LUTHOR. LET'S SEE WHAT MY DIFFERENT COLORED KRYPTONITES CAN DO TO BIG BLUE.
WE DON'T NEED KRYPTONITE, CORBEN. I COULD PERMANENTLY ABSORB HIS POWER IF YOU GAVE ME A DAY OR TWO WITH HIM ALONE.
RRR.
WE DON'T HAVE A DAY OR TWO TO WASTE, PARASITE. GENERAL ZOD AND HIS FELLOW INMATES HAVE CAPTURED SUPERMAN'S ALLIES. METROPOLIS HAS FALLEN.
I WAS PUT ON THIS WORLD TO SAVE IT FROM KRYPTONIANS--
--AND THAT'S WHAT I'M GOING TO DO.

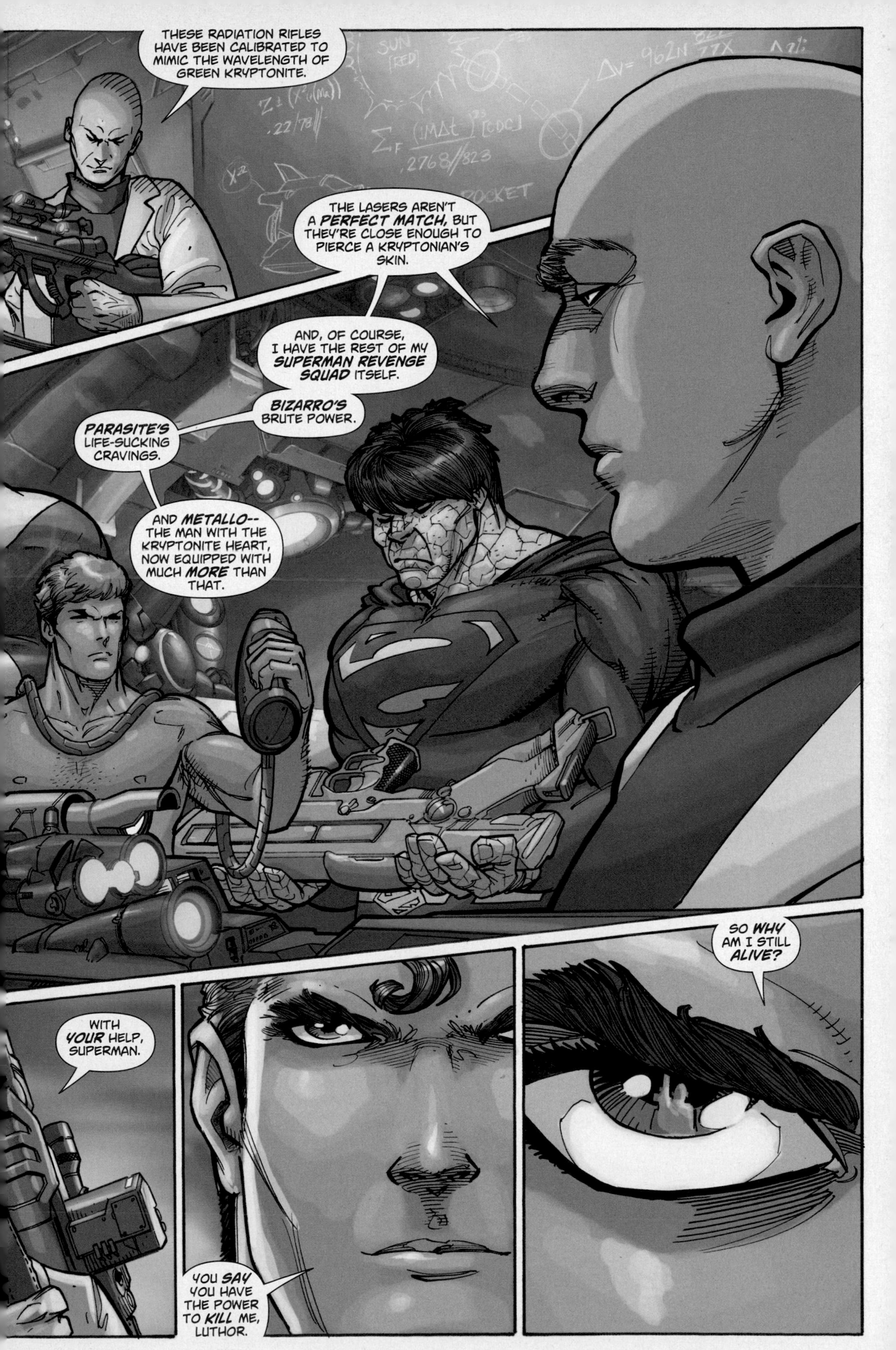
THESE RADIATION RIFLES HAVE BEEN CALIBRATED TO MIMIC THE WAVELENGTH OF GREEN KRYPTONITE.
THE LASERS AREN'T A PERFECT MATCH, BUT THEY'RE CLOSE ENOUGH TO PIERCE A KRYPTONIAN'S SKIN.
AND, OF COURSE, I HAVE THE REST OF MY SUPERMAN REVENGE SQUAD ITSELF.
BIZARRO'S BRUTE POWER.
PARASITE'S LIFE-SUCKING CRAVINGS.
AND METALLO-- THE MAN WITH THE KRYPTONITE HEART, NOW EQUIPPED WITH MUCH MORE THAN THAT.
WITH YOUR HELP, SUPERMAN.
YOU SAY YOU HAVE THE POWER TO KILL ME, LUTHOR.
SO WHY AM I STILL ALIVE?

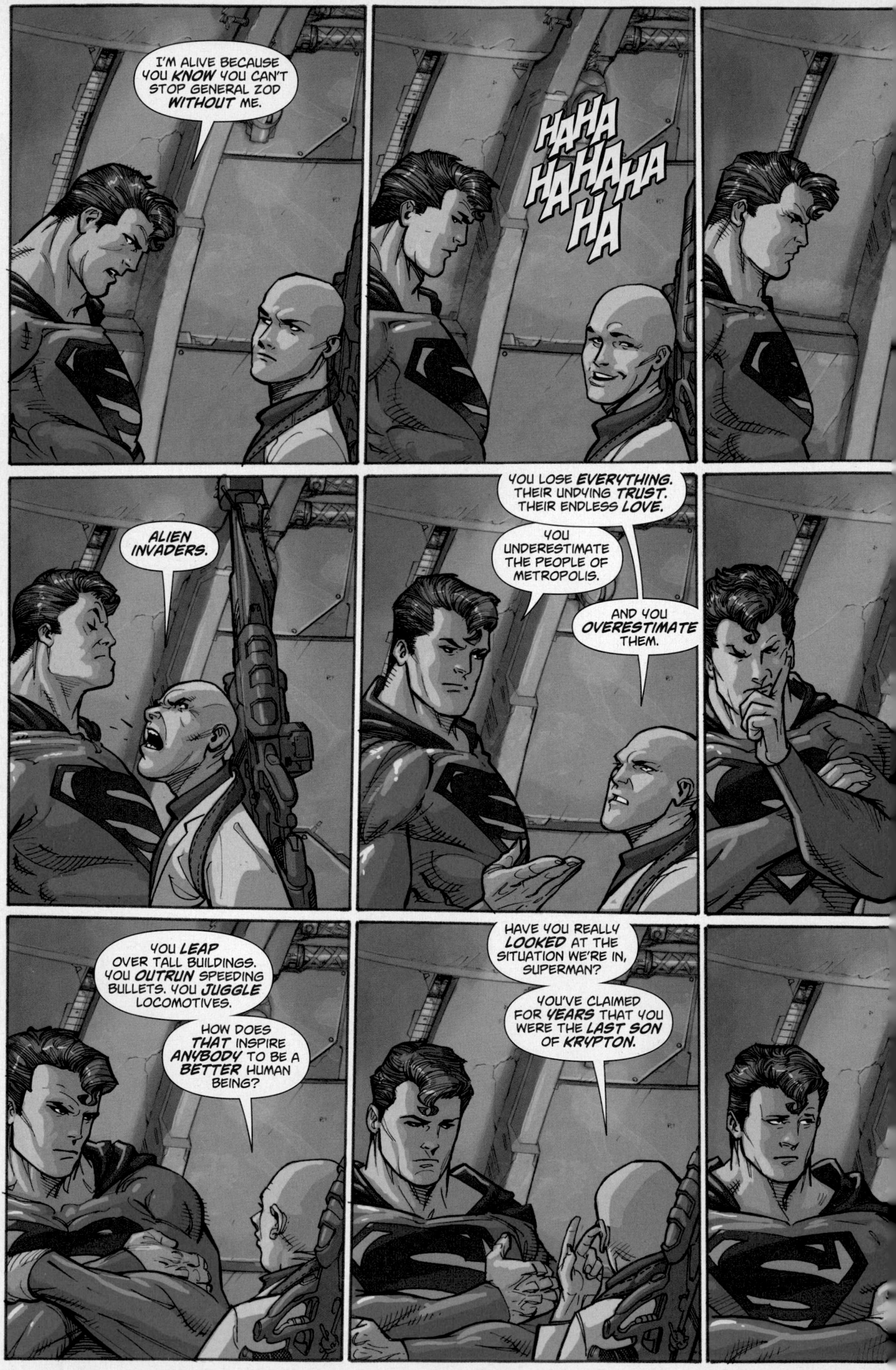
I'M ALIVE BECAUSE YOU KNOW YOU CAN'T STOP GENERAL ZOD WITHOUT ME.
HAHA HAHAHAHA HA
ALIEN INVADERS.
YOU UNDERESTIMATE THE PEOPLE OF METROPOLIS.
AND YOU OVERESTIMATE THEM.
YOU LOSE EVERYTHING. THEIR UNDYING TRUST. THEIR ENDLESS LOVE.
YOU LEAP OVER TALL BUILDINGS. YOU OUTRUN SPEEDING BULLETS. YOU JUGGLE LOCOMOTIVES.
HOW DOES THAT INSPIRE ANYBODY TO BE A BETTER HUMAN BEING?
HAVE YOU REALLY LOOKED AT THE SITUATION WE'RE IN, SUPERMAN?
YOU'VE CLAIMED FOR YEARS THAT YOU WERE THE LAST SON OF KRYPTON.

YES. YES, OF COURSE.

LIKE ALL THE *OTHER* SHEEP IN METROPOLIS, I'M AFRAID TO *STRIVE* FOR NEW HEIGHTS BECAUSE I COULD NEVER *BECOME* WHAT THE GREAT AND POWERFUL MAN OF STEEL IS.

YOU'VE TAUGHT HUMANITY TO RELY ON *YOU* AND NOT FIGHT FOR THEMSELVES.

THAT'S WHY GENERAL ZOD AND HIS ARMY WERE ABLE TO TAKE CONTROL.

I KILL YOU NOW AND YOU'RE A *MARTYR.*

YOU *SURVIVE* THIS AND THE WORLD FINALLY SEES KRYPTONIANS FOR WHAT THEY *ARE.*

THEY NEED SOMEONE TO *WAKE* THEM UP. THEY NEED SOMEONE TO SHOW THEM THEY CAN REACH THE STARS WITHOUT YOU FLYING THEM UP THERE.

THEY NEED SOMEONE *HUMAN* TO ASPIRE TO.

AND THAT'S *YOU?*

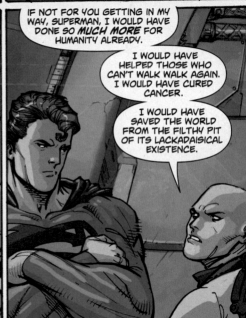

IF NOT FOR YOU GETTING IN MY WAY, SUPERMAN, I WOULD HAVE DONE SO *MUCH MORE* FOR HUMANITY ALREADY.

I WOULD HAVE HELPED THOSE WHO CAN'T WALK WALK AGAIN. I WOULD HAVE CURED CANCER.

I WOULD HAVE SAVED THE WORLD FROM THE FILTHY PIT OF ITS LACKADAISICAL EXISTENCE.

IN TRUTH, THERE ARE *DOZENS* OF OTHERS YOUR PEOPLE SIMPLY CHOSE TO *IMPRISON* AND *FORGET* ABOUT. NOW THEY'RE *FREE* FROM THIS POCKET DIMENSION.

THIS *PHANTOM ZONE.*

AND.

THEY'RE.

ALL.

CRIMINALS.

SAY WHAT YOU WANT ABOUT *ME* AND *THEM,* LUTHOR, BUT GENERAL ZOD'S *SON* IS *NOT* A CRIMINAL.

HE'S AN *INNOCENT.*

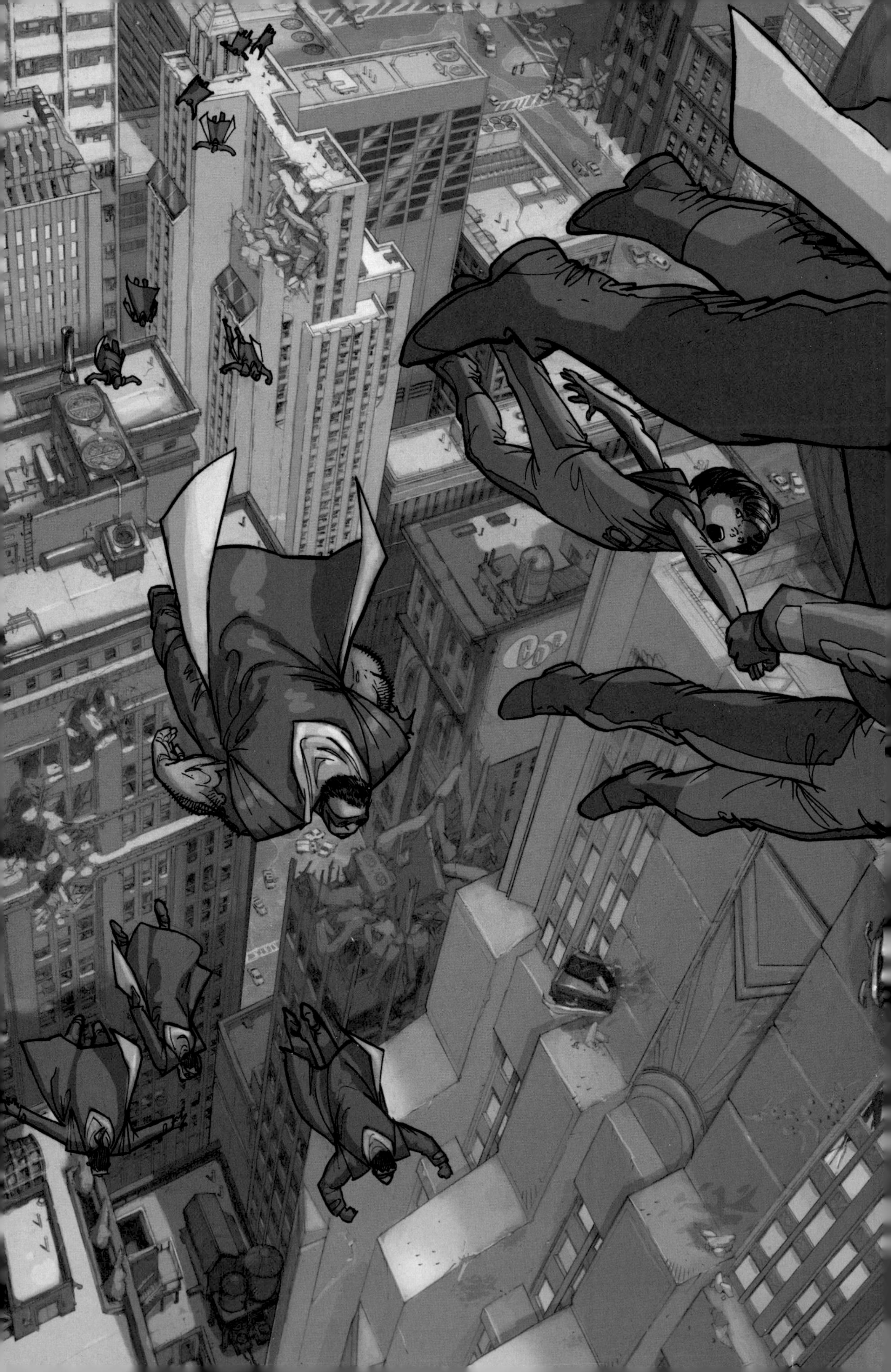

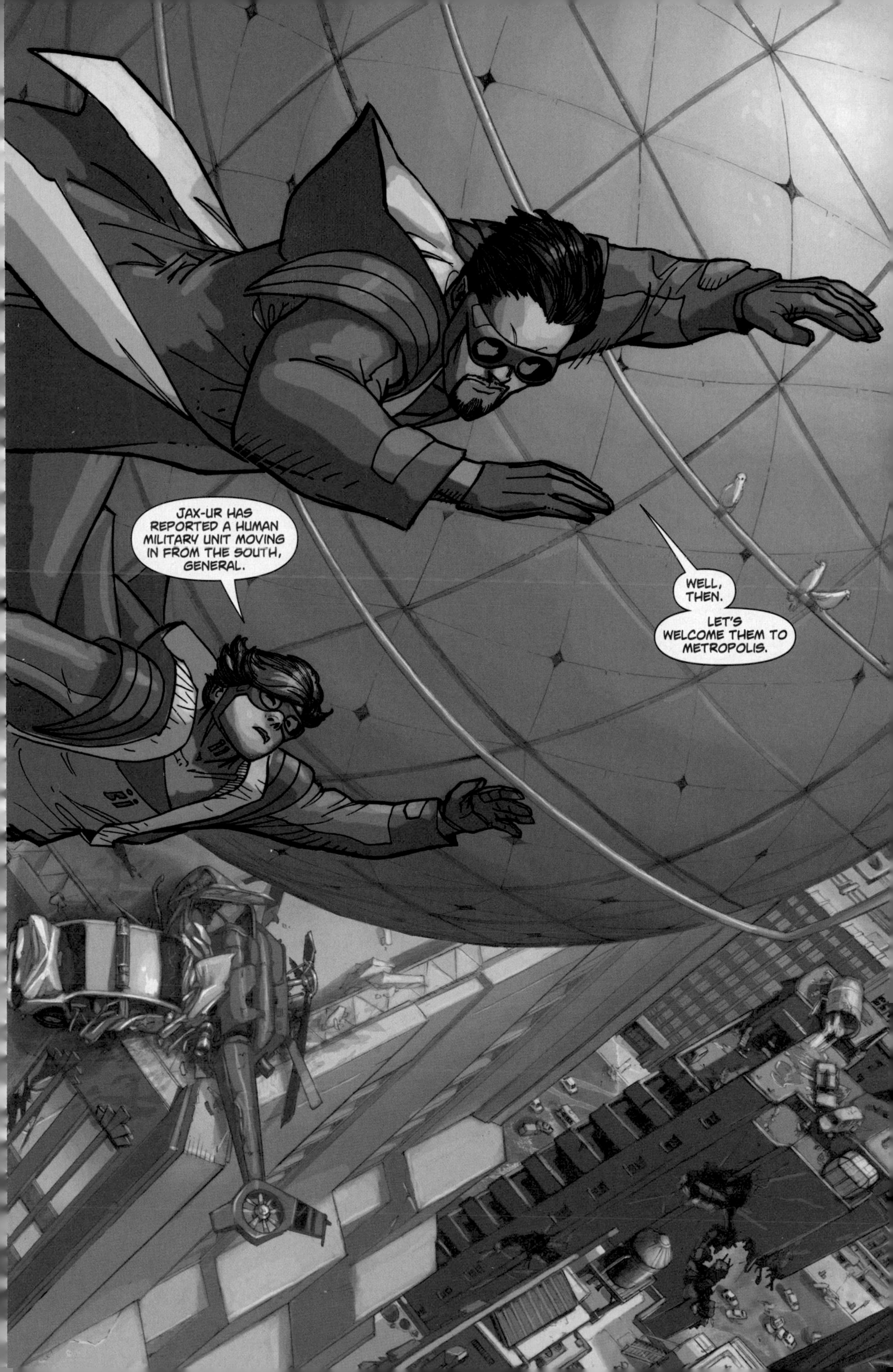

JAX-UR HAS REPORTED A HUMAN MILITARY UNIT MOVING IN FROM THE SOUTH, GENERAL.
WELL, THEN.
LET'S WELCOME THEM TO METROPOLIS.

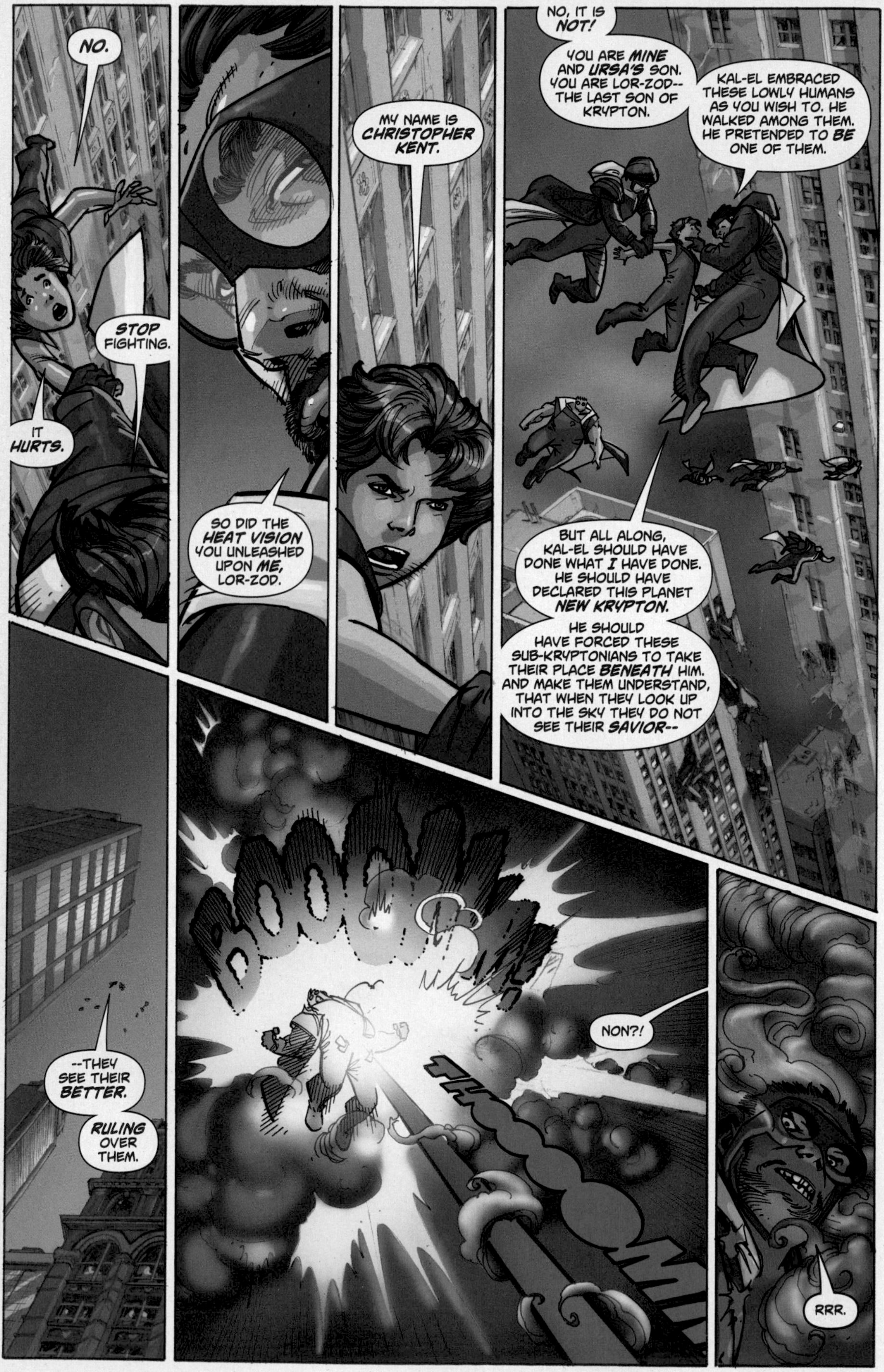
NO.
STOP FIGHTING.
IT HURTS.
SO DID THE HEAT VISION YOU UNLEASHED UPON ME, LOR-ZOD.
MY NAME IS CHRISTOPHER KENT.
NO, IT IS NOT!
YOU ARE MINE AND URSA'S SON. YOU ARE LOR-ZOD-- THE LAST SON OF KRYPTON.
KAL-EL EMBRACED THESE LOWLY HUMANS AS YOU WISH TO. HE WALKED AMONG THEM. HE PRETENDED TO BE ONE OF THEM.
BUT ALL ALONG, KAL-EL SHOULD HAVE DONE WHAT I HAVE DONE. HE SHOULD HAVE DECLARED THIS PLANET NEW KRYPTON.
HE SHOULD HAVE FORCED THESE SUB-KRYPTONIANS TO TAKE THEIR PLACE BENEATH HIM. AND MAKE THEM UNDERSTAND, THAT WHEN THEY LOOK UP INTO THE SKY THEY DO NOT SEE THEIR SAVIOR--
--THEY SEE THEIR BETTER.
RULING OVER THEM.
NON?!
RRR.

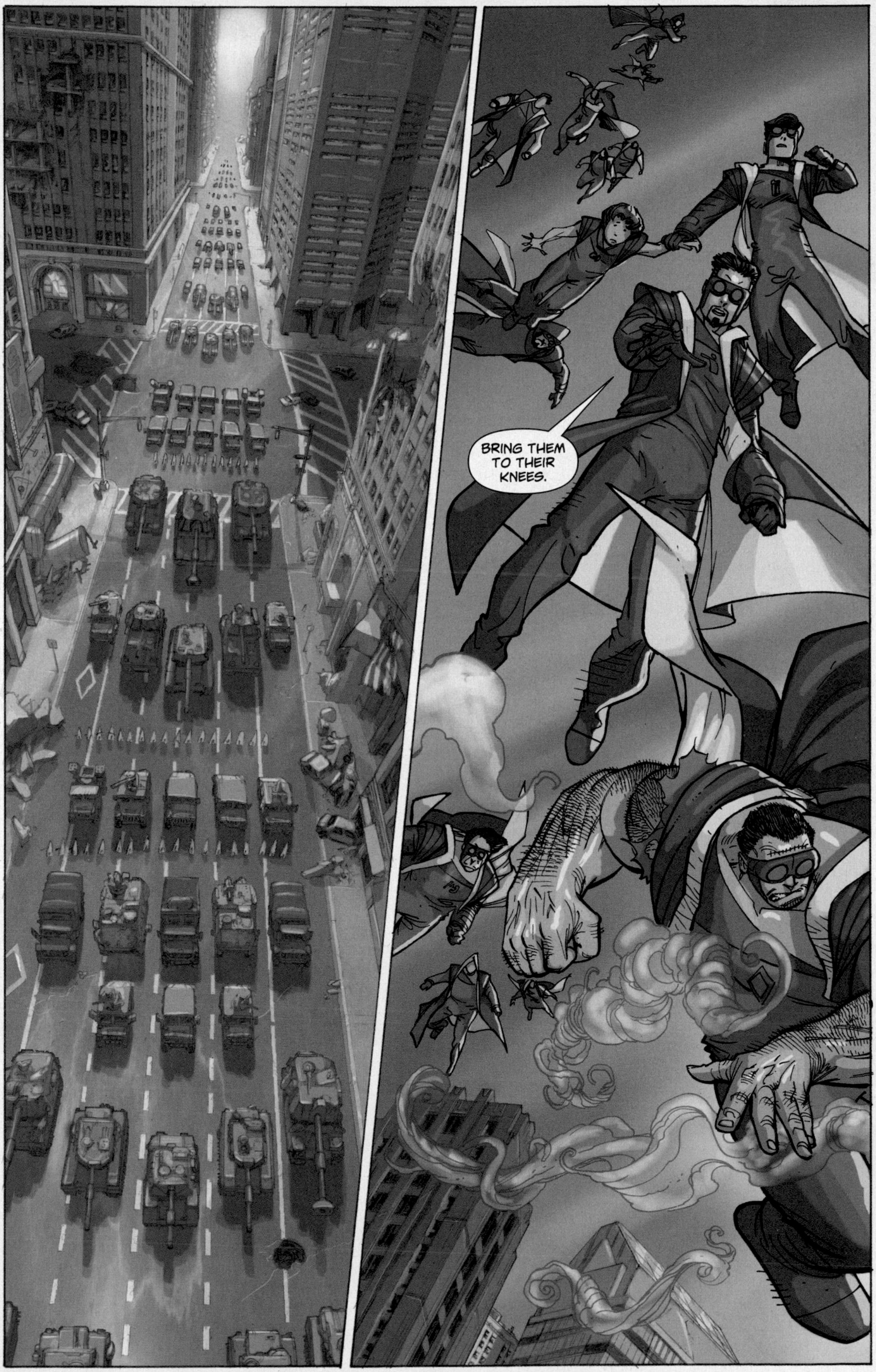
BRING THEM TO THEIR KNEES.

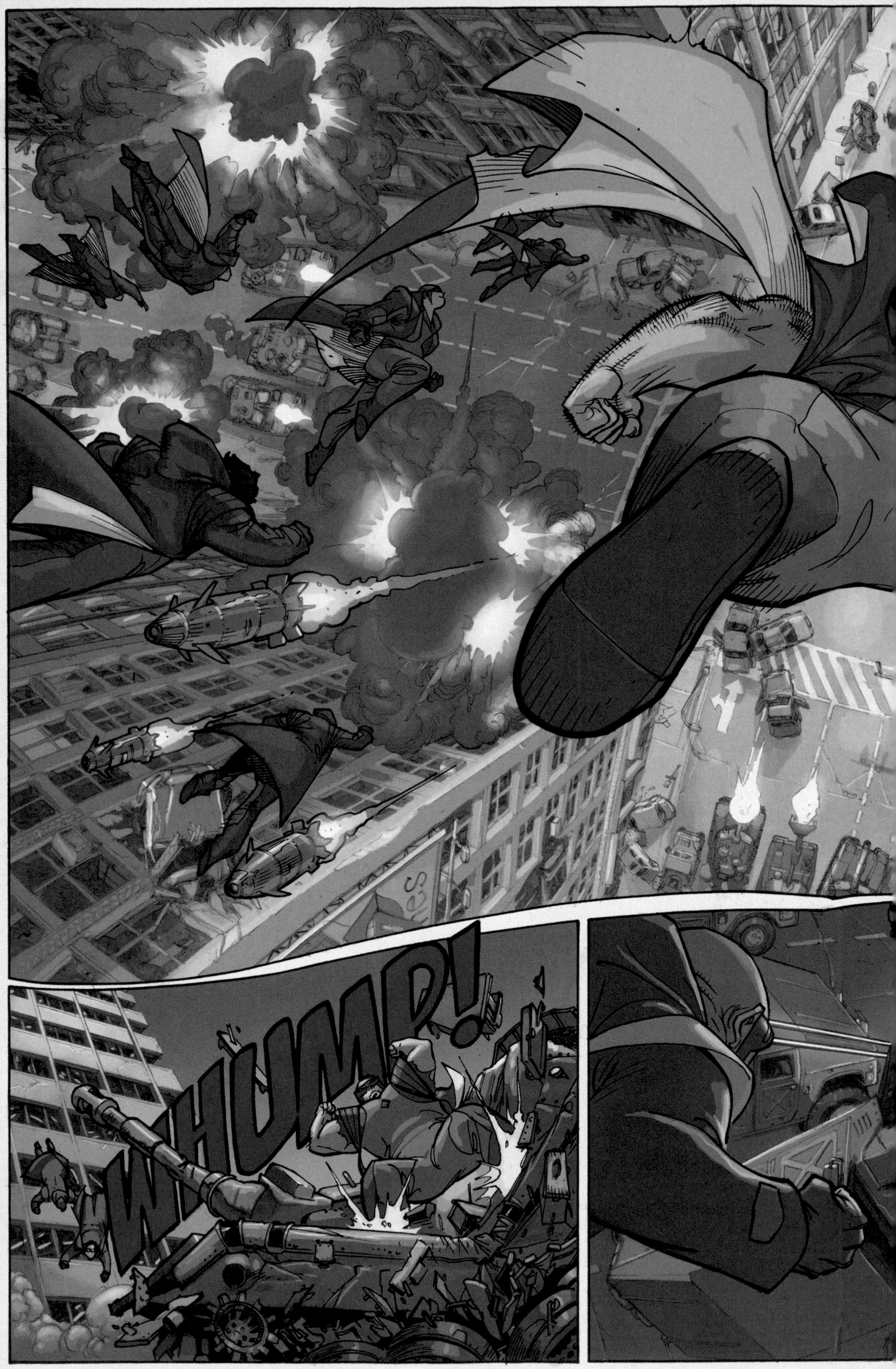
WHUMP!

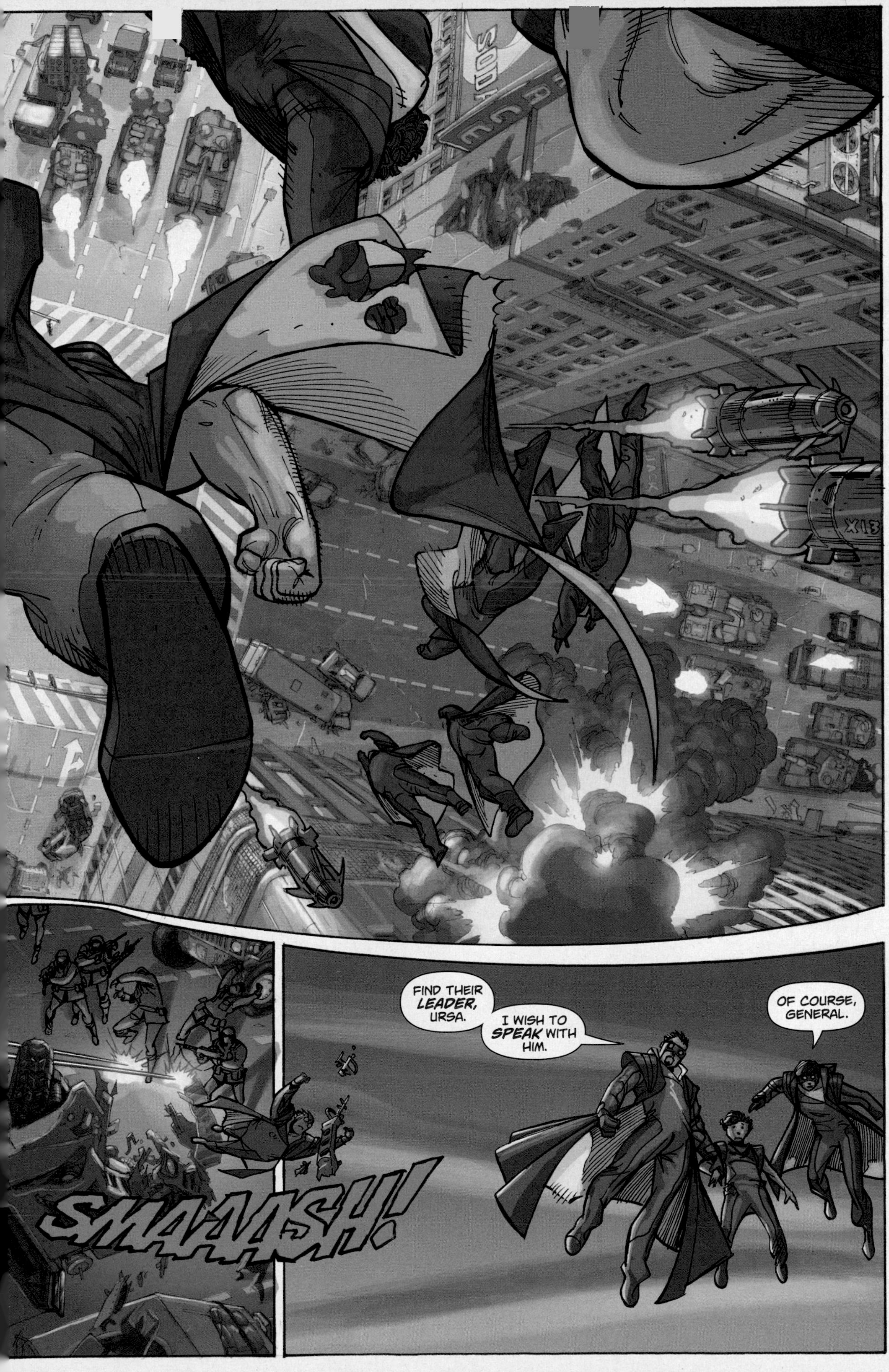
SMAAASH!
FIND THEIR LEADER, URSA.
I WISH TO SPEAK WITH HIM.
OF COURSE, GENERAL.

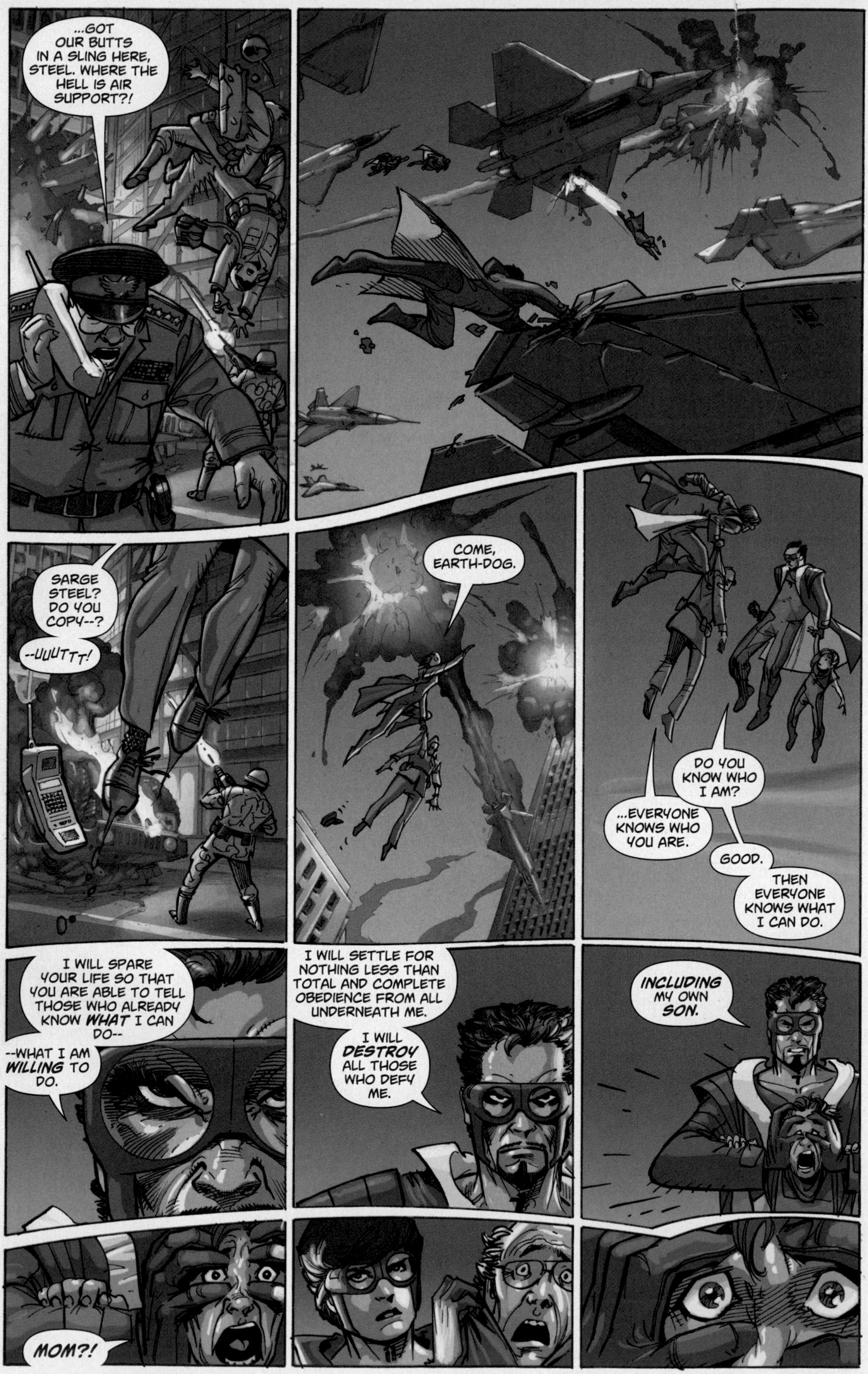

...GOT OUR BUTTS IN A SLING HERE, STEEL. WHERE THE HELL IS AIR SUPPORT?!
SARGE STEEL? DO YOU COPY--?
--UUUTTT!
COME, EARTH-DOG.
DO YOU KNOW WHO I AM?
...EVERYONE KNOWS WHO YOU ARE.
GOOD.
THEN EVERYONE KNOWS WHAT I CAN DO.
I WILL SPARE YOUR LIFE SO THAT YOU ARE ABLE TO TELL THOSE WHO ALREADY KNOW WHAT I CAN DO--
--WHAT I AM WILLING TO DO.
I WILL SETTLE FOR NOTHING LESS THAN TOTAL AND COMPLETE OBEDIENCE FROM ALL UNDERNEATH ME.
I WILL DESTROY ALL THOSE WHO DEFY ME.
INCLUDING MY OWN SON.
MOM?!

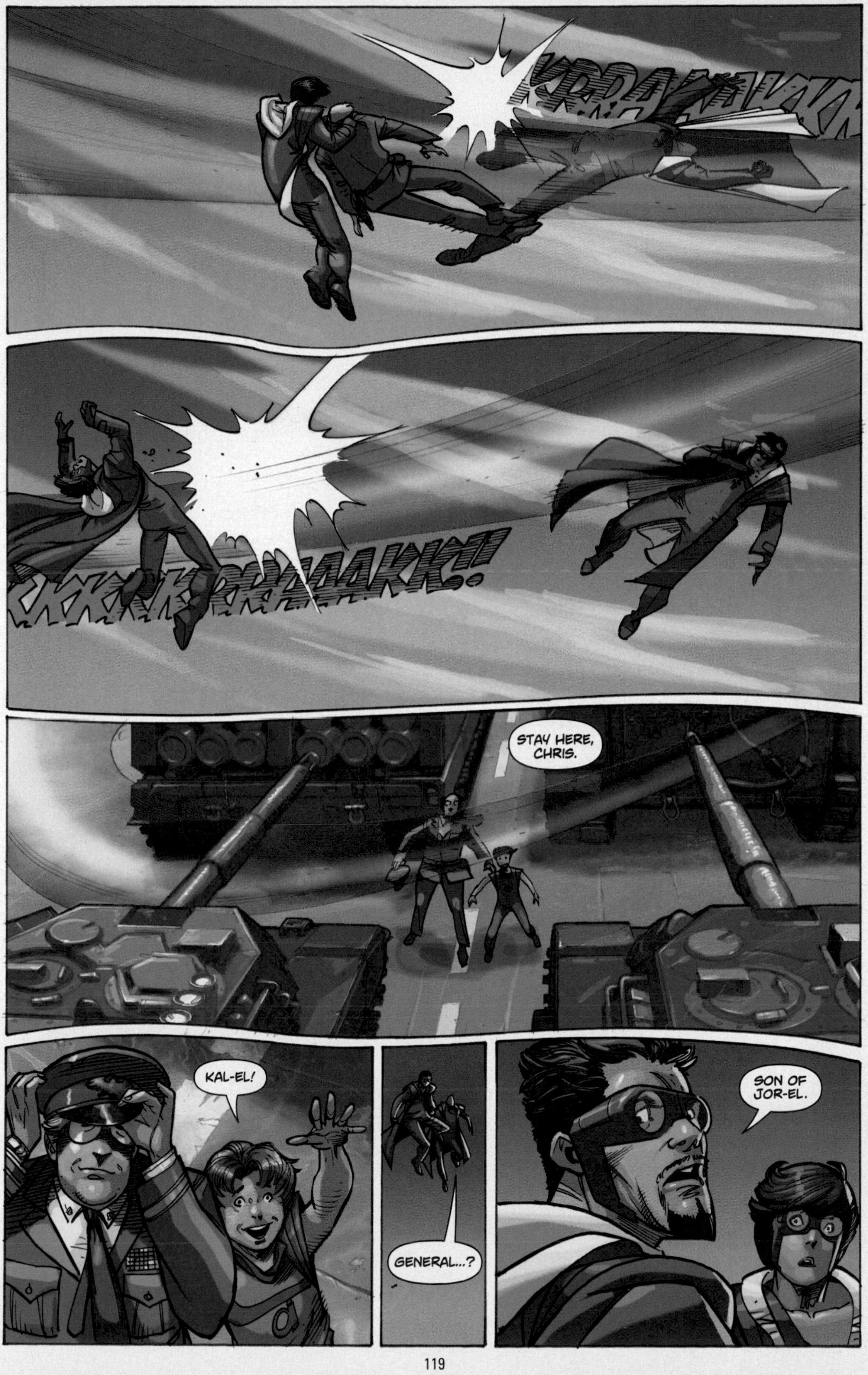
KRRAKKAKKK
KKKKKRRAAAKK!!
STAY HERE, CHRIS.
KAL-EL!
GENERAL...?
SON OF JOR-EL.

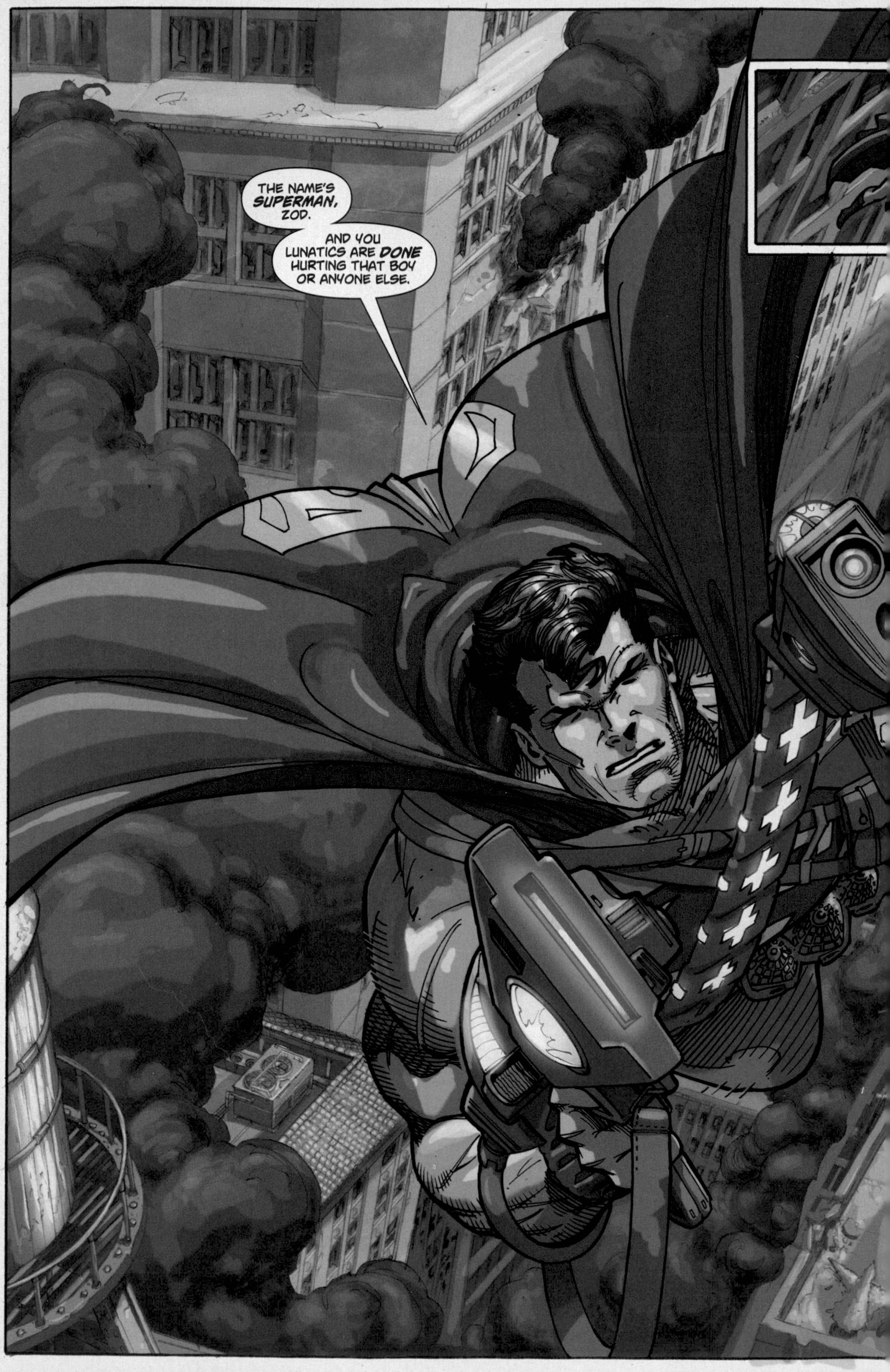
THE NAME'S **SUPERMAN,** ZOD.
AND YOU LUNATICS ARE **DONE** HURTING THAT BOY OR ANYONE ELSE.

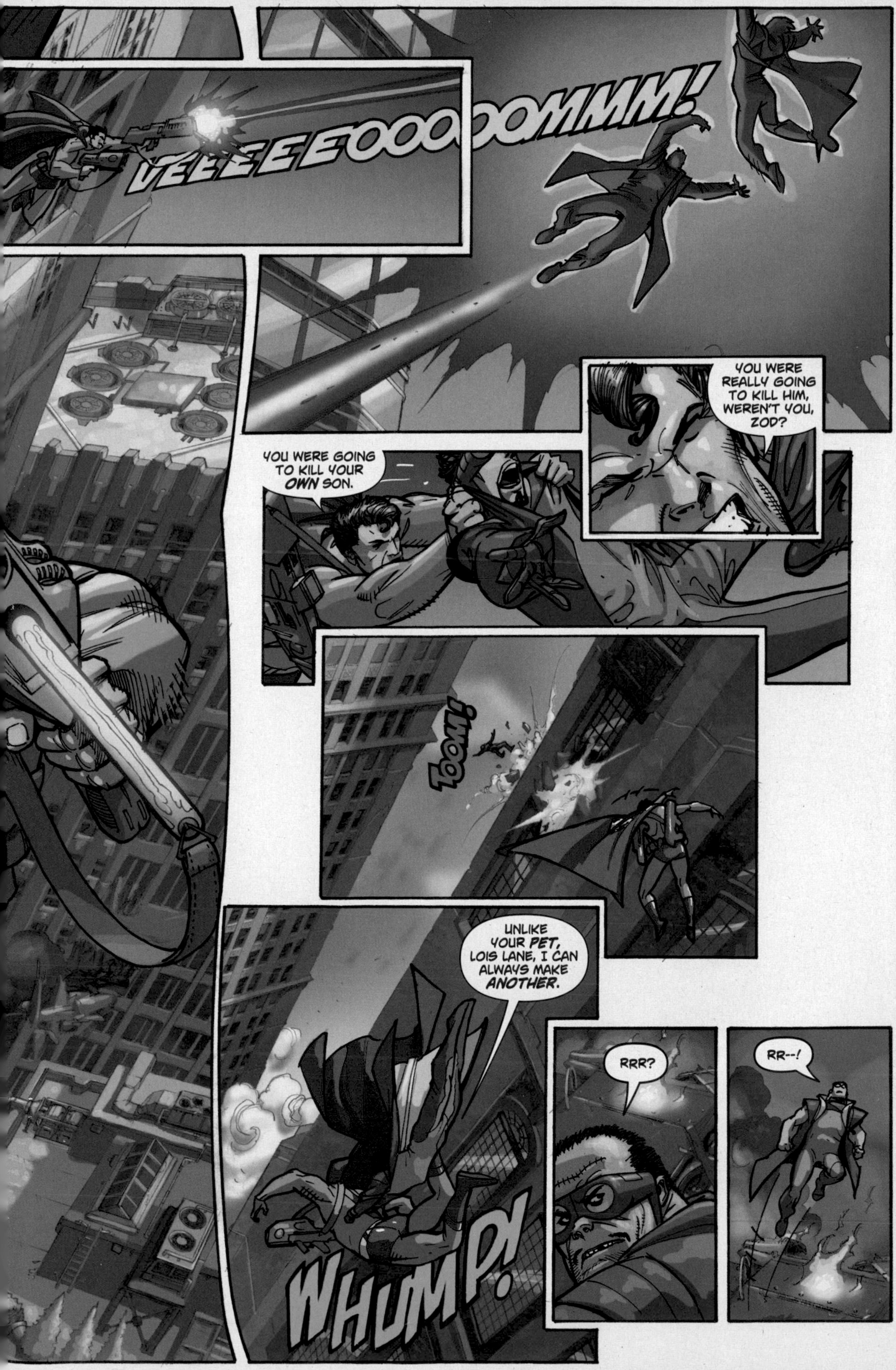
VEEEEEOOOOOOMMMM!
YOU WERE REALLY GOING TO KILL HIM, WEREN'T YOU, ZOD?
YOU WERE GOING TO KILL YOUR OWN SON.
TOOM!
UNLIKE YOUR PET, LOIS LANE, I CAN ALWAYS MAKE ANOTHER.
WHUMP!
RRR?
RR--!

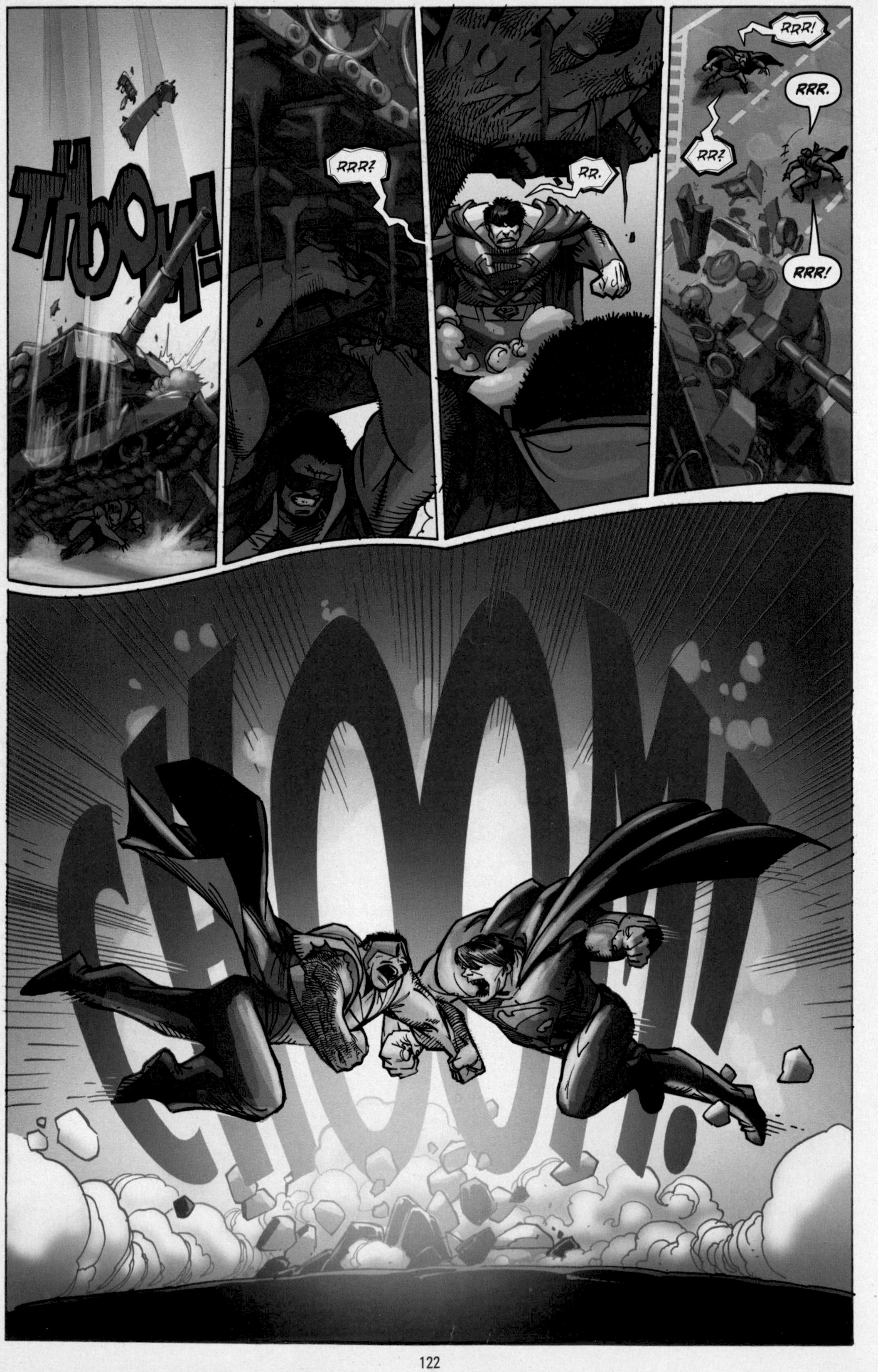
THOOM!
RRR?
RR.
RRR!
RRR.
RR?
RRR!
CHOOM!

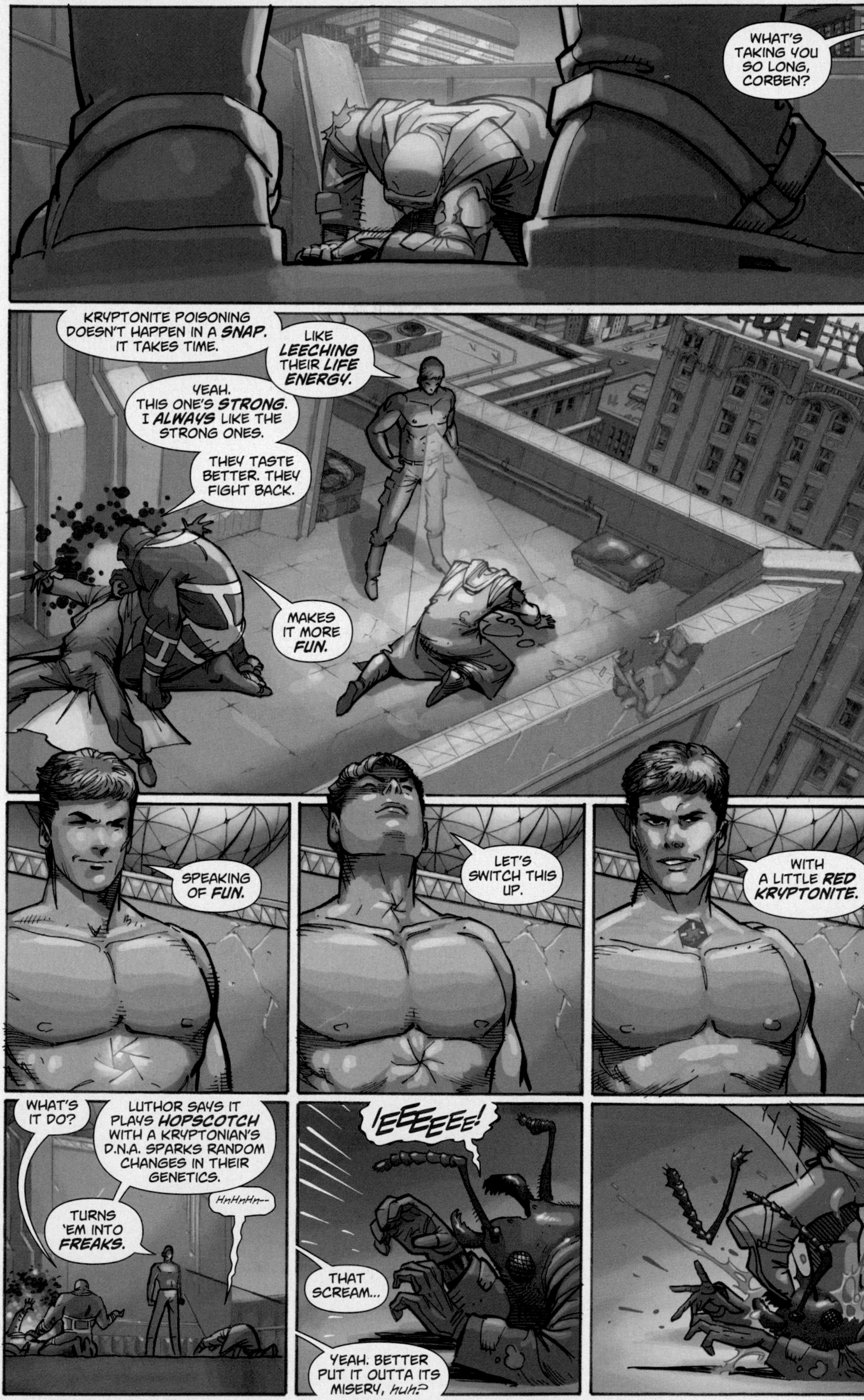
WHAT'S TAKING YOU SO LONG, CORBEN?
KRYPTONITE POISONING DOESN'T HAPPEN IN A SNAP. IT TAKES TIME.
LIKE LEECHING THEIR LIFE ENERGY.
YEAH. THIS ONE'S STRONG. I ALWAYS LIKE THE STRONG ONES.
THEY TASTE BETTER. THEY FIGHT BACK.
MAKES IT MORE FUN.
SPEAKING OF FUN.
LET'S SWITCH THIS UP.
WITH A LITTLE RED KRYPTONITE.
WHAT'S IT DO?
LUTHOR SAYS IT PLAYS HOPSCOTCH WITH A KRYPTONIAN'S D.N.A. SPARKS RANDOM CHANGES IN THEIR GENETICS.
TURNS 'EM INTO FREAKS.
HnHnHn--
IEEEEEEE!
THAT SCREAM...
YEAH. BETTER PUT IT OUTTA ITS MISERY, huh?

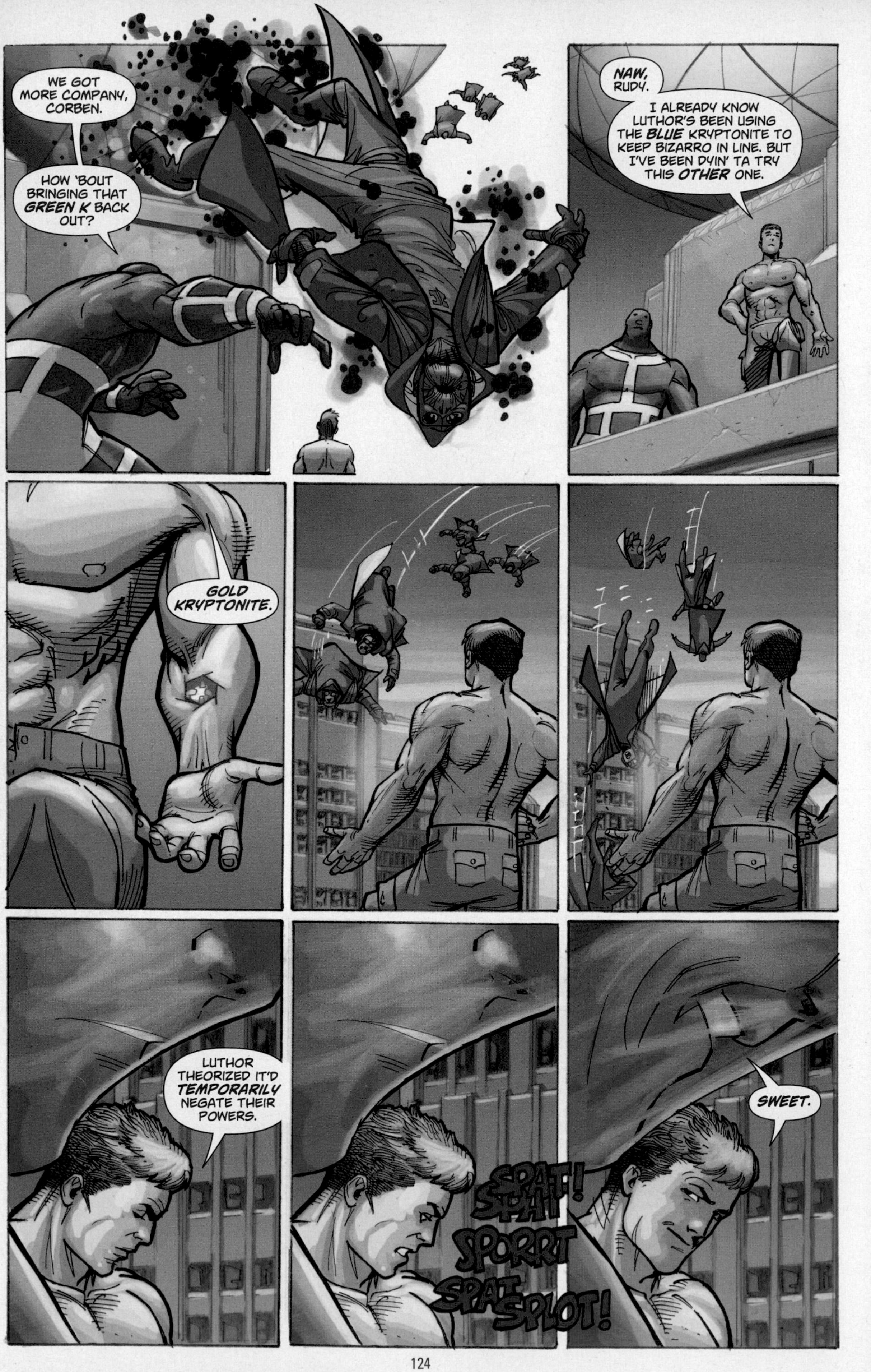
WE GOT MORE COMPANY, CORBEN.
HOW 'BOUT BRINGING THAT GREEN K BACK OUT?
NAW, RUDY.
I ALREADY KNOW LUTHOR'S BEEN USING THE BLUE KRYPTONITE TO KEEP BIZARRO IN LINE. BUT I'VE BEEN DYIN' TA TRY THIS OTHER ONE.
GOLD KRYPTONITE.
LUTHOR THEORIZED IT'D TEMPORARILY NEGATE THEIR POWERS.
SPAT! SPAT SPORRT SPAT SPLOT!
SWEET.

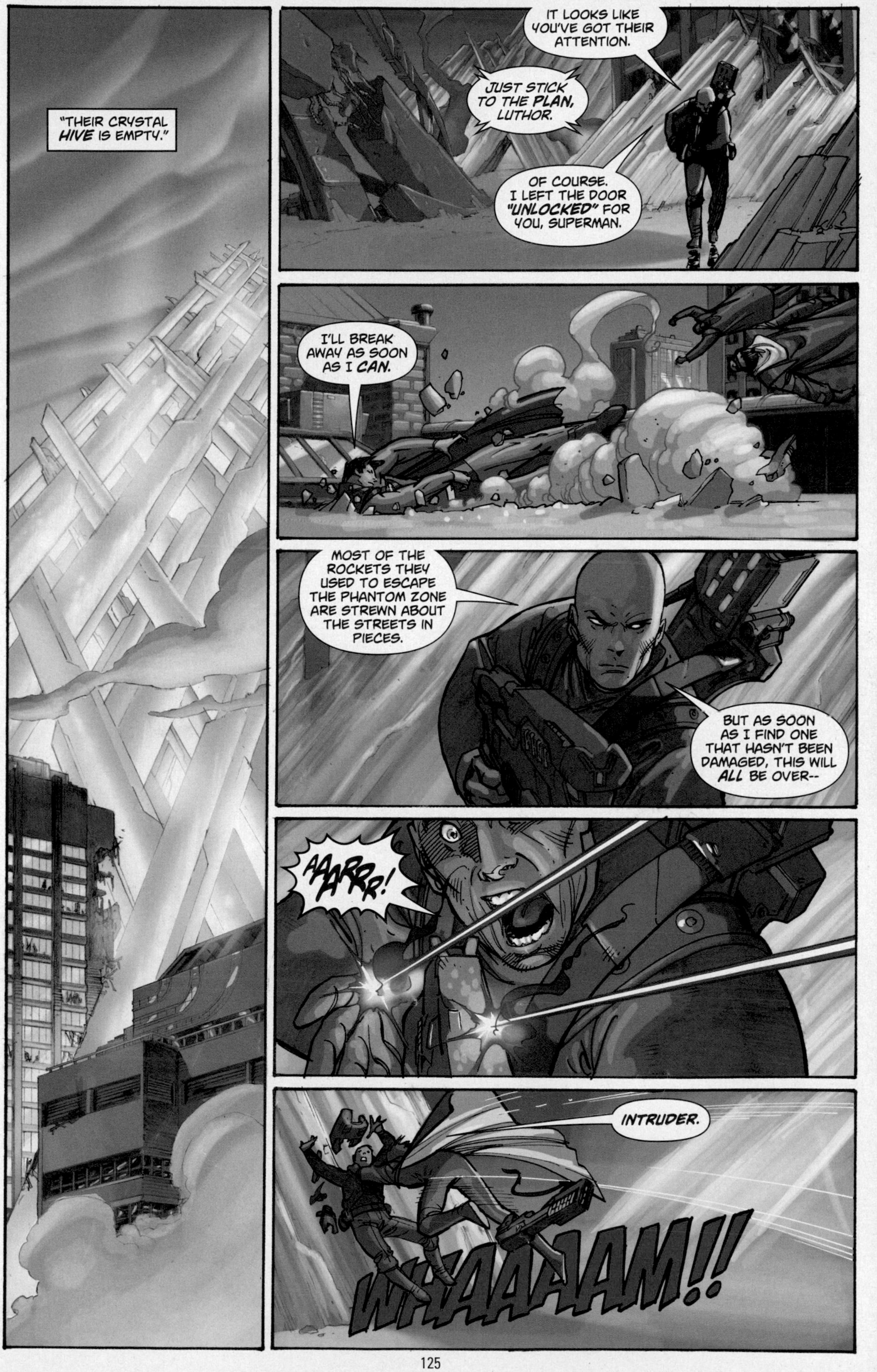
"THEIR CRYSTAL HIVE IS EMPTY."
IT LOOKS LIKE YOU'VE GOT THEIR ATTENTION.
JUST STICK TO THE PLAN, LUTHOR.
OF COURSE. I LEFT THE DOOR "UNLOCKED" FOR YOU, SUPERMAN.
I'LL BREAK AWAY AS SOON AS I CAN.
MOST OF THE ROCKETS THEY USED TO ESCAPE THE PHANTOM ZONE ARE STREWN ABOUT THE STREETS IN PIECES.
BUT AS SOON AS I FIND ONE THAT HASN'T BEEN DAMAGED, THIS WILL ALL BE OVER--
AAARRR!
INTRUDER.
WHAAAAAM!!

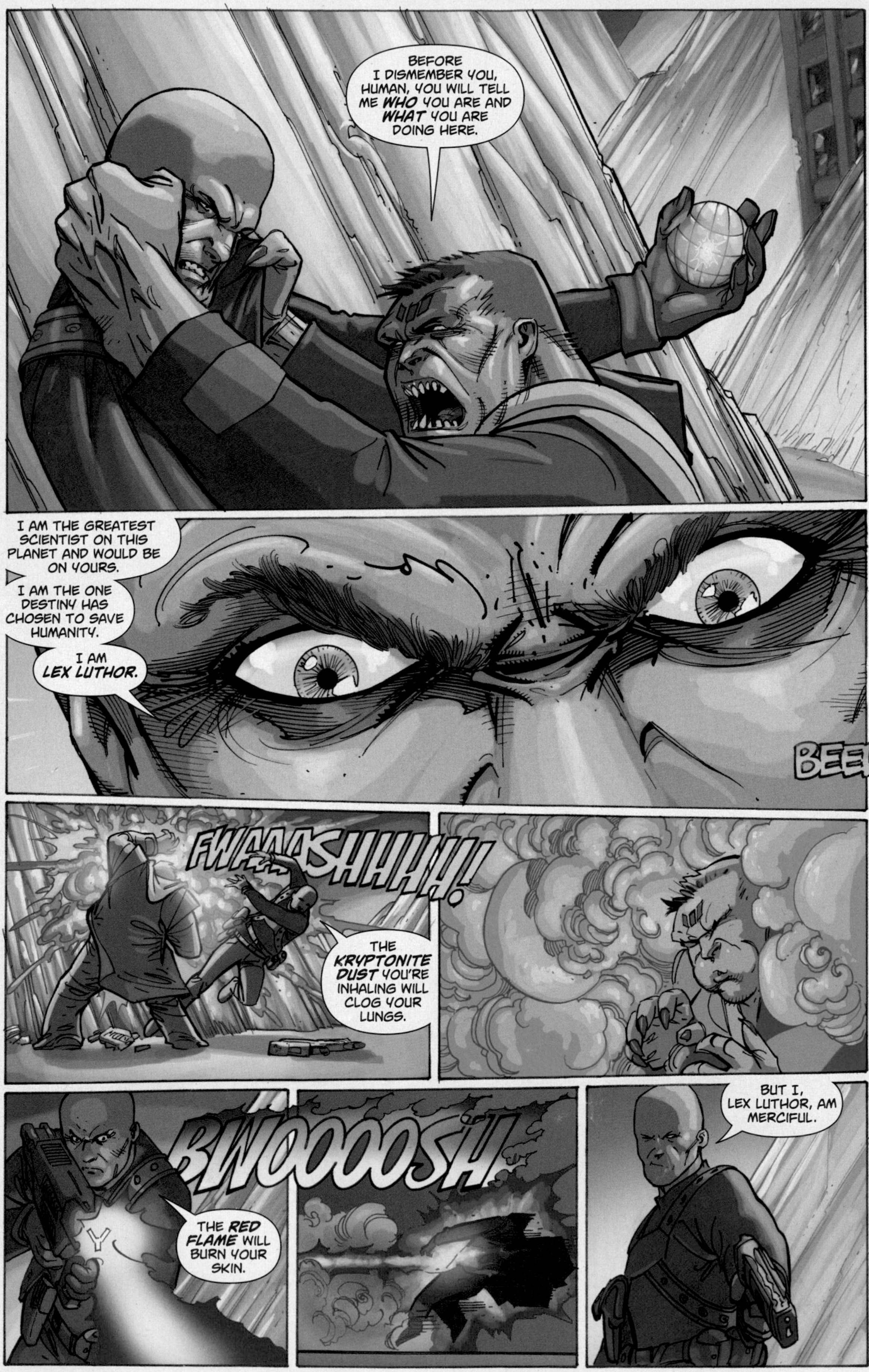

BEFORE I DISMEMBER YOU, HUMAN, YOU WILL TELL ME **WHO** YOU ARE AND **WHAT** YOU ARE DOING HERE.
I AM THE GREATEST SCIENTIST ON THIS PLANET AND WOULD BE ON YOURS.
I AM THE ONE DESTINY HAS CHOSEN TO SAVE HUMANITY.
I AM **LEX LUTHOR.**
BEEP
FWAAASHHHH!
THE **KRYPTONITE DUST** YOU'RE INHALING WILL CLOG YOUR LUNGS.
BWOOOOSH
THE **RED FLAME** WILL BURN YOUR SKIN.
BUT I, LEX LUTHOR, AM MERCIFUL.

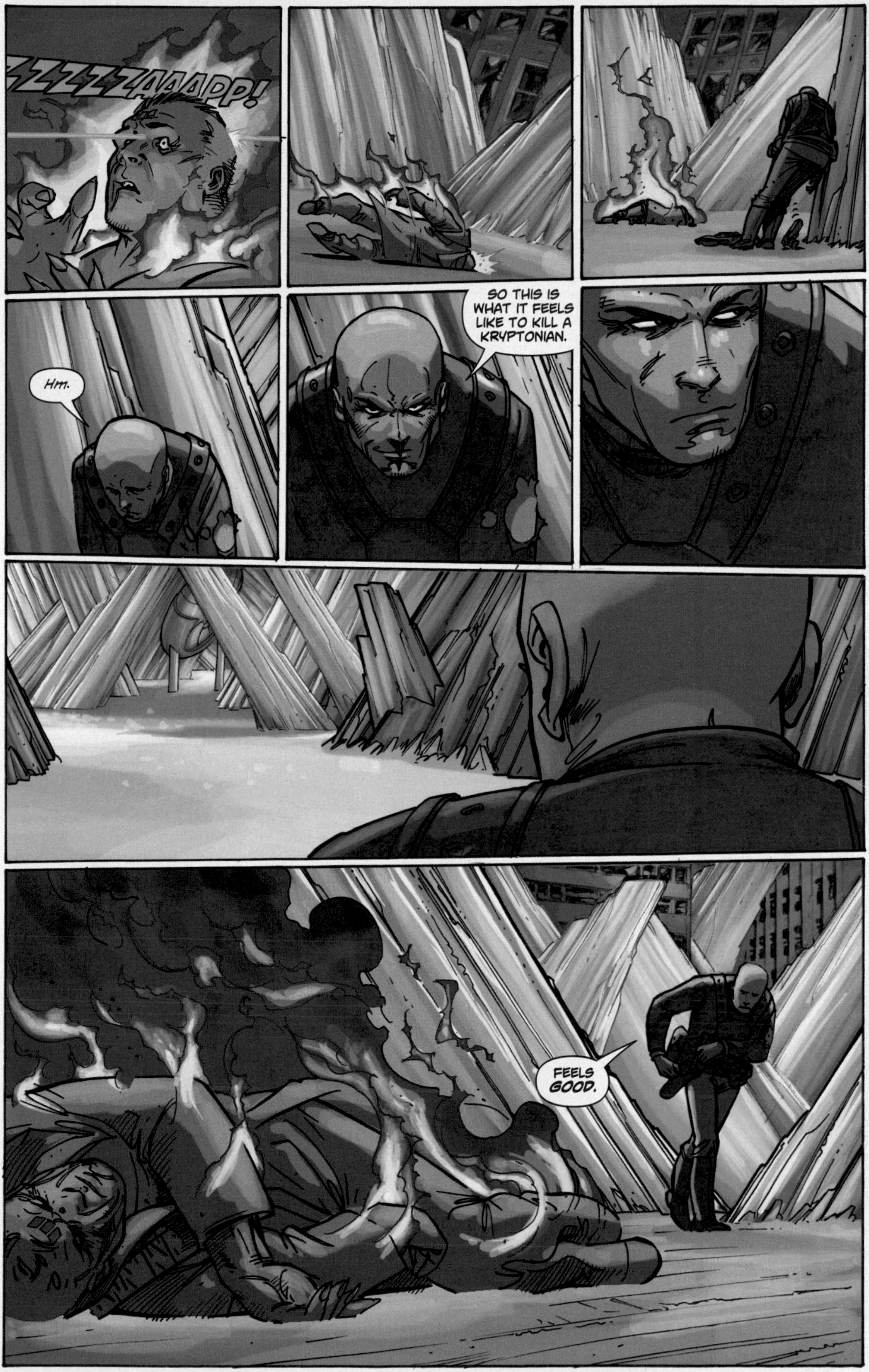
ZZZZZZAAAPP!
HM.
SO THIS IS WHAT IT FEELS LIKE TO KILL A KRYPTONIAN.
FEELS GOOD.

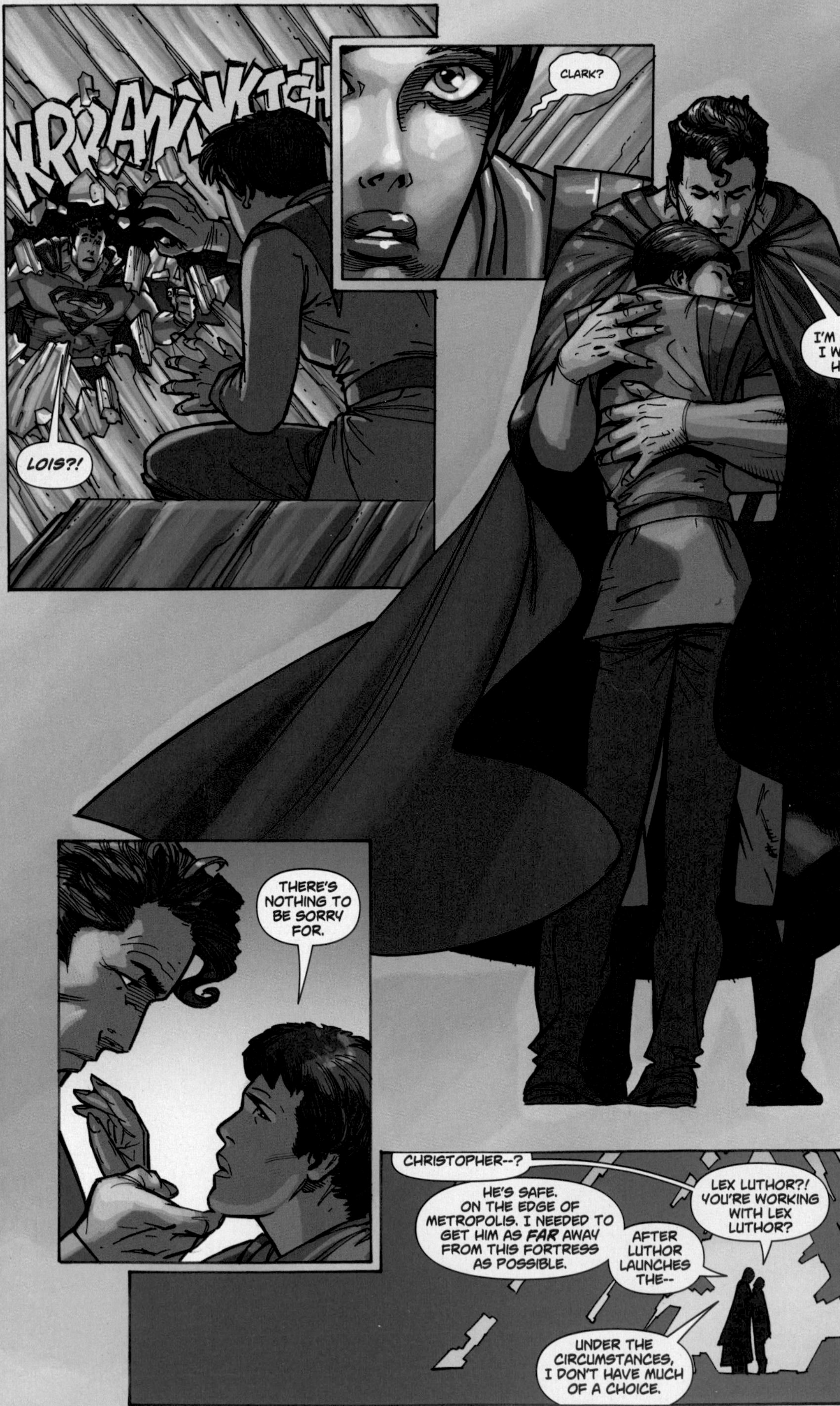
KRRANKKTCH
LOIS?!
CLARK?
I'M SORRY I WASN'T HERE.
THERE'S NOTHING TO BE SORRY FOR.
CHRISTOPHER--?
HE'S SAFE. ON THE EDGE OF METROPOLIS. I NEEDED TO GET HIM AS FAR AWAY FROM THIS FORTRESS AS POSSIBLE.
AFTER LUTHOR LAUNCHES THE--
LEX LUTHOR?! YOU'RE WORKING WITH LEX LUTHOR?
UNDER THE CIRCUMSTANCES, I DON'T HAVE MUCH OF A CHOICE.

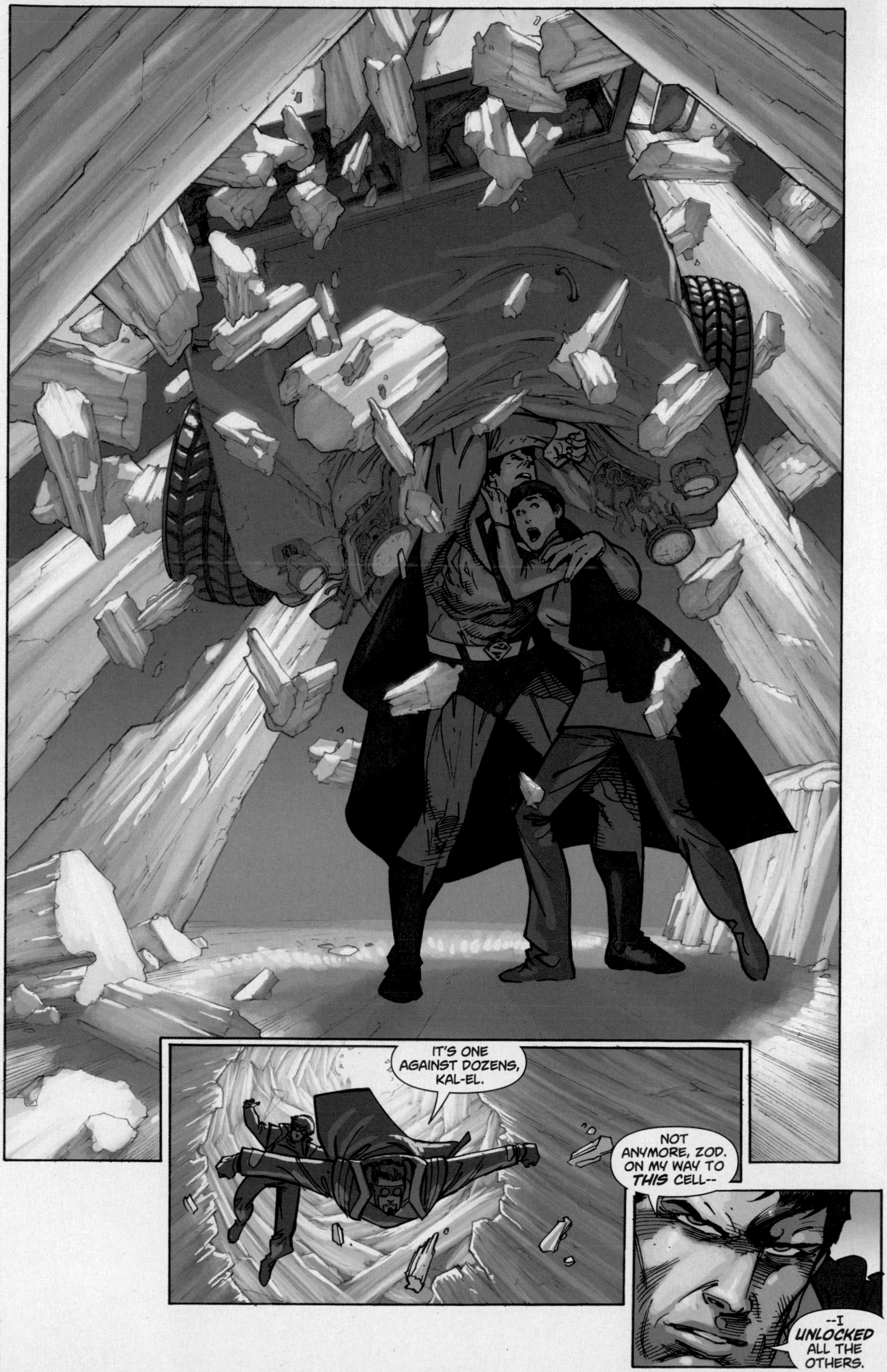
IT'S ONE AGAINST DOZENS, KAL-EL.
NOT ANYMORE, ZOD. ON MY WAY TO THIS CELL--
--I UNLOCKED ALL THE OTHERS.

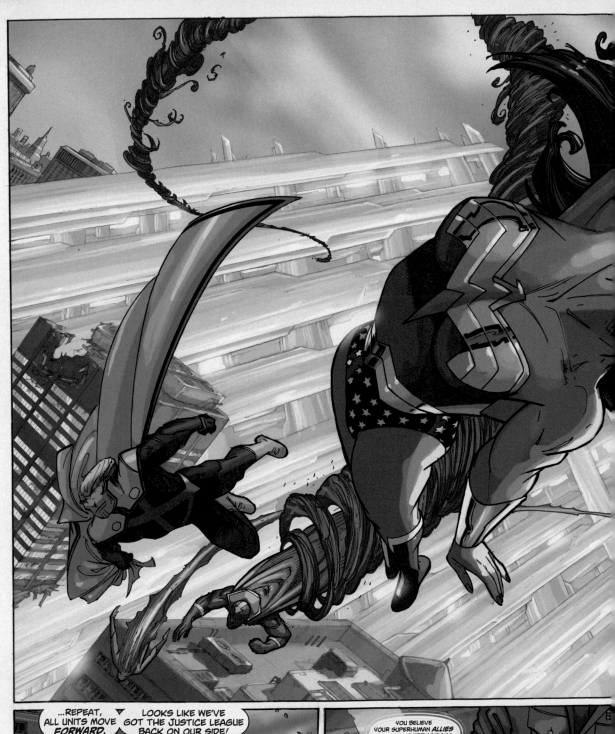

...REPEAT, ALL UNITS MOVE **FORWARD**.

LOOKS LIKE WE'VE GOT THE JUSTICE LEAGUE BACK ON OUR SIDE!

ANYONE SEE **SUPERMAN** UP THERE?

YOU BELIEVE YOUR SUPERHUMAN **ALLIES** HAVE THE **STRENGTH** TO STOP US, KAL-EL?

THEY ARE LITTLE MORE THAN **INSECTS** IN OUR WAY.

VIOLENCE IS ALL YOU **SUBSCRIBE** TO, ISN'T IT, ZOD?

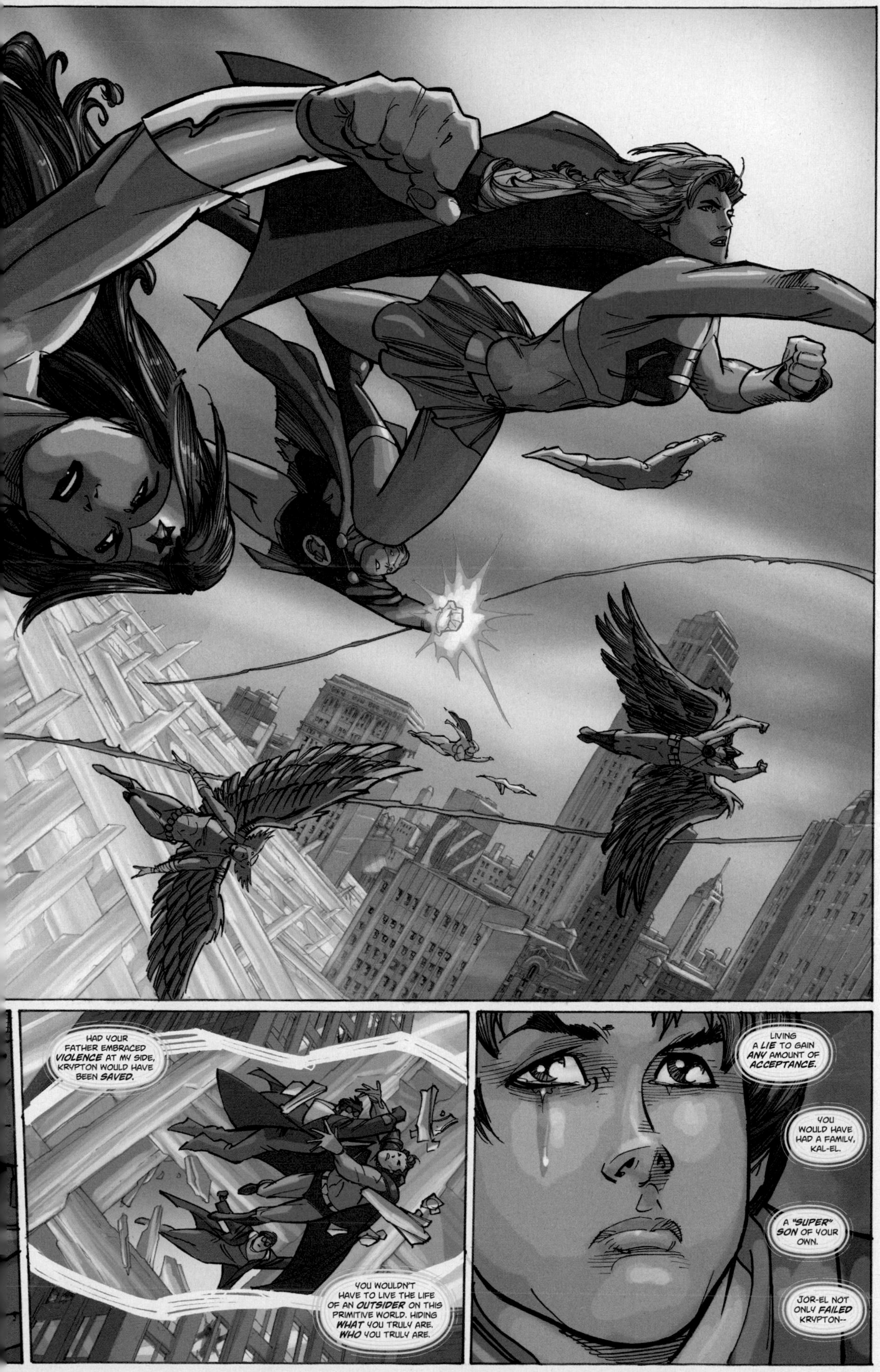
HAD YOUR FATHER EMBRACED VIOLENCE AT MY SIDE, KRYPTON WOULD HAVE BEEN SAVED.
YOU WOULDN'T HAVE TO LIVE THE LIFE OF AN OUTSIDER ON THIS PRIMITIVE WORLD. HIDING WHAT YOU TRULY ARE. WHO YOU TRULY ARE.
LIVING A LIE TO GAIN ANY AMOUNT OF ACCEPTANCE.
YOU WOULD HAVE HAD A FAMILY, KAL-EL.
A "SUPER" SON OF YOUR OWN.
JOR-EL NOT ONLY FAILED KRYPTON--

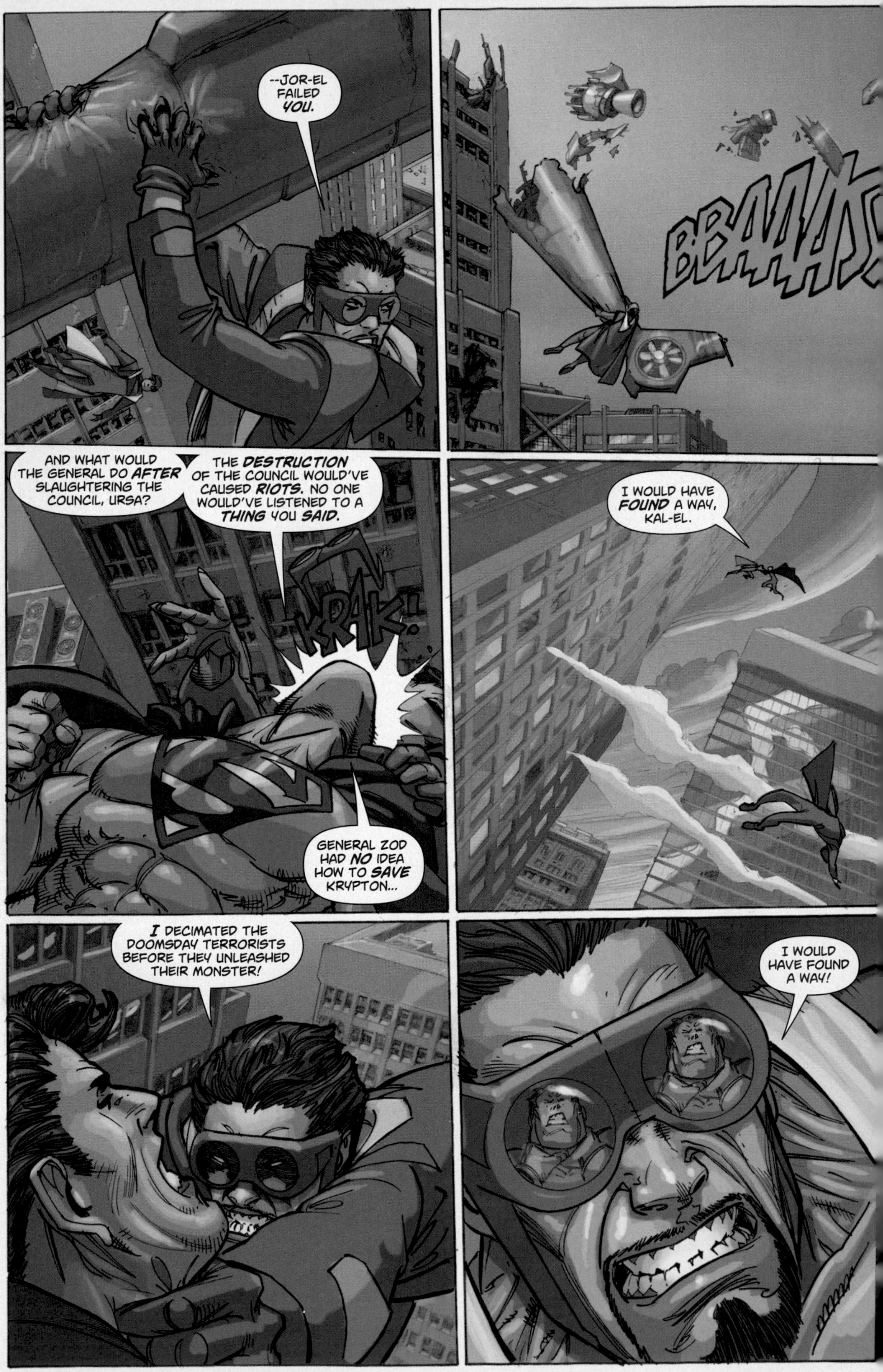
--JOR-EL FAILED YOU.
BRAAKS!
AND WHAT WOULD THE GENERAL DO AFTER SLAUGHTERING THE COUNCIL, URSA?
THE DESTRUCTION OF THE COUNCIL WOULD'VE CAUSED RIOTS. NO ONE WOULD'VE LISTENED TO A THING YOU SAID.
KRAK!
GENERAL ZOD HAD NO IDEA HOW TO SAVE KRYPTON...
I WOULD HAVE FOUND A WAY, KAL-EL.
I DECIMATED THE DOOMSDAY TERRORISTS BEFORE THEY UNLEASHED THEIR MONSTER!
I WOULD HAVE FOUND A WAY!

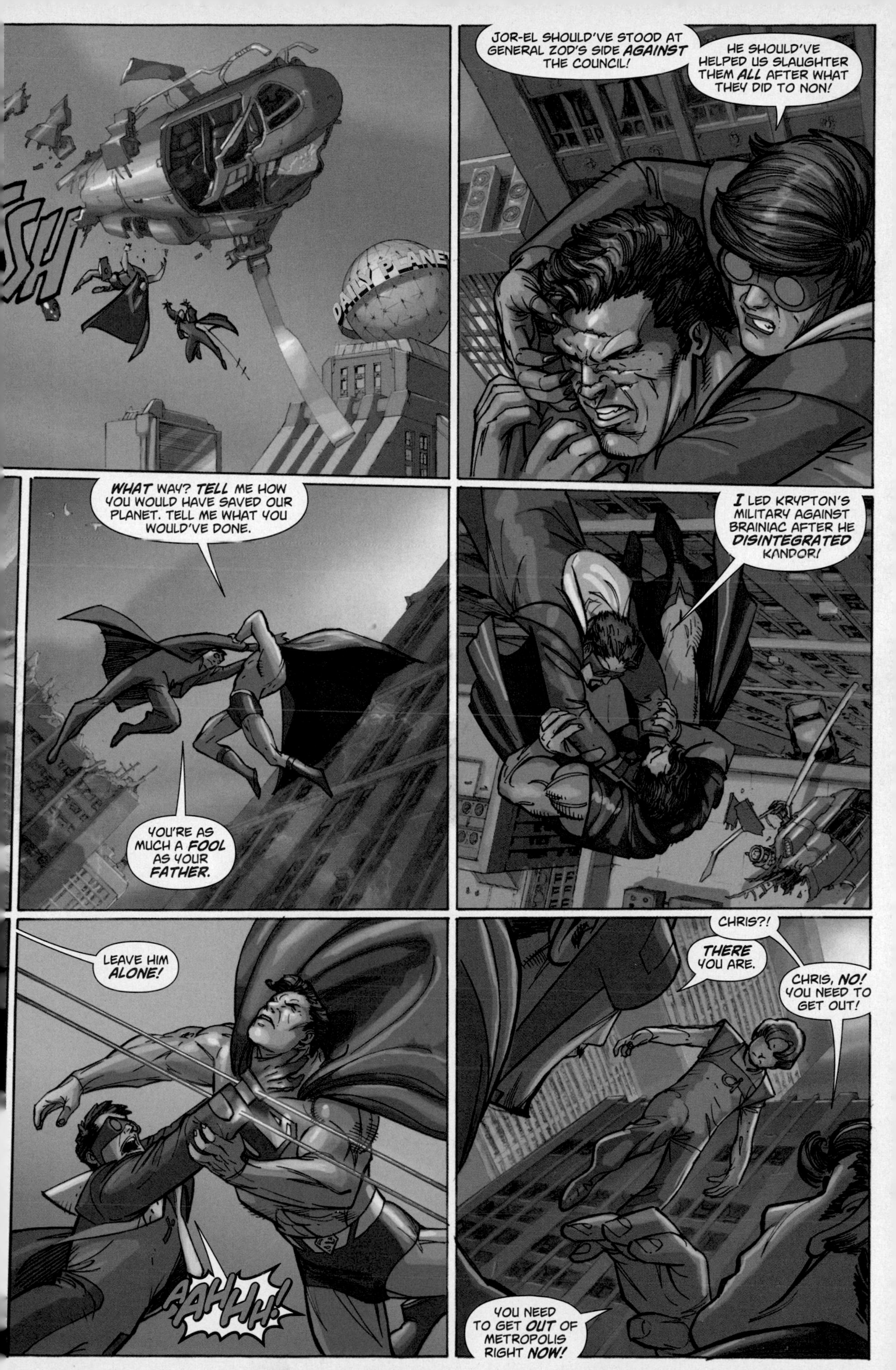

...SH
JOR-EL SHOULD'VE STOOD AT GENERAL ZOD'S SIDE AGAINST THE COUNCIL!
HE SHOULD'VE HELPED US SLAUGHTER THEM ALL AFTER WHAT THEY DID TO NON!
WHAT WAY? TELL ME HOW YOU WOULD HAVE SAVED OUR PLANET. TELL ME WHAT YOU WOULD'VE DONE.
YOU'RE AS MUCH A FOOL AS YOUR FATHER.
I LED KRYPTON'S MILITARY AGAINST BRAINIAC AFTER HE DISINTEGRATED KANDOR!
LEAVE HIM ALONE!
AAHHH!
CHRIS?!
THERE YOU ARE.
CHRIS, NO! YOU NEED TO GET OUT!
YOU NEED TO GET OUT OF METROPOLIS RIGHT NOW!

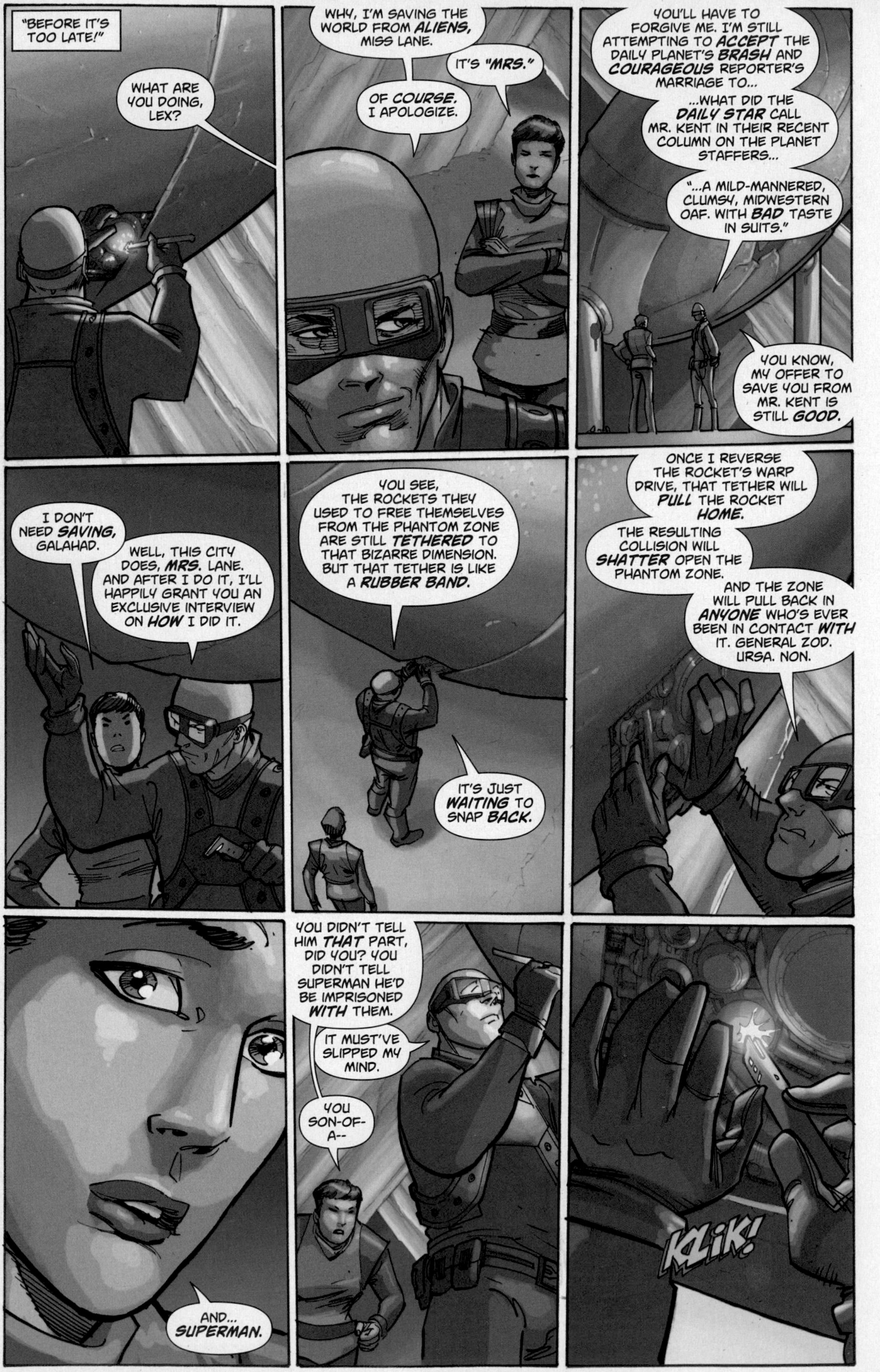
"BEFORE IT'S TOO LATE!"
WHAT ARE YOU DOING, LEX?
WHY, I'M SAVING THE WORLD FROM ALIENS, MISS LANE.
IT'S "MRS."
OF COURSE. I APOLOGIZE.
YOU'LL HAVE TO FORGIVE ME. I'M STILL ATTEMPTING TO ACCEPT THE DAILY PLANET'S BRASH AND COURAGEOUS REPORTER'S MARRIAGE TO...
...WHAT DID THE DAILY STAR CALL MR. KENT IN THEIR RECENT COLUMN ON THE PLANET STAFFERS...
"...A MILD-MANNERED, CLUMSY, MIDWESTERN OAF. WITH BAD TASTE IN SUITS."
YOU KNOW, MY OFFER TO SAVE YOU FROM MR. KENT IS STILL GOOD.
I DON'T NEED SAVING, GALAHAD.
WELL, THIS CITY DOES, MRS. LANE. AND AFTER I DO IT, I'LL HAPPILY GRANT YOU AN EXCLUSIVE INTERVIEW ON HOW I DID IT.
YOU SEE, THE ROCKETS THEY USED TO FREE THEMSELVES FROM THE PHANTOM ZONE ARE STILL TETHERED TO THAT BIZARRE DIMENSION. BUT THAT TETHER IS LIKE A RUBBER BAND.
IT'S JUST WAITING TO SNAP BACK.
ONCE I REVERSE THE ROCKET'S WARP DRIVE, THAT TETHER WILL PULL THE ROCKET HOME.
THE RESULTING COLLISION WILL SHATTER OPEN THE PHANTOM ZONE.
AND THE ZONE WILL PULL BACK IN ANYONE WHO'S EVER BEEN IN CONTACT WITH IT. GENERAL ZOD. URSA. NON.
AND... SUPERMAN.
YOU DIDN'T TELL HIM THAT PART, DID YOU? YOU DIDN'T TELL SUPERMAN HE'D BE IMPRISONED WITH THEM.
IT MUST'VE SLIPPED MY MIND.
YOU SON-OF-A--
KKLIK!

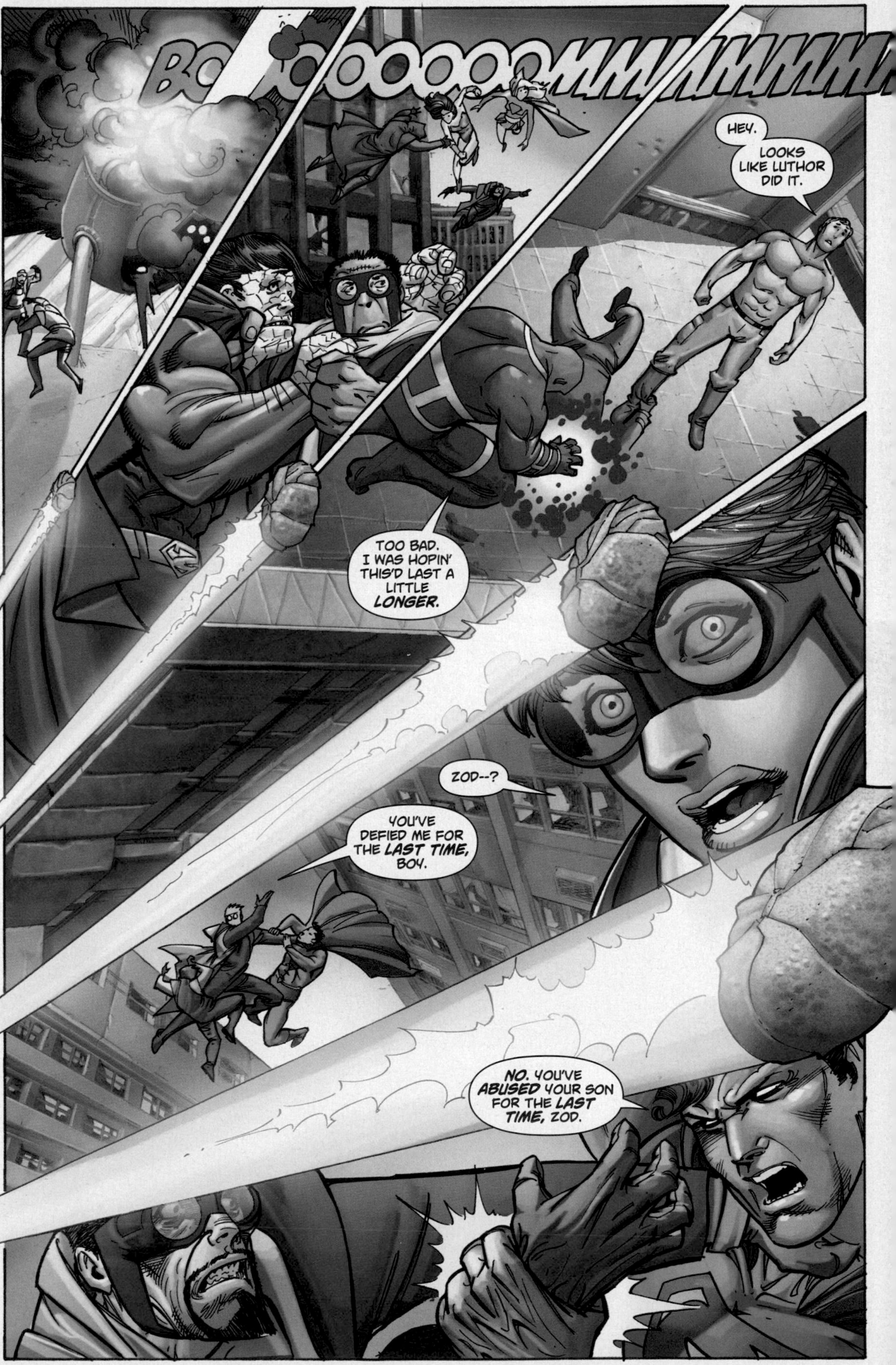
BOOOOOOOOMMMMMMMM
HEY.
LOOKS LIKE LUTHOR DID IT.
TOO BAD. I WAS HOPIN' THIS'D LAST A LITTLE LONGER.
ZOD--?
YOU'VE DEFIED ME FOR THE LAST TIME, BOY.
NO. YOU'VE ABUSED YOUR SON FOR THE LAST TIME, ZOD.

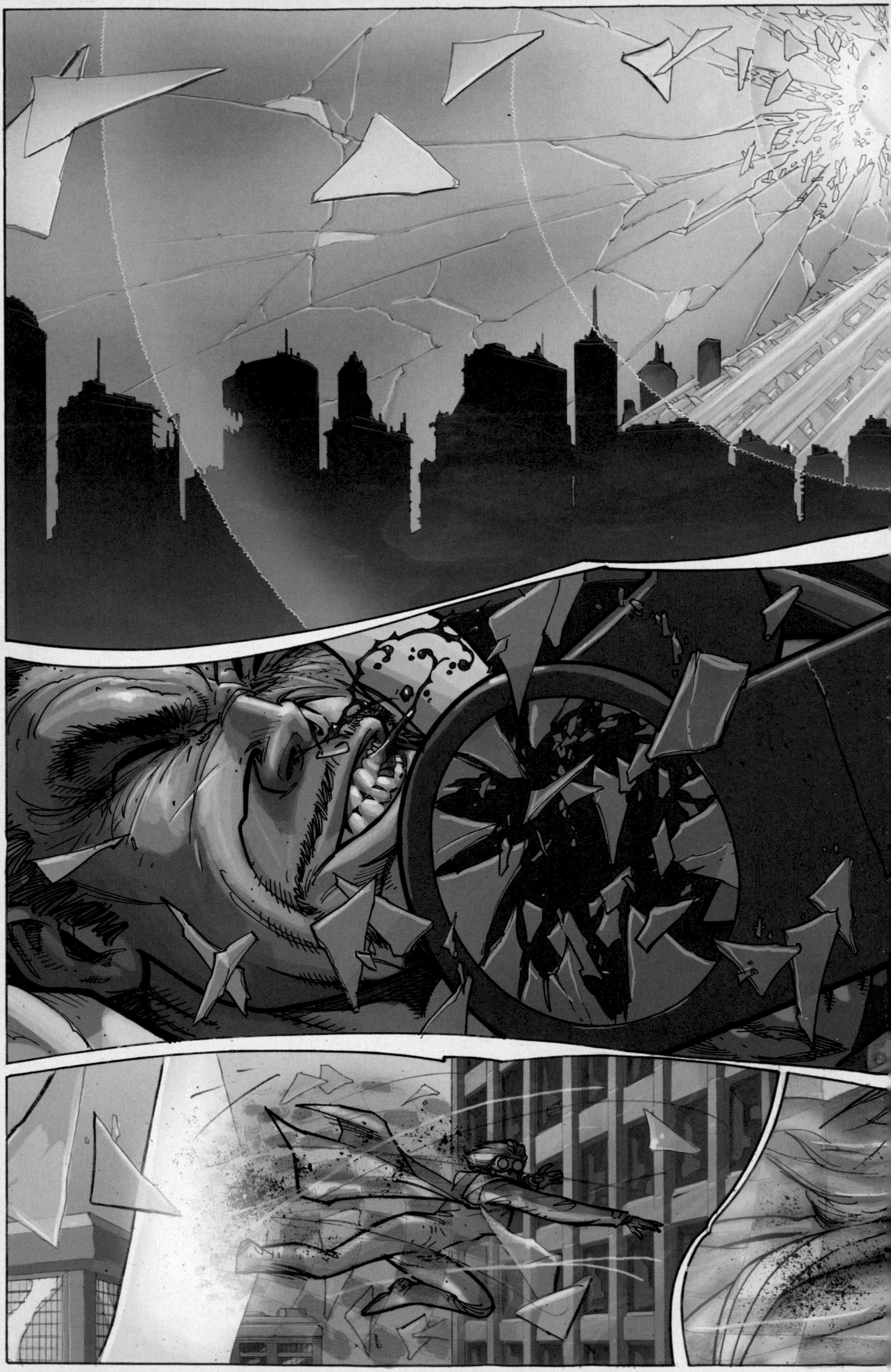

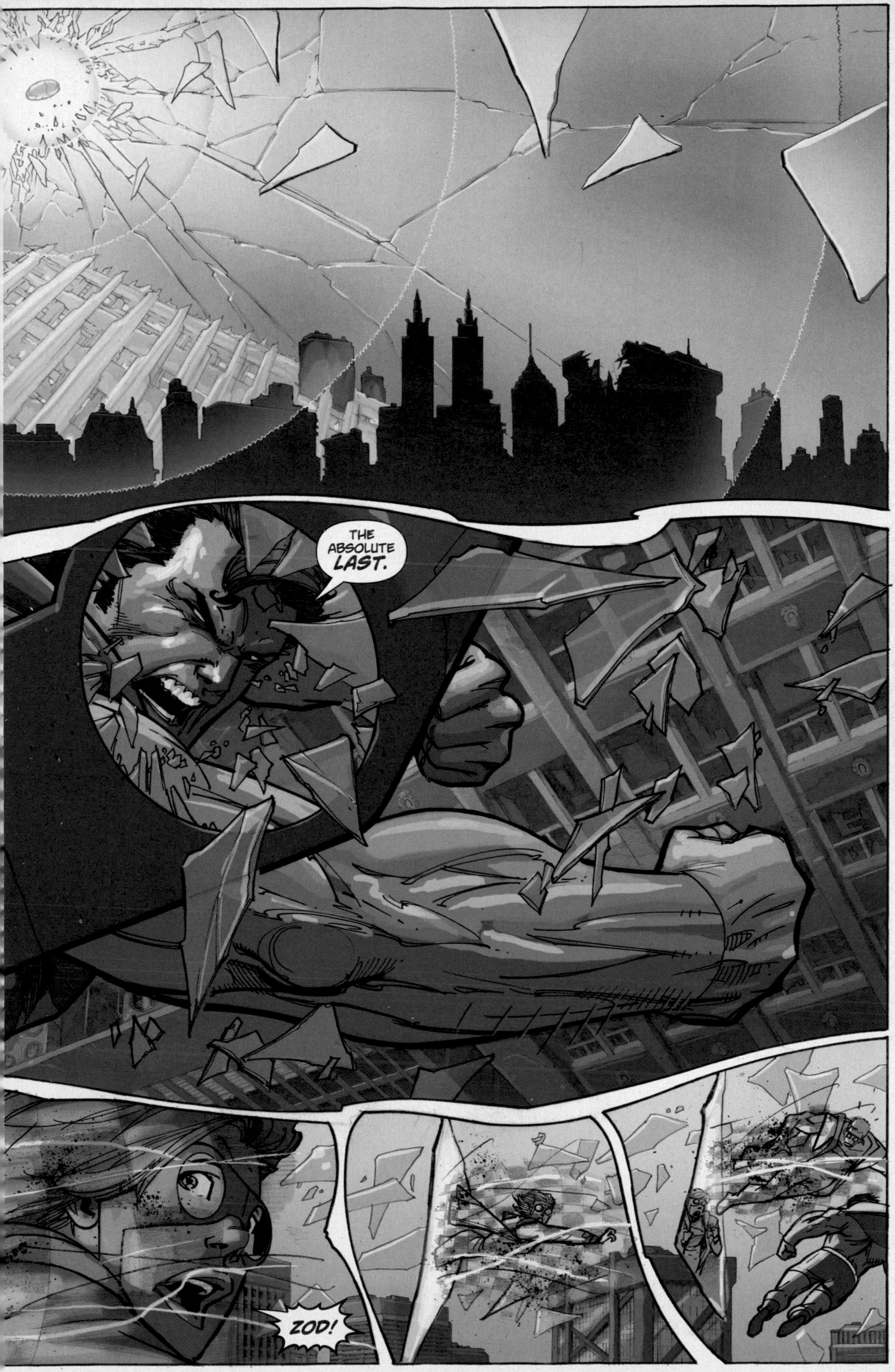
THE ABSOLUTE LAST.
ZOD!

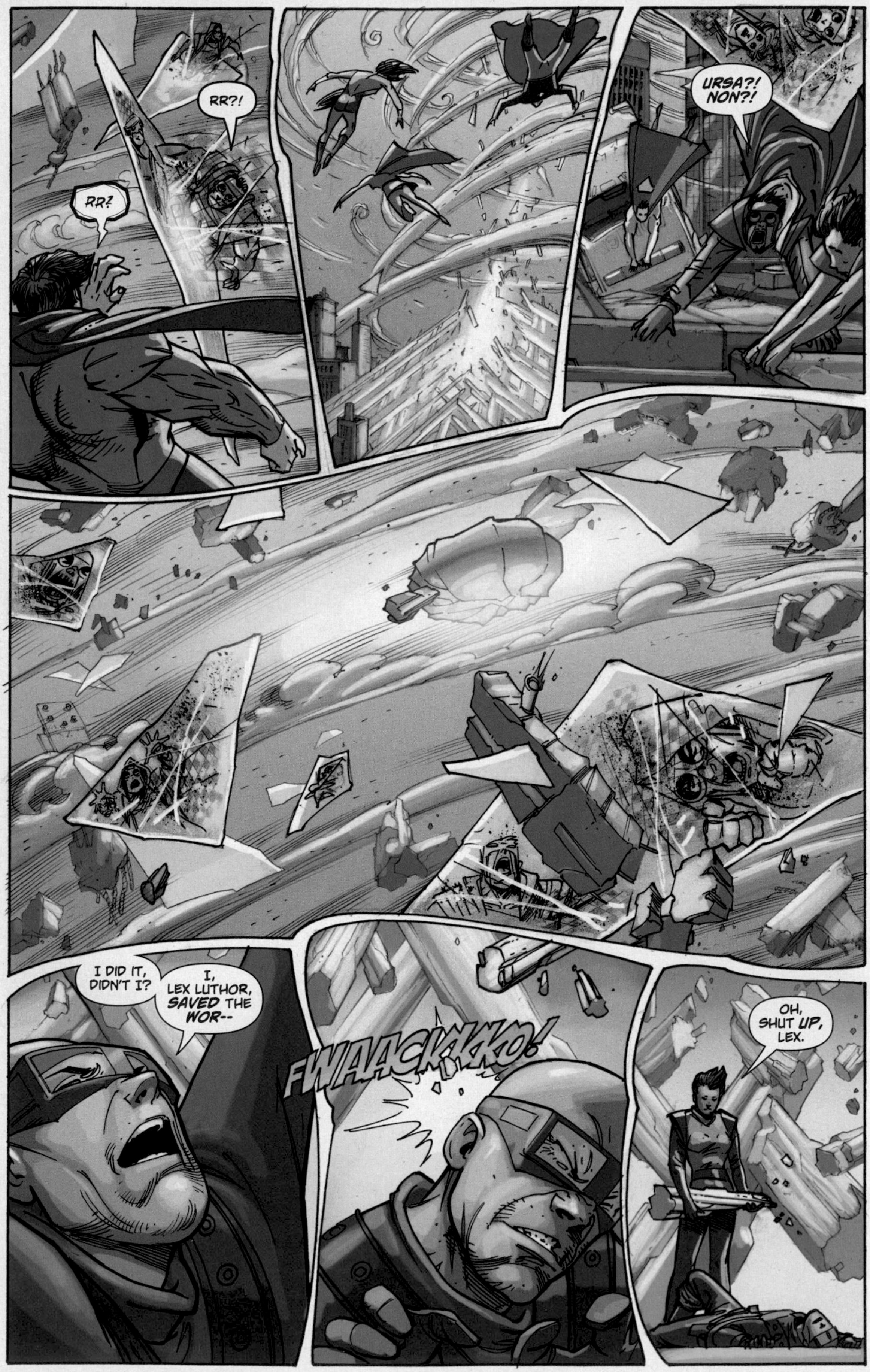
RR?!
RR?
URSA?! NON?!
I DID IT, DIDN'T I?
I, LEX LUTHOR, *SAVED* THE *WOR--*
FWAACKKKO!
OH, SHUT *UP*, LEX.

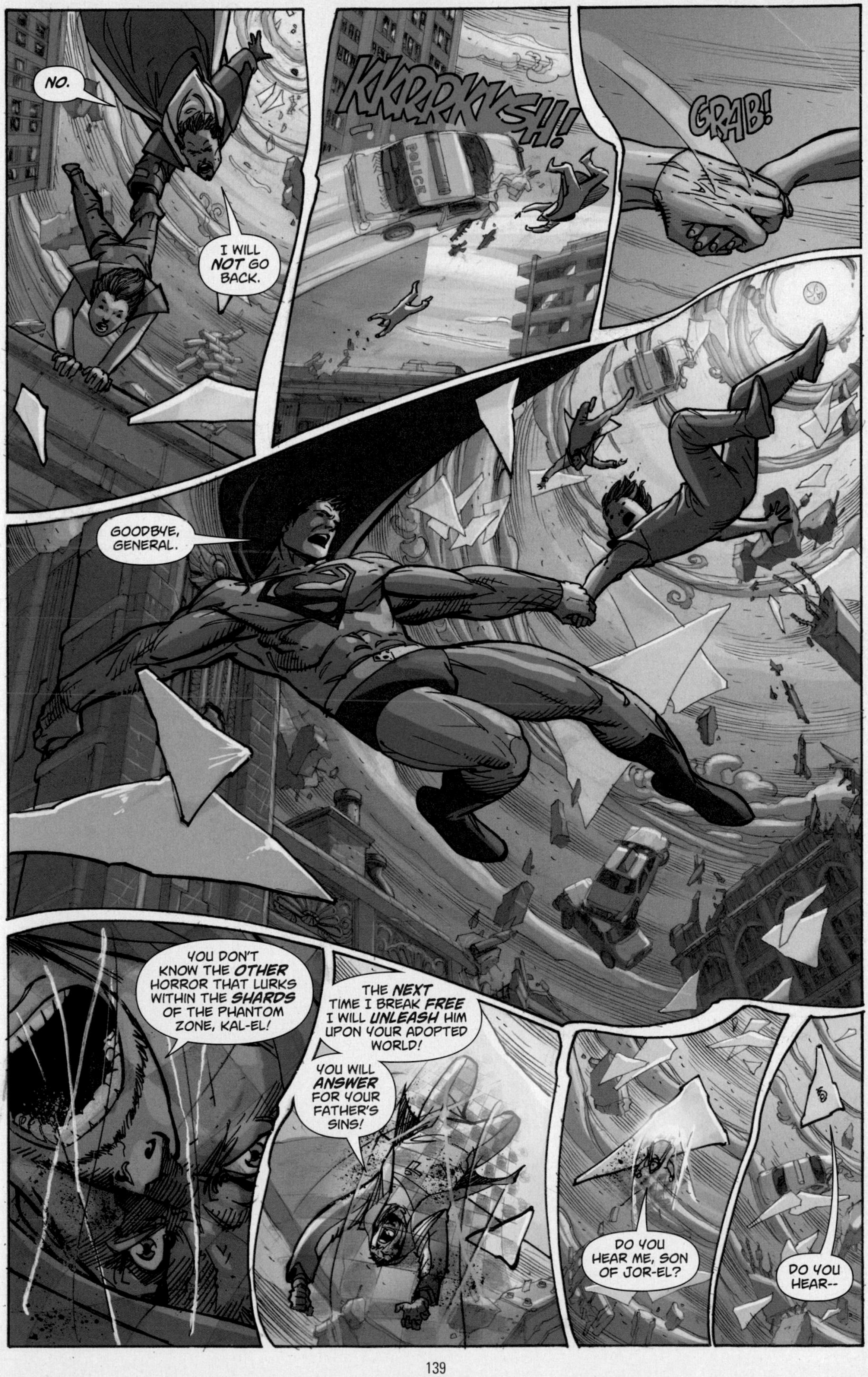
NO.
I WILL NOT GO BACK.
KKKRRRKKKSH!
POLICE
GRAB!
GOODBYE, GENERAL.
YOU DON'T KNOW THE OTHER HORROR THAT LURKS WITHIN THE SHARDS OF THE PHANTOM ZONE, KAL-EL!
THE NEXT TIME I BREAK FREE I WILL UNLEASH HIM UPON YOUR ADOPTED WORLD!
YOU WILL ANSWER FOR YOUR FATHER'S SINS!
DO YOU HEAR ME, SON OF JOR-EL?
DO YOU HEAR--

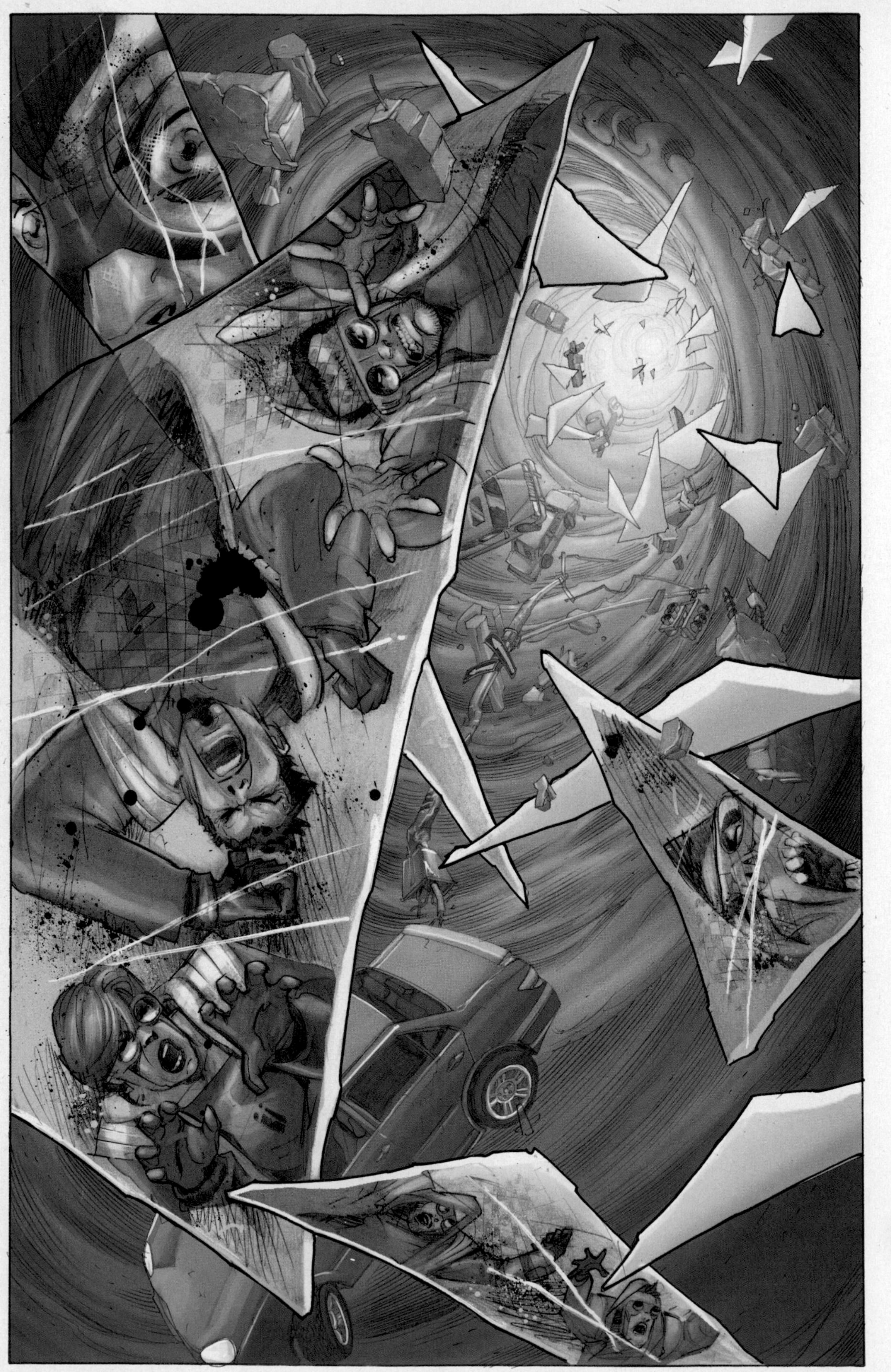

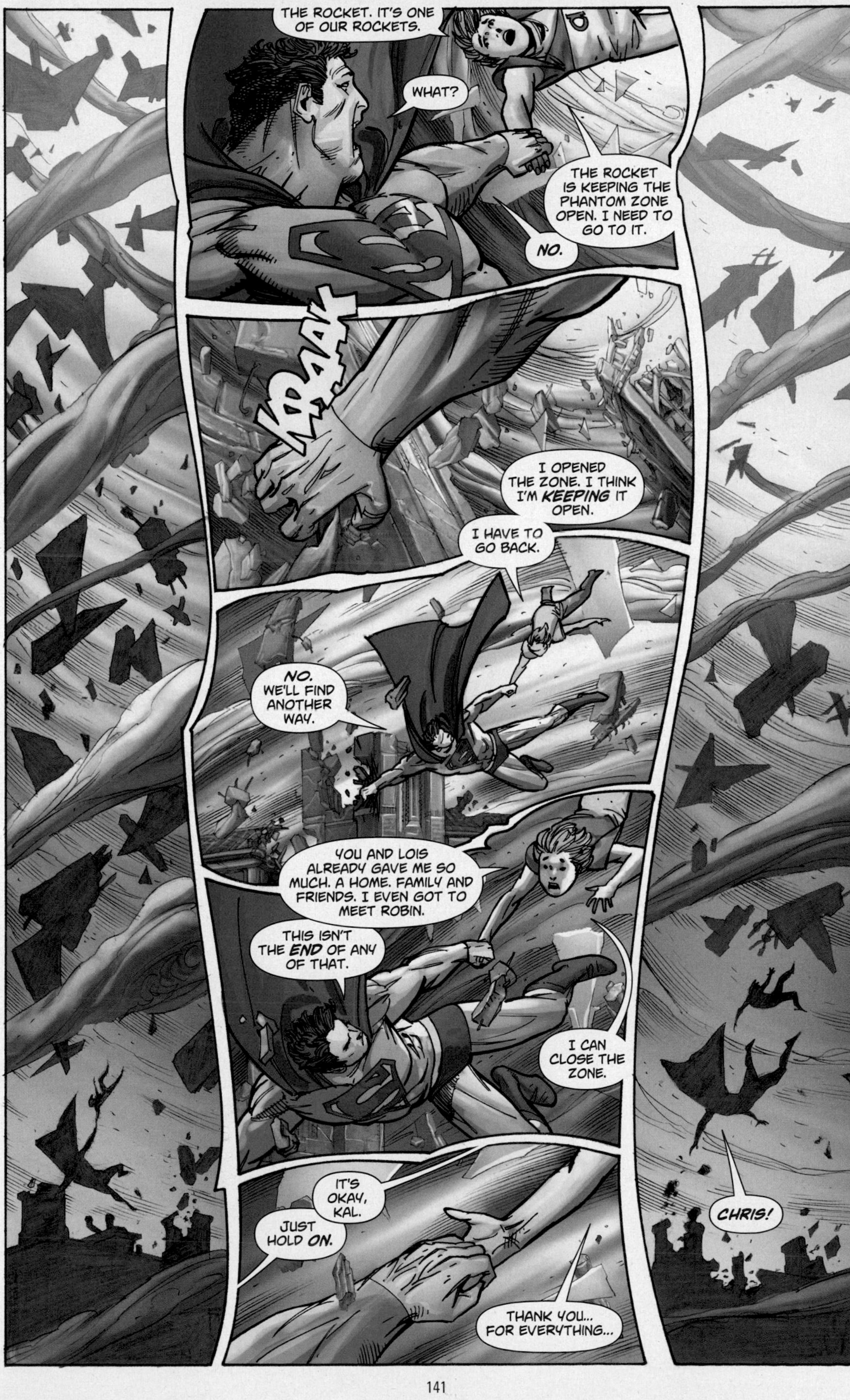
THE ROCKET. IT'S ONE OF OUR ROCKETS.
WHAT?
THE ROCKET IS KEEPING THE PHANTOM ZONE OPEN. I NEED TO GO TO IT.
NO.
KRAAK
I OPENED THE ZONE. I THINK I'M KEEPING IT OPEN.
I HAVE TO GO BACK.
NO. WE'LL FIND ANOTHER WAY.
YOU AND LOIS ALREADY GAVE ME SO MUCH. A HOME. FAMILY AND FRIENDS. I EVEN GOT TO MEET ROBIN.
THIS ISN'T THE END OF ANY OF THAT.
I CAN CLOSE THE ZONE.
IT'S OKAY, KAL.
JUST HOLD ON.
THANK YOU... FOR EVERYTHING...
CHRIS!

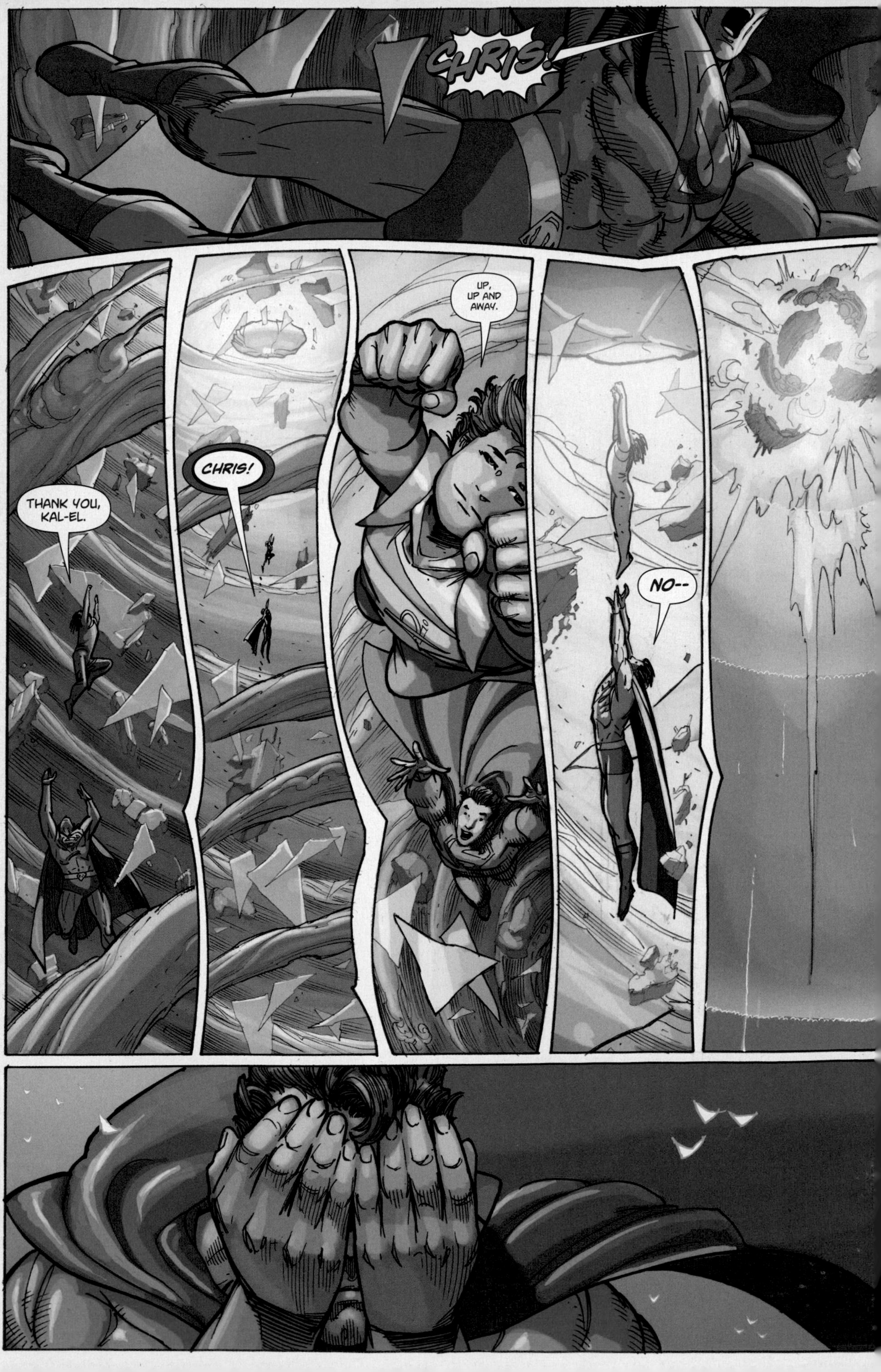
CHRIS!
THANK YOU, KAL-EL.
CHRIS!
UP, UP AND AWAY.
NO--

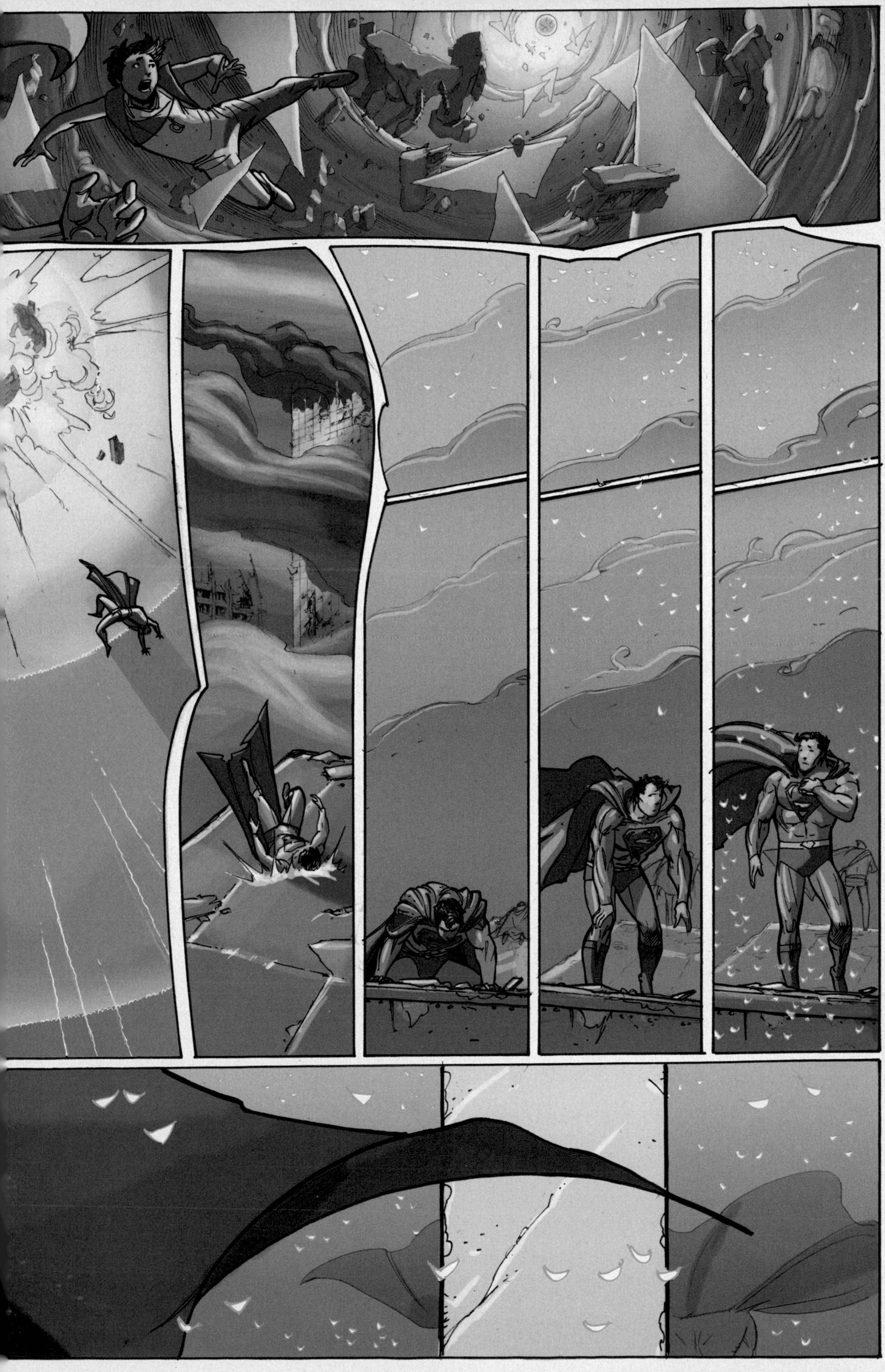

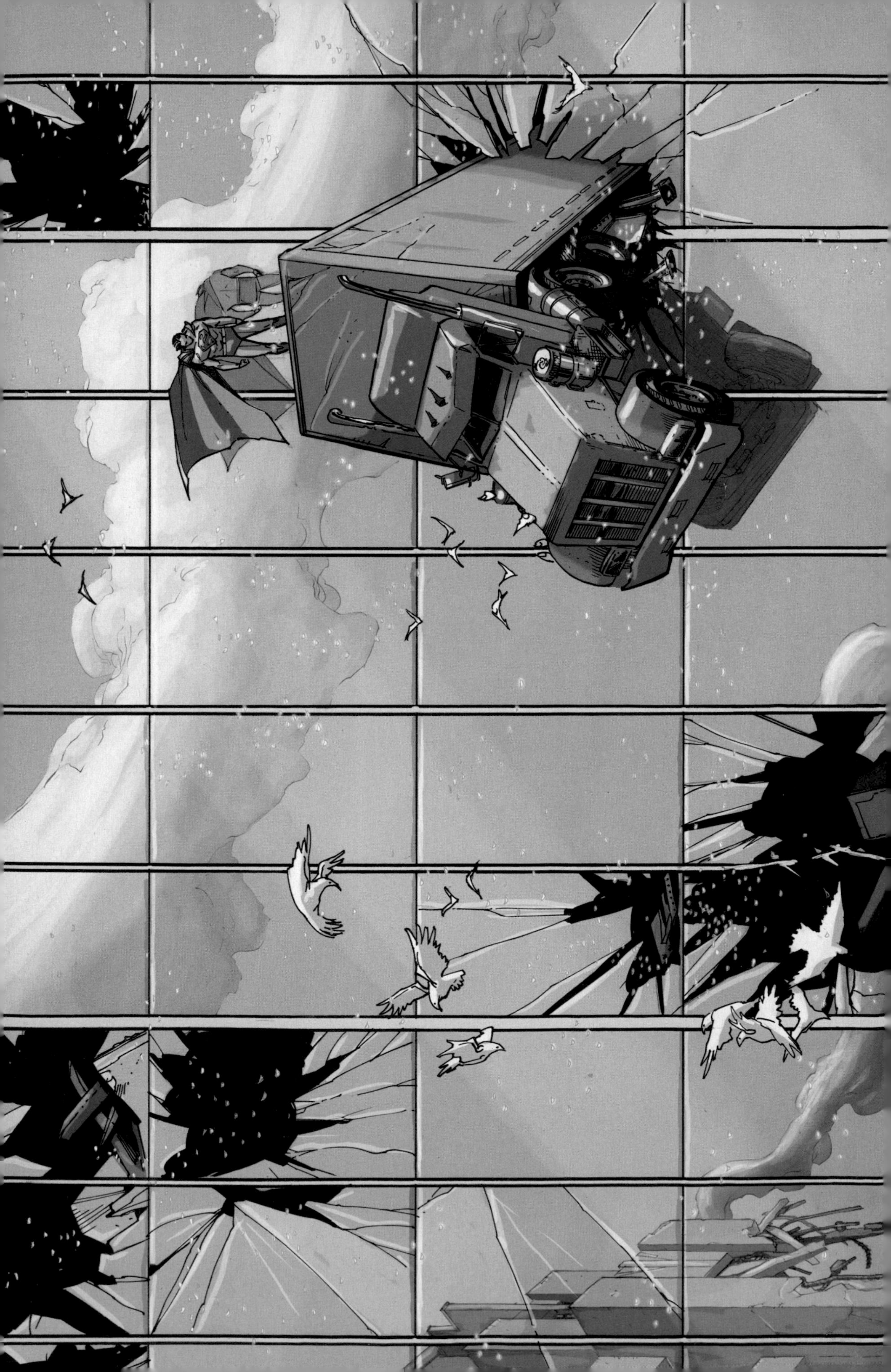

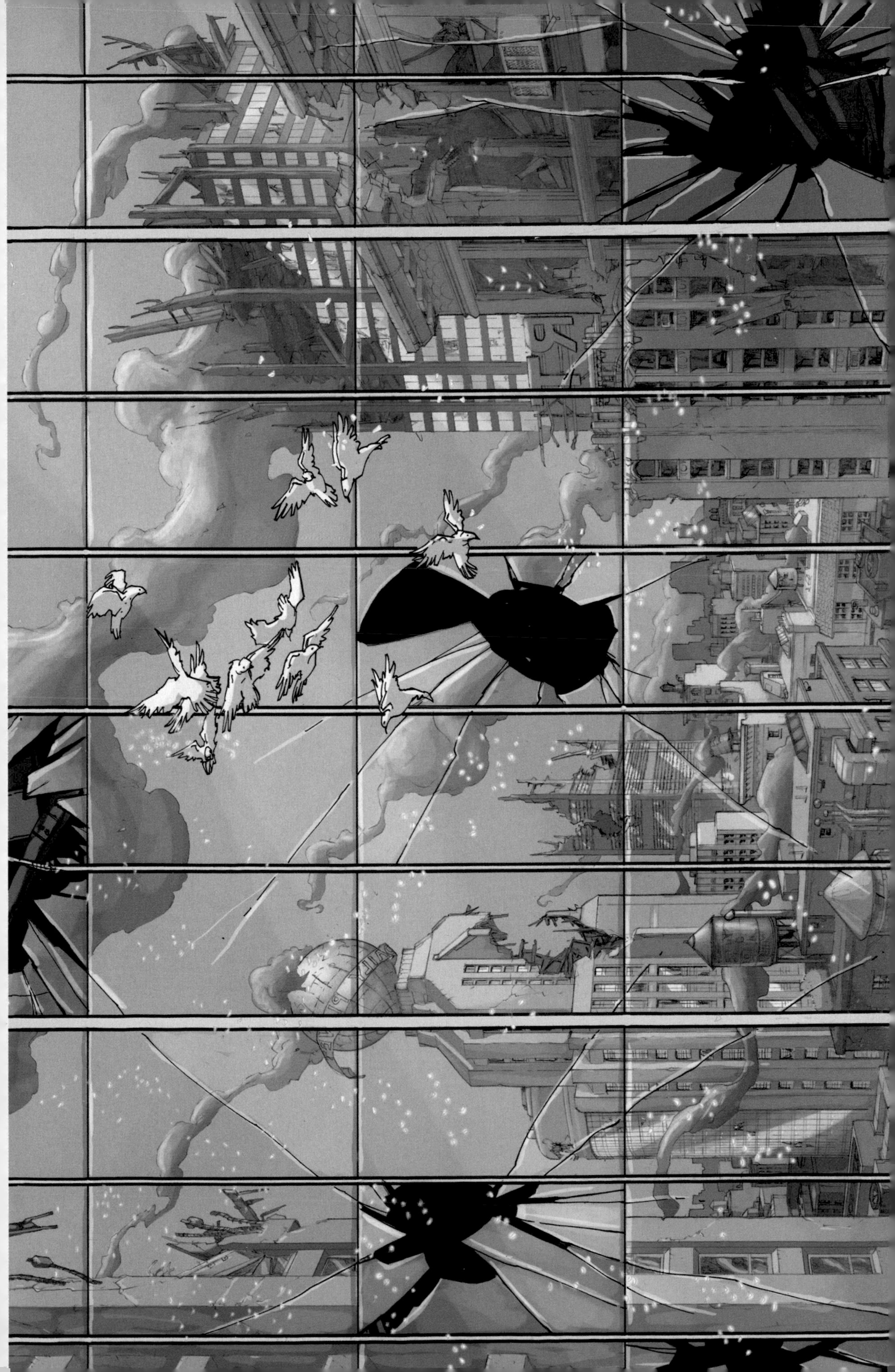

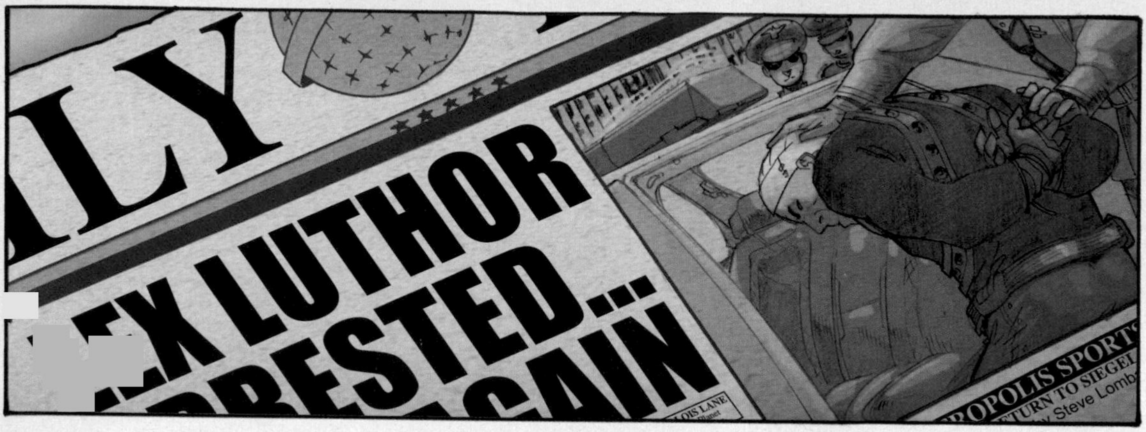
ILY
EX LUTHOR
RRESTED...
GAIN

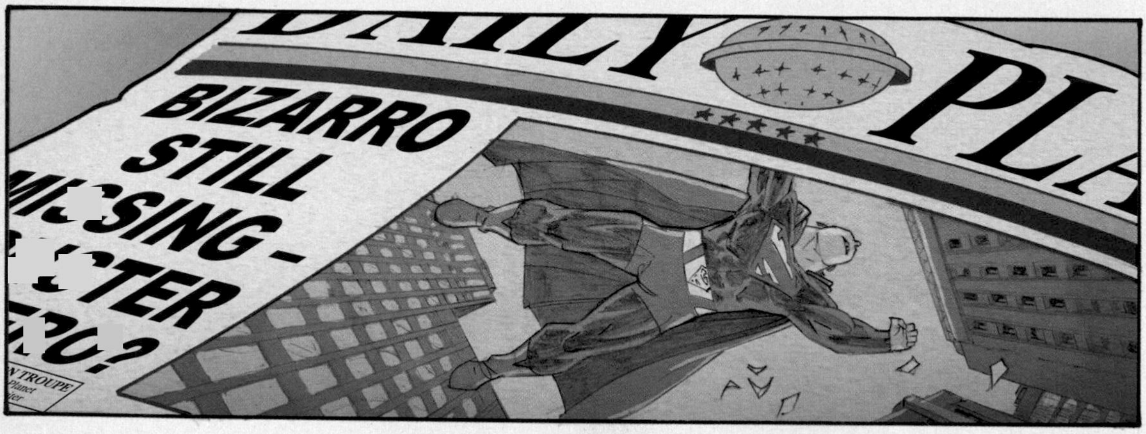
DAILY
PLA
BIZARRO
STILL
MISSING -

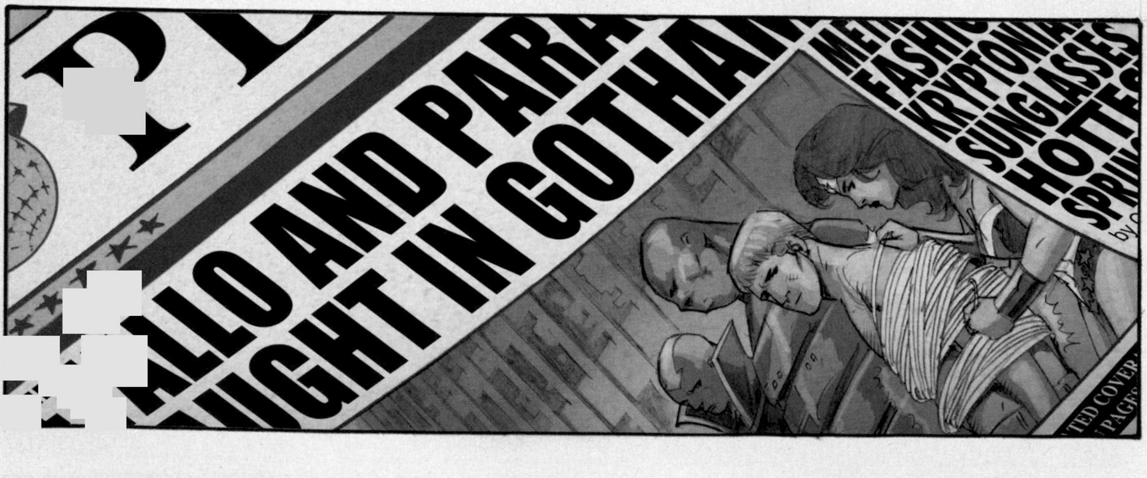
PL
LLO AND PARA
IGHT IN GOTHA
SUNGLASSES

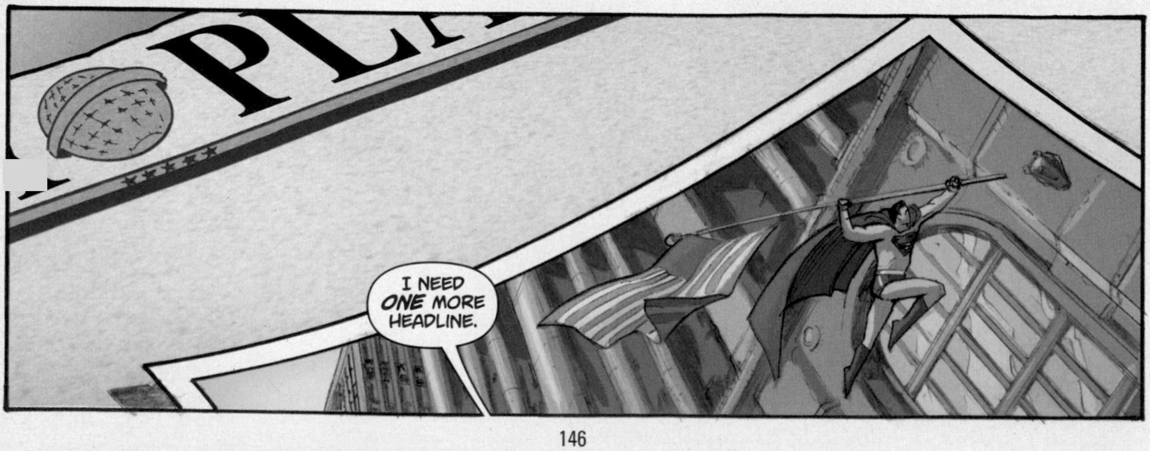
PLA
I NEED ONE MORE HEADLINE.

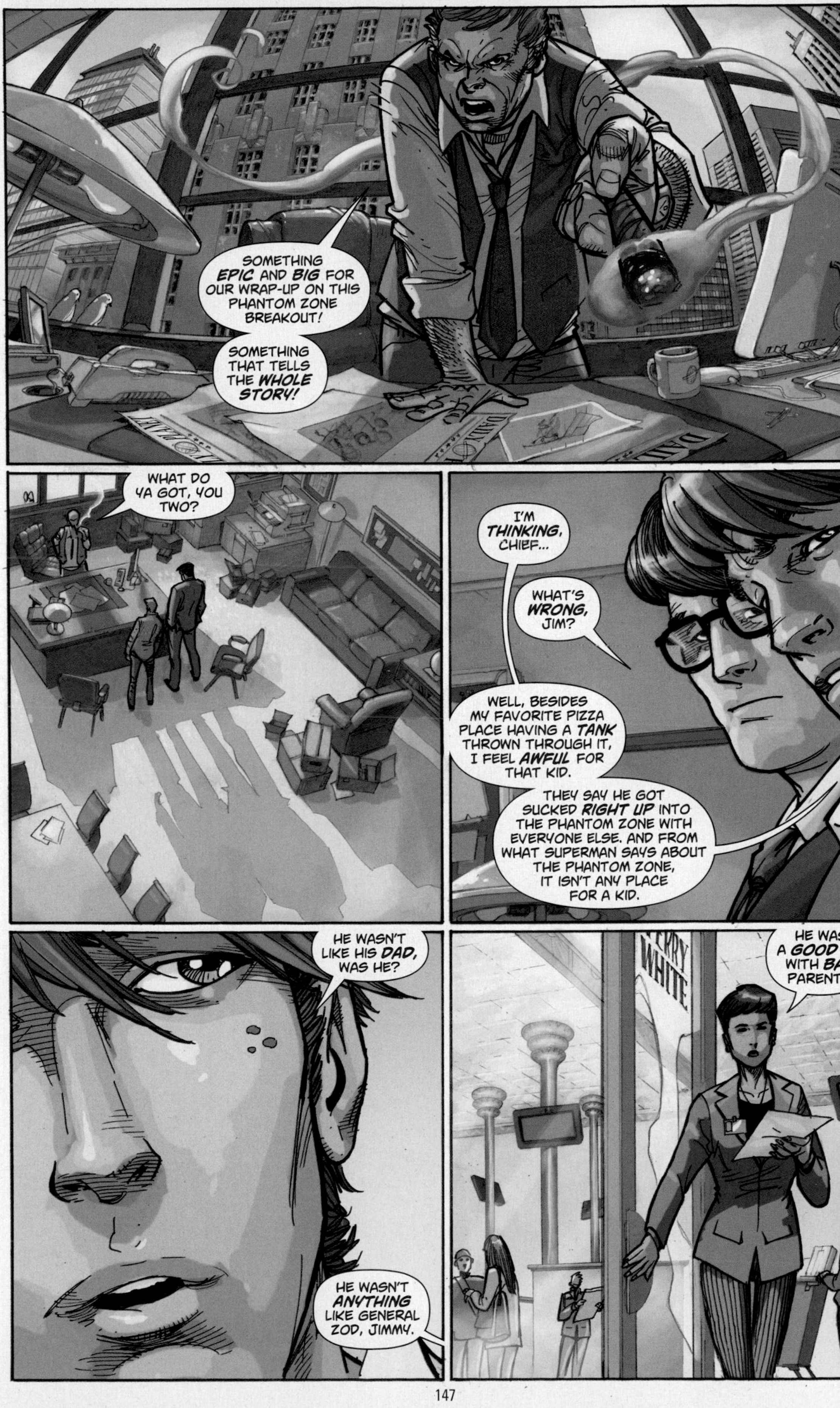
SOMETHING EPIC AND BIG FOR OUR WRAP-UP ON THIS PHANTOM ZONE BREAKOUT!
SOMETHING THAT TELLS THE WHOLE STORY!
WHAT DO YA GOT, YOU TWO?
I'M THINKING, CHIEF...
WHAT'S WRONG, JIM?
WELL, BESIDES MY FAVORITE PIZZA PLACE HAVING A TANK THROWN THROUGH IT, I FEEL AWFUL FOR THAT KID.
THEY SAY HE GOT SUCKED RIGHT UP INTO THE PHANTOM ZONE WITH EVERYONE ELSE. AND FROM WHAT SUPERMAN SAYS ABOUT THE PHANTOM ZONE, IT ISN'T ANY PLACE FOR A KID.
HE WASN'T LIKE HIS DAD, WAS HE?
HE WASN'T ANYTHING LIKE GENERAL ZOD, JIMMY.
PERRY WHITE
HE WAS A GOOD KID WITH BAD PARENTS.

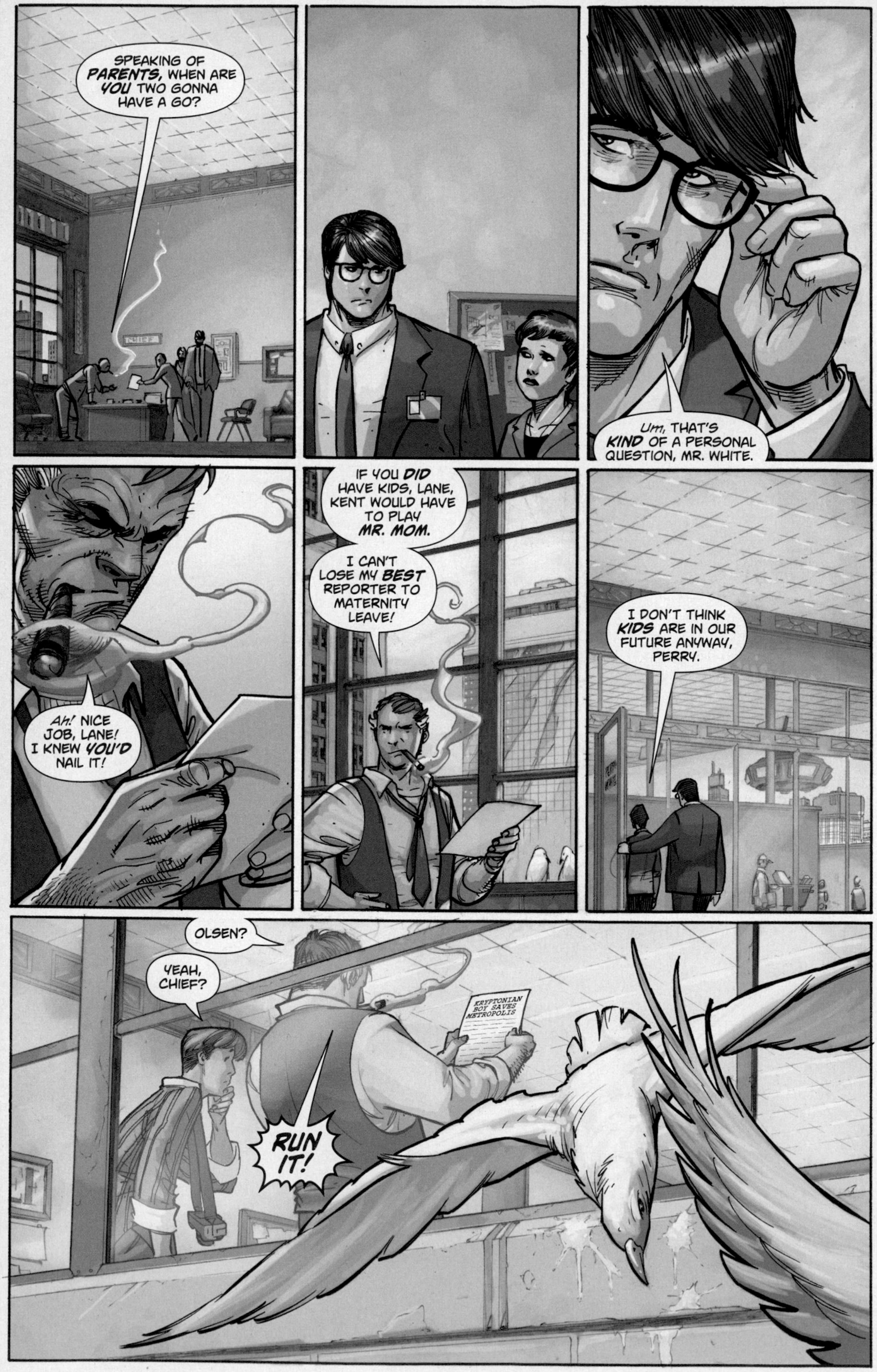
SPEAKING OF PARENTS, WHEN ARE YOU TWO GONNA HAVE A GO?
Um, THAT'S KIND OF A PERSONAL QUESTION, MR. WHITE.
Ah! NICE JOB, LANE! I KNEW YOU'D NAIL IT!
IF YOU DID HAVE KIDS, LANE, KENT WOULD HAVE TO PLAY MR. MOM.
I CAN'T LOSE MY BEST REPORTER TO MATERNITY LEAVE!
I DON'T THINK KIDS ARE IN OUR FUTURE ANYWAY, PERRY.
OLSEN?
YEAH, CHIEF?
KRYPTONIAN BOY SAVES METROPOLIS
RUN IT!

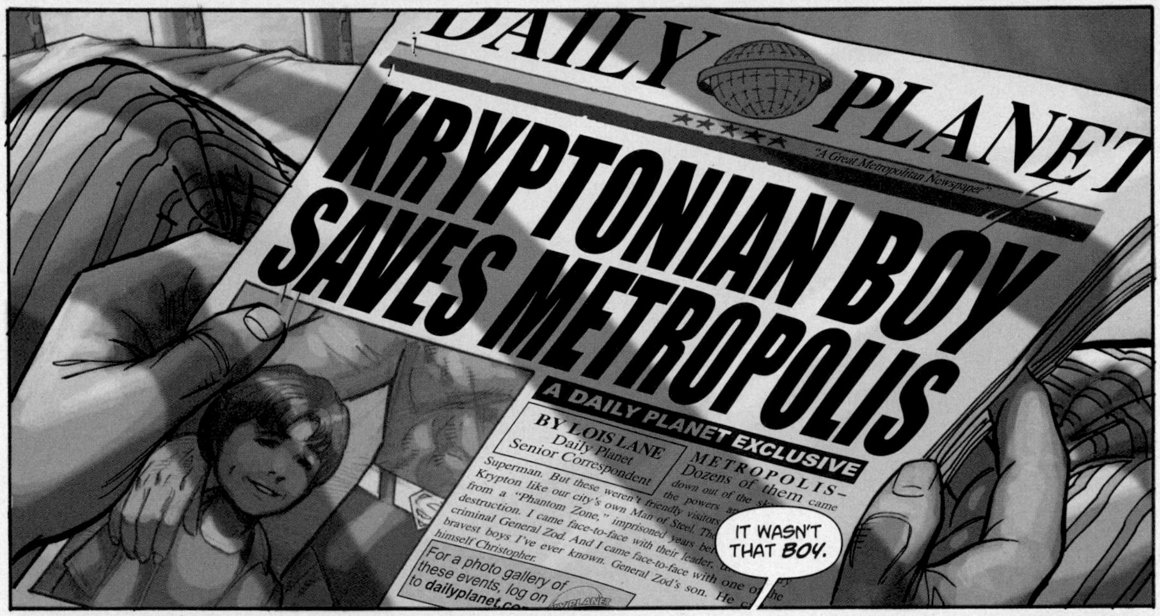
DAILY PLANET
"A Great Metropolitan Newspaper"
KRYPTONIAN BOY SAVES METROPOLIS
A DAILY PLANET EXCLUSIVE
BY LOIS LANE
Daily Planet
Senior Correspondent
METROPOLIS– Dozens of them came down out of the sk
the powers
Superman. But these weren't friendly visitors
Krypton like our city's own Man of Steel. Th
from a "Phantom Zone," imprisoned years be
destruction. I came face-to-face with their leader,
criminal General Zod. And I came face-to-face with one of the
bravest boys I've ever known. General Zod's son. He
himself Christopher.
For a photo gallery of these events, log on to dailyplanet.co
IT WASN'T THAT BOY.

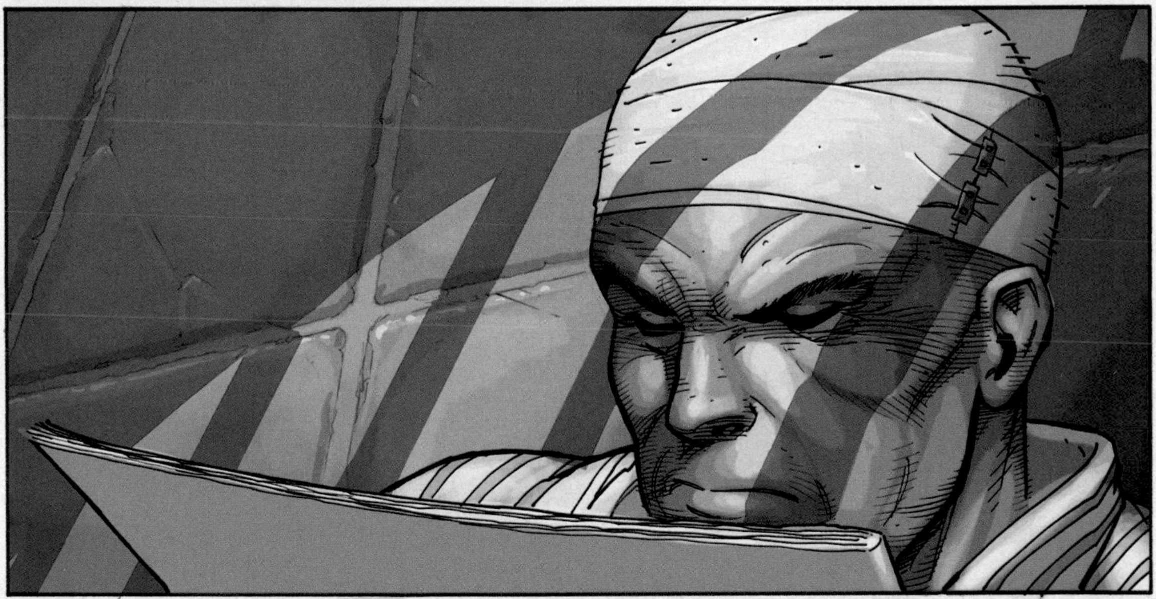

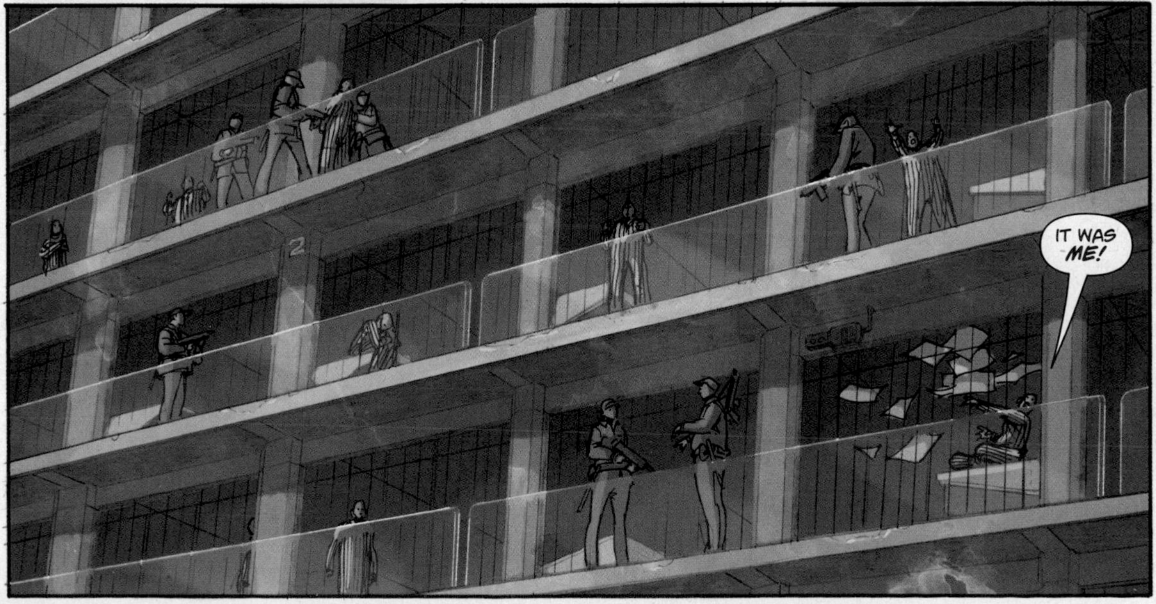
2
IT WAS ME!

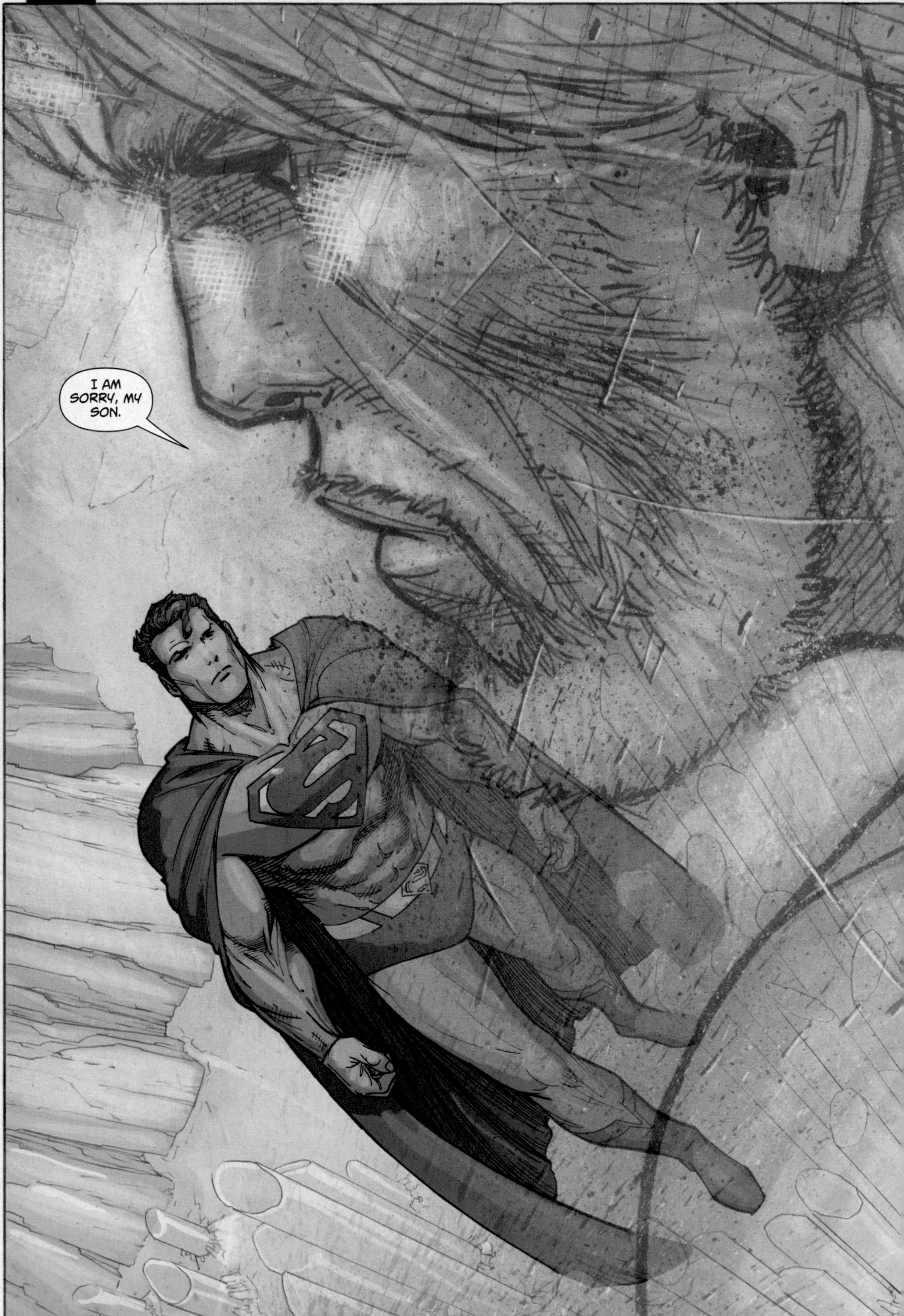
I AM SORRY, MY SON.

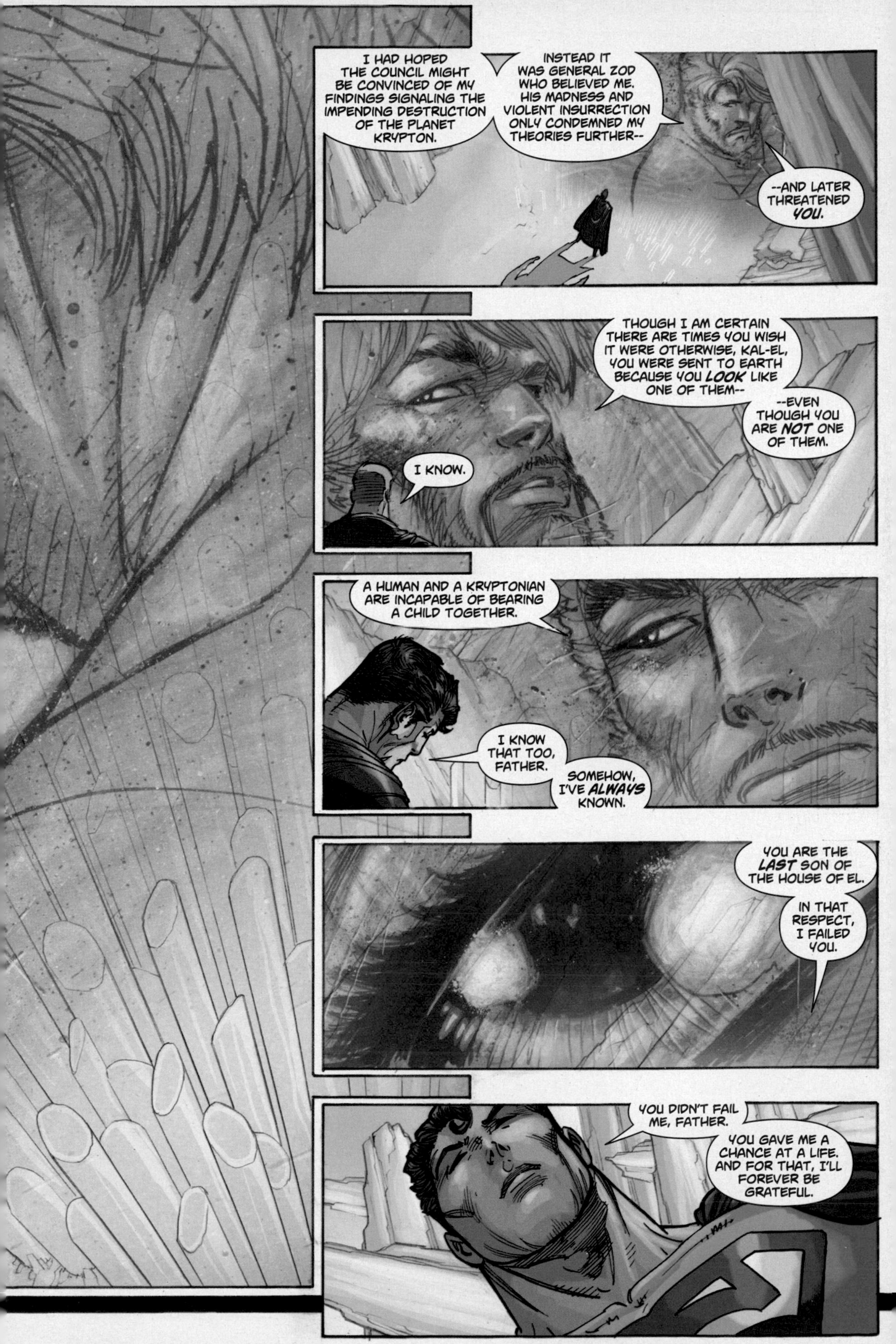
I HAD HOPED THE COUNCIL MIGHT BE CONVINCED OF MY FINDINGS SIGNALING THE IMPENDING DESTRUCTION OF THE PLANET KRYPTON.
INSTEAD IT WAS GENERAL ZOD WHO BELIEVED ME. HIS MADNESS AND VIOLENT INSURRECTION ONLY CONDEMNED MY THEORIES FURTHER--
--AND LATER THREATENED YOU.
THOUGH I AM CERTAIN THERE ARE TIMES YOU WISH IT WERE OTHERWISE, KAL-EL, YOU WERE SENT TO EARTH BECAUSE YOU LOOK LIKE ONE OF THEM--
--EVEN THOUGH YOU ARE NOT ONE OF THEM.
I KNOW.
A HUMAN AND A KRYPTONIAN ARE INCAPABLE OF BEARING A CHILD TOGETHER.
I KNOW THAT TOO, FATHER.
SOMEHOW, I'VE ALWAYS KNOWN.
YOU ARE THE LAST SON OF THE HOUSE OF EL.
IN THAT RESPECT, I FAILED YOU.
YOU DIDN'T FAIL ME, FATHER.
YOU GAVE ME A CHANCE AT A LIFE. AND FOR THAT, I'LL FOREVER BE GRATEFUL.

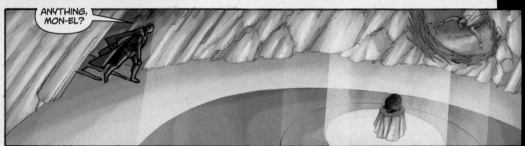

ANYTHING, MON-EL?

WHEREVER CHRIS IS, HE'S NOT WITH ZOD, URSA OR ANY OF THE OTHERS. THEY'VE RETREATED TO WHAT'S LEFT OF FORT ROZZ.

NOT YET.

THE PHANTOM ZONE'S A BIG PLACE, KAL. IT MIGHT BE ENDLESS.

BUT I'LL NEVER STOP LOOKING.

THANK YOU.

END

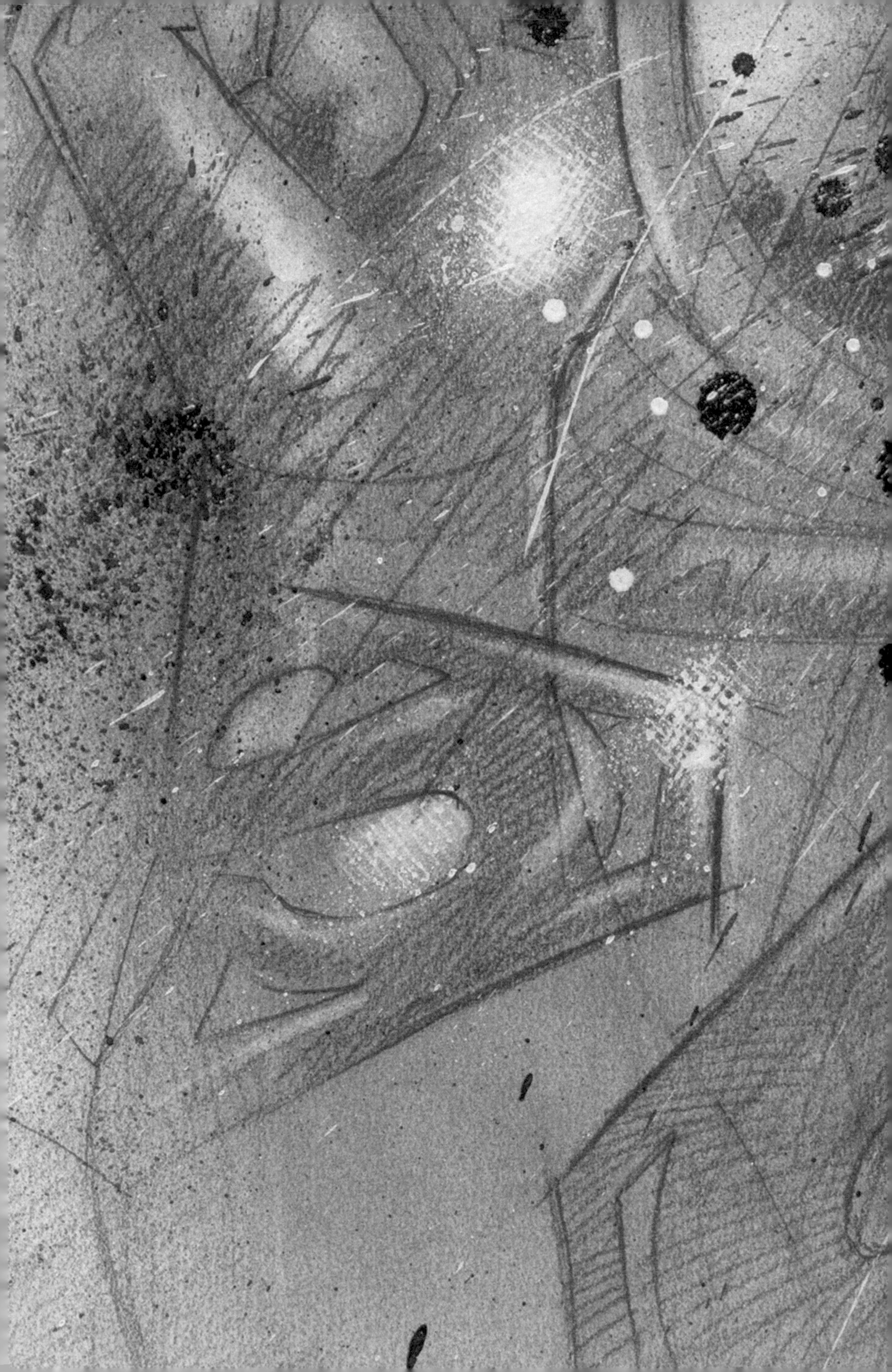

Variant cover to ACTION COMICS 844 by Andy Kubert and Jesse Delperdang

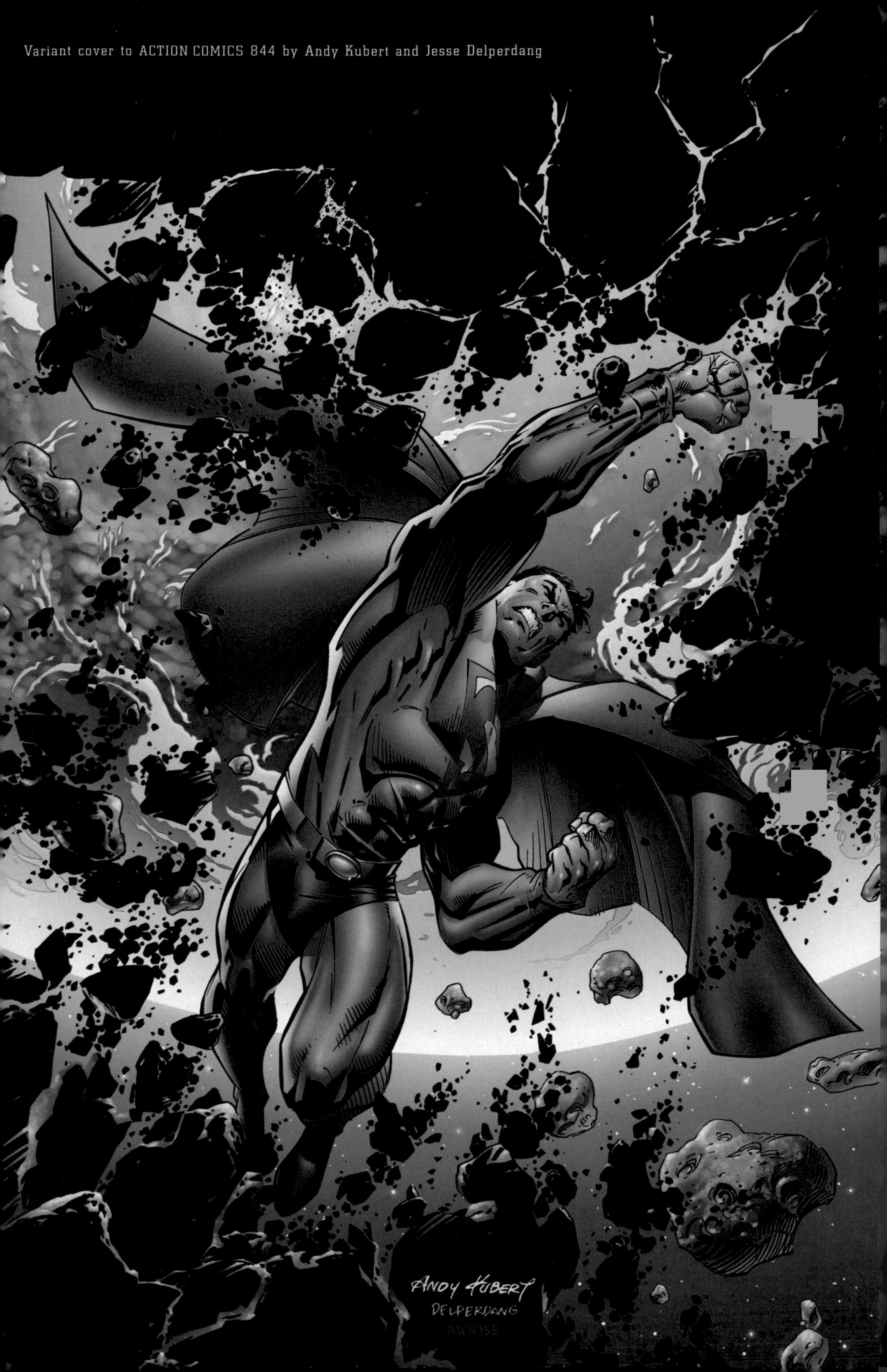
ANDY KUBERT
DELPERDANG
MOOSE

Variant cover to ACTION COMICS ANNUAL 11 by Adam Kubert

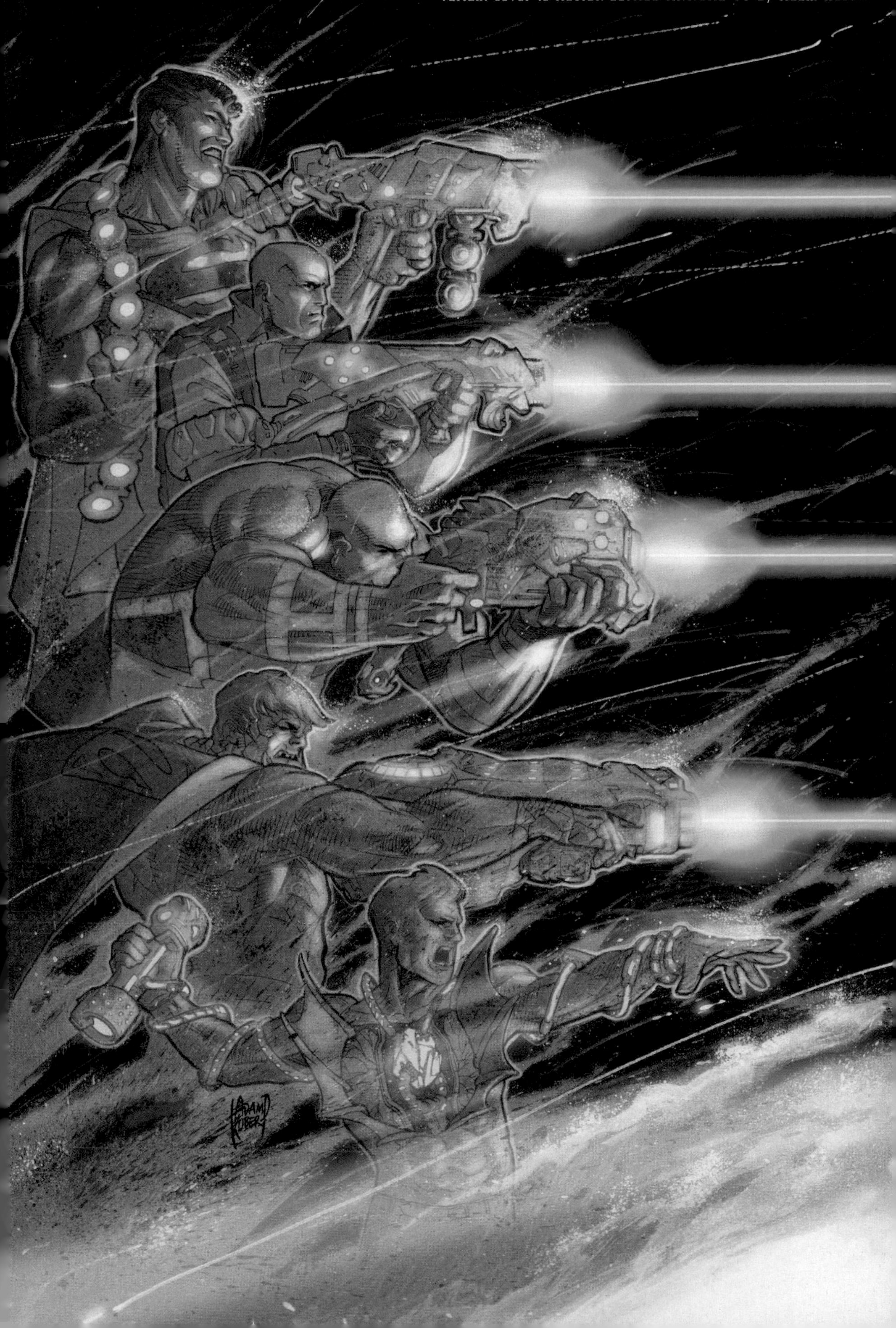

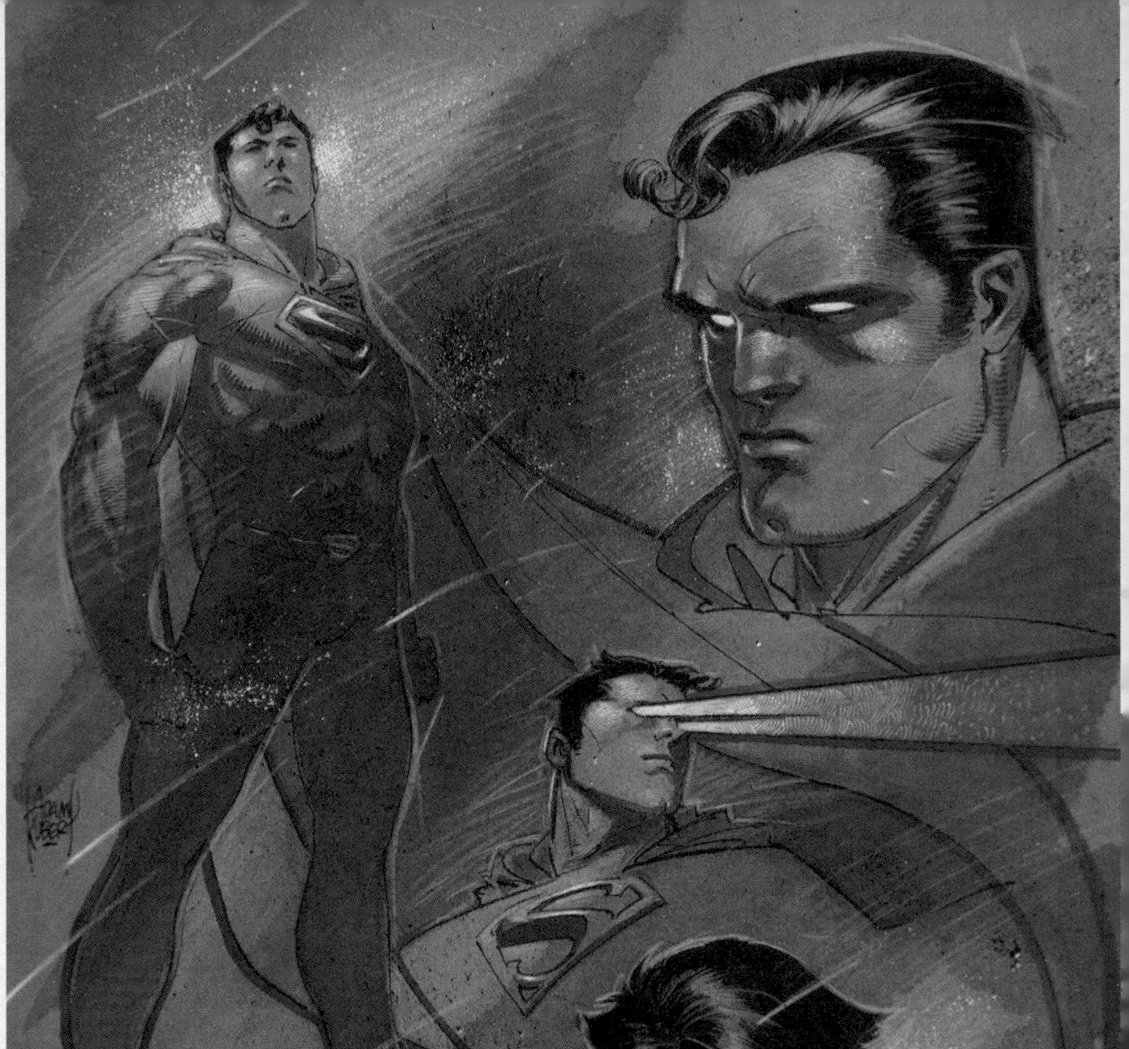

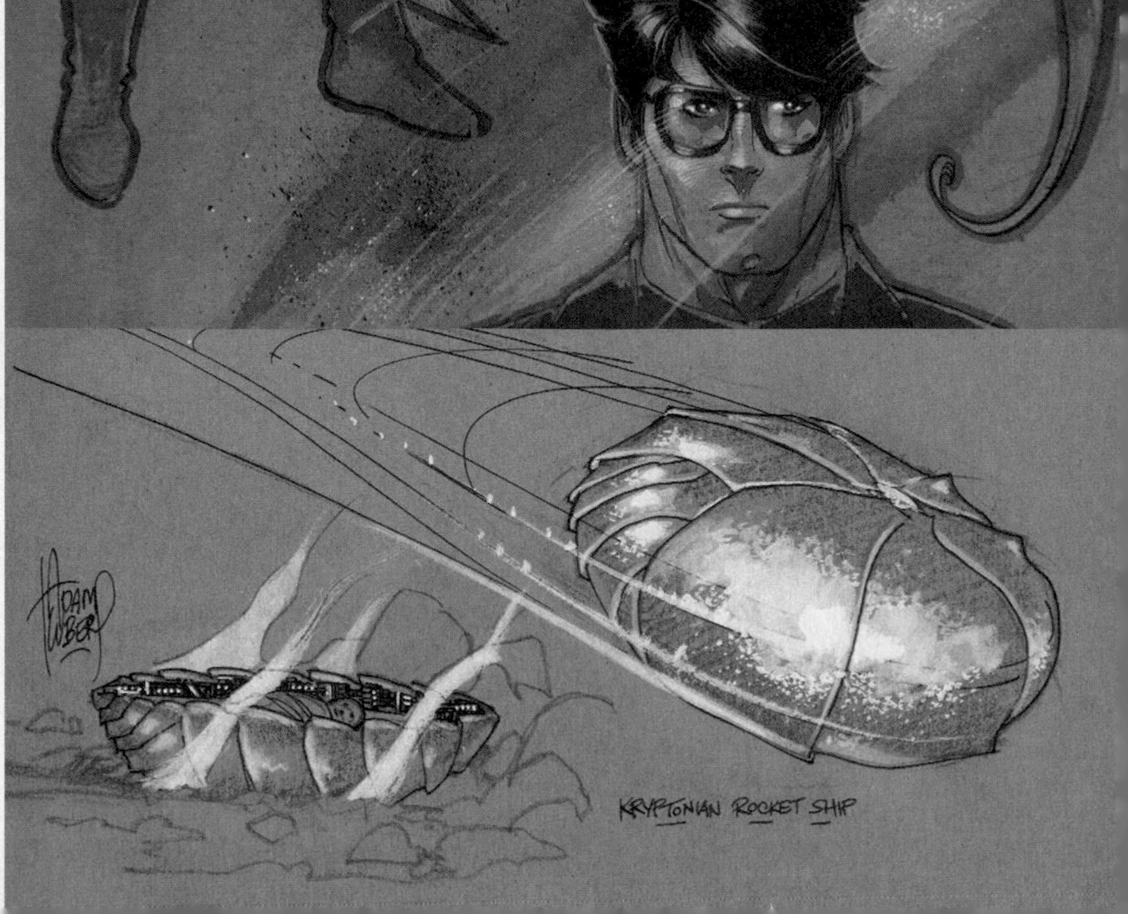
KRYPTONIAN ROCKET SHIP

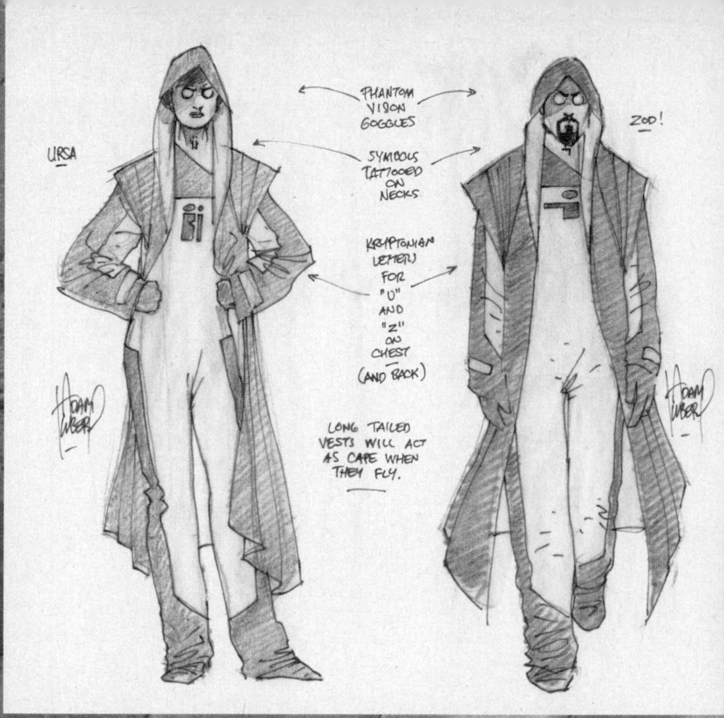
URSA
PHANTOM VISION GOGGLES
ZOD!
SYMBOLS TATTOOED ON NECKS
KRYPTONIAN LETTERS FOR "U" AND "Z" ON CHEST (AND BACK)
LONG TAILED VESTS WILL ACT AS CAPE WHEN THEY FLY.

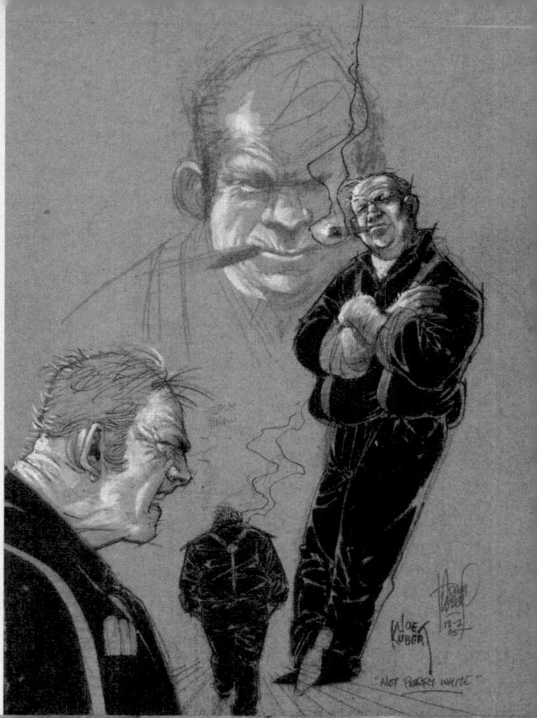
"NOT PERRY WHITE"

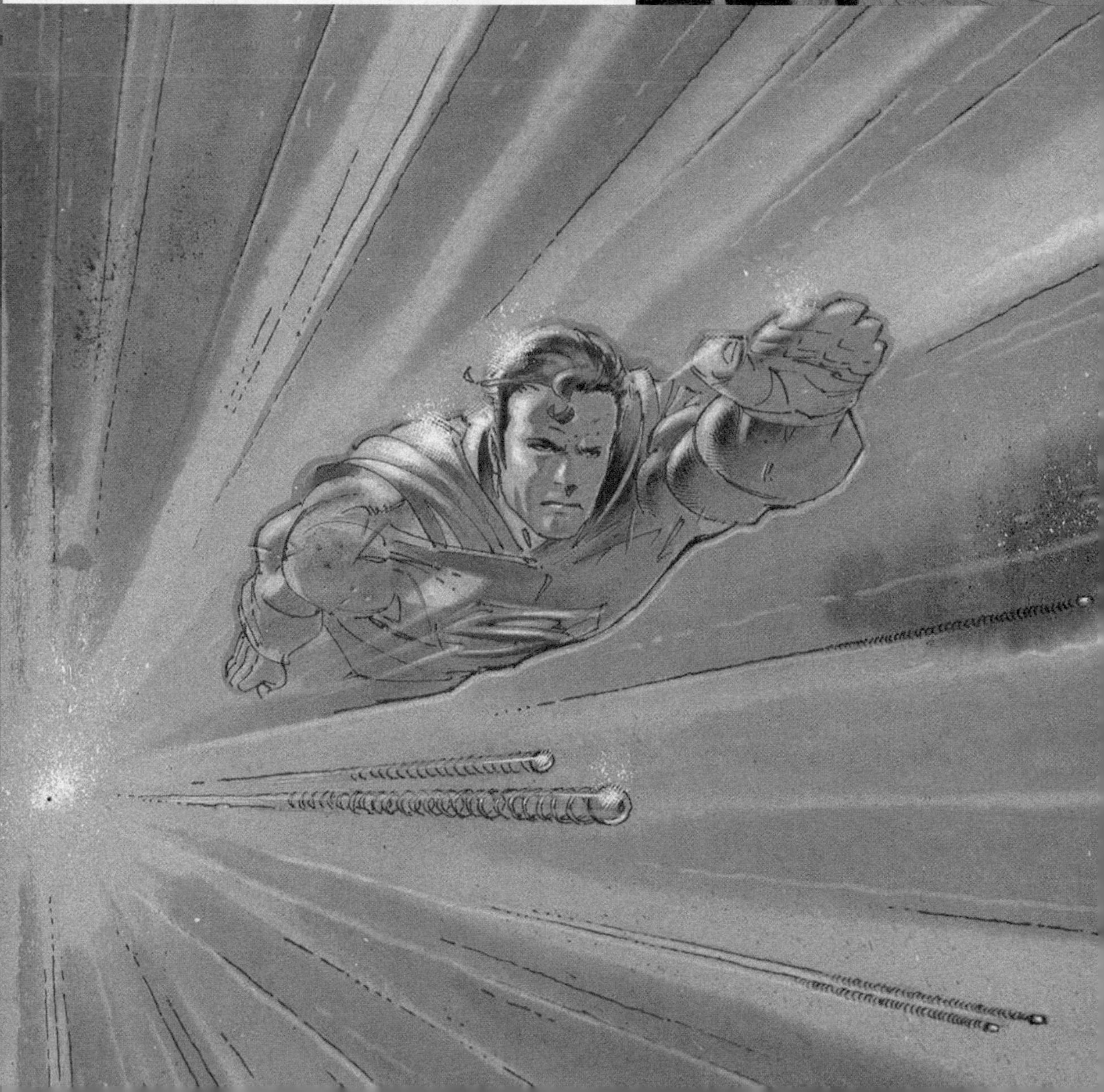

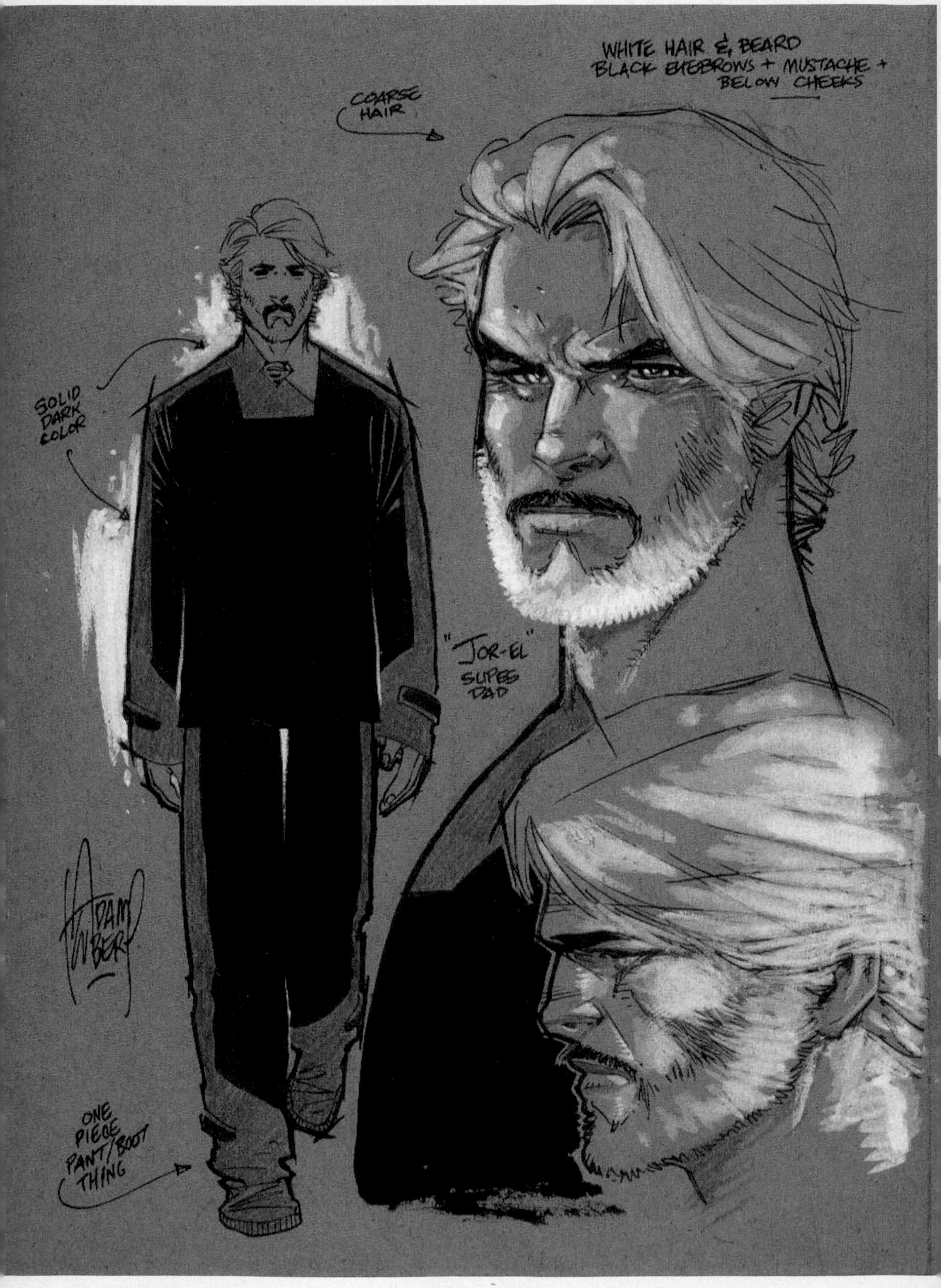
WHITE HAIR & BEARD
BLACK EYEBROWS + MUSTACHE +
BELOW CHEEKS
COARSE HAIR
SOLID DARK COLOR
"JOR-EL"
SUPES DAD
ONE PIECE PANT/BOOT THING

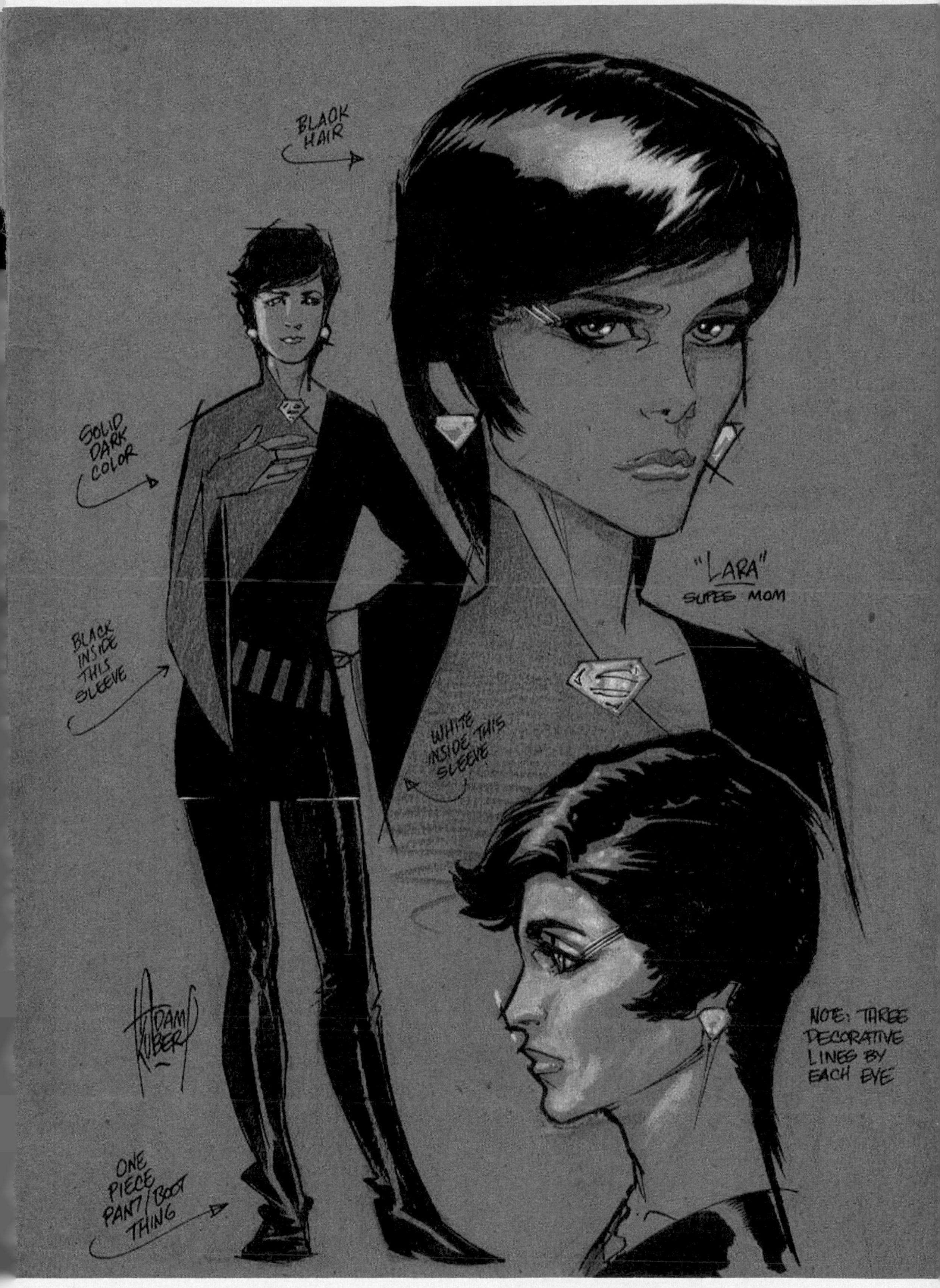
BLACK HAIR
SOLID DARK COLOR
BLACK INSIDE THIS SLEEVE
WHITE INSIDE THIS SLEEVE
"LARA" SUPES MOM
NOTE: THREE DECORATIVE LINES BY EACH EYE
ONE PIECE PANT/BOOT THING
ADAM KUBERT

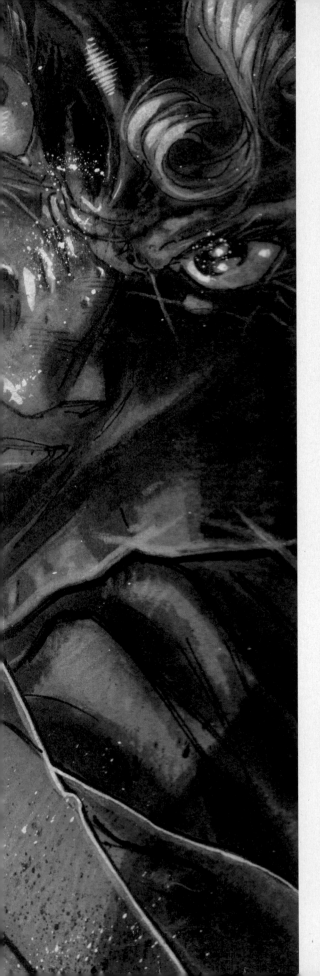

GEOFF JOHNS got his first break in comics writing STARS AND S.T.R.I.P.E. for DC Comics. He has since become one of the most prolific and popular writers in the industry, having worked on such titles as THE FLASH, TEEN TITANS, HAWKMAN, 52, INFINITE CRISIS and JUSTICE SOCIETY OF AMERICA. He reunited with his mentor, Richard Donner, to cowrite the ACTION COMICS storyline that has been collected in this volume. Johns is also currently reimagining the entire Green Lantern mythos for DC.

RICHARD DONNER, acclaimed film and television director, has been telling stories that have become part of the popular vernacular for longer than most people realize. Early in his career he was telling tales of the castaways on *Gilligan's Island*, missing it "by that much" with *Get Smart*, scaring William Shatner on an airplane in *The Twilight Zone*'s iconic episode "Nightmare at 20,000 Feet" and helping create countless other classic television series. His films such as *The Omen, Scrooged, Maverick, The Goonies* and, of course, the *Lethal Weapon* pictures helped define a generation of movie fans. But it may be his tribute to Americana that best illustrates his storytelling prowess. *Superman: The Movie*, not only made audiences believe a man can fly, but proved to the world that comic books are not only the realm of children. In 2006, Donner jumped at the chance to collaborate with friend and protégé Geoff Johns to further the adventures of Krypton's Last Son.

ADAM KUBERT was raised on DC comics, and Superman in ACTION COMICS holds a special place in his heart. Completing the picture was having the opportunity to work with the highly acclaimed writing team of Richard Donner and Geoff Johns. Adam's past work includes BATMAN VS. PREDATOR, *The X-Men, Wolverine, The Incredible Hulk, Fantastic Four, Spirits of Vengeance*, and *Doc Savage*. Adam has won many comics industry achievement awards, including an Eisner Award and multiple *Wizard Magazine* and web fan awards. When he is not teaching at the Joe Kubert School of Cartoon and Graphic Art, Adam can be found at home in New Jersey with his three children and two Harleys. Adam would like to give special thanks to Tracy, Max, Elizabeth, Jay, Scott, Andy, Geoff, Matt, Nachie, Dave, Rob, Edgar, Griz, Davo, and Mom and Dad.

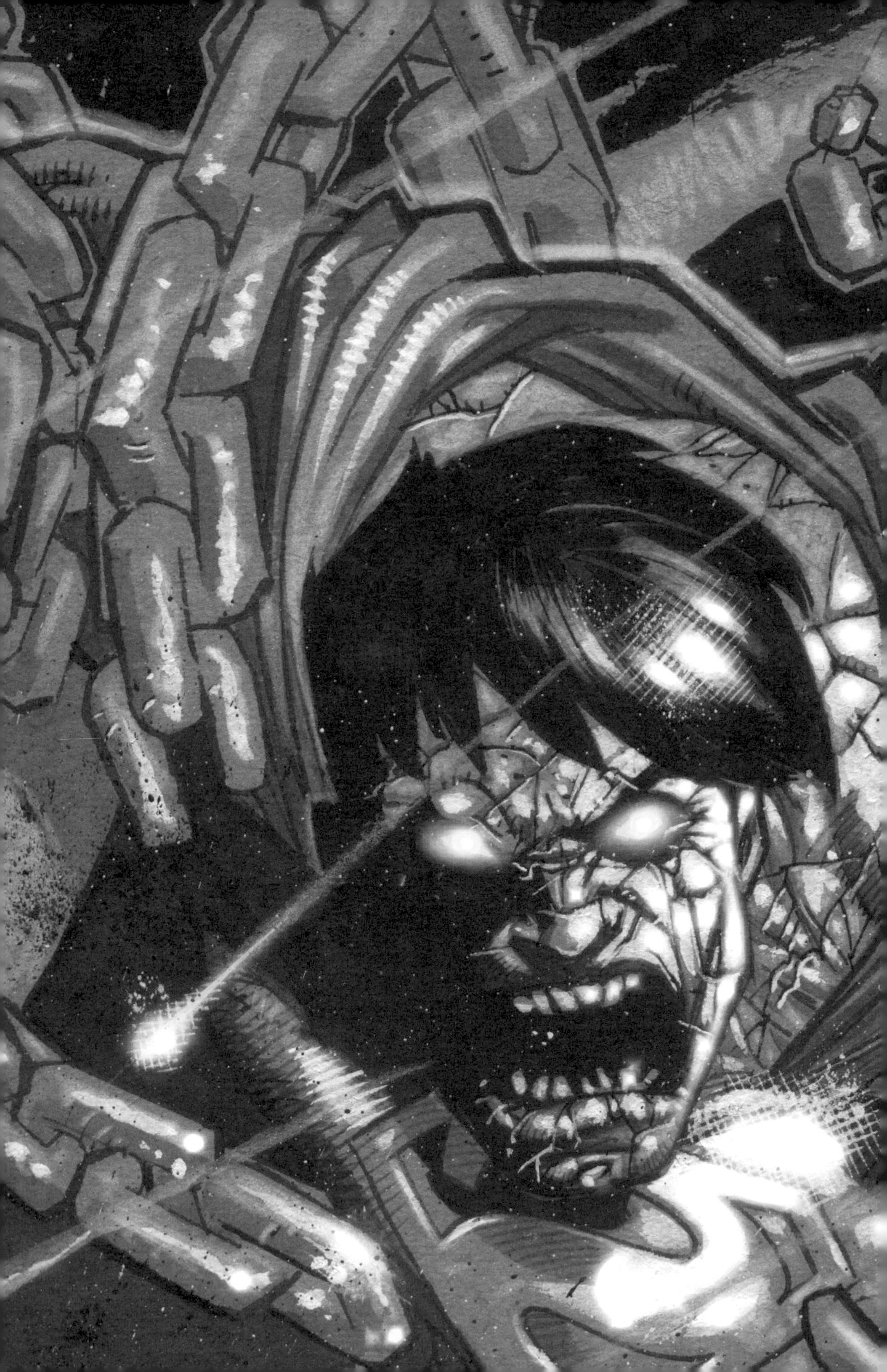